THE PRINCE

A REVISED TRANSLATION
BACKGROUNDS
INTERPRETATIONS
MARGINALIA

SECOND EDITION

W. W. NORTON & COMPANY
also publishes

THE NORTON ANTHOLOGY OF AFRICAN AMERICAN LITERATURE
edited by Henry Louis Gates Jr. and Nellie Y. McKay et. al

THE NORTON ANTHOLOGY OF AMERICAN LITERATURE
edited by Nina Baym et al.

THE NORTON ANTHOLOGY OF CONTEMPORARY FICTION
edited by R. V. Cassill

THE NORTON ANTHOLOGY OF ENGLISH LITERATURE
edited by M. H. Abrams et al.

THE NORTON ANTHOLOGY OF LITERATURE BY WOMEN
edited by Sandra M. Gilbert and Susan Gubar

THE NORTON ANTHOLOGY OF MODERN POETRY
edited by Richard Ellmann and Robert O'Clair

THE NORTON ANTHOLOGY OF POETRY
edited by Margaret Ferguson et al.

THE NORTON ANTHOLOGY OF SHORT FICTION
edited by R. V. Cassill

THE NORTON ANTHOLOGY OF WORLD MASTERPIECES
edited by Maynard Mack et al.

THE NORTON FACSIMILE OF
THE FIRST FOLIO OF SHAKESPEARE
prepared by Charlton Hinman

THE NORTON INTRODUCTION TO LITERATURE
edited by Carl E. Bain, Jerome Beaty, and J. Paul Hunter

THE NORTON INTRODUCTION TO THE SHORT NOVEL
edited by Jerome Beaty

THE NORTON READER
edited by Linda H. Peterson, John C. Brereton, and Joan E. Hartman

THE NORTON SAMPLER
edited by Thomas Cooley

THE NORTON SHAKESPEARE
edited by Stephen Greenblatt et al.

A NORTON CRITICAL EDITION

Niccolò Machiavelli
THE PRINCE

A REVISED TRANSLATION
BACKGROUNDS
INTERPRETATIONS
MARGINALIA

SECOND EDITION

Translated and Edited by

ROBERT M. ADAMS
EMERITUS PROFESSOR OF ENGLISH
UNIVERSITY OF CALIFORNIA AT LOS ANGELES

W • W • NORTON & COMPANY • *New York* • *London*

The text of this book is composed in Electra
with the display set in Bernhard Modern

Library of Congress Cataloging-in-Publication Data
Machiavelli, Niccolò, 1469–1527.
   [Principe. English]
   The prince : a revised translation, backgrounds, interpretations /
Niccolò Machiavelli ; translated and edited by Robert M. Adams.—
2nd ed.
     p. cm.—(A Norton critical edition)
   Includes bibliographical references (p. 277) and index.
   1. Political science—Early works to 1800.   2. Political ethics.
I. Adams, Robert Martin, 1915–   II. Title.
JC143.M38   1992
320.1—dc20   91-32538

ISBN 0-393-96220-2 (paper)

W.W. Norton & Company, Inc., 500 Fifth Avenue, New York, N.Y. 10110
W.W. Norton & Company Ltd., 10 Coptic Street, London WC1A 1PU

9 0

Contents

Marginalia

Historical Introduction

For as long as rulers have been ruling, they have been receiving—from laymen and clergy, from nobles and commons, from their predecessors and those who would like to be their replacements, masters, or successors—advice on how to do their jobs. Most of these manuals for statesmen and handbooks for sovereigns, since they simply rephrase, codify, and make applications of the common wisdom of the day, enjoy only an ephemeral existence. Rulers rarely read them, and even more rarely make use of their precepts; the typical manual for rulers seems to be chiefly of interest to other writers of manuals, and after a while only to students of manual writing. The major exception to all these cynicisms is a little booklet written, but not published, by Niccolò Machiavelli, citizen of Florence, in 1513. *The Prince* is not far from its five hundredth birthday, and it continues as vital, as much discussed, as influential, as any book only a tenth of its age.

Many of the reasons for this exceptional vitality are apparent to the most casual reader of Machiavelli's text. They are literary, dramatic, and moral qualities that stand out boldly on the page. They are implicit in the personality and voice of Machiavelli himself. But Machiavelli and his book were very much the product of their times, and it may be useful for the reader to have in mind a minimal outline sketch of the historical circumstances that formed both.

Machiavelli was born in 1469 and died in 1527; he was a Florentine. The city of Florence, straddling the Arno in northwest Italy, was in those days both a commercial center of European importance and the politico-military capital of the surrounding district, known as Tuscany. The Tuscans are a story all by themselves: they think themselves, and probably are, smarter than most other Italians. They tend to be ironic if not cynical, and rather proud of the fact that nobody likes them—which they take to be evident proof of their superior intelligence. Dante's is a characteristically Tuscan imagination—dry, clear, proud, and severely logical in its poetry. Machiavelli's mind has many of the same traits.

During the Renaissance, the Florentines exercised direct or indirect power over a great many other Tuscan cities, such as Prato, Pistoia, Pisa, Lucca, San Gimignano, and Siena. Like it or not, and many did not, these cities, and many of the country folk in the surrounding countryside, were ruled by the smart, quick Florentines. The city proper had been a republic as far back as historical records reached (before the year A.D. 1000), though with occasional intervals when a particular family or individual gained enough power to set up, uneasily and temporarily, as ruler. Thus the struggle between rich and poor, between centralized authoritarian rule and more popular, participatory forms of government, was a constant feature of Florentine history. During Machiavelli's lifetime, the chief family menacing the republican institutions of Florence was the Medici. Relevant portions of their family tree are outlined in the genealogical table on page x.

Cosimo, Piero, and Lorenzo, three successive generations of the Medici, ruled over Florence through the greater part of the fifteenth century, without altogether abolishing representative government, yet while clearly dominating it. They did so through a combination of force, persuasion, leniency, deception, and social astuteness. But the skills required to manage, without actual dictatorship, so restive and independent a city were exceptional, and without them even a Medici was helpless. When Lorenzo died in 1492, his son Pietro proved quite incapable, and within two years he and his supporters were forced into exile. A republican government replaced him. Machiavelli was then just twenty-three years old, and for the next eighteen years, until just before the writing of *The Prince*, it was a republican government under which he lived and for which he worked.

This is no place to describe the detailed machinery of Florentine city government and politics; a vivid impression of its working will be found in N. Rubenstein, *The Government of Florence under the Medici 1434–94* (Oxford, 1966); or Jean Lucas-Dubreton, *Daily Life in Florence in the Time of the Medici*, chapter 2. What cannot fail to amaze a modern reader is the extraordinary intensity of political life in this moderately sized city of one hundred thousand or so inhabitants. Even under the Medici, and to a much greater degree under the republic, Florence was like a swarm of political bees. Because they feared that administrations long in power would become entrenched and tyrannical, the Florentines limited most of their officials to short terms in office: a man might be elected to some major bodies for a term as brief as two months. As a result, the city was constantly involved in election campaigns, and politics was a constant preoccupation of every citizen. There were parties based upon ancient though nebulous principles, like the old Guelfs, who were tolerant of papal power and anti-German; they opposed the Ghibellines, who tended to favor the Holy Roman emperor, a German, and to distrust the pope. There were religious reformers, notably the Dominican monk Savonarola, who preached up a storm during the years 1494–98, till Alexander VI caused him to be burned in the public square. These were massive public events. But down among the grass roots—or at least in the narrow, cobblestoned alleys of the walled city —Florence was in constant ferment. The various wards and districts were in political conflict with one another; the rich and poor were often at each other's throats; the various families gathered and broke up into factions; the guilds and trades were politically active; and because they were all crowded together in a tight little town behind walls, the Florentines were subject to gusty rumors and surges of passion that sent them raging through the streets to howl or hammer at the high towers and massive palazzi within which lay hidden their heroes or hated enemies of the moment.

The systematic chaos here described was modified, however, by some stabilizing institutions. In 1502 a widely respected and constitutionally moderate man named Piero Soderini was elected for life to the highest office of the republic (gonfalonier); it was a deliberate effort to confer stability on the regime. On another level entirely, the family structures were strong forces making for stability. Young men were trained in politics by the elders of their family and party; only after a long period of initiation and trial in minor offices did men become eligible to run for major ones. And in areas where experience and continuity were essential, as in foreign policy, there was an ongoing bureaucracy of trained civil servants. At the age of twenty-nine in the year 1498, Machiavelli joined this staff, and he remained a valued servant in the diplomatic corps till the events of 1512 brought about the downfall of the republic as a whole, and the return of the Medici. Sometimes he served in the home office, transmitting instructions to, and receiving messages from, ambassadors abroad; on several occasions of no slight importance he was himself dispatched to represent the republic at the court of some foreign power. This work constituted his training to write *The Prince*, and we provide, in the Backgrounds section (pp. 75–88), a sampling of the reports he wrote on these missions. He knew his business well; his reports were much admired, and he himself rose in the service to be a valued agent of Piero Soderini.

The chief interest of Machiavelli's professional life was foreign policy, and not surprisingly the subject bulks large in *The Prince*. It behooves us therefore to know something of the world within which he and his employers had to operate. Florence, the city from which he saw everything, and in whose interests he always wrote, was neither large nor warlike; it was not protected by the sea, like Venice, nor was it an international center of religious authority, like Rome. To a great extent it depended on the skill of its craftsmen, the shrewdness of its merchants and bankers, and the political astuteness of its leaders. Until the death of Lorenzo in 1492, it survived and competed successfully in the little world of Italian power politics. Partly this was because of its strong points, noted above, and partly it was because the world of Italian politics was indeed a fairly autonomous world. There were five chief power units

Medici Family Tree—A Rough Diagram

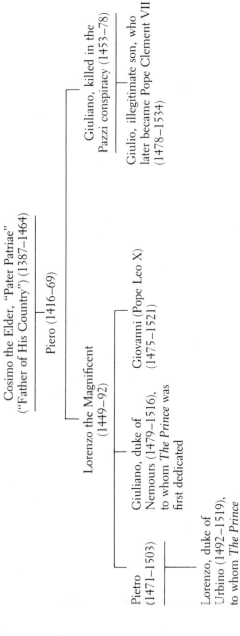

Cosimo the Elder, "Pater Patriae"
("Father of His Country") (1387–1464)

Piero (1416–69)

Lorenzo the Magnificent
(1449–92)

Giuliano, killed in the
Pazzi conspiracy (1453–78)

Giulio, illegitimate son, who
later became Pope Clement VII
(1478–1534)

Giovanni (Pope Leo X)
(1475–1521)

Giuliano, duke of
Nemours (1479–1516),
to whom *The Prince* was
first dedicated

Pietro
(1471–1503)

Lorenzo, duke of
Urbino (1492–1519),
to whom *The Prince*
was dedicated after the
death of Giuliano

on the peninsula, consisting, in addition to Florence, of Milan, Venice, the Papal States (an unruly district of semi-autonomous chieftains under the theoretical dominion of the pope in Rome), and the kingdom of Naples, also known sometimes as the kingdom of the Two Sicilies, or just the Kingdom. Because they had fairly well defined areas of interest, because no one of them was ever strong enough to dominate the other four, and because their wars were fought largely by professional soldiers who had no great interest in making things tough on one another, these five units managed to maintain, throughout the fifteenth century, an uneasy balance of power, tempered by frequent squabbles but never seriously shaken. They were not, after all, very much like modern nations. Ethnically, they were very similar; they all called themselves Italians. In religion, they were all Catholics, who accepted at least nominally the authority of the pope. They all spoke dialects of the same language. Socially, they were not too different. The kingdom of Naples was a royal state of sorts, though its dynastic affairs were an incredible tangle, with the French, the Spanish, and the papacy all laying claim to the royal power via various pretexts. The doge of Venice and the pope in Rome were elected to their offices, though by very different procedures. Milan was for many years under the command of the Visconti, local tyrants; they were replaced in 1450 by their former employee, Francesco Sforza, who was a professional soldier by trade, and the son of another professional soldier, who began life as a peasant. All these rulers were, for Machiavelli and his contemporaries, "princes"; it was a catchall term. But not one of them was the head of a nation in the modern sense.

Such nations did exist, however, and just two years after the death of Lorenzo, they began to intrude into Italy's little world of small-power political balances and neighborly squabbles. All through the fifteenth century, the kings of France had been consolidating their territories, taking over independent duchies like Burgundy and Brittany, and reducing their feudal lords to the service of a centralized monarchy. Much the same thing happened in Spain, though by a different process. The marriage of Ferdinand of Aragon with Isabella of Castile in 1469 led directly to the final expulsion of the Moors from Spain and a whole series of foreign adventures in Europe and the New World, to which the formidably centralized bureaucracy of Spain contributed support on an unprecedented scale. To put it with Machiavelli's bluntness, Ferdinand was always ready to start a new military adventure because he had a ruthlessly efficient system of tax collection. In Germany, centralization of power did not take the same form or proceed quite as far as in France and Spain; but under the Holy Roman emperor Maximilian I, the Germans were able to muster from their vast territories armies of tough professional soldiers (Landsknechte), before which the small Italian armies were ultimately helpless.

The influx of foreign armies into Italy was triggered by Ludovico Sforza of Milan. He invited the French, under Charles VIII, to invade Italy in order to assert their claim to the kingdom of Naples. This they in fact did (1494), and though they were forced to withdraw almost at once (by a coalition that included the treacherous Sforza himself), the ease with which they advanced the length of the peninsula alerted the other European powers to the fact that Italy was a plum for the picking. In 1499 the French were back again, this time under Louis XII—first to seize Milan from their old friend Sforza, then to assert their claim to Naples. And this time it was the Venetians who half encouraged the French invasion, as a way of getting back at their old enemies the Milanese; but the pope helped too, because he wanted French troops to support his bid for temporal power. Seeing Naples on the point of falling to the French, the Spanish moved in to cut them off; by the Treaty of Granada (1500) they got a share of Naples, and three years later they grabbed the whole thing. And thus the various Italian states began struggling to get themselves powerful foreign allies, and to protect themselves by hiring more and more foreign mercenaries—Swiss, Germans, Albanians, Gascons, Croatians, any bloodthirsty thugs whatever. Everybody deplored the arrival of these brutal freebooters, but the fact was that they won battles. In the last chapter of *The Prince*, Machiavelli recites a mournful litany of battles lost by Italian armies to invading foreigners; over a period of twenty years, he lists seven major battles lost or cities destroyed, and could have doubled or tripled the list without difficulty.

For Florence—rich, without natural protection, lying on the main road south, and without either a big army or a strong military tradition—things were particularly difficult. In the very first French invasion, Florence lost control of Pisa, which guarded the mouth of the Arno and thus was vital to Florentine trade. The struggle to get Pisa back was infinitely painful, expensive, and frustrating. Meanwhile, every gang of soldiers that appeared before the city gates meant a new levy on the citizens. Florence had to pay so many powerful "friends" to protect it, and powerful "enemies" not to attack it, that the difference between friends and enemies evaporated altogether. In the end, the Florentine republic suffered more as a result of its traditional loyalty to the French than from its traditional enemies. With blind obstinacy, and despite Machiavelli's repeated objections, the republic insisted on reaffirming its loyalty to its French allies, at the very moment when they were on the point of packing up and leaving Italy altogether. Their departure, in 1512, left the Florentines at the mercy of a hostile pope who was under the influence of the exiled Medici and allied with the tremendous power of Spain. For years Machiavelli had been calling for a citizen's army or militia, which would make the city independent of the hated and treacherous mercenaries. He had actually recruited and begun training this body. But in 1512, they came up prematurely against some veteran Spanish infantry, who smashed them with contemptuous ease. The republic fell, and Machiavelli with it; the Medici returned; and Machiavelli, after an uncomfortable interval during which he was tortured in connection with a suspected plot, was allowed to retire to the country, where he composed *The Prince*. His retirement from active politics did not of course stop the terrible process of decay and disintegration against which he had protested. Mercenaries continued to pour into Italy, the city states continued to fight one another instead of the invaders, and the climactic act of the whole squalid drama came in 1527, the year of Machiavelli's death. This was the infamous Sack of Rome, when a huge, disorderly mob of mercenary soldiers, mostly German and many Lutheran, but completely out of control by their officers or anybody else, surrounded, besieged, captured and for an entire summer looted, raped, murdered, burned, smashed, and vandalized the Holy City. Pope Clement VII was forced to seek shelter in the Castel San Angelo and pay a giant ransom to regain his liberty. The humiliation of Italy was complete.

In this entire story, one institution peculiar to the Italian scene played a constant part, which calls for a bit of extra explanation: this was of course the papacy. *The Prince* weaves the story of the various popes so deftly into the texture of its argument, and alludes to them so lightly, that it may be useful to have here a list of them, covering the period of Machiavelli's life:

> Sixtus IV (Francesco della Rovere), pope from 1471 to 1484
> Innocent VIII (Giovanni Battista Cibo), pope from 1484 to 1492
> Alexander VI (Rodrigo Borgia), pope from 1492 to 1503
> Pius III (Francesco Todeschini-Piccolomini), pope for eight weeks in 1503
> Julius II (Giuliano della Rovere, nephew of Sixtus IV, above), pope from 1503 to 1513
> Leo X (Giovanni de' Medici), pope from 1513 to 1521
> Adrian VI (Adrian Dedel), pope from 1522 to 1523
> Clement VII (Giulio de' Medici, cousin of Leo X above), pope from 1523 to 1534

All these popes were alike in combining enormous spiritual power with a certain measure of temporal power. It is customary to date the beginning of the Lutheran revolt from 1517; before that the spiritual power of the popes was largely unquestioned; and even after that, in most of the Latin countries, it remained supreme as a practical matter. On the other hand, the temporal power of the popes varied enormously, depending on Italian circumstances; and its application varied enormously, depending on the pope who occupied the seat of Peter, and his concerns. Machiavelli estimates the average life span of a sitting pope at about ten years, and as will be seen from the dates above, that figure is high. So changes of policy were inevitable and very frequent. Three strong, ambitious popes among the first five listed above embroiled the papacy deeply in the Italian political process that Machiavelli was trying to teach his prince to master. But as they took very different lines, and each policy was cut short in mid-career by the death of its maker, the papacy had an erratic, inconsistent influence on Italian politics that Machiavelli bitterly deplores.

Sixtus IV, the first of the three restless and ambitious popes, came to the office with little diplomatic or ecclesiastical experience, because he was the newest of the cardinals when they elected him pope. He began by arranging large international adventures, like an expedition against the Turks and a reconciliation with the Russian Church, but turned to Italian politics as more feasible, and involved his Papal States in successive wars against the Florentines and the Venetians. To finance his military campaigns, his building programs (including the Sistine Chapel, made famous later by Michelangelo), and a whole flock of hungry relatives, he began the process of milking the church's power to extract money from believers by the sale of indulgences, and the promulgation of new taxes, direct and indirect, on the faithful.

Alexander VI, the second of the activist popes, calls for more specific discussion. Like his predecessor Sixtus, he strained the moneygathering powers of the church to their absolute limits and beyond; like his predecessor Sixtus, he was a lavish and shameless nepotist, pouring money on his relatives. But those relatives were not just nieces and nephews; they were his own illegitimate children. And one of them, Cesare Borgia, duke of Valentino, is of central importance to Machiavelli's book.

Cesare seems originally to have been destined for the Church; through his father's influence, he was made an archbishop and a cardinal at the age of seventeen. But after only five years he gave up these offices "for the good of his soul," as he said; in fact, he was a reckless, violent man, with a deep streak of personal cruelty. Whether or not all the stories of incest, fratricide, poisoning, and so on that are told about the domestic life of the Borgias are true, we need not decide here. That Cesare Borgia was a formidable fellow in an age of very hard cases indeed is apparent from the record. And from the first he was the agent of his father's political schemes. These can be roughly outlined as follows. In October 1498, Cesare went to France as legate (agent) for his father; he brought with him a papal bull entitling Louis XII to set aside his first wife and marry Anne of Brittany, thereby completing the unification of France. Louis also got papal permission, if not encouragement, to assert his claim to the dukedom of Milan at the expense of Ludovico Sforza. In exchange, Cesare got the dukedom of Valentinois in France (hence the

Italians always called him Duke Valentino), and a promise of French assistance in his own military affairs in Italy. These affairs called first of all for the unification and strengthening of the Papal States; and then, though Louis was not told this, and would not have liked it had he guessed, for the unification of all Italy under the leadership of Cesare Borgia.

The Papal States comprised a large group of semi-feudal domains and semi-independent cities across the middle of the Italian peninsula. In two campaigns that are carefully described in *The Prince* (they took place in 1499 and 1500–1501), Cesare subdued this area, known as the Romagna. In 1502 a conspiracy was raised against him, by the petty war lords of the district and the powerful Roman family of the Orsini, who saw too late that he was threatening their independent survival. But he put down the conspiracy, trapped its leaders in the little town of Sinigaglia, and on the last day of December 1502, had the two most dangerous of them strangled in their dungeon. As spring turned to summer of 1503, Cesare and his father Alexander stood on the verge of success in their bold and venturesome scheme. One more campaign in northern Italy would enable Cesare to dictate terms to the Italian states, and then to deal on more or less equal terms between France and Spain. But at that crucial moment, Alexander unexpectedly died, just at the time when Cesare himself was deathly ill. Everything depended on the choice of Alexander's successor; and though Cesare was able to manipulate one stopgap pope into office, the wretched man did not live a month; and in the next election, Julius II was named without opposition. He was an old and inveterate enemy of all the Borgias; without support in the Vatican, Cesare was doomed, and he faded away, to die a few years later in an obscure scuffle in Spain.

Meanwhile, though Julius, the third activist pope, retained many of the same general objectives as his predecessor, he pursued them in an entirely different way. Headstrong and volatile, he bullied the Florentines and made war on the Venetians in order to persuade them to join with him in driving the French out of Italy. In many of his projects he was successful, partly because nobody expected to see a graybearded Vicar of Christ campaigning at the head of his army through winter mud and snow. But because he was committed to a wholly new set of feuds and loyalties, Julius built his policies at complete cross-purposes with those of the Borgias. Where they had tried to use the French against the Spanish, he tried to use the Spanish against the French, and enlisted the Swiss against both; where they had tried to crush the Orsini family and the magnates of the Romagna, Julius raised many of them up. And as he was sixty years old when he became pope, it was apparent to one and all that his policies would almost certainly be soon reversed by a successor. Hence the fatal conclusion described above, the total prostration of Italy, less than fifteen years after his death.

This, then, in bare outline, is the school in which Machiavelli learned his trade. His was a lean, acute mind to begin with; years of struggle against complex and dangerous circumstances honed it to razor sharpness. Two other influences on it should perhaps be cited. Machiavelli was a learned man; he read widely in the classical authors, especially the historians of the republics, reading Greek authors in Latin translations and Latin authors in the original. He was proud of his learning, and often used it, after the manner of his day, to buttress a contemporary argument. At the same time, he was an instinctive dramatist, and one of the dramatic effects he most enjoyed producing was shock and outrage. Even when writing in private to his friends, he often chose to depict himself in more villainous colors than he could have used, and professed more desperate opinions than he really held. Like a great many Tuscans, he had a horror of being taken for a dupe, and to avoid that appearance did not mind sometimes being considered a monster. Readers who have carefully studied *The Prince* will be able to make their own estimates of Machiavelli's character; but when they have studied the *Discorsi* and the other writings as well, they will be able to make better ones.

ROBERT M. ADAMS

Translator's Note

Readers of *The Prince* who study it in Italian after first becoming acquainted with it in English translation are likely to be a little surprised at the complex and various quality of Machiavelli's prose. It is not of a piece throughout, as translations make it seem. There are indeed epigrams and aphorisms with the brief, cruel point of a stiletto; there are also, and more characteristically, complex sentences overburdened by modifiers, laden with subordinate clauses, and serpentine in their length. Machiavelli likes to balance concepts and phrases, to build the structure of his thought out of elegantly juxtaposed contrasts, and to draw out the tenor of his thought through a long, linked, circumstantial sentence. By contrast with the Ciceronianisms of his humanist contemporaries, Machiavelli's periods may have seemed brutally swift and abrupt; but standards have changed, and I have not thought it improper to render, on occasion, one of my author's poised yet labyrinthine periods, by four or five separate English sentences. Given a choice between the lucid poise of Machiavelli's ideas, and their close syntactical knotting, I have generally opted for the former. It is, after all, partly a matter of convention; in some ways, Machiavelli used the full stop as we use the paragraph (which was not at his disposal), and the only way to preserve his main intention is to alter the convention by which he punctuated. Besides, a modest advantage really does attach, in translation, to readability. So I have sinned like most of my predecessors, and surrendered one of my author's many qualities in the hope of making the others shine forth more cleanly.

For a couple of crucial words in *Il Principe*, modern English has no true equivalent. The pair *principe-principato* is of course perfectly easy to translate as "prince-principality"; but neither equivalent is very accurate. Machiavelli's prince is not our prince by a long shot—he may, for example, be what we would call a king or he may be a mercenary soldier; he may be elected, like a doge, or be a churchman like a pope. A "principality" in English doesn't include a kingdom or a baronial fief, as "principato" does in Italian; but its worst defect is that it is a learned, cautious word, a kind of neutral word in English. A "principality" is what a "prince" governs, and he is defined chiefly as not a king, not a duke, not a president, not a pope, not a condottiere—not even a prince, really, because in English usage a prince (like the Prince of Wales) doesn't govern, and that is one thing that Machiavelli's *principe* emphatically does. "Prince" and "principality" are chiefly defined in English by negatives, whereas for Machiavelli they are nothing if not positive and inclusive. I have generally translated *principe* as "prince," simply for lack of a better term, though I have turned occasionally to "ruler" or "governor"; and *principato* has become a variety of words, depending on circumstances—"principate," "princedom," "princely state," or just plain "state" when the context has permitted. Further dilemmas arise in translating the words *stato, dominio, paese, provincia, regno, città* and *patria* (but never *nazione*), which I have had to adjudicate with nothing more decisive than tact. A last, long-standing problem in translating Machiavelli is posed by the word *virtù*, which can mean anything from "strength," "ability," "courage," "manliness," or "ingenuity" to "character," "wisdom," or even (last resort) "virtue." I have translated it in all of these senses and several others; but to preserve an awareness that it is really the same original word behind all these manifestations, I have retained it (in brackets, in the original Italian) next to each different translation.

This diphthong effect (which must be exaggerated if it is to be caught at all) suggests another special stylistic quality of Machiavelli's prose, which is bound to cost a translator a few extra twinges. This is his trick of using adjectives or nouns in carefully distanced pairs, so that one undercuts as well as complements the other. Cesare Borgia, for instance, was gifted with "tanta ferocità e tanta virtù" that with a little luck he might have survived the catastrophe of his father's death. The débacle of Louis in Lombardy is described as no miracle, but "molto ordinario e ragionevole"—where both adjectives imply, though from different points of view, a wonderfully remote and serene perspective. A virtuoso performance on the double adjective is that which begins with the description of Remirro de Orco's murder as having left the people both "satisfatti e stupidi"; the phrase is picked up, in intricate counterpoint, twelve chapters later, when Septimius Severus is said to have rendered the soldiers "attoniti e stupidi," while leaving the people "reverenti e satisfatti." One translates here for a finely mingled concord and discord: the words are isometric, so to speak.

Another oddity in the original, which there is no reason to do more than mention in passing, is Machiavelli's habit of titling his chapters in Latin and using occasional Latin words in his text, above all when defining logical relationships. *Praeterea, in exemplis, tamen, quodam modo,* and so forth—they give the treatise a slightly dry and schoolmasterish tonality. At the same time, Machiavelli is not above slang and popular metaphors, as when Charles took Italy "with chalk" (*col gesso*); and he is capable of extended passages of rather broad irony, as in his description of the felicity of ecclesiastical states. Among other pleasures of the translator's task is the swift dexterity with which Machiavelli can sketch a story like that of Oliverotto da Fermo, in chapter VIII, with its magnificently climactic last word, *strangolato*; or slash an argument down to the dimensions he has chosen for it:

> E perchè e' non può essere buone legge dove non sono buone arme, e dove sono buone arme conviene sieno buone legge, io lascerò indrieto il ragionare delle legge e parlerò delle arme.

> ("And since there can't be good laws where there aren't good soldiers, and where there are good soldiers there are bound to be good laws, I shall set aside the topic of laws and talk about soldiers.")

Since the question of laws would never have come up if Machiavelli himself hadn't raised it, the ruthless speed with which he here disposes of it suggests a certain impatience with pedagogic formulae that is itself profoundly pedagogic. A prince must learn to look under the surface of antithetical constructs (such as Machiavelli himself has used freely in the first chapters of his book) in order to distinguish the mere formula (the either-or for its own sake) from genuine alternatives. In addition to practical precepts, Machiavelli's language offers the prince a severe model of the lean Tuscan style.

But these are pleasures to be appreciated in the text itself. A book so lucid and taut in its phrasings offers relatively few problems to the translator who has opted for a plain style. The book has been many times rendered, and while some versions are better than others, the spectrum of their variation is not particularly wide, as it generally is in translations of lyric poetry. The problems of Machiavelli's text lie less in its verbal complexities than in its practical implications and applications.

R. M. A.

The Text of
THE PRINCE

Niccolò Machiavelli to the Magnificent Lorenzo de' Medici:[1]

It is a frequent custom for those who seek the favor of a prince to make him presents of those things they value most highly or which they know are most pleasing to him. Hence one often sees gifts consisting of horses, weapons, cloth of gold, precious stones, and similar ornaments suitable for men of noble rank. I too would like to commend myself to Your Magnificence with some token of my readiness to serve you; and I have not found among my belongings anything I prize so much or value so highly as my knowledge of the actions of great men, acquired through long experience of contemporary affairs and extended reading in antiquity. For a long time I have thought carefully about these matters and examined them minutely; now I have condensed my thoughts into a little volume, and send it to Your Magnificence. Though I know it is unworthy to enter your presence, still I hope you will be graciously pleased to accept this work; since I could give no greater gift than this, which will enable you to grasp in short order everything I have learned over many years and come to understand through many trials and troubles. My book is not stuffed with pompous phrases or elaborate, magnificent words, neither is it decorated with any form of extrinsic rhetorical embroidery, such as many authors use to present or adorn their materials. I wanted my book to be absolutely plain, or at least distinguished only by the variety of the examples and the importance of the subject.

I hope it will not be thought presumptuous if a man of low social rank undertakes to discuss the rule of princes and lay down instructions for them. When painters want to represent landscapes, they stand on low ground to get a true view of the mountains and hills; they climb to the tops of the mountains to get a panorama over the valleys. Similarly, to know the people well one must be a prince, and to know princes well one must be, oneself, of the people.

Will Your Magnificence, then, deign to accept this little gift in the same spirit that I send it? If you will read it over and study it carefully, you will recognize in it my most earnest desire that you may achieve that summit of grandeur to which your happy destiny and your other capacities predestine you. And if from that summit Your Magnificence will occasionally glance down at these humble places, you will recognize how unjustly I suffer the bitter and sustained malignity of fortune.

1. When he first wrote it, Machiavelli dedicated his book to Giuliano de' Medici, third son of Lorenzo the Magnificent; after Giuliano's death in 1516, he rededicated it to Lorenzo, duke of Urbino, one of the original Lorenzo's grandsons, here called the magnificent but never half as magnificent as his grandfather. See the genealogical table in the Historical Introduction, p. x.

The form of the dedication reveals Machiavelli's devotion to antiquity; it is an imitation of the Address to Nicocles by the ancient Greek rhetorician Isocrates.

I /

DIFFERENT KINDS OF STATES, AND THE DIFFERENT WAYS TO GET THEM

All the states and governments that ever had or now have power over men were and are of two sorts: either republics or princely states. And princely states also are of two sorts: either hereditary, where the family of the ruler has been in control for a long time, or else new. And the new ones are either brand-new, as Milan was for Francesco Sforza,[2] or they are like grafts freshly joined to the hereditary state of a prince who has acquired them, as the kingdom of Naples was to the kingdom of Spain.[3] New acquisitions of this sort are either accustomed to living under a prince, or used to being free; they may be acquired either by force of other people's arms or with one's own, either by fortune or by strength [*virtù*].

II 2

ON HEREDITARY PRINCIPATES

Setting aside republics, about which I have spoken at length elsewhere,[4] I shall concern myself only with princely states; and, following the outline set down above, I shall describe how these states may be governed and kept in hand.

Let me say, then, that hereditary states which have grown used to the family of their ruler are much less trouble to keep in hand than new ones are; it is simply a matter of not upsetting ancient customs, and of accommodating oneself to meet new circumstances. Hence, if a prince is just ordinarily industrious, he can always keep his position, unless some unusual or excessive act of force deprives him of it. And even if he is dethroned, the slightest mistake by the usurper will enable him to get it back.

We have an Italian example in the duke of Ferrara,[5] who stood up

2. Francesco Sforza (1401–66), second of the name. The father, originally named Giacomo or Muzio Attendolo, was a tough peasant who when he became a professional soldier took the name of Sforza, implying energy and ambition. His bastard son Francesco was also a professional soldier for many years, often on both sides of the same feud. When the ancient line of the Visconti expired in Milan (1447), he first defended, then betrayed the republic that replaced it, and in 1450 had himself declared duke of Milan.

3. As noted in the Historical Introduction, the kingdom of Naples, including southern Italy and Sicily, had a tangled succession to which practically everybody in Europe had some sort of claim. After being partitioned between France and Spain by the Treaty of Granada (1500), it was captured for Spain and King Ferdinand by brute force of arms (1503). This is the annexation to which Machiavelli alludes. See chapters III and XVIII.

4. In book 1 of the *Discorsi* on Livy's history,

Machiavelli discusses, among other things, republics.

5. Two dukes of Ferrara were involved in the two assaults. Ercole d' Este (1471–1505) had to yield a district of his territory to the Venetians in 1484 as a result of a dispute over a tax on salt. His successor, Alfonso (1486–1534), refused to join the Venetians and the pope in a holy league against the French, and had to defend himself against both of them. He too lost a couple of cities, but held out, and was ultimately able to regain them. The house of Este had been established in Ferrara for four centuries, but Machiavelli's point would have been less clear-cut had he told us that Alfonso d' Este was a wily diplomat, a master strategist, a superb gunner, and one of the most skilled soldiers in Europe. His conflating of the gentle, culturally minded Ercole with the tough, resourceful Alfonso makes more impressive his point that a long-established regime is a stable one.

against attacks from the Venetians in 1484, and those of Pope Julius in 1510,[6] for no better reason than that his family had ruled in that district for a long time. Since a prince by birth has fewer reasons and less need to offend his subjects, it follows that he should be better liked; if he has no extravagant vices to make him hateful, it is only natural that he should be popular with his own people. And in the antiquity and continuity of the government, people forget not only the reason for innovations, but their very existence, because every new change provides a footing to build on another.[7]

III 3

ON MIXED PRINCIPALITIES

But it is the new state that makes troubles. To begin with, if it is not entirely new but like a graft freshly joined to an old kingdom (so that the two bodies together may be considered mixed), its problems derive from a natural difficulty, common to all new states, which is that all men are ready to change masters in the hope of bettering themselves. In this belief they take up arms against their master, but find themselves deceived when they discover by experience that instead things have got worse. And the reason for this is another natural and ordinary necessity, which is that a new prince must always harm those over whom he assumes authority, both with his soldiers and with a thousand other hardships that are entailed in a new conquest. Thus you have as enemies all those you have harmed in seizing power, and you cannot stay friends with those who put you in power, because you can never satisfy them as they expected. Nor can you use strong medicines against them, because you are under obligations to them. However strong your armies may be, you always need the backing of local people to take over a province. This was why Louis XII of France took Milan quickly and lost it just as quickly. The first time, Ludovico's[8] own troops were able to take it back without any help, because those who had opened the gates to Louis were deceived in their hopes, disappointed in the rewards they had expected, and so refused to put up with the annoyances of the new prince.[9]

It is true, of course, that once lands which have rebelled are conquered a second time, they are not so easily lost, because the ruler who has

✓

6. Julius II, the pope who attacked Alfonso, was the most warlike Vicar of Christ ever to hold the office. Machiavelli summarizes his rash, adventurous character in chapter XXV.
7. Machiavelli uses the technical term *l'addentellato* ("crenellation") to express the way in which one policy of a long-continuing government can deliberately be designed to provide a footing on which to construct the next.
8. Ludovico Sforza's.
9. The calamitous story of how the French were first called into Italy by Ludovico Sforza is sketched in the Historical Introduction. The historical details to which Machiavelli is referring are that Louis XII took Milan in the fall of 1499, that Ludovico recovered it on February 5, 1500, and lost it for the second time only a couple of months later. Ludovico ended his life gloomily, a prisoner in remote exile at the lovely but alien castle of Loches, not far from Tours.

learned from the revolt will be less hesitant about securing his position
by punishing culprits, exposing suspects, and strengthening his own weak
points. So that though France could be driven out of Milan the first
time by nothing more than Duke Ludovico blustering on the borders
of the territory, the second time it was necessary for the whole world to
unite against her, destroying her armies or chasing them out of Italy.[1]
The reasons for this difference were stated above. In any case, Milan
was taken away from France the second time as well as the first.

I have described the general reasons for the first loss; I must now
describe the reasons for the second, and see what devices were available
to Louis, or to someone else in his position, to keep better hold on his
new possessions than the French king did. Let me say, then, that new
states which are acquired by, or annexed to, an already existing state
are either of the same district and language, or else not. When they are,
it is perfectly easy to hold onto them, especially when they are not used
to independence. To keep a secure hold, it suffices to have extinguished
the line of the previous prince, because in other matters, as long as you
keep their old way of life and do not change their customs, men will
live quietly enough. And this has been demonstrated in the cases of
Burgundy, Brittany, Gascony, and Normandy, which have been joined
with France for so long.[2] There is indeed some difference of language,
but the customs are much the same, and so they have been able to get
along easily. Whoever has acquired such lands and wants to hold onto
them must keep just two things in mind: one is that the line of the
previous prince be extinguished, and the other is to avoid changing
either the laws or the taxes, so that the new acquisitions may become
incorporated, in the shortest possible time, with the old kingdom as one
single body.

But when one acquires new possessions in a district that differs from
one's own in language, customs, and laws, that is where troubles arise,
and where one needs good luck and plenty of resolution to hold onto
them. One of the best and most effective policies would be for the new
possessor of territories to go there and live. This would make his possession more secure and longer-lasting, as it did for the Turks in Greece.[3]

---

1. After the French captured Milan for a second time (April 1500), they held it for more
than a decade, and could be dislodged only by
Julius II's Lega Santa. Effectively, this was a
coalition of papal troops with those of Spain
and Venice; on paper it also included the emperor Maximilian I and Henry VIII of
England—hence Machiavelli's phrase, "the
whole world." (It was Alfonso d' Este's refusal
to join this league that led to Pope Julius's
attack on him; see chapter II, note 5, p. 4.)
2. Normandy became part of France in 1204,
but the other semi-independent duchies and
provinces were all incorporated with France
over the last half of the fifteenth century—

Gascony in 1453, Burgundy in 1477, and Brittany in 1491. The last of these annexations took
place in connection with the marriage of
Charles VIII to Anne of Brittany. By completing the consolidation of France, it paved
the way for Charles's and Louis's Italian
adventures.
3. After the Turks captured Constantinople in
1453, under Muhammad II, "the Conqueror,"
their power was rapidly extended, not only over
modern Greece but throughout the Balkans; by
deliberate policy, the new occupiers settled
onto the land, not to be uprooted till the nineteenth century.

These people would never have been able to hold onto their new possessions, whatever precautions they took, if they had not gone there to live themselves. When you are on the spot, you can see troubles getting started, and take care of them right away; when you do not live there, you hear of them only when they have grown great and there is no longer a cure. Besides this, the new province will not be looted by your officials, and the citizens will be satisfied because they have easy access to the prince. If they want to be good citizens, they have more reason to love him, and if they do not, they have more reason to fear him. Any foreigner who thinks of attacking that state will think twice about it; for the prince who lives on his new possessions can be deprived of them only with the greatest of difficulty.

Another, and even better policy, is to set up colonies in one or two places which will serve, so to speak, as the shackles of the state. If he does not do this, the prince will have to maintain immense forces of cavalry and infantry. Colonies are not expensive; for little or nothing you can send them out and keep them up. The only people hurt are those who lose their houses and fields to the new possessors, and they are a very small part of the new state. The ones who are actually hurt, being poor and scattered, cannot possibly do any harm. All the others remain untouched, which is a persuasion to keep quiet; yet they also become fearful of making a mistake and suffering like those who have already been despoiled. I conclude that these colonies are cheaper, do better service, and commit less damage than any other method. Those whom they harm can take no reprisals, because they are left poor and scattered, as I said. And in this connection it should be remarked that men ought either to be caressed or destroyed, since they will seek revenge for minor hurts but will not be able to revenge major ones. Any harm you do to a man should be done in such a way that you need not fear his revenge. If you maintain an army instead of colonies, the expense will be much greater, so that you may have to spend all the money you get from a state in standing guard over it: the profit may even turn to a loss. An army is also much more offensive to the subjects, because the whole state is harmed when the prince drags his army about with him from place to place. Everyone feels this inconvenience, every man becomes an enemy; and these are enemies who can do harm, because, even though beaten, they remain in their own homes. On every count, then, defense by armies is useless, as defense by colonies is useful.

In addition, the man who comes into an alien province of this sort ought to set up at once as head and protector of his weak neighbors, should try to weaken his strong neighbors, and should make sure at all costs that no foreigner gets in who is as powerful as he is. You can always count on the foreigner's being invited in by those who are discontented, through either excess ambition or fear, as was seen long ago when the Aetolians[4] first brought the Romans into Greece. Wherever the Romans went in other provinces, they were always sent for by the local inhabitants. The rule is that as soon as a powerful foreigner enters a district, those in the area who are least powerful flock to him, out of hatred for the strong man who had been ruling over them. Thus the foreigner need be at no pains to gain over these people, because they will quickly and gladly join in the new state he has acquired. He need only take care not to let them have too much strength and authority of their own; then, with his own strength and their support, he can easily put down the powerful men of the district, to become master of the province in all things. Anybody who does not follow this line will quickly lose what he has acquired, or as long as he manages to keep it will find it a source of infinite problems and annoyances.

Whenever the Romans took over a province, this was the policy they followed; they sent out colonies, indulged the less powerful without increasing their strength, broke the powerful, and never allowed any strong foreigners to pick up a following in their lands. I will limit my examples to the Romans in their dealings with the province of Greece, where they indulged the Achaeans and Aetolians, humbled the kingdom of Macedon, and drove Antiochus out of the land.[5] Yet they never let the merits of the Achaeans and Aetolians gain them any authority in the region, never let Philip talk them into being friends till they had reduced his strength, and never let the power of Antiochus gain any foothold in their territory. In each of these instances, the Romans did just what every wise ruler ought to do: you have to keep an eye, not only on present troubles, but on those of the future, and make every effort to avoid them. When you see the trouble in advance, it is easily remedied, but when you wait till it is on top of you, the antidote is useless, the disease has become incurable. What doctors say about consumption applies here: in the early stages it is hard to recognize and easy to cure, but in the later stages, if you have done nothing about it, it becomes easy to recognize and hard to cure. That is how it goes in affairs of state: when you recognize evils in advance, as they take shape (which requires some prudence to do), you can quickly cure them; but when you have not seen them, and so let them grow till anyone can recognize them, there is no longer a remedy.

Thus the Romans, who could see troubles at a distance, always found remedies for them. They never allowed a trouble spot to remain simply

---

4. In 211 B.C. the Aetolians, a relatively weak confederacy of cities and states in north and central Greece, called in the Romans to help them against Philip of Macedon. Once established in Greece, the Romans easily controlled a balance of power, by means indicated below. 5. The Achaeans were a federal league, similar to the Aetolians and opposed to them. Antiochus III of Syria, invited by the Aetolians and incited by Hannibal (who had taken refuge in the Middle East after his defeat in the Second Punic War), invaded Greece in 196 B.C.; he provided a natural counterweight to Philip V of Macedon. The decisive battle in which the Romans gained control of Greece by defeating Philip was that of Cynoscephelae (197 B.C.); seven years later they destroyed the power of Antiochus at Magnesia in Asia Minor.

to avoid going to war over it, because they knew that wars don't just go away, they are only postponed to someone else's advantage. Therefore they made war with Philip and Antiochus in Greece, in order not to have to fight them in Italy. At the time, they could have avoided both wars, but they chose not to. They never went by that saying which you hear constantly from the wiseacres of our day, that time heals all things. They trusted rather to their own character [*virtù*] and prudence—knowing perfectly well that time contains the seeds of all things, good as well as bad, bad as well as good. ✓

But, returning to France, let us see if she did any of the things we have described; and I shall talk of Louis rather than Charles, because he controlled Italy for a longer period of time and wrote a more considerable record.[6] You will see that he did exactly the opposite of what should be done to control an alien province.

King Louis was brought into Italy by the ambition of the Venetians, who expected by his coming to get control of half the state of Lombardy. I don't mean to blame the king for his part in the scheme; he wanted a foothold in Italy, and not only had no friends in the province, but found all doors barred against him because of King Charles's behavior.[7] Hence he had to take what friendships he could get; and if he had made no further mistakes in his other arrangements, he might have carried things off very successfully. By taking Lombardy, the king quickly regained the reputation lost by Charles. Genoa yielded, and the Florentines turned friendly; the marquis of Mantua, the duke of Ferrara, the Bentivogli (of Bologna), the countess Forlì, the lords of Faenza, Pesaro, Rimini, Camerino, Piombino, and the people of Lucca, Pisa, and Siena all sought him out with professions of friendship.[8] At this point the Venetians began to see the folly of what they had done, since in order to gain for themselves a couple of districts in Lombardy, they had now made the king master of a third of Italy.

Consider now how easy it would have been for the king to maintain his position in Italy if he had observed the rules laid down above, and become the protector and defender of his new friends. They were many, they were weak, some of them were afraid of the Venetians, others of the Church, hence they were bound to stick by him; and with their help, he could easily have protected himself against the remaining great

6. Charles VIII, a thoroughly impractical, visionary fellow, was in Italy for little more than a year (1494–95). Neither Charles nor Louis, both of whom were unprepossessing men physically and intellectually, could have failed to impress Machiavelli. If national organization could raise men like these to positions of power and authority, what could it not do for Cesare Borgia?
7. Starting from his idea of claiming Naples, Charles dreamed of recapturing Constantinople from the Turks and then advancing through the East like another Alexander; no sooner had he actually appeared in Italy than the Italians joined with Maximilian I, the Holy Roman Emperor, to drive him out.
8. Machiavelli's list of Louis's friends deliberately includes both big and little *signori*, the rulers of important cities like Bologna and of very little towns indeed, people from every area of northern Italy. In throwing away their support, Louis weakened himself everywhere.

powers. But no sooner was he established in Milan than he took exactly
the wrong tack, helping Pope Alexander to occupy the Romagna. And
he never realized that by this decision he was weakening himself, driving
away his friends and those who had flocked to him, while strengthening
the Church by adding vast temporal power to the spiritual power which
gives it so much authority. Having made his first mistake, he was forced
into others. To limit the ambition of Alexander and keep him from
becoming master of Tuscany, he was forced to come to Italy himself.[9]
Not satisfied with having made the Church powerful and deprived himself of his friends, he went after the kingdom of Naples and divided it
with the king of Spain.[1] And where before he alone had been the arbiter
of Italy, he brought in a rival to whom everyone in the kingdom who
was ambitious on his own account or dissatisfied with Louis could have
recourse. He could have left in Naples a caretaker king of his own, but
he threw him out, and substituted a man capable of driving out Louis
himself.[2]

It is perfectly natural and ordinary that men should want to acquire
things; and always when men do what they can, they will be praised or
not blamed; but when something is beyond them and they try to get it
anyhow, then they are in error, and deserve blame. If France could
have taken Naples with her own power, she should have done so; if she
could not, she should have split the kingdom with the Spaniards. The
division of Lombardy that she made with the Venetians was excusable,
since it gave Louis a foothold in Italy; the division of Naples with Spain
was an error, since there was no such necessity for it.

Thus Louis had committed these five errors: he put down the weaker
powers; he increased the strength of a major power; he introduced a very
powerful foreigner in the midst of his new subjects; he never took up
residence among them; and he never set up any colonies. And yet all
these mistakes, if he had lived, might not have ruined him, if he had
not made a sixth, in depriving the Venetians of their power.[3] Indeed,
if he had not previously made the Church powerful, or brought Spain

---

9. Alexander VI was Rodrigo Borgia, father of
Cesare and Lucrezia. The armies of Louis XII,
led by Gian Giorgio Trivulzio during the first
expeditions against Ludovico Sforza, required
the presence of the king himself in August
1502, as a result of Cesare's menacing
presence.
1. Charles VIII's claim to the throne of Naples
was based on dynastic arguments involving his
connection with the house of Anjou; but Naples, as the most remote of the Italian states,
was obviously the hardest for a French army to
annex or defend. Ferdinand II of Spain was
the king with whom Louis arranged (by the
treaty of Granada, in 1500) to share Naples.
2. He could have left Frederick of Aragon, the
original ruler, in Naples, taking the real power
from him but leaving him nominal command

of his kingdom; instead, he installed Ferdinand, who promptly drove him out. The modern historian, summarizing the treaty of
Granada, assigns most of the disgrace to Ferdinand, most of the folly to Louis: John S.
Bridge, *History of France* (Oxford, 1929)
3.137–40.
3. When he joined in the League of Cambrai
(1508) under the leadership of Julius II to take
part in a war against the Venetians, Louis
sealed his own doom. The victory of Vailà or
Agnadello (May 14, 1509), which put the
Venetians out of circulation on the mainland,
led directly to the formation of the Lega Santa
(see note 1, page 6), in which Venetian armies
were allowed to take a subordinate role for the
purpose of driving the French from Italy.

into Italy, putting down the Venetians might have been perfectly reasonable and necessary. But when he had taken the other steps, he should never have agreed to their ruin, because while they remained powerful, they would have kept everyone else out of Lombardy. The reason is simply that the Venetians would never have let anyone else into Lombardy unless they were in control; nobody would have wanted to take Lombardy from France just to give it to the Venetians; and nobody would have had courage enough to attack the two of them together. And if someone puts up the argument that King Louis gave the Romagna to Pope Alexander, and the kingdom of Naples to Spain, in order to avoid a war, I would answer as I did before: that you should never let things get out of hand in order to avoid war. You don't avoid such a war, you merely postpone it, to your own disadvantage. And if someone else should cite the oath that the king swore to the pope,[4] promising to undertake this enterprise in exchange for the annulment of his marriage and the post of cardinal for Rouen, my answer will be given later on, when I discuss the promises of princes and how they should be kept.

In this way King Louis lost Lombardy because he did not observe any of the rules established by others who have taken provinces and tried to keep them. None of this is in any way miraculous, but perfectly ordinary and reasonable. And I talked over this whole subject at Nantes with the cardinal of Rouen when Valentino (as people generally called Cesare Borgia, the son of Pope Alexander) was occupying the Romagna.[5] Actually, the cardinal told me that Italians knew nothing about war, and I told him that the French knew nothing about politics; since, if they knew the first thing about it, they would never allow the Church to grow so great. It has been our experience in Italy that the Church and Spain have grown powerful through the influence of France, and that their power caused her ruin. From this we can draw a general rule, which never fails or only rarely: the man who makes another powerful ruins himself. The reason is that he gets power either by shrewdness or by strength, and both qualities are suspect to the man who has been given the power.

---

4. In order to retain possession of Brittany by marrying Anne of Brittany, widow of Charles VIII (see note 2, page 6), Louix XII had to get a dispensation from Alexander VI to divorce his first wife, Jeanne. In addition, he wanted his favorite, George d' Amboise, archbishop of Rouen, to be made cardinal. In exchange for these papal favors, Louis agreed with Alexander VI to help the pope get the Romagna, and to undertake the expedition against Naples—to which both pope and king asserted a historic claim. Louis felt he had to honor this promise—which, as made to Alexander, might have been merely very dangerous—with his successor Julius II, with whom it was disastrous.

5. Machiavelli was on a diplomatic mission to France in 1500, i.e., just when Cesare Borgia and his father were starting to gain control of the Romagna, and must have talked with George d'Amboise, the cardinal of Rouen, at that time.

IV 4

WHY THE SUCCESSORS OF ALEXANDER AFTER HIS DEATH DID NOT LOSE
THE KINGDOM HE HAD CONQUERED FROM DARIUS

Seeing how hard it is to hold onto a newly acquired state, somebody
might wonder why after the death of Alexander, when he had conquered
Asia in just a few years and had barely settled into power, the land did
not rebel, as you might have thought it would; on the contrary, Alexander's successors kept their hold on it, and had no problems in keeping
it other than those arising from their own ambitions and consequent
difficulties with one another.[6] I answer that all kingdoms of which we
have any knowledge are governed in one of two ways: either by a single
prince with everyone else as servants, who by his appointment and
permission assist him in the task of ruling; or by a prince with the aid
of barons, who hold that rank, not by the prince's grace, but by right
of birth in an ancient family. Barons of this sort have states and subjects
of their own, who recognize them as masters and are naturally fond of
them. States governed by a prince and his servants grant the prince more
authority because in the whole district there is nobody who can claim
real power except the prince; when other people are obeyed, they are
obeyed as ministers and officials, and command no affection in their
own persons.

Contemporary examples of these two different sorts of government
are to be found in Turkey and France. The whole monarchy of Turkey
is governed by a single master; everyone else is his servant; he divides
his kingdom into districts, sending different administrators to each, and
changing them around as he thinks best.[7] But the king of France is
placed in the midst of a great many noblemen of long standing, each
recognized by his own subjects in his own district, and held in esteem
by them. They have their different privileges; the king himself cannot
meddle with these, except at his peril. Comparing the two states, anyone
can see that, though conquering the Turkish state might be hard, once
conquered, it would be easy to hold. On the other hand, to take the
state of France would be relatively easy in some ways, but to hold onto
it would be very hard.

6. When Alexander died abruptly in 323 B.C.,
power was divided among his main lieutenants,
Antipater, Antigonus, Ptolemy, and Perdiccas.
As these men had already been granted wide
governmental as well as military power (they
were satraps of districts as well as generals of
the army), they adapted easily to independent
rule. The exception that Machiavelli makes (in
saying the only trouble they got into came from
their own quarrels) is accurate but it is not
insignificant; their quarrels were continuous,
immensely complex, and brutally destructive.

7. Two great sultans ruled Turkey in Machiavelli's time: Muhammad II the Conqueror
(1451–81) and Bayezid II (1481–1512). The
first instituted and the second consolidated a
highly efficient organization of centralized government, and both made use of the newly created elite corps of janizaries to control enemies
at home and abroad. Machiavelli evidently
equates their government with that of Darius
as hard to take but easy to hold. For the "districts" into which Turkey is divided, Machiavelli uses the proper Turkish word, "sanjaks."

The problem in gaining control of Turkey is that you cannot hope to be invited in by the district rulers, or to make use of a palace revolt in gaining a foothold. The reasons are given above: since they are all the slaves of their master and obliged to him, there is no easy way of corrupting them; and even if you succeeded, there is not much advantage to be hoped from it, because the man you corrupt cannot bring along many followers, as noted above. Hence, anyone who attacks the Turks may expect to find them completely united, and had better count on his own strength rather than any internal disorders. But once they are thoroughly beaten and crushed so their army cannot reform, there is nothing more to fear except the family of the prince; once his line is extinct, there is no other danger, since nobody else has any standing with the people; and as the victor before his victory could expect no help from them, so, after it, he has nothing to fear from them.

Quite the other way in a kingdom like France, which you can easily get into by winning over to your cause some baron of the kingdom; one or another of them will always be discontented or restless for a change.[8] As I said before, these people can open the way for you, and make your victory an easy one. But after that, holding onto the power will involve you in infinite difficulties, both with those who helped you in and with those you have beaten. Extinguishing the royal house will not suffice, because those local nobles will remain to head up new rebellions against you; and since you can neither make them happy nor wipe them out completely, you will lose control at the first unlucky accident.

Now, if you ask yourself what kind of government Darius had, you will find it very much like that of Turkey, and so Alexander had to smash the whole thing, and take control of the country. But when that was done, and Darius was dead, the state was securely in Alexander's hands, for the reasons described above. And if his successors had remained united, they could have ruled the empire at their leisure, because the only disorders that arose were those they stirred up themselves. But states organized like that of France cannot possibly be held so easily. Hence the frequent rebellions of Spain, France, and Greece against the Romans—they were due to the many local powers in those districts.[9] As long as the memory of those powers persisted, the Romans were always uneasy in their control of the provinces; they became secure

8. Henry V of England had, for example, made expert use of the dukes of Burgundy to gain a foothold in France early in the fifteenth century; even as Machiavelli wrote, the duke of Savoy was intriguing with Austria for protection against annexation by France.
9. Spain was a long time being Romanized, and resisted (especially among the mountain tribes) well into the empire. But Gaul, after its conquest by Caesar, was almost a model of

docility—there were few and only short-lived revolts against the Roman power; and Greece, apart from the Mithridatic incursion of 88–84 B.C., was almost as well behaved. Historical inaccuracy is unusual in Machiavelli and his several overstatements here suggest that he may be concerned to make a categorical distinction between oriental dynasties (Darius, the sultans) and European governments (less centralized and more like a confederation of local powers).

masters only after memories faded in the course of the empire's long duration and as a result of its great strength. Even afterward, when the Romans began fighting among themselves, each one was able to attract a following in the provinces, depending on the authority he had built up there; and the provinces, once the family line of their former rulers was extinct, refused to recognize anyone but Romans. All these things considered, no one should be surprised at the ease with which Alexander grasped the whole government of Asia, nor at the difficulties other men have had in maintaining possession, like Pyrrhus and many others.[1] Success in this matter depends not on the greater or lesser skill [*virtù*] of the conqueror, but on the different circumstances of the vanquished.

5 V 4

HOW CITIES OR STATES SHOULD BE RULED WHICH LIVED BY THEIR OWN LAWS BEFORE BEING TAKEN

When states are acquired, as I have said, which have got in the way of living at liberty and under their own laws, there are just three ways to hold onto them: the first is to destroy them;[2] the second is to go there and live in person; and the third is to let them continue living under their own laws, levying tribute on them, and creating a government of a few people who will keep the state friendly toward you. Such a government, being the prince's actual creation, knows it cannot stand without his friendship and power; therefore it will do anything to maintain him in authority. And a city which is used to freedom can be held more easily by means of its own citizens than in any other manner—always supposing you want it to survive at all.

Examples are to be found among the Spartans and Romans. The Spartans held onto Athens and Thebes by creating oligarchies there, though in the end they lost both cities.[3] The Romans, in order to hold onto Capua, Carthage, and Numantia, destroyed them, and therefore

1. Pyrrhus of Epirus (died 272 B.C.) was a Greek kinglet related to Alexander the Great. He was called to Italy in 281 by the city of Tarentum, to help defend Magna Graecia against encroaching Roman power. Both in Greece and in Italy, he mounted dashing and momentarily successful military campaigns, but could strike no permanent roots anywhere.
2. What Machiavelli means by this deliberately bitter phrase is not quite unequivocal. He could mean physical demolition of the captured cities and dispersal of their inhabitants, and instances of this sort of thing are cited below. But there is no example of anything like that happening during the Renaissance, in Italy; and Machiavelli is particularly unlikely to

have recommended this policy "seriously" because all through this chapter it is apparent that Florence herself (as a city still vibrant with republican instincts) is the city he has in mind. Writing to a Medici, he would recommend demolition of Florence only as a way of saying, "*unless* you go to live there, you may actually have to destroy your city."
3. After the fall of Athens in 405 B.C., a brief oligarchy under Spartan control replaced the previously democratic government, and Sparta's relation to Thebes, previously amicable, changed sharply. In 382 B.C., a Spartan force occupied the citadel of Thebes, and held possession for three years.

never lost them.[4] They wanted to hold Greece in about the same way the Spartans did, making it free and leaving it under its own laws, but they were not successful; so that in the end, they had to destroy many cities in the province in order to hold it. And in fact there is no sure way to hold onto cities except to destroy them. Any man who becomes master of a city accustomed to freedom, and does not destroy it, may expect to be destroyed by it. Because such a city, when it rebels, can always call on the name of liberty and its ancient ordinances, which no passage of time or bestowal of gifts can ever cause to be forgotten. No matter what measures one takes for the present or future, if one does not divide or disperse the inhabitants, they will never forget that name or those ordinances; and, at the slightest incident, they will instantly have recourse to them. That was what happened in Pisa a full hundred years after it had first been placed in subjection to the Florentines.[5] But when cities and provinces are used to living under a prince, and his line is destroyed, they fall on great difficulties: on the one hand, they are used to obeying, yet they no longer have their old prince; they cannot agree among themselves to set up a new prince, yet they do not know how to live in freedom. As a result, they are slow to take up arms, and a prince can easily take them over and make himself sure of them. But in republics, you will find greater life, greater hate, more desire of revenge; memories of ancient liberties cannot and will not give them any rest; so that the safest way with them is either to wipe them out or to settle among them.

6 **5**

VI

ABOUT NEW PRINCEDOMS ACQUIRED WITH ONE'S OWN ARMS AND ENERGY [*Virtù*]

No one should be surprised if, in talking about states completely new in their rulers and constitutions, I make use of the very greatest examples. Men almost always prefer to walk in paths marked out by others and pattern their actions through imitation. Even if he cannot follow other people's paths in every respect, or attain to the merit [*virtù*] of his originals, a prudent man should always follow the footsteps of the great and imitate those who have been supreme. His own talent [*virtù*] may

---

4. These three cities, Capua in Italy (211 B.C.), Carthage in Africa (146 B.C.), and Numantia in Spain (133 B.C.), were captured after long and desperate sieges, and actually dismantled as municipalities: the physical plant was torn down, the population dispersed, the laws and constitutions abrogated. All three were later reconstituted, but from scratch.

It is possible that behind the apparently classical reference of Capua, a potent contemporary allusion may lie. In the course of the Neapolitan war between France and Spain, Capua was captured on July 24, 1501, by a French army under D'Aubigny and Cesare Borgia. While the city was not exactly "destroyed," estimates place the number of casualties in the general massacre, orgy, and looting spree that followed capitulation, at about seven thousand.

5. Pisa, purchased by Florence in 1405, subjugated in 1406, and very harshly treated through the fifteenth century, asserted its liberty as a result of the invasion of Charles VIII in 1494; after four bitter campaigns and sieges, the Florentines finally won it back again in June 1509.

not come up to theirs, but at least it will have a sniff of it. Thus he will resemble skilled archers who, seeing how far away the target lies, and knowing the strength [*virtù*] of their bow, aim much higher than the real target, not because they expect the arrow to fly that far, but to accomplish their real end by aiming beyond it.

Let me say, then, that a new prince taking charge of a completely new kingdom will have more or less trouble in holding onto it, as he himself is more or less capable [*virtuoso*]. And since this transition, from private citizen to prince, presupposes either skill [*virtù*] or luck, it would seem that either one or other of these two qualities might ease some of the difficulties, at least partly. Still, the less one trusts to chance, the better one's hope of holding on. It helps, too, if the prince is forced, for lack of other states, to come and live personally among his new subjects. Turning to those who have become princes by their own powers [*virtù*] and not by accident, I would say that the most notable were Moses, Cyrus, Romulus, Theseus, and a few others.[6] And though we should not consider Moses, because he was simply an agent sent by God to do certain things, he still should be admired, if only for that special grace which made him worthy of talking with God. But let us turn to Cyrus and the others who acquired or founded kingdoms. You will find them all deserving of admiration; and if you consider their individual actions and decrees, they will be found not much different from those of Moses, who had such a great teacher. When we look into their actions and their lives, we will find that fortune provided nothing for them but an opportunity; that gave them material, on which they could impose whatever form they chose.[7] Without the opportunity their strength [*virtù*] of mind would have been vain, and without that strength [*virtù*] the opportunity would have been lost.

Hence it was necessary for Moses to find the children of Israel in Egypt, enslaved and oppressed by the Egyptians, so that they should be disposed to follow him, in order to escape from that servitude.[8] For Romulus it was necessary that he not remain in Alba, but should be exposed at birth, so that he might become ruler of Rome and founder of that country.[9] It was necessary that Cyrus should find the Persians unhappy with the rule of the Medes, and the Medes soft and effeminate from years of peace.[1] Theseus could never have exercised his energy

---

6. The heroes on whom Machiavelli proposes that the realistically minded prince pattern his behavior are all more or less mythical; they all founded, not simply national organizations, but enduring civilizations. Machiavelli plants these great, vague prototypes here, at least in part, for the rhetorical effect he will get from reinvoking them in chapter XXVI.

7. The scholastic distinction of *materia* and *forma* carried with it the overtone that the former was feminine, the latter masculine; the male provided shape and soul for what, without

him, would be mere inchoate shape or mass (*mola*). Thus the prince's *virtus* is the male principle of the marriage between ruler and people.

8. On the bondage of the children of Israel, see Exodus 2–6.

9. The story of Romulus is familiar from the first books of Livy and from Plutarch.

1. Herodotus, notoriously devoted to fables, is one major authority for the life of Cyrus; Xenophon's *Cyropaedia* is also full of moral purpose and hence of pious legend.

[*virtù*] if he had not found the Athenians in confusion.[2] Specific occasions brought these happy men to power, and their unusual abilities [*virtù*] enabled them to seize the occasion and so to make their countries noble and prosperous.

These men and men of this sort, who become princes through their own strength of character [*per vie virtuose*] may have troubles gaining power, but they find it easy to hold onto. Their troubles in getting power derive partly from the new laws and measures they have to adopt in order to set up their state and secure themselves. And it is worth noting that nothing is harder to manage, more risky in the undertaking, or more doubtful of success than to set up as the introducer of a new order. Such an innovator has as enemies all the people who were doing well under the old order, and only halfhearted defenders in those who hope to profit from the new. This halfheartedness derives partly from fear of opponents who have the law on their side, and partly from human skepticism, since men don't really believe in anything new till they have solid experience of it. This is why, whenever the enemies of a new state have occasion to attack it, they do so furiously, while its friends come only languidly to its defense, so that the venture and it supporters are likely to collapse together.[3]

Still, if we are to discuss the matter thoroughly, we shall have to ask if these innovators stand on their own feet or depend on the help of others—that is, whether they have to go begging in order to carry out their work, or can use force of their own. In the first case, they are bound to fail without accomplishing anything; but when they depend on their own energies and can make use of force, then they hardly ever come to grief. This is why armed prophets always win and unarmed prophets lose. Apart from all the factors considered above, it is the nature of people to be fickle; to persuade them of something is easy, but to make them stand fast in that conviction is hard. Hence things must be arranged so that when they no longer believe they can be compelled to believe by force.[4] If Moses, Cyrus, Theseus, and Romulus had had no weapons, they could never have imposed their institutions on their peoples for so long. In our own times, there is the example of Fra Girolamo Savonarola, who collapsed with all his new ordinances as soon as the people ceased to believe in him; he had no way of keeping the

2. Theseus, who is even more fabulous than any of the others, is known to us through the collection of legends summarized by Plutarch —who makes the comparison with Romulus. 3. It is a surprisingly rational view of human nature that Machiavelli takes here; actually, men often attribute strictly irrational values to things of which they have no experience at all—as Machiavelli explicitly recognizes in the *Discorsi* 1.53.

4. Practically the first act of Moses when he descended from Sinai with the tablets was to get the sons of Levi to massacre three thousand worshippers of the Golden Calf; see Exodus 32.19–28. Romulus murdered Remus and his associate Titus Tatius, acts that Plutarch describes and Machiavelli warmly endorses in the *Discorsi* 1.9.

backsliders in line or of converting the doubters.[5] Such men meet with great difficulties in their rise to power; all their dangers are on the way up, and must be overcome by their talents [*virtù*]; but once they are on top, once they are held in veneration, and have destroyed all their envious rivals, they remain powerful, secure, honored, and prosperous.

To these exalted examples, I'd like to add a lesser one; but it parallels the others, in a way, and may stand for a whole class. It is Hiero of Syracuse.[6] When he rose from a private citizen to prince, he owed nothing to fortune except the opportunity; the Syracusans were oppressed, and elected him general, then raised him to prince when he proved worthy. He was a man of such character [*virtù*], even as a private citizen, that somebody said of him "the only thing he needs to be a ruler is a kingdom." He abolished the old army and formed a new one, broke the old alliances and formed new ones; and, when he had his own soldiers and his own allies, he could build on that foundation any structure he wanted. For him too the throne was hard to acquire but easy to keep.

7

VII

ABOUT NEW STATES ACQUIRED WITH OTHER PEOPLE'S ARMS AND BY GOOD LUCK

When simple good luck raises private citizens to the rank of prince, they have little trouble in rising, but plenty in holding onto their positions. They have no troubles along the way, because they are practically flying; all the problems arise when they are in place. These are the people who get control of a state either by buying it, or as a gift from someone. Such things happened often in Greece, in the cities of Ionia and Hellespont, where Darius created a great many princes to augment his own glory and security;[7] and some Roman emperors attained that rank after starting as private citizens, by corrupting the soldiers.[8] Men of this sort depend entirely on the good will and good fortune of those who raised them up, and these are two extremely volatile, unstable things. The new rulers do not know how to hold what they have been given, and they could not do it if they did know. They don't know because, unless they are men of great shrewdness and vigor [*virtù*], they

---

5. Savonarola was undone, less by the fickleness of his followers, than by the hostility of Alexander VI and the great houses of Florence, among whom, primarily, were the Medici. Given the sort of followers to whom Savonarola appealed, it is doubtful if force on his part would have persuaded them of anything: Machiavelli himself condemns as self-destructive the one infraction of the law that Savonarola condoned (*Discorsi* 1.45).

6. This was Hiero II of Syracuse, who lived in the third century B.C., and about whom Machiavelli could have learned in Livy 21. 49–51, and in Polybius 1.8, and 7.7; but the phrase that he quotes is from the historian Justin.

7. Darius the Great (died 485 B.C.) created many local princedoms and satrapies throughout his extensive realms: see Herodotus 3.

8. Reviewing the Roman emperors in chapter XIX, Machiavelli particularly emphasizes Septimius Severus as one who rose to power and maintained his rule by gratifying the soldiery.

cannot be expected to have the knack of command after living all their lives as private citizens. And they cannot, because they have no troops of their own, who are devoted to them and trustworthy. Besides, states which spring up suddenly, like everything else in nature which springs up in a day, cannot have a network of roots and branches; they are destroyed by the first storm that strikes. Of course it may be that men who become princes overnight have so much natural astuteness [*virtù*] that they quickly prepare themselves to preserve what fortune has showered on them; the foundations that other men construct before becoming princes, they may be able to construct afterwards.

I'd like to illustrate these two ways of becoming prince, by strength [*virtù*] or by luck, with two examples taken from our own times: they are Francesco Sforza and Cesare Borgia. Francesco started as a private citizen, and used the appropriate means with great shrewdness [*virtù*] to become duke of Milan: he won power in the teeth of a thousand difficulties, and maintained it with little effort.[9] On the other hand, Cesare Borgia, popularly called Duke Valentino, acquired authority through his father's fortune and lost it in the same way: he did so in spite of the fact that he used every means and took all the precautions that a wise and able [*virtuoso*] man should, to root himself in those states which had been granted him by the arms and fortune of others. As I noted above, the man who does not lay his foundations in advance may with great effort [*virtù*] build them later—but he will always do so with inconvenience to the architect and danger to the structure. If, then, we consider all the duke's proceedings, we shall see that he laid strong foundations for future power; and I do not consider it irrelevant to describe them, since I cannot imagine better advice to give a new prince than the example of his actions. If he failed to profit by his own measures, the fault was not his, but resulted from an extraordinary and extreme piece of bad luck.

When Alexander VI set out to make his son the duke a great man, he faced many difficulties, both immediate and long-term. First, he saw no way to make him master of any state except one of those belonging to the Church; and, looking over the Papal States, he realized that the duke of Milan and the Venetians would never consent to that, because Faenza and Rimini were already under the protection of the Venetians.[1] Besides, he saw the armies of Italy, especially those that he might have been able to use himself, were under the control of those who had reason to fear the Pope's power and whom he therefore could not trust— members of the Orsini and Colonna families, and their allies.[2] Therefore he was first obliged to upset existing arrangements and create disorder

9. On Francesco Sforza, see above, chapter I, note 2, p. 4.
1. On Cesare Borgia, natural son of Pope Alexander VI, see the Historical Introduction.
2. The Orsini and Colonna families were fa-

mous Roman tribes or gangs, in immemorial feud with one another; on the Pope's traditional trouble in putting down one without exalting the other, see chapter XI.

among the Italian states in order to gain secure control over some of them. This was easy enough because he found that the Venetians, for reasons of their own, had decided to let the French back into Italy. Far from opposing this project, the pope hastened it along by dissolving the first marriage of King Louis.[3] Thus the king entered Italy with the help of the Venetians and the consent of Alexander; and he was no sooner in Milan than the pope got from him troops for the conquest of the Romagna, which he quickly overcame with the help of the king's reputation.[4]

Now when the duke was possessed of the Romagna, and the Colonna people were beaten, he wanted to keep his winnings and push ahead, but two things held him back: one was that his army did not seem trustworthy, and the other was the French position. That is, the Orsini troops he had been using might play him false, endangering not only his new projects but his old winnings; and the king also could not be trusted. He had a hint of the mood among the Orsini when, after storming Faenza, he attacked Bologna, and found them very halfhearted in the assault. As for the king, he learned his mind when, after taking Urbino, he moved on Tuscany, and the king made him pull back from that enterprise.[5] Hence the duke decided he would no longer depend on the weapons and fortune of others. So first he moved to weaken the Orsini and Colonna factions in Rome, by recruiting to his cause all their followers who were of noble rank, enrolling them in his party, and giving them generous pensions and posts, according to their station, in the army or the government. In a few months, therefore, all factional enthusiasm faded from their minds, and their devotion turned toward the duke. After this he watched for a chance to wipe out the Orsini family, as he had already broken up the house of Colonna. A good occasion turned up, and he made even better use of it. For when the Orsini realized, too late, that the power of the duke and the Church was making for their ruin, they called a gathering of the clan at La Magione near Perugia.[6] This was the reason why Urbino rebelled and

---

3. Cesare was the papal legate who, in a spectacularly lavish expedition (October–December 1498) brought Louis papal permission to set aside his first wife, Jeanne, in order to marry Anne of Brittany. Many basic decisions about the future of Italy must have been reached during the visit, but we must guess at them from the tangled and perhaps unintended results.

4. Cesare Borgia made two formal campaigns in the Romagna, the first May 1499 to February 1500; his army consisted mostly of French, Gascon, and Swiss troops, and with these forces he captured Imola (Nov. 24) and Forlì (Dec. 17). The second campaign was October 1500 to June 1501, with a larger army, better equipped and better disciplined, and including a good many Italian mercenaries among the usual miscellaneous cosmopolites. At the head of this crowd he took Rimini (Oct.

10), Pesaro (Oct. 27), and Faenza after a longer siege (April 25, 1501).

5. After the fall of Faenza, Bologna was menaced in late April and early May, but never put to the assault. Urbino fell to the duke in June 1502; on May 15 Florence had had to hire the duke as its general and "protector" (promising him thirty-six thousand ducats a year for three years) in order to preserve its independence. But Florence was already, supposedly, under the "protection" of the king of France. "Protection" seems to have meant in Renaissance Italy very much what it means today to a New York bookmaker or brothelkeeper.

6. Present at the gathering at La Magione near Perugia in early October 1502 were various Orsini, Pandolfo Petrucci of Siena, Ermete Bentivoglio, and various Baglioni of Perugia.

all those disorders occured in the Romagna, with infinite peril to the duke; but he overcame them all, with the aid of the French. Once he had regained his reputation, he put no further trust in the French, nor in any other outside forces, since he found them too risky; so he turned to trickery. And he was so skillful in disguising his intentions that the Orsini themselves sought to be reconciled with him through the mediation of Signor Paolo,[7] whom the duke tried to placate in every way conceivable, giving him money, fine clothes, and horses. Thus the simple-mindedness of the Orsini brought them to Sinigaglia, and into the duke's hands. And when he had killed all the leaders, and won over their followers to be his friends, the duke had laid excellent foundations for his power, since he possessed the entire Romagna, along with the duchy of Urbino; most important of all, he not only controlled the Romagna, but controlled it as a friend, and won over the people of the district as soon as they began to savor the benefits of his rule.

The next point is worthy of special note, and of imitation by others; I don't want to pass lightly over it. When the duke took over the Romagna, he found it had been controlled by impotent masters, who instead of ruling their subjects had plundered them, and had given them more reason for strife than unity, so that the whole province was full of robbers, feuds, and lawlessness of every description. To establish peace and reduce the land to obedience, he decided good government was needed; and he named Messer Remirro de Orco, a cruel and vigorous man, to whom he gave absolute powers. In short order this man pacified and unified the whole district, winning thereby great renown. But then the duke decided such excessive authority was no longer necessary, and feared it might become odious; so he set up a civil court in the middle of the province, with an excellent judge and a representative from each city. And because he knew that the recent harshness had generated some hatred, in order to clear the minds of the people and gain them over to his cause completely, he determined to make plain that whatever cruelty had occurred had come, not from him, but from the brutal character of the minister. Taking a proper occasion, therefore, he had him placed on the public square of Cesena one morning, in two pieces, with a piece of wood beside him and a bloody knife.[8] The ferocity of this scene left the people at once stunned and satisfied.

But, to return from our digression, let me say that the duke now found himself powerful, fairly safe from immediate dangers, and in charge of his own armies; he had largely destroyed those forces which, if they were near, might have destroyed him. But he still had to look to the king of

7. Signor Paolo is Paolo Orsini, head of the house; Vitellozzo Vitelli and Oliverotto da Fermo were strangled at Sinigaglia on the last day of December 1502; the duke of Gravina and Paolo Orsini a few days later.

8. Remirro de Orco (or Ramiro de Lorqua, to call him by his native Spanish name) was appointed lieutenant general of the Romagna March 1500, imprisoned December 22, 1502, and put to death the morning after Christmas day.

France, before going on with his program; because he knew that the king, who had belatedly recognized his error, would not now support him. For this reason, he began to look for new alliances and to temporize with the French during their expedition toward the kingdom of Naples against the Spaniards who were besieging Gaeta. His intention was to gain Spanish support; and he would quickly have done it, if Alexander had lived. [9]

Such were his policies with regard to present matters. As for the future, he had to be concerned lest a new successor to the Church prove hostile to him, and try to take back what Alexander had given. Against this possibility he tried to secure himself in four ways: first he planned to wipe out all the families of those noblemen he had ruined, so the [new] pope would not be able to use them as pretexts to strike at him; second, he proposed to enlist all the gentry of Rome, as I said before, and use them to keep the pope in check; third, to make the College of Cardinals his own creatures, so far as he could; and fourth, to acquire so much power of his own, before the pope died, that he could resist a first onslaught. Of these four projects, by the death of Alexander, he had completed three, and the fourth he was still working on. He had killed as many of the ruined nobles as he could reach, and very few escaped; he had all the Roman bravos; and in the College, he controlled a good majority. As for new power, he had plans to control Tuscany, and he was already master of Perugia and Piombino, while Pisa was under his protection. And since he no longer needed to be concerned with France (because the French had already been stripped of Naples by the Span-iards, so that both of them now needed his friendship), he was ready to grasp at Pisa. [1] After that, Lucca and Siena would quickly have given in, partly to spite the Florentines, and partly from fear; and the Flor-entines could never have done anything about it. If he had carried this off (and in fact he was doing so in the very year when Alexander died), he would have had such strength and prestige that he could have stood alone, depending no longer on other people's fortunes and forces, but only on his own power and skill [virtù]. But Alexander died just five years after the duke first drew his sword, leaving him with the government of Romagna in good order, but with all the rest up in the air, between two very powerful hostile armies; and the duke himself was deathly sick. Yet the duke was a man of such savagery and courage [virtù], and he understood so perfectly how to win men over or ruin them, and the

9. Gaeta, a few miles north of Naples, was a first center of fighting between French and Spanish troops after the breakdown of the Treaty of Granada. Alexander VI died August 18, 1503, of a sudden fever, and Pius III was not elected till September 22.

1. Perugia came under Cesare's control in February 1503; Piombino had been his since September 3, 1501; Pisa was under his "con-dotta" because, having declared itself indepen-dent of Florence, it had looked to France for protection, and when the French position be-came untenable (because the Spaniards had driven them out of Naples), only Cesare could restrain the Florentines.

foundations were so strong that he had laid down in so short a period, that if he had not had those armies on his back, or had not been sick himself, he would have pulled through all his difficulties. And that his foundations were solid was obvious, since the Romagna waited more than a month for him; in Rome, even when he was half-dead, he was safe from attack; and though the Baglioni, the Vitelli, and the Orsini came to Rome, they could not raise any force against him.[2] Perhaps he could not have made pope the man he wanted, but he could have kept from the office anyone he did not want. If he had been in good health the day of Alexander's death, everything would have been easy for him. He told me himself, on the day Julius II was made pope, that he had thought of everything which could happen at his father's death, and had found a solution for everything; only he never thought that when his father was dying he too would be at death's door.

Looking over all the duke's actions, then, I find nothing with which to reproach him; rather I think I'm right in proposing him, as I have done, as a model for all those who rise to power by means of the fortune and arms of others. Being a magnanimous man of lofty ambitions, he was bound to govern in that way; and the only obstacles to his plan were the cutting short of Alexander's life and his own illness. Any man coming into a new state, therefore, who finds it necessary to guard against enemies and win friends, to overcome by force or fraud, to make himself loved and feared by the people, followed and respected by his troops—if you have to destroy those who can or might hurt you, revamp old laws with new measures, be severe and indulgent, magnanimous and liberal, disband old armies and replace them with new, meanwhile managing your relations with other princes and kings in such a way that they will be glad to help you and cautious about harming you, you can find no better recent examples than those of his career. His only error lay in making Julius pope, where he simply made a bad choice; because, as I said, though he couldn't make his own man pope, he could keep anyone else from the office.[3] And he should never have allowed any of those cardinals to become pope whom he had injured, or who, on their election, might have had reason to fear him. For men injure others either through fear or hate. Those whom he had already injured were, among others, San Pietro in Vincoli, Colonna, San Giorgio, and Ascanio; all the others, if elected, would have had reason to fear him,

2. Cesare had many enemies, and when he was sick they all came to finish him off; but indeed they could make little headway against him. Pius III, who succeeded Alexander, was moribund when elected, and survived his coronation by a matter of only ten days (October 8–18, 1503).

3. In the elections of September 1503, which led to the brief papacy of Pius, there were orig-inally fifteen votes for Carvajal (a Spaniard), fourteen for della Rovere, and thirteen for Rouen; Pius was elected as a compromise candidate when all three leaders agreed to withdraw. In the October elections, which resulted in the election of Julius II, there was no significant division, since Rouen had given up hope; thus Julius was elected on the first ballot.

except for Rouen and the Spaniards.[4] The latter were all bound to him
by nationality and obligation; the former had nothing to fear, being
closely bound to the king of France. And so the duke, first and foremost,
should have tried to make a Spaniard pope, and if he could not do that,
should have accepted Rouen and not San Pietro in Vincoli.[5] Anyone
who thinks that recent benefits make great people forget old injuries is
simply deluding himself. Thus the duke made a mistake in this election,
and it was the cause of his final ruin.

4 VIII

ON THOSE WHO HAVE BECOME PRINCES BY CRIME

But as there are two other ways to rise from private citizen to prince
which cannot be assigned altogether to luck or ability [virtù], I cannot
omit them, even though one could be handled more fully in a discussion
of republics. These are: ascent to princely power by some criminal or
evil conduct; and the rise of a private citizen to supreme authority in
his land through the choice of his fellow citizens. In describing the first,
I will use just two examples, one ancient, one modern, without further
declaiming on the method itself, since I think the examples will suffice
for anyone who needs to follow them.

Agathocles the Sicilian became prince of Syracuse, not simply from
the rank of a private citizen, but from a base and abject position in life.[6]
Born the son of a potter, he led a life of complete iniquity at every stage
of his career; yet he joined to his villainies such powers [virtù] of mind
and body that after enlisting in the army he rose through the ranks to
become military governor of Syracuse. Once settled in this post, he

---

4. Cardinals may be known by the Roman
church to which they are assigned, by their
family names, or even by their given (Christian)
names:

San Pietro in Vincoli was Giuliano della
Rovere (later Julius II); his uncle had been Sixtus IV, who appointed him early to eight or
ten major ecclesiastical offices.

Colonna was Giovanni Colonna, of the great
Roman house, named cardinal in 1480, died
in 1508.

San Giorgio was Raffaello Riario, a nephew
of Sixtus IV and patron of the arts, born in
1451, died in 1521.

Ascanio was Ascanio Sforza, son of Francesco and thus brother of Lodovico Il Moro.
Captured by the French in the collapse of
Milan, he was released by influence of the cardinal of Rouen, who wanted his vote to be
made pope. He was devoted to his brother,
whose fondness for an opulent life-style he
shared.

Rouen was George d'Amboise, favored ad-
viser of Louis XII. Machiavelli thinks Cesare

might have controlled the eleven Spanish cardinals in the college, since the Borgias were of
Spanish origin; but the clerics were beyond sentiments of that sort, and never worked with him
as a bloc.

5. Giuliano della Rovere, who became Julius
the Second, had cherished his grudge against
the Borgias during ten years of bitter exile in
France (1494–1503). His election after the
death of Pius III was a foregone conclusion;
but Machiavelli is of opinion that Cesare might
have done more for Rouen (obviously by manipulating the Spanish faction) during the elections of September, thus forestalling the
elections of both Pius and Julius. The French
king agreed; when he heard of the election of
Pius, he is said to have shouted, "That son of
a whore [Cesare] has kept Rouen from the
papacy!"

6. The story of Agathocles the tyrant of Syracuse (361–289 B.C.) was known to Machiavelli
through the historians Justin and Diodorus Si-
culus; the latter is himself scandalized at the
misdeeds of the tyrant.

decided to make himself prince, and take violent possession, without obligation to others, of what had already been freely granted to him. First he told his plan to Hamilcar the Carthaginian, who was campaigning in Sicily with his armies; then one morning he convoked all the people and the full senate of Syracuse, as if he had some announcement of public concern to make. At a prearranged signal, he then had his soldiers butcher all the senators and the richest of the people; and after they were dead, he took and kept the office of prince over that city without the slightest public protest. And even though the Carthaginians twice defeated him, and at last brought him under siege, he was not only able to defend his city; but, leaving some of his people to defend against the besiegers, he led the others off to assault Africa. In short order, he was able to lift the siege of Syracuse and reduce the Carthaginians to desperate straits; and in the end, they had to come to terms with him, content themselves with their African possessions, and leave Sicily to Agathocles.

Considering the deeds and career of this man, one finds little or nothing that can be attributed to luck; for, as I noted above, he did not come to power through anyone's help, but rose through the ranks of the army, passed through a thousand hardships and perils to become prince, and held onto the office by the spirited and dangerous means described. Yet it certainly cannot be called "virtue" [virtù] to murder his fellow citizens, betray his friends, to be devoid of truth, pity, or religion; a man may get power by means like these, but not glory. If we consider simply the courage [virtù] of Agathocles in facing and escaping from dangers, and the greatness of his soul in sustaining and overcoming adversity, it is hard to see why he should be considered inferior to the greatest of captains. Nonetheless, his fearful cruelty and inhumanity, along with his innumerable crimes, prevent us from placing him among the really excellent men. For we can scarcely attribute to either fortune or virtue [virtù] a conquest which he owed to neither.

In our own days, during the papacy of Alexander VI, there is the example of Oliverotto da Fermo.[7] His father having died when he was young, he was raised by a maternal uncle named Giovanni Fogliani, and sent off as a young man to soldier with Paolo Vitelli, so that he might learn the discipline and qualify for a good post in the army. After Paolo's death, he served under Vitellozzo his brother; and before long, being clever and a gallant fellow in mind as well as body, he advanced

---

7. Oliverotto da Fermo killed, in the coup of Fermo, not only his uncle Giovanni Fogliani, but Giovanni's son Gennario, his son-in-law Raffaello della Rovere, and four other persons. Paolo Vitelli had been killed by the Florentines in 1499 on suspicion of double-dealing in their campaigns against Pisa; see below, chapter XII, note 5, p. 36. Cesare Borgia, when he allowed Vitellozzo Vitelli to take Arezzo from the Flor- entines (June 1502), explained to the Florentines (including their ambassador, Machiavelli himself) that Vitellozzo was acting on his own, to revenge his brother. But nobody believed this story. As indicated above (chapter VII, note 5, p. 20), Cesare was blackmailing the Florentines into naming him their chosen, and very well paid, "protector."

to head of the army. But as he considered it slavish to depend on others, he plotted with various citizens of Fermo who preferred to see their native land enslaved rather than free; and they resolved, with Vitellozzo's help to capture Fermo. Therefore he wrote to Giovanni Fogliani, saying that as he had been away from home for several years, he would now like to see his uncle and his native town, in addition to looking over his estate there. And he added that since he had sought only honor and would like his fellow citizens to see that he hadn't altogether failed of it, he would like to make a state visit, and bring along a hundred of his friends and followers on horseback. He hoped the people of Fermo would give them an honorable reception, one that would bring credit not only to Oliverotto but to his former guardian. Giovanni, on his part, omitted no ceremony that would gratify his nephew; he persuaded the people of Fermo to receive him in high style, and took him into his own house. After he had been there a few days, and made all those secret preparations necessary for his crime, Oliverotto announced a splendid banquet to which he invited Giovanni Fogliani and all the most important men of Fermo. When the meal was finished, and the entertainments usual on such occasions were completed, Oliverotto deliberately raised certain grave topics, speaking of Alexander's greatness and that of Cesare, his son, and of all their undertakings.[8] When Giovanni and the others ventured certain comments, he rose abruptly, saying that these were things to be discussed in a less public place; and he moved to another room, followd by Giovanni and the other citizens. No sooner were they all seated than soldiers appeared from secret places where they lay concealed; they killed Giovanni and all the rest. After this slaughter, Oliverotto mounted his horse, rode through the city, and blockaded the town council in their palace, terrorizing them into obedience and forcing them to form a government of which Oliverotto became chief. Once everyone was dead whose discontent might have been dangerous, he strengthened his position with new laws and regulations, to such effect that in the single year of his rule, he not only secured the city of Fermo, but became the terror of his neighbors. Getting rid of him would have been as hard as getting rid of Agathocles, if he hadn't let himself be tricked by Cesare Borgia when he trapped all the Orsini and Vitelli at Sinigaglia, as described above. There he was taken, along with the others, just a year after he committed the parricide, and there, along with Vitellozzo, who had been the teacher, both of his craft [virtù] and of his crime, he was strangled.[9]

Somebody might wonder how it happened that Agathocles and others of his ilk, after they had committed so many acts of treachery and cruelty,

---

8. At the time of this story, both Oliverotto and Vitellozzo were in the service of Cesare; the date, if it was just a year before the trap at Sinigaglia, must have been late 1501. Some of the flavor of this tale depends on the fact that Fermo was then (as it is today) a very small town indeed, a lesser satellite of Ascoli Piceno, which is also small, but can be found on a map.

9. Cf. chapter VII, note 7, p. 21.

could live long, secure lives in their native cities, defend themselves from foreign enemies, and never be conspired against by their fellow citizens. And yet many other princes were unable, because of their cruelty, to maintain their power, even in time of peace, not to speak of the troubled times of war. I believe this depends on whether the cruelty is used well or badly. Cruelty can be described as well used (if it is permissible to say good words about something evil in itself) when it is performed all at once, for reasons of self-preservation; and when the acts are not repeated after that, but rather are turned as much as possible to the advantage of the subjects. Cruelty is badly used, when it is infrequent at first, but increases with time instead of diminishing. Those who use the first method may find some excuse before God and man for their state, as Agathocles did; the others cannot possibly stay in power.

We may add this note that when a prince takes a new state, he should calculate the sum of all the injuries he will have to do, and do them all at once, so as not to have to do new ones every day; simply by not repeating them, he will be able to reassure people, and win them over to his side with benefits. Whoever believes otherwise, either through fearfulness or bad advice, must always keep his knife in hand, and he can never count on his subjects, because their fresh and recurring injuries keep them suspicious of him. In a word, injuries should be committed all at once, because the less time there is to dwell on them, the less they offend; but benefits should be distributed very gradually, so the taste will last longer. Above all, a prince should live with his subjects on such terms that no accident, whether favorable or unfavorable, can force him to change his conduct. When misfortune strikes, harsh measures are too late, and the good things you do are not counted to your credit because you seem to have acted under compulsion, and no one will thank you for that.

9

IX
ON THE CIVIL PRINCIPATE

Turning now to the other alternative, when a private citizen becomes a prince, not through crimes or other intolerable violence, but by the choice of his fellow citizens (and this may be called a civil princedom, success in which depends neither completely on skill [*virtù*] nor completely on fortune, but rather on a kind of lucky shrewdness), let me say that one rises in such a state either by the favor of the people or by that of the nobles. In every city there are two different humors, one rising from the people's desire not to be ordered and commanded by the nobles, and the other from the desire of the nobles to command and oppress the people. From these two different impulses we get one of three consequences: either the rule of a prince, or liberty, or license.

The rule of a prince results either from the power of the people or that of the nobles, depending on which has a chance to prevail. When the nobles see they cannot resist the people, they start to build up one of their own, and make him prince so that in the shadow of his power they can satisfy their own wants. In the same way, the people, when they see they cannot resist the nobles, build up one of *their* own, and make him prince to have his authority as a shield. The man who becomes prince with the help of the nobles has more trouble holding onto his power than the man who rises with the aid of the people, because as prince he is surrounded by many who think themselves his equals, and for this reason he cannot give orders or manage his agents as he would like. But the man who becomes prince by popular favor reaches the pinnacle alone, and finds no one around him, or very few, who are not prepared to take orders. Apart from this, you cannot satisfy the nobles honestly and without harming others, but you certainly can satisfy the people. In fact, the aim of the common people is more honest than that of the nobles, since the nobles want to oppress others, while the people simply want not to be oppressed.[1] Besides, a prince can never be sure of his position when the people are against him, because there are so many of them; but he knows where to find hostile nobles, because they are few. The worst thing a prince can expect from a hostile population is that they will abandon him; but hostile nobles may not only abandon him, but attack him directly. They are more farsighted and shrewder, taking timely steps to protect themselves and ingratiate themselves with the man they expect to win. Besides, the prince must always live among the same people, but he can do very well without a particular set of noblemen, since it is in his power to make or unmake them every day, abolishing honors or creating them, just as he pleases.

And to make this point clearer, let me say that noblemen can be seen as essentially of two sorts: either they manage their affairs in such a way as to be entirely at your disposal, or they do not. Those who are devoted to you and who are not greedy, you should honor and cherish; those who are not devoted to you may again be seen in two ways. They may hold back from pusillanimity and innate lack of spirit; then you should make use of them, especially as counsellors, since in times of prosperity they will hold you in honor, and in times of adversity there is no need to fear them. But when they deliberately refuse to commit themselves for reasons of ambition, that is a clear sign they are thinking more of themselves than of you; and the prince should beware of men like this, and fear them as if they were open enemies, because in times of adversity they will certainly join in trying to ruin him.

Of course a man who becomes prince through the good will of the

---

1. Machiavelli's strong democratic and popular feelings here are echoed in that unit of the *Discorsi* showing that a prince is more likely to be ungrateful than are the people (1. 29); "ungrateful" in this context equates with "untrustworthy."

people ought to keep them well disposed toward him; and this should not be hard, since all they ask is not to be oppressed. But even a man who becomes prince against the will of the people, with the aid of the nobles, should try above all things to win over the populace; he can do this quite easily by taking them under his protection. And because men, when they receive benefits from a prince whom they expected to harm them, are especially obliged to him, such a prince's subjects may feel more warmly toward him than if he had risen to power with their help. The prince can earn the good will of his subjects in many ways, but as they vary according to circumstances, I can give no fixed rules and will say nothing of them. One conclusion only can be drawn: the prince must have the people well disposed toward him; otherwise in times of adversity there is no hope.

Nabis, prince of Sparta, held out against the attacks of all the rest of Greece and a Roman army that had always been victorious, defending his country and his state against them; and when danger threatened, there were very few Spartans against whom he had to protect himself.[2] If he had had the people against him, his measures would never have sufficed. And let nobody pretend to answer me with that trite proverb that "The man who builds on the people builds his house on mud." That may be true when a private citizen plants his foundations amid the people and lets himself think that the people will come to his aid when he is in trouble with his enemies or the magistrates. In such a case one can easily find himself deluded, as happened in Rome with the Gracchi and in Florence with Messer Giorgio Scali.[3] But if it is a prince who puts his trust in the people, one who knows how to command, who is a man of courage and does not lose his head in adversity, if he will make the necessary practical preparations and can rouse his people to action by his own example and orders, he will never find himself betrayed, and his foundations will prove to have been well laid.

These principalities are generally in most danger when they are just passing from a civil to an absolute form of government. In such circumstances, a prince commands either in his own person or through the magistrates; in the latter case, his position is much weaker and more dangerous, because he depends entirely on the good will of those citizens who have been put in office. Especially in time of trouble, they can easily depose him, either by opposing him directly or by not obeying him. And the prince has no chance to seize absolute command once

2. Nabis, tyrant of Sparta from 205 to 192 B.C., was a very crude fellow; what Machiavelli probably has in mind is the story that before engaging in his first war with Flamininus the Roman, he had eighty suspected citizens murdered in Sparta; Livy 34.27.

3. The two Gracchi, Tiberius and Gaius, were popular Roman reformers of the second century B.C., who both met violent ends as a result of bitter aristocratic resistance. Giorgio Scali took part in the so-called "revolt of the Ciompi" (wool carders) in 1378; after a brief success, he and his fellow leaders were thrown out of power, and Scali was beheaded. In his History of Florence (3.5), Machiavelli makes much of Giorgio Scali's complaints against the fickleness of the people.

his rule is endangered, because citizen-subjects who are used to obeying the magistrates will not take orders from him in times of crisis. At crucial moments a prince always finds himself short of trustworthy men. This is why a prince should never count on what he sees in times of quiet, when the citizens find the state useful to them, and everyone pushes forward, making big promises and professing readiness to die for the prince—as long as death is far away; but when times are tough, when the state really needs its citizens, few are to be found. And a crisis of this sort is particularly dangerous, as a prince never experiences it a second time. Thus a wise prince will think of ways to keep his citizens of every sort and under every circumstance dependent on the state and on him; and then they will always be trustworthy.

X

HOW TO MEASURE THE STRENGTH OF ANY PRINCE'S STATE

There is one other consideration to bear in mind regarding these civil principates; that is, whether a prince is strong enough to stand on his own feet in case of need, or whether he is in constant need of help from others. And to make the matter clearer, let me say that in my opinion princes control their own destiny when they command enough money or men to assemble an adequate army and make a stand against anyone who attacks them. I think princes who need outside protection are those who cannot take the field against their foes, but have to hide behind their walls and defend themselves there. I have already mentioned the first class,[4] and will save whatever else I have to say about them till later. As for the others, all I can say is that they should keep their cities well fortified and well supplied, and pay no heed to the surrounding countryside. Whenever a man has fortified his city strongly, and has dealt with his subjects as I described above and will describe further below, people will be slow to attack him; men are always wary of tasks that seem hard, and it can never seem easy to attack a prince whose city is in fine fettle, and whose people do not hate him.

In Germany the cities are perfectly free, though their territories are small; they obey the emperor when they feel like it, and have no fear of him or any other neighbors, because they are so well fortified that everyone realizes it would be slow, hard work to capture them. They all have moats and walls of good size, plenty of artillery, and in the public warehouses food, drink, and fuel for a full year; besides which, to keep the workers occupied without draining the public treasury, they always hold in reserve a year's supply of raw materials for the crafts which are the city's vital nerves—the industries by which the common people

---

4. The "first class" seems to consist of those who, like Cesare Borgia, have no army of their own, but go out to get one; that group is described in chapter VII. The second group is those who have no army of their own, and don't even try to get one; they lurk behind walls, and to them alone Machiavelli directs the advice that follows.

make a living. They also respect military training, and have many ordinances to keep people active in this way.[5]

Thus a prince who has a strong city and does not earn his people's hatred cannot be attacked, or if he were, that attacker would be driven off to his own disgrace; because the way things keep changing in this world, it is almost impossible for a prince with his armies to devote an entire year to a siege while doing nothing else. Maybe someone will object: when the people see their possessions outside the walls being burnt up, they will get impatient; a long siege and their own self-interest will make them forget the prince.[6] But to this I answer that a brave, strong prince will overcome all these problems, giving his subjects hope at one minute that the storm will soon pass, stirring them up at another moment to fear the enemy's cruelty, and on still other occasions restraining those who seem too rash. Besides, the enemy will generally do his burning and ravishing of the countryside as soon as he begins the siege, when men's minds are still passionate and earnest for the defense; thus the prince has less reason to worry, because, after a few days, when tempers have cooled, the harm will already have been done, the losses inflicted, and there will clearly be no cure. At that point, the people will rally even more strongly behind their prince, because they will feel he owes them something, since their houses were burnt and their fields ravaged in defense of his cause. Indeed, men are so constructed that they feel themselves committed as much by the benefits they grant as by those they receive. Hence, all things considered, it should not be hard for a prudent prince to keep his subjects in good spirits throughout a siege, as long as he does not run short of food or weapons.

XI

OF ECCLESIASTICAL STATES

It remains for us now only to discuss ecclesiastical states, which present their worst difficulties before one takes possession of them; for though they are gained either by virtue [*virtù*] or fortune,[7] they can be held without either of those qualities. They are sustained by the ancient principles of religion, which are so powerful and of such authority that

5. In 1507 Machiavelli had been sent by the Florentines to treat with Maximilian, and had ventured into Austria perhaps as far as Innsbruck, writing (perhaps some years later) a little *Portrait of Things of Germany*. The cities he saw were thus Swiss and Tyrolean, though he called them all German; and their self-sufficiency is the quality he emphasizes.

6. In a classic passage (2.6.21) Thucydides describes the rage of the Athenians when they saw the lands outside their walls being ravaged; but Machiavelli probably had in mind the more

immediate instance of the Pisans, from whose city the Florentines in their fury once actually tried to divert the river Arno.

7. With Alexander VI and Julius II in mind, it might seem inappropriate to translate the word *virtù* in this passage as "virtue." But as Leo X was pope when Machiavelli wrote (a Medici and a decent man, if not especially holy), if Machiavelli had had to separate the meanings of *virtù* he would probably have opted for "virtue" here.

they keep their princes in power whatever they do, however they live.
These are the only princes who have states that they do not defend and
subjects that they do not govern; the states, though undefended, are
never taken from them, and the subjects, though ungoverned, neither
protest, nor try to break away, nor could revolt if they had a mind to.
These, then, are the only safe and happy governments. But since they
are ruled by a heavenly providence to which human reason cannot reach,
I shall say nothing of them. Instituted as they are by God, and sustained
by him, it would be a rash and imprudent man who ventured to discuss
them.[8]

Still, someone might wonder how it happened that the Church became so powerful, since before Alexander's time, the rulers of Italy—
and not just those who were known as potentates, but every minor baron
and lord down to the smallest—had little respect for its temporal power.
Yet now a king of France trembles before it, and the papacy was actually
able to throw him out of Italy and ruin the Venetians at the same
time[9]—in view of which, well known though the events are, I do not
think it superfluous to recall some of them to memory.

Before Charles, king of France, came into Italy, this part of the world
was divided between the pope, the Venetians, the king of Naples, the
duke of Milan, and the Florentines. These rulers were bound to keep
two principal ends in view: one, to ensure that no foreign armies entered
Italy; the other, to ensure that none of the five became overly powerful.[1]
The two most to be feared were the pope and the Venetians. To hold
the Venetians in check, a union of all the others was required, such as
was formed for the defense of Ferrara.[2] And to keep the pope down, the
nobles of Rome were very useful; they were divided in two factions, the
houses of Orsini and Colonna, which always had good reason to feel
hostile toward one another, and thus stood armed to the teeth under
the pope's very nose, keeping him weak and impotent. Occasionally,
no doubt, a pope of courage came along, like Sixtus, but neither fortune
nor wisdom could free him from this predicament.[3] One reason for this
was simply the shortness of papal lives; because in ten years, which is
all the average pope lives, he might barely put down one of the factions,
but then when he had about put down the Colonnas, for example, in

8. Machiavelli's bitter view of the Church in
politics found fullest expression in *Discorsi* 1.12
(see pp. 98–100).
9. Julius II defeated the Venetians at Vailà (or
Agnadello) May 14, 1509; he drove the French
out of Italy in 1512, and was assembling at the
time of his death the Fifth Lateran Council,
which proposed to condemn both the French
Church and the French king.
1. Guicciardini's *History* opens with a long
and eloquent picture of the peace and pros-

perity prevailing in Italy at the moment when
Lorenzo the Magnificent died (1492).
2. In 1484 the pope (Sixtus IV), the king of
Naples, the duke of Milan, and the Florentines
all combined to help defend Ferrara against the
Venetians in the so-called "war of salt." See
chapter II, note 5, p. 4.
3. Sixtus IV, pope from 1471 to 1484, was a
member of the aggressive family of della Rovere; Julius II, his nephew, inherited his disposition and a number of his quarrels.

would come another pope hostile to the Orsini, and in raising one faction he would not have time to put down the other.

For these reasons, the temporal power of the pope was little respected in Italy. Then Alexander VI was raised to the papacy, and he showed, more than any other pope that ever was, how much can be done in that office with money and arms. Using Duke Valentino as his instrument and the coming of the French as his occasion, he did all those things that I described above in talking of the duke's actions. His intent, to be sure, was to aggrandize the duke and not the Church; still what he did served the Church's ends; and after his death, when the duke was out of the way, the Church profited from his efforts. Pope Julius followed, and he found the Church in flourishing estate, controlling the whole of the Romagna, with the Roman nobles crushed and the two factions beaten down by Alexander. What was more, he found handy ways of accumulating money, that before Alexander had never been used.[4] Julius not only followed his predecessor but pushed beyond him; he planned to take Bologna, crush the Venetians, and drive the French out of Italy. In fact he accomplished all these things, and what is even more to his credit, he did them all for the benefit of the Church and not of any private individual.[5] Moreover, he kept the Orsini and Colonna factions in the same lowly condition in which he found them; and though among these families one leader or another has since tried to stir things up, two things kept them quiet: one was the power of the Church, which awed them; and the other was that they had no cardinals, who start most of the quarrels between them. As long as they have cardinals, these factions will never be at ease; the churchmen stir up trouble, inside Rome as well as outside it, and then the barons have to back them up; thus ambitious prelates inflame quarrels and tumults among the barons. These are the reasons why his present holiness Pope Leo has found the papacy so strong; and we may hope that as his predecessors made it great by force of arms, he by his generosity and countless other talents [virtù] will make it even greater and more to be revered.[6]

XII

ON DIFFERENT KINDS OF TROOPS, ESPECIALLY MERCENARIES

Now that I have described in detail the natures of the various states that are my topic; now that I have considered some of the reasons for

4. Alexander pronounced 1500 a special jubilee year, and created cardinals wholesale in order to support his son Cesare's campaigns in the Romagna; Julius also sold Church offices and indulgences, perhaps less spectacularly, but on a wider scale.

5. Even his enemies agreed that Julius II wanted money for political, not personal purposes; though known before his elevation as a lavish man, he followed as pope the policies recommended in Machiavelli's chapter XVI, as Machiavelli himself indicates.

6. The compliment is barely polite; writing to a Medici about a Medici pope, Machiavelli could hardly say less.

their prosperity and decline, and have shown how they have often been won and held—I must discuss in general the offensive and defensive actions that princes may be called on to undertake. I said before that a prince must lay strong foundations, otherwise he is bound to come to grief. The chief foundations on which all states rest, whether they are new, old, or mixed, are good laws and good arms. And since there cannot be good laws where there are not good arms, and where there are good arms there are bound to be good laws, I shall set aside the topic of laws and talk about arms.

Let me say, then, that the armies with which a prince defends his state are either his own or are mercenaries, auxilaries, or mixed. Mercenaries and auxilaries are useless and dangerous. Any man who founds his state on mercenaries can never be safe or secure, because they are disunited, ambitious, undisciplined, and untrustworthy—bold fellows among their friends, but cowardly in the face of the enemy; they have no fear of God, nor loyalty to men. They will protect you from ruin only as long as nobody assaults you; in peace you are at their mercy, and in war at the mercy of your enemies. The reason is that they have no other passions or incentives to hold the field, except their desire for a bit of money, and that is not enough to make them die for you. They are all eagerness to be your soldiers as long as you are not waging war; when war breaks out, they either turn tail or disappear. And this should not be hard to believe, because the present ruin of Italy is caused by nothing else than its having trusted for so long to mercenary armies. For some individuals they were indeed useful, and they seemed fierce enough when they had only one another to fight; but when outsiders appeared, they showed themselves for what they were. For this reason Charles of France was allowed to take Italy "with chalk."[7] And the man who said our sins were the cause of our defeats, said the truth; but they were not the sins he thought, they were those I described, and because princes committed them, princes have suffered for them.

To demonstrate further the ill effect of these troops, let me say that either mercenary leaders are skilled soldiers, or they are not; if they are, they cannot be trusted, because they will always be trying to increase their own authority, either by attacking you, their employer, or by oppressing people with whom you have no quarrel. But if your mercenary is not a brave [*virtuoso*] leader, he will ruin you with his incompetence. And if you object that any leader may do this, whether mercenary or not, my answer is that armies are controlled by either a prince or a republic. The prince should go to war in his own person, and assume the captain's post; the republic has to send its citizens. When one of

7. Charles VIII took Italy "with chalk" and without fighting by simply marking the doors of houses requisitioned as quarters for his troops. Alexander VI made the remark about chalk being the only weapon he needed. Savonarola was the man who attributed the French invasion to Italian sinfulness.

those it sends does not prove a valiant leader, it must change him; when he does well, it must check him with laws, to keep him in line. Experience teaches that independent princes and well-armed republics accomplish great things, but mercenary armies do nothing but lose; and a republic with its own armies holds out longer against the tyranny of one of its citizens than does a republic with foreign armies. For many centuries the Romans and the Spartans were well armed and free; the Swiss are heavily armed and live in the greatest freedom.

The Carthaginians are an example from antiquity of a people who used mercenary armies: even though they had Carthaginian leaders, those armies nearly overran the city after the first war with the Romans.[8] After the death of Epaminondas, the Thebans appointed Philip of Macedon head of their armies; he won a victory for them, and took away their liberty.[9] After the death of Duke Philip, the Milanese used Francesco Sforza against the Venetians; after he had beaten the enemy at Caravaggio, he joined with them to put down the Milanese, his employers.[1] When Sforza his father was soldiering for Queen Joanna of Naples, he deliberately left her unprotected on one occasion, so that, to keep from losing her kingdom, she was forced to throw herself on the mercies of the king of Aragon.[2] No doubt the Venetians and the Florentines have recently increased their empires by means of mercenary armies, the leaders of which did not make themselves princes, but defended their employers. But I answer that the Florentines were just lucky in this matter; because the good leaders whom they might have had to fear sometimes were not victorious, sometimes had rivals, and sometimes turned their ambition elsewhere. Giovanni Acuto was not victorious, and for that reason we cannot tell how he would have kept his word; but everyone concedes that if he had won a victory, the Florentines would have been at his mercy.[3] Sforza always had the Braccio crowd as his rivals, and they kept an eye on one another. Francesco[4] turned his ambition against Lombardy, while Braccio went against the Church and the kingdom of Naples.

But let us turn to events of recent history. The Florentines made Paolo Vitelli their military leader; he was a very shrewd man, who had risen

8. In the so-called "servile war," which broke out in 241 B.C., directly after the First Punic War, the Carthaginian mercenaries turned on their own masters. This struggle provides the background for Flaubert's novel, *Salammbô*; Machiavelli read of it in the less gaudy pages of Polybius.

9. The Thebans accepted help from Philip of Macedon (Alexander's father) against the Phocians, and less than ten years later he took away their liberty at the battle of Chaeronea (338 B.C.).

1. Duke Philip was the last of the Visconti line: he died in 1447. The republic that followed in Milan employed Francesco Sforza, with the

results indicated. See above, p. 4.

2. The tangled relationships between Joanna II of Naples and Sforza the elder included an erotic episode, in the course of which, as part of a lovers' quarrel, Sforza deliberately left the lady at the mercy of her enemies.

3. Sir John Hawkwood (1320–94), originally of England but known in Italy as "Giovanni Acuto," served the Florentines for many years, with his "White Company." Braccio da Montone and Sforza the elder were contemporaries, fellow-students, and professional rivals among the condottieri of the early fifteenth-century Romagna.

4. Francesco Sforza.

from private life to a position of the greatest renown. If he had taken Pisa, there is no denying that the Florentines would have had to stick with him; since if he had taken service with their enemies their cause would have become hopeless, and as long as they kept him they had to obey him.[5] As for the Venetians, if we consider their career, we will see that they made steady, splendid progress with their own people, before they began to fight on land; using their own gentry and armed populace, they campaigned very successfully [*virtuosissamente*]. But when they began to fight on land, they abandoned these good customs [*virtù*], and began to follow the military traditions of Italy. When they first began to expand on land, because their country was still small and their reputation great, they had no special need to fear their captains; but as they expanded in power under the leadership of Carmagnola,[6] they got a sniff of their danger. They knew he was a man of great ability [*virtuosissimo*], and recalled that under his leadership they had beaten the duke of Milan; on the other hand, they saw that he was cooling in his conduct of the war. Thus they judged that they could not win the war with him, because he did not want to win; yet they could not dismiss him either, for fear of losing what they had won. So, finally, to be sure of him they had to have him murdered. Thereafter they had as their captains Bartolomeo da Bergamo, Roberto da San Severino, the count of Pitigliano, and suchlike—men who gave them more reason to worry over losses than gains. That happened shortly at Vailá,[7] where in a single day they lost everything that their incessant labors over eight hundred years had earned them. Armies of this [mercenary] sort make only slow, weak, late conquests; their losses are sudden, amazing.

As these examples have all brought me to the consideration of Italy, which for many years has been controlled by mercenary armies, I would like to look into the backgrounds, so that when we have seen the origin and progress of this warfare, we can take steps to change it. I must explain, then, that when the empire began to lose its hold on Italy and the pope's temporal power began to increase, Italy was divided into several states. Many of the big cities took arms against their nobles who previously, with the help of the emperor, had kept them under. The

---

5. Paolo Vitelli, who commanded the Florentine armies against Pisa but did not make satisfactory progress with that enterprise, was accused of treason and executed in 1499. It was his brother Vitellozzo, who had never forgiven the Florentines, who was strangled three years later at Sinigaglia by Cesare Borgia.
6. Francesco Bussone, count of Carmagnola (ca. 1380–1432), was not in reality as successful as Machiavelli describes him; during most of his later campaigns, he was either inept or deliberately dilatory. The Venetians chose the second horn of that dilemma, and had him executed.
7. Bartolomeo Colleoni da Bergamo, a rela-

tively able commander, is best known now for the splendid equestrian statue by Verrocchio erected by the Venetians after his death in 1475. The other Venetian generals mentioned by Machiavelli were his associates and subordinates. The battle of Vailà (also known as Agnadello, also known as Ghiaradadda) was fought against forces assembled by Pope Julius II, on May 14, 1509; in this engagement the Venetians lost their entire land empire—which was not, indeed, *all* they had gained in eight hundred years of struggle, but, in conjunction with their recent losses at sea to the Turks, represented a staggering blow.

Church favored these risings as a way of increasing its temporal power; and thus private citizens became princes in many cities. Thus almost all Italy came into the hands of the Church and of a few republics; and since neither priests nor ordinary citizens know much about military matters, they began to hire foreigners. The first to bring this sort of soldiering into reputation was Alberigo da Conio, from the Romagna.[8] Among those trained in his school were Braccio and Sforza, who in their day were arbiters of Italy. After them came the whole crew who have directed Italian armies down to the present day; and the result of their prowess [virtù] has been that Italy has been overrun by Charles, sacked by Louis, raped by Ferdinand, and disgraced by the Swiss.

Their policy was, first of all, to raise their own reputation by diminishing that of the infantry. They did this because they had no estates or native lands, but lived on salaries; a few infantry would have given them little prestige, and a large number they could never have supported. So they limited themselves to cavalry, a moderate number of which could give them both strength and high repute. And before long, they had so arranged things that in an army of twenty thousand soldiers, not two thousand infantrymen were to be found. Besides, they went to great lengths to avoid disturbing themselves or their soldiers with work or danger, never killing one another in skirmishes, but only taking one another prisoner and never asking any ransom. They never attacked a fortification at night, and the besieged never counterattacked; around their camps they built neither palisades nor ditches; and they never campaigned in winter. All these things were permitted by the rules of their warfare, and deliberately contrived, in order to avoid work and danger, as we said; so that they have brought Italy to a state of slavery and contempt.

13

XIII

ON AUXILIARY TROOPS, MIXED TROOPS, AND YOUR OWN TROOPS

Armies of auxiliaries, the other useless sort, are the kind that come when you ask a powerful neighbor to help with his soldiers in your defense. Pope Julius tried this only recently; he had learned a gloomy lesson at Ferrara as a result of using mercenary troops, and now turned to auxiliaries, getting Ferdinand, king of Spain, to help with his soldiers and armies.[9] Troops of this sort may be perfectly good and useful in their own right, but to the man who calls them in they are almost always harmful, because when they lose they carry your cause down with them,

8. Alberigo da Barbiano, count of Conio (?–1409) founded the first Italian mercenary company, and gave instruction in the art of mercenary warfare to both Braccio da Montone and Sforza the elder (see note 3 above).
9. Julius assaulted Ferrara in 1510, using

troops of several different nationalities, including three hundred Spanish lances supplied by Ferdinand. As noted above in chapter II, note 5, p. 4, Alfonso, duke of Ferrara, who stood off this attack, was one of the great soldiers of Europe.

and when they win, you remain their prisoner. And though ancient history is full of instances, I don't want to set aside the fresh example of Pope Julius. His behavior could scarcely have been more ill-advised: just because he wanted Ferrara, he put his whole destiny in the hands of a foreigner. Only his good luck enabled him to escape the consequences of his bad judgment, through the operation of a third force. For when his auxiliaries had been beaten at Ravenna, the Swiss suddenly appeared and drove off the victors, much to his surprise and everyone else's.[1] So he was not captured either by his enemies, because they had fled, or by his auxiliaries, because he was victorious through the efforts of somebody else. Likewise the Florentines, when they had no arms of their own, brought ten thousand Frenchmen to attack Pisa; and this project of theirs brought greater dangers upon them than any of their other tribulations.[2] The emperor of Constantinople, in order to put down his neighbors, brought into Greece an army of ten thousand Turks; when the war was over, they refused to leave, and thus began the enslavement of Greece by the infidels.[3]

Anyone who wants to make dead sure of not winning, then, had better make use of armies like these, since they are much more dangerous than mercenaries. In these you get your ruin ready-made; they come to you a compact body, all trained to obey somebody else. Mercenaries after a victory need a little time and a better occasion before they attack you, since they are not a unified body, but a group of individuals picked and paid by you. Hence a third party, even if you name him as head, cannot immediately gain enough authority to do you serious harm. In a word, when you have mercenaries, their cowardice is most dangerous to you; when you have auxiliaries, it is their courage [virtù] you must fear. Hence a wise prince has always kept away from troops like these, and made use of his own, preferring to lose under his own power than to win with other people's troops—since it isn't a real victory when alien armies win it for you. I am never reluctant to cite Cesare Borgia and his deeds. The duke entered the Romagna with auxiliary troops, consisting entirely of Frenchmen; and with them he took Imola and Forlì.[4] But then when he found they were not to be trusted, he adopted mer-

1. At the desperate battle of Ravenna, on April 11, 1512, the French defeated Julius and his auxiliaries; but in May, twenty thousand Swiss descended on Italy, compelling the victorious French to retreat. Machiavelli is forcing his case here; though defeated at Ravenna, the Spaniards fought like lions, inflicting crippling losses on the French even before the Swiss invasion.

2. Gascon and Swiss troops, borrowed by the Florentines from the French king for use against Pisa in the summer of 1500, mutinied for more pay, so the whole enterprise collapsed; Machiavelli himself was one of the commis-

sioners who had to explain the fiasco to Louis XII.

3. For his third example, Machiavelli leaps back more than 150 years; it was 1353 when Emperor John V Cantacuzene first made the fatal error of inviting the Turks to help him against his European enemies.

4. Cf. above chapter VII, note 4, p. 20. When he says "it is not a real victory when alien armies win it for you," Machiavelli isn't invoking the rules of sportsmanship or fair play; he means that prizes gained by other peoples' energies belong to them, when they are strong enough to hold onto them.

cenaries as less dangerous, and hired the Orsini and Vitelli. When he found they too were undependable, treacherous, and dangerous to his service, he got rid of them, and turned to troops of his own. And you can easily see the difference there is between these various armies by the difference in the duke's reputation when he had only French soldiers, when he had the Orsini and Vitelli, and when he had his own soldiers and could stand on his own feet. His reputation grew steadily more impressive, and it never stood higher than when everyone saw he was the complete master of his own troops.

Though I don't want to stop using Italian examples which are fresh in mind, I cannot omit Hiero of Syracuse, whom I mentioned earlier. When the Syracusans made this man head of their armies, as I said before, he recognized at once that mercenary soldiers were useless, being formed on the same pattern as our Italian condottieri; and since he couldn't safely keep them, nor yet let them go, he had them cut to bits, and after that he made war with his own armies, not with those of other people.[5] I'd like also to call to mind a parable from the Old Testament which bears on the point. When David volunteered before Saul to fight with Goliath the Philistine challenger, Saul, to give the young man courage, offered him his own royal armor. But David, after trying it on, refused, saying he could never do himself justice in that armor. He preferred to meet the enemy armed simply with his own sling and a knife. In a word, other men's armor will either slip off your back, or weigh you down, or constrict your actions. When Charles VII, father of King Louis XI, had freed France from the English by his own energy [virtù] and good luck, he realized how necessary it was to have his own armies, and established laws in his kingdom for training cavalry and infantry. But afterwards his son, King Louis, gave up the infantry and began to hire Swiss;[6] that mistake was followed by others, and brought the country into the dangers which we can now observe. By giving the Swiss a great reputation, he lowered that of his own armies; he abolished all his own infantry, and forced his cavalry into dependence on outsiders—for when they became accustomed to fight with the help of Swiss infantry, they began to suppose they could not win without them. And now the French are no longer strong enough to oppose the Swiss, while without Swiss in their ranks they cannot stand up to anyone else. Thus the French armies have become mixed, part mercenary and part

5. The mercenaries with whom Hiero had to struggle were known as Mamertines; actually, they were first hired by Agathocles. Hiero had to attack them, not because they were ineffectual, but because they were threatening his rule of Syracuse. See Polybius 1.7–9. The story of Saul and David is found in 1 Samuel 17.38–39.

6. In a Renaissance army, everyone wanted to be a horseman because the pay was better.

Charles VII, made king of France by Joan of Arc, had to reform the French army to end the war with England. He formed a kind of national militia, but in 1474 his successor, Louis XI, repealed the ordinance and began hiring Swiss mercenaries. The dangers facing the French in 1513 grew out of their losses at Ravenna (1512) and Novara (1513), which Machiavelli attributes to their poor infantry.

native troops. Taken all in all, these troops are much better than mere auxiliaries or mere mercenaries, but they are much inferior to armies of one's own people. The example already given will suffice; the kingdom of France would be invincible if the laws of Charles had been kept in force or strengthened. But shortsighted men undertake policies for their immediate advantage, paying no heed to the slow poison hidden within them, as I said before regarding consumptive fevers.

So a prince who does not recognize the evils of a state the minute they are born is not really wise; and such ability to look ahead is given to very few. If you try to seek out the basic reason for the fall of the Roman Empire, you will find it began with the hiring of Goths as soldiers; from that moment, the forces of the Roman Empire began to grow slack, and all the energy [*virtù*] taken from them accrued to the outsiders.

I conclude, then, that unless it has its own armies, no state is really secure; in that case, it depends entirely on fortune, having no power [*virtù*] to put up a reliable defense in times of trouble. Wise men have always thought and said "that nothing is so weak and unstable as a reputation for power not founded on strength of one's own."[7] Your own armies are defined as those composed of your own subjects, citizens, or dependents: all others are either mercenary or auxiliary. You will have no trouble creating your own armies if you study the regulations of the four men noted above,[8] and note how Philip, father of Alexander the Great, levied and organized his armies. Many other republics and kingdoms have done the same; and to their precedents I refer you without further remark.

XIV

MILITARY DUTIES OF THE PRINCE

A prince, therefore, should have no other object, no other thought, no other subject of study, than war, its rules and disciplines; this is the only art for a man who commands, and it is of such value [*virtù*] that is not only keeps born princes in place, but often raises men from private citizens to princely fortune. On the other hand, it is clear that when princes have thought more about the refinements of life than about war, they have lost their positions. The quickest way to lose a state is to neglect this art; the quickest way to get one is to study it. Because he was a soldier, Francesco Sforza raised himself from private citizen to duke of Milan; his successors, who tried to avoid the hardships of warfare, became private citizens after being dukes.[9] Apart from the other evils it

---

7. The quotation is from Tacitus, *Annals* 13.19.

8. The examples make a curious quartet: Cesare Borgia, Hiero of Syracuse, King David, and Charles VII of France. The point seems to be that the rule holds good whatever the moral status of the person to whom it may be applied.

9. The Sforzas passed, with spectacular abruptness, from barbarism to decadence in a generation; Machiavelli's exhortations, however necessary he supposed them, were not borne out by Medici history—they generally lost by warfare what they gained by diplomacy and trade.

brings with it, being defenseless makes you contemptible. This is one of the disgraces from which a prince must guard himself, as we shall see later. Between a man with arms and a man without them there is no proportion at all. It is not reasonable to expect an armed man to obey one who is unarmed, nor an unarmed man to be safe among armed servants; because, what with the contempt of the former and the mistrust of the latter, there is no living together. Thus a prince who knows nothing of warfare, apart from his other troubles already described, cannot hope for respect from his soldiers or put any trust in them.

Therefore the prince should never turn his mind from the study of war; in times of peace he should think about it even more than in wartime. He can do this in two ways, by training the body and training the mind. As for physical training, apart from keeping his troops well disciplined and exercised, he should do a great deal of hunting, and thus harden his body to strenuous exercise, meanwhile learning to read terrain. He will see how the mountains rise, how the valleys open out, and how the plains lie; he will know about rivers and swamps—and to this study he should devote the greatest attention. What he learns will be doubly useful; first, he will become acquainted with his own land, and understand better how to defend it; and then, because he knows his own country thoroughly, he can easily understand any other country that he is forced to look over for the first time. For example, in Tuscany the hills, valleys, plains, and swamps are pretty much like those in other provinces, so that, knowing one, you can easily get to know the others. Any prince who lacks this experience lacks the main thing a captain should have, that is, a knowledge of how to find the enemy, pick a campsite, draw up an army, prepare it for battle, and organize sieges for his own advantage.

Among the other good things that historians report of Philopoemon, prince of the Achaeans, they say that in peacetime he thought of nothing but how to make war;[1] and when he was in the country with his friends, he would sometimes stop and ask them: "Suppose there were enemies up in those hills, and we were here with our army, who would have the advantage? How could we get at them, without breaking ranks? If we wanted to get away, how would we do it? If they tried to get away, how could we cut them off?" Thus, as they traveled along he would raise every tactical problem that could confront an army; he listened to their opinions and put forth his own, supporting them with reasons. As a result of this constant practice, no unexpected difficulty could ever arise, when he was at the head of his army, for which he did not have a ready remedy.

As for exercising the mind, a prince should read history and reflect

1. The story of Philopoemon, leader of the Achaean league, and his single-minded strategic training program is told by Plutarch among the *Parallel Lives*, where the Greek general is compared with the Roman Flamininus; and also by Livy 35.28.

on the actions of great men. He can see how they carried themselves during their wars, and study what made them win, what made them lose, so that he can imitate their successes and avoid their defeats. Above all, he should do as great men have done before him, and take as a model for his conduct some great historical figure who achieved the highest praise and glory by constantly holding before himself the deeds and achievements of a predecessor. They say Alexander the Great imitated Achilles, Caesar imitated Alexander, and Scipio imitated Cyrus. Anyone who reads Xenophon's life of Cyrus must realize how closely Scipio modelled himself on Cyrus, how much that imitation contributed to his glory, and how closely he conformed, in temperance, affability, humanity, and liberality to the things that Xenophon wrote about Cyrus.[2]

Such are the rules that a wise prince should observe. He must never idle away his days of peace, but vigorously make capital that will pay off in times of adversity; thus, when fortune changes, it will find him in a position to resist.

XV

ON THE REASONS WHY MEN ARE PRAISED OR BLAMED—ESPECIALLY PRINCES

It remains now to be seen what style and principles a prince ought to adopt in dealing with his subjects and friends. I know the subject has been treated frequently before, and I fear people will think me rash for trying to do so again, especially since I intend to differ in this discussion from what others have said. But since I intend to write something useful to an understanding reader, it seemed better to go after the real truth of the matter than to repeat what people have imagined. A great many men have imagined states and princedoms such as nobody ever saw or knew in the real world,[3] and there's such a difference between the way we really live and the way we ought to live that the man who neglects the real to study the ideal will learn how to accomplish his ruin, not his salvation. Any man who tries to be good all the time is bound to come to ruin among the great number who are not good. Hence a prince who wants to keep his authority must learn how not to be good, and use that knowledge, or refrain from using it, as necessity requires.

Putting aside, then, all the imaginary things that are said about

2. These various stories of classical figures imitating other classical figures are all taken from books—the story of Alexander imitating Achilles from Plutarch, the story of Caesar imitating Alexander from Suetonius, the story of Cato imitating Cyrus from a passage of Cicero. Even Xenophon's ostensible "life" of Cyrus is really a didactic novel, with only the slightest basis in historical fact.

3. Plato's *Republic* was certainly in Machiavelli's mind; More's *Utopia* was not yet published. But Machiavelli was doubtless thinking, as well, of previous books giving advice to princes, which dealt in realistic terms with impractical situations. Egidio Colonna had said, for example, that to lack just one of the princely virtues was to lack them all.

princes, and getting down to the truth, let me say that whenever men are discussed (and especially princes because they are prominent), there are certain qualities that bring them either praise or blame. Thus some are considered generous, others stingy (I use a Tuscan term, since "greedy" in our speech means a man who wants to take other people's goods; we call a man "stingy" who clings to his own);[4] some are givers, others grabbers; some cruel, others humane; one man is treacherous, another faithful; one is feeble and effeminate, another fierce and spirited; one modest, another proud; one lustful, another chaste; one straight-forward, another sly; one harsh, another gentle; one serious, another playful; one religious, another skeptical, and so on. I know everyone will agree that among these many qualities a prince certainly ought to have all those that are considered good. But since it is impossible to have and exercise them all, because the conditions of human life simply do not allow it, a prince must be shrewd enough to avoid the public disgrace of those vices that would lose him his state. If he possibly can, he should also guard against vices that will not lose him his state; but if he cannot prevent them, he should not be too worried about indulging them. And further-more, he should not be too worried about incurring blame for any vice without which he would find it hard to save his state. For if you look at matters carefully, you will see that something resembling virtue, if you follow it, may be your ruin, while something else resembling vice will lead, if you follow it, to your security and well-being.

XVI

ON LIBERALITY AND STINGINESS

Let me begin, then, with the first of the qualities mentioned above, by saying that a reputation for liberality is doubtless very fine; but the generosity that earns you that reputation can do you great harm. For if you exercise your generosity in a really virtuous way [*virtuosamente*],[5] as you should, nobody will know of it, and you cannot escape the odium of the opposite vice. Hence if you wish to be widely known as a generous man, you must seize every opportunity to make a big display of your giving. A prince of this character is bound to use up his entire revenue in works of ostentation. In the end, if he wants to keep a name for generosity, he will have to load his people with exorbitant taxes and squeeze money out of them in every way he can. This is the first step in making him odious to his subjects; for when he is poor, nobody will

---

4. The two words in Italian are *avaro* and *mis-ero*. Machiavelli seems to derive the first by mistaken etymology from the verb *avere*, ("to possess"); the "avaro" is he who "per rapina desidera di avere." The "misero," by contrast, is the true miser; and that's a legitimate etymological link.

5. This phrase marks one extreme in Machia-velli's handling of the word *virtù*. It means here, not simply doing a charitable thing, but doing it without ulterior motives, from a sin-cere, inward, and personal sense of "caritas." Contrast phrases like "tanta ferocità e tanta virtù" (chapter VII) or "maestro delle virtù e scelleratezze sua" (chapter VIII).

respect him. Then, when his generosity has angered many and brought rewards to a few, the slightest difficulty will trouble him, and at the first approach of danger, down he goes. If by chance he foresees this, and tries to change his ways, he will immediately be labelled a miser.

Since a prince cannot use this virtue [*virtù*] of liberality in such a way as to become known for it unless he harms his own security, he will not mind, if he judges prudently of things, being known as a miser. In due course he will be thought the more liberal man, when people see that his parsimony enables him to live on his income, to defend himself against his enemies, and to undertake major projects without burdening his people with taxes. Thus he will be acting liberally toward all those people from whom he takes nothing (and there are an immense number of them), and in a stingy way toward those people on whom he bestows nothing (and they are very few). In our times, we have seen great things being accomplished only by men who have had the name of misers; all the others have gone under. Pope Julius II, though he used his reputation as a generous man to gain the papacy, sacrificed it in order to be able to make war; the present king of France has waged many wars without levying a single extra tax on his people, simply because he could take care of the extra expenses out of the savings from his long parsimony.[6] If the present king of Spain had a reputation for generosity, he would never have been able to undertake so many campaigns, or win so many of them.

Hence a prince who prefers not to rob his subjects, who wants to be able to defend himself, who wants to avoid poverty and contempt, and who has no desire to become a plunderer, should not mind in the least if people consider him a miser; this is simply one of the vices that enable him to reign. Someone may object that Caesar used a reputation for generosity to become emperor, and many other people have also risen in the world, because they were generous or were supposed to be so. Well, I answer, either you are a prince already, or you are in the process of becoming one; in the first case, this reputation for generosity is harmful to you, in the second case it is very necessary. Caesar was one of those who wanted to become ruler in Rome; but after he had reached his goal, if he had lived, and had not cut down on his expenses, he would have ruined the empire itself. Someone may say: there have been plenty of princes, very successful in warfare, who have had a reputation for generosity. But I answer: either the prince is spending his own money and that of his subjects, or he is spending someone else's. In the first case, he ought to be sparing; in the second case, he ought to spend

6. Louis XII, though afflicted like his predecessor Charles VIII with a mania for foreign conquest (a work for which both were largely incompetent), ran a thrifty shop at home. Starting with an empty treasury, he accumulated within a year after his accession enough money to support two years of war in Italy; and, as Machiavelli remarks, he imposed no new taxes. Ferdinand of Spain was equally prudent in money matters, and though he is not mentioned here, Henry VII of England was as famous for stinginess as his son Henry VIII became for extravagance.

money like water. Any prince at the head of his army, which lives on loot, extortion, and plunder, disposes of other people's property, and is bound to be very generous; otherwise, his soldiers would desert him. You can always be a more generous giver when what you give is not yours or your subjects'; Cyrus, Caesar, and Alexander were generous in this way. Spending what belongs to other people does no harm to your reputation, rather it enhances it; only spending your own substance harms you. And there is nothing that wears out faster than generosity; even as you practice it, you lose the means of practicing it, and you become either poor and contemptible or (in the course of escaping poverty) rapacious and hateful. The thing above all against which a prince must protect himself is being contemptible and hateful; generosity leads to both. Thus, it is much wiser to put up with the reputation of being a miser, which brings you shame without hate, than to be forced—just because you want to appear generous—into a reputation for rapacity, whch brings shame on you and hate along with it.

XVII

ON CRUELTY AND CLEMENCY: WHETHER IT IS BETTER TO BE LOVED OR FEARED

Continuing now with our list of qualities, let me say that every prince should prefer to be considered merciful rather than cruel, yet he should be careful not to mismanage this clemency of his. People thought Cesare Borgia was cruel, but that cruelty of his reorganized the Romagna, united it, and established it in peace and loyalty. Anyone who views the matter realistically will see that this prince was much more merciful than the people of Florence, who, to avoid the reputation of cruelty, allowed Pistoia to be destroyed.[7] Thus, no prince should mind being called cruel for what he does to keep his subjects united and loyal; he may make examples of a very few, but he will be more merciful in reality than those who, in their tenderheartedness, allow disorders to occur, with their attendant murders and lootings. Such turbulence brings harm to an entire community, while the executions ordered by a prince affect only one individual at a time. A new prince, above all others, cannot possibly avoid a name for cruelty, since new states are always in danger. And Virgil, speaking through the mouth of Dido, says:

> Res dura et regni novitas me talia cogunt
> Moliri, et late fines custode tueri.[8]

7. In 1501–2 the Pistoians broke out in a small but desperate civil war between two factions, the "Panciatichi" and the "Cancellieri"; though the nearby Florentines were in control of the city, and actually sent Machiavelli to investigate, they were afraid to intervene effec-tually, and so the townspeople hacked one another to pieces.
8. "Harsh pressures and the newness of my reign / Compel me to these steps; I must maintain / My borders against foreign foes. . . ." (Aeneid 1.563–64) [Editor's translation].

Yet a prince should be slow to believe rumors and to commit himself
to action on the basis of them. He should not be afraid of his own
thoughts; he ought to proceed cautiously, moderating his conduct with
prudence and humanity, allowing neither overconfidence to make him
careless, nor excess suspicion to make him intolerable.

Here the question arises: is it better to be loved than feared, or vice
versa? I don't doubt that every prince would like to be both; but since
it is hard to accommodate these qualities, if you have to make a choice,
to be feared is much safer than to be loved. For it is a good general rule
about men, that they are ungrateful, fickle, liars and deceivers, fearful
of danger and greedy for gain. While you serve their welfare, they are
all yours, offering their blood, their belongings, their lives, and their
children's lives, as we noted above—so long as the danger is remote.
But when the danger is close at hand, they turn against you. Then, any
prince who has relied on their words and has made no other preparations
will come to grief; because friendships that are bought at a price, and
not with greatness and nobility of soul, may be paid for but they are not
acquired, and they cannot be used in time of need. People are less
concerned with offending a man who makes himself loved than one
who makes himself feared: the reason is that love is a link of obligation
which men, because they are rotten, will break any time they think
doing so serves their advantage; but fear involves dread of punishment,
from which they can never escape.

Still, a prince should make himself feared in such a way that, even
if he gets no love, he gets no hate either; because it is perfectly possible
to be feared and not hated, and this will be the result if only the prince
will keep his hands off the property of his subjects or citizens, and off
their women. When he does have to shed blood, he should be sure to
have a strong justification and manifest cause; but above all, he should
not confiscate people's property, because men are quicker to forget the
death of a father than the loss of a patrimony. Besides, pretexts for
confiscation are always plentiful; it never fails that a prince who starts
to live by plunder can find reasons to rob someone else. Excuses for
proceeding against someone's life are much rarer and more quickly
exhausted.

But a prince at the head of his armies and commanding a multitude
of soldiers should not care a bit if he is considered cruel; without such
a reputation, he could never hold his army together and ready for action.
Among the marvelous deeds of Hannibal, this was prime: that, having
an immense army, which included men of many different races and
nations, and which he led to battle in distant countries, he never allowed
them to fight among themselves or to rise against him, whether his
fortune was good or bad. The reason for this could only be his inhuman
cruelty, which, along with his countless other talents [*virtù*], made him
an object of awe and terror to his soldiers; and without the cruelty, his

other qualities [*le altre sua virtù*] would never have sufficed. The historians who pass snap judgments on these matters admire his accomplishments and at the same time condemn the cruelty which was their main cause.[9]

When I say, "His other qualities would never have sufficed," we can see that this is true from the example of Scipio, an outstanding man not only among those of his own time, but in all recorded history; yet his armies revolted in Spain, for no other reason than his excessive leniency in allowing his soldiers more freedom than military discipline permits.[1] Fabius Maximus rebuked him in the senate for this failing, calling him the corrupter of the Roman armies. When a lieutenant of Scipio's plundered the Locrians, he took no action in behalf of the people, and did nothing to discipline that insolent lieutenant; again, this was the result of his easygoing nature. Indeed, when someone in the senate wanted to excuse him on this occasion, he said there are many men who know better how to avoid error themselves than how to correct error in others.[2] Such a soft temper would in time have tarnished the fame and glory of Scipio, had he brought it to the office of emperor; but as he lived under the control of the senate, this harmful quality of his not only remained hidden but was considered creditable.

Returning to the question of being feared or loved, I conclude that since men love at their own inclination but can be made to fear at the inclination of the prince, a shrewd prince will lay his foundations on what is under his own control, not on what is controlled by others. He should simply take pains not to be hated, as I said.

XVIII

THE WAY PRINCES SHOULD KEEP THEIR WORD

How praiseworthy it is for a prince to keep his word and live with integrity rather than by craftiness, everyone understands; yet we see from recent experience that those princes have accomplished most who paid little heed to keeping their promises, but who knew how to manipulate the minds of men craftily. In the end, they won out over those who tried to act honestly.

You should consider then, that there are two ways of fighting, one with laws and the other with force. The first is properly a human method, the second belongs to beasts. But as the first method does not always suffice, you sometimes have to turn to the second. Thus a prince must

9. Among the historians who applauded Hannibal's feats but deplored the "inhuman cruelty" that made them possible was Livy himself, whom Machiavelli admired, but not uncritically.
1. In balancing Hannibal, the great Carthaginian commander, with his chief antagonist, Scipio Africanus, Machiavelli seems to be imitating the method of Plutarch, but he got most of his details from Livy.
2. The city of Locri in southern Italy was captured by Scipio in 205 B.C. and placed under Q. Pleminius. Livy tells how he outdid even the Carthaginians in wanton brutality without suffering so much as a minor rebuke from Scipio.

know how to make good use of both the beast and man. Ancient writers made subtle note of this fact when they wrote that Achilles and many other princes of antiquity were sent to be reared by Chiron the centaur, who trained them in his discipline.[3] Having a teacher who is half man and half beast can only mean that a prince must know how to use both these two natures, and that one without the other has no lasting effect.

Since a prince must know how to use the character of beasts, he should pick for imitation the fox and the lion. As the lion cannot protect himself from traps, and the fox cannot defend himself from wolves, you have to be a fox in order to be wary of traps, and a lion to overawe the wolves. Those who try to live by the lion alone are badly mistaken. Thus a prudent prince cannot and should not keep his word when to do so would go against his interest, or when the reasons that made him pledge it no longer apply.[4] Doubtless if all men were good, this rule would be bad; but since they are a sad lot, and keep no faith with you, you in your turn are under no obligation to keep it with them.

Besides, a prince will never lack for legitimate excuses to explain away his breaches of faith. Modern history will furnish innumerable examples of this behavior, showing how many treaties and promises have been made null and void by the faithlessness of princes, and how the man succeeded best who knew best how to play the fox. But it is necessary in playing this part that you conceal it carefully; you must be a great liar and hypocrite. Men are so simple of mind, and so much dominated by their immediate needs, that a deceitful man will always find plenty who are ready to be deceived. One of many recent examples calls for mention. Alexander VI never did anything else, never had another thought, except to deceive men, and he always found fresh material to work on. Never was there a man more convincing in his assertions, who sealed his promises with more solemn oaths, and who observed them less. Yet his deceptions were always successful, because he knew exactly how to manage this sort of business.

In actual fact, a prince may not have all the admirable qualities listed above, but it is very necessary that he should seem to have them. Indeed, I will venture to say that when you have them and exercise them all the time, they are harmful to you; when you just seem to have them, they are useful. It is good to appear merciful, truthful, humane, sincere, and religious; it is good to be so in reality. But you must keep your mind so disposed that, in case of need, you can turn to the exact contrary.[5] This

3. In allegorizing Chiron as he does, Machiavelli is relatively original. If the mythographers know any such moral for the myth, they have hidden it in very remote places. A later writer, like Natale Conti (1568), follows Machiavelli. 4. Machiavelli perhaps had in mind the folly of Louis XII of France in trying to honor with one pope a pledge he had made to another: see chapter III, note 4, p. 11. But truth to one's word was not the usual fault of princes in the Renaissance. 5. This recommendation that the prince should deliberately play the hypocrite has perhaps done more than any other passage of *The Prince* to darken Machiavelli's reputation. But it says nothing worse than what youthful Cyrus was required to learn in the first book of Xenophon's *Cyropaedia*.

has to be understood: a prince, and especially a new prince, cannot possibly exercise all those virtues for which men are called "good." To preserve the state, he often has to do things against his word, against charity, against humanity, against religion. Thus he has to have a mind ready to shift as the winds of fortune and the varying circumstances of life may dictate. And as I said above, he should not depart from the good if he can hold to it, but he should be ready to enter on evil if he has to.

Hence a prince should take great care never to drop a word that does not seem imbued with the five good qualities noted above; to anyone who sees or hears him, he should appear all compassion, all honor, all humanity, all integrity, all religion. Nothing is more necessary than to seem to have this last virtue. Men in general judge more by the sense of sight than by the sense of touch, because everyone can see but only a few can test by feeling. Everyone sees what you seem to be, few know what you really are; and those few do not dare take a stand against the general opinion, supported by the majesty of the government. In the actions of all men, and especially of princes who are not subject to a court of appeal, we must always look to the end. Let a prince, therefore, win victories and uphold his state; his methods will always be considered worthy, and everyone will praise them, because the masses are always impressed by the superficial appearance of things, and by the outcome of an enterprise. And the world consists of nothing but the masses; the few have no influence when the many feel secure. A certain prince of our own time, whom it is just as well not to name,[6] preaches nothing but peace and mutual trust, yet he is the determined enemy of both; and if on several different occasions he had observed either, he would have lost both his reputation and his throne.

XIX

ON AVOIDING CONTEMPT AND HATRED

Now that I have talked in detail about the most important of the qualities mentioned above, I'd like to discuss the others briefly under this general heading: that the prince should try to avoid anything which makes him hateful or contemptible, as was suggested above.[7] When he has avoided actions that will have this effect, he has done his best, and he will run no risks from his other vices. What makes him hated above all, as I said,[8] is his confiscating the property of his subjects or taking their women. He must not commit these acts, since most men, if you

---

6. The not-very-covert allusion is to Ferdinand of Spain, a political animal who is said to have boasted toward the end of his life that he had deceived Louis XII twelve times hand running. Machiavelli actively disliked Ferdinand, calling him a shifty, shameless, tricky ruler, rather than a proper prince.
7. See chapter XVI.
8. See chapter XVII.

don't touch their property or their honor, will live contentedly. Then you have only to contend with the ambition of the few, which can easily be checked in a number of ways. What makes the prince contemptible is being considered changeable, trifling, effeminate, cowardly, or indecisive; he should avoid this as a pilot does a reef, and make sure that his actions bespeak greatness, courage, seriousness of purpose, and strength. In the private controversies of his subjects, he should be sure that his judgment once passed is irrevocable; indeed, he should maintain such a reputation that nobody will even dream of trying to trick or manage him.

Any prince who gives such an impression is bound to be highly esteemed, and a man with such a reputation is hard to conspire against, hard to assail, as long as everyone knows he is a man of character and respected by his own people. For a prince must be on his guard in two directions: domestically, against his own subjects; and abroad, against foreign powers. From the latter he can defend himself with good weapons and good friends; if he has good weapons, he will never lack for good friends. And domestic affairs will always be secure, as long as foreign policy is successful, unless the situation is disturbed by a conspiracy. Indeed, even when foreigners turn on him, if he has organized his defenses and his life as I suggested, and does not lose his head, he will withstand every assault, just as I said Nabis the Spartan did. [9]

As for one's own subjects; even when no outside disturbance occurs, there is danger they may form a secret conspiracy; from such a plot the prince's best protection lies in not being hated or despised, and keeping himself in popular favor. In a previous passage I explained the necessity for this at length. [1] One of the strongest counters that a prince has against conspiracies is not to be hated by the mass of the people, because every man who conspires always thinks that by killing the prince he will be pleasing the people. But when he thinks his act will enrage them, he no longer has any stomach for the work, because the problems of a conspirator are enormous at best. Experience teaches us that, of many conspiracies attempted, few turn out successfully; because a man who conspires can hardly do so alone, and can take as co-conspirators only those whom he judges to be discontented. Yet as soon as you explain your plot to a malcontent, you have furnished him with a means to be very content indeed. For he has everything to gain by giving you away; and when he has everything to gain one way, and so much danger and loss the other way, he must be either a very special friend of yours or a bitter enemy of the prince, if he is to keep faith with you. In a word, there is nothing in the conspirator's life but fear, jealousy, and the awful

9. See chapter IX.
1. See chapters XV–XVIII. These several ref-   erences to previous chapters of the book suggest review and summary.

prospect of punishment; while the prince is defended by the majesty of his office, by the laws, by the help of his allies, and by the state itself. And if to all this you add the good will of the people, it is impossible that any man will be rash enough to conspire against you.[2] Every conspirator is bound to live in fear before he executes his plot; but the man who conspires against a popular prince must also be fearful after his crime is committed—since then he will have the whole people against him, and from their hate he can hope for no refuge whatever.

I could give innumerable examples of this point, but one will suffice, that took place within the memory of our fathers. Messer Hannibal Bentivoglio, grandfather of the present Messer Hannibal, was murdered when he was prince of Bologna by a conspiracy of the Canneschi; he left behind only Messer Giovanni, then in his swaddling bands.[3] Immediately after the prince's murder, the people rose up and massacred all the Canneschi. The reason for this was simply the people's devotion to the house of Bentivogli, which was so great at that time that, when nobody was left in Bologna who could rule the state after Hannibal's death, the Bolognesi went to Florence to seek out a man of the Bentivogli family (though he had previously been regarded as the son of a blacksmith), and entrusted him with the governing of their city. He governed it till Messer Giovanni was of age to rule.

Thus I conclude that a prince should not worry too much about conspiracies, as long as his people are devoted to him; but when they are hostile, and feel hatred toward him, he should fear everything and everybody. Well-ordered states and prudent princes have made every effort to keep the aristocracy from desperation and to satisfy the populace by making them happy; this is one of the most important of a prince's duties.

Among the well-ordered and -governed kingdoms of our time is that of France, where one can observe a great many good institutions making for the liberty and security of the king. Outstanding among these is the parliament, and its authority.[4] The founder of the kingdom, clearly knowing the ambition of the nobility and their insolence, saw the necessity of putting a bit in their teeth by which they could be managed. At the same time he understood the hatred of the common people for

2. Machiavelli who dismisses conspiracies rather lightly here, is more impressed by them elsewhere; *Discorsi* 3.6 is an extended analysis of several different historical conspiracies, and of the elements involved in them.
3. The murder of Hannibal Bentivoglio took place in 1445; his son Giovanni did not come of age till seventeen years later, in 1462. Santi Bentivoglio, who filled the gap, was probably a bastard son of Hercules, Hannibal's cousin; but for the Bolognesi a left-handed Bentivoglio

was clearly better than none.
4. Machiavelli's ideas on the form and function of the French Paliament are not very historical. It began under the early Capets as a court of law, where the king in person gave judgment in the presence of his vassals. The idea of using it to balance off the various estates did not occur till later, and certainly never had the importance that Machiavelli assigns it.

the nobles, a hatred grounded in fear, and tried to reassure them. Yet he did not want this to be a particular responsibility of the king, lest he be accused of partiality—by the nobles for favoring the people, or by the people for favoring the nobles. Thus he established a third judicial force which, while it was not the king's direct responsibility, could hold down the nobility and favor the commons. There could hardly be a wiser or more prudent arrangement than this, nor one serving better to promote the security of king and kingdom. And from this we can draw another notable lesson: princes should delegate unpleasant jobs to other people and reserve the pleasant functions for themselves.[5] Again let me conclude by saying that a prince should respect his nobles, but not let himself be hated by the people.

Many people who have studied the lives and deaths of the Roman emperors may think that they provide examples contrary to this opinion of mine, since some of them lived exemplary lives and showed great strength [*virtù*] of mind, yet lost the empire or were killed by subjects who conspired against them. By way of answering these objections, let me describe some of these emperors and show the reasons for which they came to grief; they will not be found much different from those I proposed. In passing, I will try to point out the most notable events in the history of those times, limiting myself to those emperors who came to the purple between Marcus the philosopher and Maximin. They were Marcus himself, Commodus his son, Pertinax, Julian, Severus, Antoninus Caracalla his son, Macrinus, Heliogabalus, Alexander, and Maximin.[6]

Now the first thing to note is that, unlike other princes who had to contend only with the ambition of nobles and the insolence of the people, the Roman emperors had a third difficulty: they had to cope with a cruel and avaricious soldiery. Satisfying both the soldiers and the populace at the same time proved so difficult that it cost many of the emperors their thrones. For the people generally wanted quiet, and thus were pleased with unambitious princes, while the soldiers loved a prince of warlike spirit, who was domineering, greedy, and cruel; they wanted to see these qualities exercised on the people, because that meant double wages for them, and satisfied their cruelty as well as their greed. These were the reasons why those emperors who had not a great reputation (granted by nature or acquired by political practice) could not keep the two factions

5. The somewhat cynical principle that Machiavelli is recommending here, to let nasty jobs be done by expendable agents, can be found as early as Xenophon's *Hiero*, a dialogue on the tyrant; it is timeless piece of common sense.

6. This period of Roman history, from the accession of Marcus Aurelius (A.D. 161) to the death of Maximin (A.D. 238) is later than that covered by the great Roman historians. The fragmented history of Dio Cassius and that of Herodian (both in Greek) and the Latin biographies of the six *Scriptores historiae Augustae* are the chief authorities for the seventy-year period that Machiavelli covers; he used primarily Herodian, probably in Poliziano's Latin version.

in hand, and so came invariably to grief. Most of them, especially when they were new in office, recognized that they could not reconcile these two humors, so they chose to please the soldiers at the cost of doing harm to the people. This was a choice they had to make; because when princes cannot help being hated by someone, they ought first of all to try to avoid universal hatred, and when they cannot escape some hatred, they should try as hard as they can to avoid the hatred of the most powerful group around. Thus emperors who were new in office and needed special support, turned to the soldiers rather than the people, that policy serving them well or badly according to whether they maintained control over their troops or not.

These are the reasons why Marcus, Pertinax, and Alexander, who were all men of decent lives, lovers of justice, enemies of cruelty, humane, and benevolent, all came to bad ends—except for Marcus. Marcus alone lived and died in the highest honor, because he came to the purple by the law of heredity, and had nobody to thank for it, either soldiers or people. Besides, his many virtues [virtù], which made him an object of reverence to all, enabled him to keep both factions within bounds as long as he lived, and he was never hated or despised. But Pertinax was created emperor against the will of the army; the soldiers were accustomed to a licentious life under Commodus, and could not endure the honest life toward which Pertinax tried to direct them. In this way he made himself hated, and to hate was added contempt because he was old, and this ruined him at the very beginning of his administration.

And here it should be noted that hatred may be earned by doing good just as much as by doing evil; and so, as I said above, a prince who wants to keep his state, is often bound to do what is not good. Because when that group is corrupt whose support you think you need—whether the people or the army or the nobility—then you have to follow their humors to satisfy them; and in that case, good deeds are harmful to you. But let us now consider Alexander, who was such a good man that, among his other praises, this one is recorded: that in the fourteen years of his reign, no man was ever put to death by his orders without a trial. Yet, being considered effeminate and under his mother's thumb, he fell into contempt, the army conspired against him, and murdered him.[7]

Turning now for contrast to the emperors Commodus, Severus, Antoninus Caracalla, and Maximin, you will find that they were extremely cruel and rapacious men; to satisfy their soldiery, they condoned every

7. Pertinax was forced to become emperor in his old age and against his will; he lasted just three months in the job. Alexander Severus was just fourteen years old when the murder of Heliogabalus propelled him to the purple. But Machiavelli is making points to which these untidy individual circumstances are irrelevant.

sort of lawlessness against the people; and yet they all came to a wretched end, except for Severus. The reason was that Severus was a man of such character [*tanta virtù*] that, by keeping the soldiers friendly to him, and oppressing the people, he was able to reign in prosperity all his life long: his talents [*virtù*] made him so remarkable, in the eyes of the people as well as the soldiery, that the former remained awestruck and appeased, the latter astonished and abashed.[8]

And since his actions were so striking and worthy of study by a new prince, I would like to show in brief what good use he made of the fox and the lion; which are the two natures that I said above must be simulated by a successful prince. When Severus realized that the Emperor Julian was a weakling, he persuaded the army he was leading in Sclavonia[9] that it was a good idea to go to Rome, in order to avenge the death of Pertinax, who had been killed by the Praetorian Guards. Under this pretext, and without any indication that he aspired to the purple, he led his army against Rome, and was in Italy before anyone there knew he had set out. As soon as he reached Rome, the senate, acting out of fear, elected him emperor and ordered Julian killed. After taking this first step, Severus faced two other difficulties in making himself master of the entire state: one was in Asia, where Pescennius Niger, leader of the Asiatic armies, had had himself proclaimed emperor, and the other was in the west, where Albinus also aspired to the empire. Seeing it would be rash to engage both these enemies at once, he decided to attack Niger and deceive Albinus. So he wrote the latter, saying that though the senate had elected him emperor, he wanted a partner in that dignity; he hailed him as Caesar and got the senate to declare him a colleague. Albinus took all this at face value. But then when Severus had defeated Niger, killed him, and pacified the East, he went back to Rome and complained in the senate that Albinus, unmindful of all the benefits showered on him, had treacherously tried to murder him. For this reason, Severus was bound to seek him out and punish his ingratitude. Whereupon, he hunted him down in France, deprived him of his authority, and took his life.

Whoever examines carefully the action of this man will find that he was a most ferocious lion and a very clever fox; he was feared and respected by all, and his army did not hate him. Even though he was a new man, it is no wonder that he could successfully hold onto so great an empire, since his splendid reputation always protected him from that

8. The virtues [*virtù*] of Severus, which amounted to cold and ruthless decisiveness, are perceptibly different from the virtues [*virtù*] of Marcus Aurelius; in thus deliberately equating them, Machiavelli is in effect declaring that the moral qualities of a prince are virtues or vices only as they help or hinder his political functioning.

9. Severus was commanding a Roman army not far from modern Vienna; the "Julian" in question was not Julian the Apostate, emperor 361–63, but a certain Didius Julianus who in 193 bought the Roman Empire at public auction and enjoyed his prize for just sixty-six days before Severus took it away from him and cut off his head.

popular hatred which might have been the consquences of his looting.[1]
His son, Antoninus Caracalla, was also a man of great talents, well
suited to make him admirable in the eyes of the people and popular
with soldiers; he was a man of arms, who could stand any kind of fatigue
or hardship, who despised fine food and all sorts of delicate living; and
this made him very popular with the army. But his cruelty was so
ferocious, so unheard-of (after endless individual murders, he killed most
of the population of Rome and the entire population of Alexandria),
that he became hateful to everyone, and even his intimate associates
began to fear him—so that he was finally murdered by a centurion in
the middle of his army. We should note here that assassinations of this
sort, long meditated by a fanatical mind, are impossible for a prince to
avert, because anyone who does not fear to die himself can carry out
such a deed. But since such episodes are very rare, the prince need not
be too much concerned about them. He ought only to beware of inflicting serious injury on any of his personal servants or those who are
employed near him in the service of the state. That was the mistake of
Antoninus, who had imposed a shameful death on a brother of this
centurion, and threatened the man himself every day, though he still
kept him in his bodyguard; this was a rash thing to do, and, as it
happened, brought about the emperor's death.

Now let us come to Commodus, who found the empire easy to
acquire, since it descended to him by hereditary right, as son of Marcus
Aurelius; and if he had simply been content to follow his father's footsteps, he would have satisfied both the populace and the soldiers. But
he was a cruel and beastly man, who, to exercise his rapacity on the
people, indulged his armies to the limit, and encouraged their excesses.
On the other hand, he took no care for his own dignity, descending
many times into the theater to fight with gladiators, and doing other
completely vulgar things unworthy of imperial majesty, till at last he
became contemptible to his own soldiers. Then, when he was hated by
one faction and despised by the other, a conspiracy was formed against
him, and he perished.

It remains now to describe Maximin. He was a man much practiced
in war; and as the armies were disgusted by the effeminacy of Alexander,
whom we described above, after his death they elected Maximin emperor. He was not long in power, because two things caused him to be
hated and despised: one was his base birth (he had once been a shepherd
in Thrace, everyone knew it, and it was much held against him); the

1. Machiavelli omits any mention of Severus's
ruthless terrorizing of the Roman senate. As
he himself had created a law punishing anyone
who murdered a senator, he was careful to expel his enemies from the senate first, and then
murder them when they were no longer senators. This did a good deal for his splendid
reputation. His son Caracalla seems to have
been more than half insane; having murdered
his brother Geta in their mother's arms, he
turned over the government to her, and spent
the last years of his life wandering from one
remote military frontier to another, seeking the
death with which his own soldiers at last
obliged him. Macrinus, who murdered him
and thereby gained the throne, retained it for
less than a year.

other was his delay in entering Rome at the beginning of his reign to take possession of the royal throne. His prefects in Rome and other parts of the empire meanwhile carried out many harsh acts; and these gave everyone an impression of terrible personal cruelty. Thus everyone turned against him, some because of his base birth, others for fear of his bloodthirstiness; Africa was first to rebel, then the senate and all the Roman people followed, and all Italy conspired against him. Even his own army joined in; they were besieging Aquileia, found the assault difficult, were disgusted with his cruelty, feared him the less because he had so many enemies, and thus killed him.

I shall say nothing of Heliogabalus, Macrinus, and Julian because everyone despised them, and so they were quickly done away with. To conclude this discourse, let me say that the princes of our day have less trouble in satisfying the excessive demands of the soldiers under their command; though you have to have some concern for them, the conflicts are easily resolved, because modern princes do not have armies involved with provincial governments and administrators, like the armies of the Roman Empire. At that time, it was necessary to gratify the soldiers rather than the people because the soldiers represented the greater power; nowadays, it is necessary to gratify the people rather than the soldiers, because the people have more power except in the lands of the Turk and the sultan.[2] I except the Turk here, because he always keeps near the court twelve thousand infantry and fifteen thousand cavalry, on whom the strength and security of his rule depend; and, before anything else, he must keep these armies satisfied. So too with the realm of the sultan, which is all under military rule; he also has to keep the soldiers on his side without regard to the people. And it is to be noted that the sultan's state is unlike all others in one respect, where it most resembles the Christian pontificate. It cannot be called a hereditary monarchy, nor yet a new monarchy, because the sons of the old prince do not inherit the throne and assume command; instead a man is elected to the office by those who have authority to do so. Since the system is traditional, the monarchy cannot be called a new one; it has none of the difficulties inherent in new regimes, for even though the prince himself may be new, the laws of the state are old, and are set up to receive him just as if he were a hereditary monarch.

But, to return to our topic, let me say that whoever studies the record described above will see that either hatred or contempt was the ruin of the Roman emperors we mentioned; and he will understand how the very different paths they took led each of them to his destined end,

2. "The Turk" is the hereditary monarchy of the Ottoman Empire, under the direction, as it happened, of successive sultans—Muhammad II the Conqueror, Bayezid II, Selim I, son regularly succeeding father. By "the sultan" Machiavelli evidently means the caliphate, as established by Muhammad the prophet in the pattern of an elective monarchy, but radically modified, in its later Egyptian manifestations, by frequent assassinations, insurrections, depositions, and efforts by the caliphs to get their sons appointed to succeed them.

whether happy or unhappy. For Pertinax and Alexander, since they were new princes, it was useless and harmful to imitate Marcus Aurelius, who was emperor by hereditary right; so too it would have been fatal for Caracalla, Commodus, and Maximin to imitate Severus, since they had not sufficient character [*virtù*] to follow in his footsteps. Thus a new prince, coming to power in a new state, cannot imitate the actions of Marcus Aurelius, nor indeed is he bound to follow after Severus; but he should take from Severus those elements of his conduct that are necessary to found his state, and from Marcus those that are useful and creditable in preserving a state already stabilized and secure.[3]

 XX

WHETHER BUILDING FORTRESSES AND OTHER DEFENSIVE POLICIES OFTEN ADOPTED BY PRINCES ARE USEFUL OR NOT

In order to keep a tight grasp on the state, some princes have disarmed their subjects; others have tried to control their captured cities by dividing them into factions; still others have deliberately fomented hostilities against themselves; others again have made a point of winning over those who were suspect at the beginning of their reign; some have built new fortresses, other have torn down old ones. And though there is no formulating a definite rule about these many alternatives without knowing the particular circumstances of the state to be managed, still I will discuss these topics as generally as the nature of the subject allows.

There never was a new prince who disarmed his subjects; on the contrary, when he found them without weapons, he always armed them. The reason is that when you arm them, their arms become yours; those who were suspect become your faithful supporters, and those who were faithful before continue so, and from merely being your subjects become your partisans. Naturally, you cannot arm all your subjects, but when those whom you have armed are well treated, you can consider yourself safer from the others. Those you select for special favor will think themselves obliged to you, and the others will forgive you, judging that men deserve special rewards when they assume special risks and obligations. But when you disarm them, you begin to alienate them; you advertise your mistrust of them, which may come from your suspecting them of cowardice or treachery; both these insinuations will raise hatred agaist you. And since you cannot remain unarmed yourself, you will have to turn to mercenary armies, the quality of which was discussed above:

3. This perfunctory and superficial chapter concludes with some perfunctory and superficial moral generalities. In reality the downfall of Alexander Severus had nothing to do with his being a new prince: he was not, and the virtues fatal to him contributed to the success of Marcus Aurelius. The judgment about Caracalla, Commodus, and Maximin is an obvious begging of the question; if they had acted like Severus, Machiavelli would have concluded that they had his *virtù*. Finally, it is apparent that in all these judgments, Machiavelli is making liberal use of historical hindsight, and tailoring his account of the different men's careers to the different fates he knows they met.

even if they were good, they could not possibly defend you from powerful enemies and treacherous subjects. Therefore, as I've said, a new prince in a new kingdom has always armed the citizens; the histories are full of examples. But when a prince acquires a new state and attaches it, like a fresh graft, on his old state, then the new acquisition must be disarmed, except for those who actively helped you acquire it; even those people, as time and occasions allow, must be rendered soft and compliant. Things have to be arranged so that all the arms in your new state are in the hands of your own soldiers, who used to live in your own state, under your eye.

The so-called wise men among our ancestors used to say that Pistoia was to be held by factions and Pisa by fortresses; on this principle, they encouraged factionalism in various cities that they possessed, in order to control them more easily.[4] In those days, when a kind of balance of powers prevailed in Italy, this may well have been a good idea; but I doubt if we can take it as a precedent nowadays. As a matter of fact, I do not believe factions ever did any good; on the contrary, it is inevitable, when an enemy approaches, that divided cities will collapse immediately, since the weaker faction will join with the invader, and the stronger faction will not be able to hold out against them both.

It was on this logic, I suppose, that the Venetians fostered the Guelf and Ghibelline parties in the cities they controlled; and though they never let matters come to bloodshed, still they encouraged the quarrel, thinking that when the citizens were occupied in their feuds, they would not unite against the Venetians. But things did not turn out according to their plan, as everyone knows; after their defeat at Vailà, one of the factions took fire and snatched the whole state from them.[5] Besides, these policies are an argument of weakness in the prince. In a strong state, divisions of this sort would never be permitted. They serve only in times of peace, when indeed subjects can be managed more easily; but when war breaks out, the weakness comes to the surface.

Princes become great, no doubt about it, by overcoming the difficulties and obstacles placed in their way; thus fortune, when it wants to favor a new prince (who has more need of gaining a personal reputation than a hereditary prince), gives him enemies who are active against him, so that he can overcome them and climb even higher on the ladder that his enemies have brought to him. For this reason, many hold that a shrewd prince will, when he can, subtly encourage some enmity to

4. Machiavelli is often impatient with wise saws and ancient adages, and particularly this one about Pistoia, since he had seen first-hand the consequences of factional rioting there: see chapter XVII, note 7, page 45.
5. After the defeat at Vailà, the Venetians were not exactly overrun by a faction; for a mixture of selfish and generous reasons, they released their tributary cities to their own devices, and tried to equivocate for themselves between pope and emperor.

himself, so that by overcoming it he can augment his own reputation.[6]

Especially when they are new, princes have often found more fidelity and serviceability in men who at first were suspect than in men who originally enjoyed the royal confidence. Pandolfo Petrucci, prince of Siena, ruled his state more with men he did not trust than with men whom he did.[7] But there is no general rule in this matter, because it varies with circumstances. I shall say only this: that if the men who at the beginning of a regime are considered its enemies are in need of support to maintain themselves, the prince will have no trouble at all in winning them over. They are the more deeply obliged to serve him faithfully because they know that only good service will cancel the bad impression he had of them. Thus the prince always gets better service from them than from men who feel too sure of their jobs, and so neglect his interests. In connection with this matter, I feel impelled to remind princes who have acquired a new state with the help of the local in-habitants, that they should consider carefully what motives stirred their supporters. If it was not native affection for the new prince, but just discontent with the previous state, then he will have great difficulty keeping them friendly, because he will not be able to satisfy them. Considering carefully the principle at work here, in the light of ancient and modern examples, you will see that it is much easier to gain as friends those men who were satisfied with the earlier state, and therefore were hostile to the conqueror, than those men who, because they were discontented in the earlier state, looked with favor on the new prince and helped him take over.[8]

It has been customary for princes who want to keep a tight grasp on their states to build fortresses for use as a checkrein on those who might want to rise against them, and as a place of secure refuge against a first attack. I approve of this policy, because it has been used since ancient times; yet in our own days Messer Niccolò Vitelli has been observed to demolish two fortresses in Città di Castello as a means of holding onto that state. Guidobaldo, duke of Urbino, when he returned to his kingdom after being driven out by Cesare Borgia, razed all the fortresses in the kingdom to the ground, and thought himself much less likely to lose his kingdom a second time without them; the Bentivogli did the same

6. Machiavelli passes no judgment on the princely practice of fomenting insurrections in order to make a reputation by crushing them. What he describes is the functioning of the agent provocateur, familiar in repressive re-gimes of all sorts, and serving many different functions.

7. Pandolfo Petrucci, leader of the aristocratic faction in Siena, may well have ruled with the aid of men he did not trust, but no other his-torian records this judgment. (See the judg-ment, in chapter XXII below, of Petrucci's long-time instructor Antonio da Venafro.) In

making the point, Machiavelli can scarcely have been unaware that the Medici, to whom he was addressing his book, did not much trust *him*, Machiavelli. Petrucci, highly respected, very successful, and only recently dead, pro-vided good precedent for an action in which Machiavelli had a certain interest.

8. The major principle set forth here (that rev-olutionary regimes, once established, depend for their survival, not on revolutionaries, but on docile managerial types) has been many times verified, as in the English, French, and Russian revolutions.

thing when they returned to Bologna.[9] Thus fortresses may be useful or otherwise, according to circumstances; if they help you one way, they hurt you another. And the matter may be summarized as follows: the prince who fears his own people more than he does foreigners ought to build fortresses, but a prince who is more afraid of foreigners than of his own people can neglect them. The castle that Francesco Sforza built in Milan has been and will be the cause of more disturbance to the house of Sforza than anything else in that state.[1]

Actually, the best fortress of all consists in not being hated by your people. However many fortresses you hold, if the people hate you, the forts will not save you, because once the people have taken up arms, they will never lack for foreigners to come to their aid. In our own day, the only prince who profited by forts was the countess of Forlì, when her husband Count Girolamo died; by taking refuge in the fortress she was able to escape the rising of the people, hold out till aid came from Milan, and thus regain her state. At that time, there were no foreign powers around who could come to the aid of the people. But later on her forts were of little value when Cesare Borgia attacked her, and her people in their hostility joined with the outsider. So on both occasions, it would have been safer for her if, instead of trusting to fortresses, she had managed not to be hated by her people.[2]

All things considered, then, I may approve of those who build fortresses or of those who do not, depending on the circumstances; but it is a foolish man who, because he puts his trust in fortresses, thinks he need not worry about the enmity of his people.

XXI
HOW A PRINCE SHOULD ACT TO ACQUIRE REPUTATION

Nothing gives a prince more prestige than undertaking great enterprises and setting a splendid example for his people. In our day we have Ferdinand of Aragon, the present king of Spain.[3] He may be considered

---

9. These various instances of fortress razing point somewhat different morals. Niccolò, father of Vitellozzo and Paolo Vitelli, destroyed castles at Città de Castello at a time when he had just returned from exile—as a gesture of confidence in his people. Guidobaldo, duke of Urbino, destroyed fortifications because he found by bitter experience that they were more useful to an invader than to him. The Bentivogli when they got back to Bologna in 1511 destroyed a castle that Pope Julius had built there to command the city—destroying thus an emblem of the invader's power. In each instance, smashing the fortress meant something different, politically.
1. Francesco Sforza built the Castello, which still stands, shortly after becoming duke of Milan; within Machiavelli's recent memory, Ludovico had lost it twice without a shot being fired.

2. The countess of Forlì was Caterina Sforza, niece of Il Moro. After her husband was murdered in 1488, Caterina held out in the fortress till help came from her uncle. But in 1500 Cesare Borgia, in the course of his first campaign, compelled her to surrender. Machiavelli admired her courage but deplored her lack of popular support. See below, pp. 255–59.
3. Admiration mingles with repugnance in this sketch of Ferdinand the Catholic. Ferdinand was a "new prince" in a sense not explicitly noted by Machiavelli, since the throne of Castille really belonged to Isabella; the unification of Aragon and Castille was what some Castilian barons might have objected to, if he had not distracted them with a series of wars. Ferdinand's boldness was thus even greater than it seemed.

a new prince, since from being a weak king he has risen to become, for fame and glory, the first prince of Christendom; and if you consider his actions, you will find all of them very great and some of them extraordinary. At the beginning of his rule he attacked Granada, and that enterprise was the cornerstone of his reign. For some time he carried on the siege in a leisurely way, and without any outside distractions; he kept all the barons of Castille preoccupied with it, and while they were thinking of the war, they never considered the changes he was making in the state. Thus he acquired reputation and authority over them without their being aware of it. Money from the Church and the people enabled him to recruit big armies, and in the course of this long war to build a military establishment which has since won him much honor. Apart from this, he made use of the pretext of religion to prepare the way for still greater projects, and adopted a policy of pious cruelty in expelling the Moors from his kingdom and despoiling them; his conduct here could not have been more despicable nor more unusual.[4] On the same pretext, he attacked Africa; he carried out a campaign in Italy; and finally he assaulted France.[5] Thus he has always been planning and carrying out some great design which has enthralled and preoccupied the minds of his subjects, and kept them fascinated with the outcome of his schemes. And his various projects have risen one out of the other, so that they have never allowed men leisure to take concerted action against him.

It is also helpful for a prince to give special evidence of his ability in internal affairs, as we hear about Messer Bernabò of Milan;[6] whenever anyone did anything special affecting the state, whether for good or evil, he chose a way of rewarding or punishing him that gave rise to comment. It should be a prince's major concern in everything he does to give the impression of being a great man and of possessing excellent insight.

A prince will also be well thought of when he is a true friend or an honest enemy, that is, when, without any hedging, he takes a stand for one side and against another. It is always better to do this than to stand on one's neutrality; because if two of your powerful neighbors come to blows, they are either such people that you have to fear the winner, or

---

4. The adjective are *miserabile* and *raro*. The expulsion of the Moors (and simultaneously of the Jews) deprived Spain of two energetic and intelligent minorities, who might have done something to avert the blight that fell on Spain after her golden age.

5. Dates here suggest the pace of Ferdinand's activity and the casualness of Machivelli's chronology. The conquest of Granada was completed after ten years of war in 1492; the expulsion of the Moors in 1502; the Italian campaign, begun in 1495, culminated in the war with France over Naples 1502–4 and the assault on Navarre in 1512; the conquest of Tripoli took place in 1510. In most of these undertakings Ferdinand made a mighty show of religious motives, but it was hardly more than a show.

6. Bernabò Visconti divided rule of Milan in the late fourteenth century with his nephew (later to become his executioner) Gian Galeazzo. All the Visconti were infamous for the hideous ingenuity and cruelty of their punishments but Messer Bernabò was the worst; in addition, he sired over thirty children, legitimate and illegitimate, whom he tended to marry off for their advantage or his own. Machiavelli may have had this profuse generosity in mind when he selected Bernabò to exemplify skill in internal affairs, "e governi di dentro."

they are not. In either case, it will be better for you to assert yourself and wage open war; because, in the first case, when you do not take sides, you are bound to be the prey of the winner, to the pleasure and satisfaction of the loser. Then you have no excuse, nothing to defend you, nobody to take you in; a winner has no use for doubtful friends, who would not support him in adversity, and a loser will not take you in because you were not willing to take your chances with him, sword in hand.

When Antiochus came into Greece, brought there by the Aetolians to drive out the Romans, he sent ambassadors to the Achaeans to persuade them to neutrality; meanwhile the Romans were persuading the Achaeans to take up arms on their side. The matter came up for consideration in the Achaean council, and when Antiochus's envoy had spoken for neutrality, the Roman ambassador answered: "What these people tell you about not getting mixed up in a war could not be more opposed to your real interests; if you do that, whatever the outcome of the war, you will fall prey to the victors, without any hope of mercy."[7]

As a general thing, anyone who is not your friend will advise neutrality, while anyone who is your friend will ask you to join him, weapon in hand. Weak-minded princes who want to avoid present dangers generally follow the path of neutrality and generally come to grief. But when the prince declares himself like a man in favor of one side, even if this ally wins and becomes so powerful that you are at his mercy, still he owes you something, he is your friend. Men are never so dishonest that they will show gross ingratitude by turning immediately on their helpers. Besides, victories are never so decisive that the victor does not have to maintain some moderation, some show of justice. But even if your ally loses, you will still be dear to him, he will help you as long as he can, and be a staunch friend when your fortune rises again.

As for the second case, when neither of the two powers who are at odds is so strong that you have to be afraid of his winning, it is all the more sensible for you to take sides, since you are now able to ruin one with the aid of the other, who would have saved him if he had any sense. The winner, whoever he is, will be at your mercy, and the side to which you throw your weight is bound to win. And here let me say that a prince should never ally himself with someone more powerful than himself in order to attack a third party, except in cases of absolute necessity. As I said before, when your ally wins, you remain his prisoner; and princes ought to avoid, as far as they can, being under the control of other people. The Venetians joined with the king of France against the duke of Milan;[8] they could perfectly well have avoided this alliance, which led directly to their ruin. There are of course times when an alliance cannot be avoided (for example, the Florentines had to join in

---

7. The episode is described by Livy 35.48.

8. In 1499, when Louis XII first expelled Ludovico from Milan.

when the pope and the king of Spain sent armies to subdue Lombardy),[9] and then the prince must take sides, for the reasons given above. No leader should ever suppose he can invariably take the safe course, since all choices involve risks. In the nature of things, you can never try to escape one danger without encountering another; but prudence consists in knowing how to recognize the nature of the different dangers and in accepting the least bad as good.

A prince ought also to show himself an admirer of talent [*virtù*], giving recognition to men of ability [*uomini virtuosi*] and honoring those who excel in a particular art. Moreover, he should encourage his citizens to ply their callings in peace, whether in commerce, agriculture, or in any other business. The man who improves his holdings should not be made to fear that they will be taken away from him; the man who opens up a branch of trade should not have to fear that he will be taxed out of existence. Instead, the prince should bestow prizes on the men who do these things, and on anyone else who takes pains to enrich the city or state in some special way. He should also, at fitting times of the year, entertain his people with festivals and spectacles. And because every city is divided into professional guilds and family groupings, he should be inward with these people, and attend their gatherings from time to time, giving evidence of his humanity and munificence, yet avoiding any compromise to his dignity, for that must be preserved at all costs.[1]

XXII

ON A PRINCE'S PRIVATE COUNSELORS

Choosing his ministers is a matter of no small importance to a prince, since they will be good or bad, depending on his judgment. The first notion one gets of a prince's intelligence comes from the men around him; when they are able and loyal, you may be sure he is wise, because he knew enough to recognize their ability and command their loyalty. When they are otherwise, you can always form a poor opinion of the prince, because he made an error in his very first choice.

Nobody who knew that Messer Antonio da Venafro was a minister of Pandolfo Petrucci, prince of Siena, could fail to consider Pandolfo a thoroughly worthy man, since he had this sort of minister.[2] There are, in fact, three sorts of brains: one understands on its own, another un-

9. In 1512, when Julius II and Ferdinand united to drive out the French. Machiavelli discreetly avoids saying that the Florentine government with which he was involved backed the wrong horse, holding to the French alliance and thus bringing about the defeat of Machiavelli's militia by Spanish regulars at Prato, and the return of the Medici. The platitudes that follow, about choosing the lesser of two evils, date back at least to Cicero, *De officiis* 3.1.
1. In his advice about how the prince should

seek popularity among his subjects, Machiavelli is largely repeating commonplace wisdom of his own day and of antiquity. The last part of the paragraph paraphrases Xenophon, *Hiero*, chapter IX.
2. Antonio da Venafro was a lawyer long in the employ of Pandolfo Petrucci, prince of Siena; Machiavelli's friend, Francesco Vettori, says he was the most persuasive man he ever heard. See chapter XX, note 7, p. 59.

derstands what others tell it, and the third understands neither itself nor other people. The first sort is superb, the second sort very good, the third sort useless.[3] Thus it necessarily followed that if Pandolfo was not of the first sort, he must have been of the second; since a man who has wit enough to distinguish good words and deeds from bad ones, even if he could not invent the good himself, can tell his minister's good ideas from his bad ones, encourage the former and correct the latter. The minister cannot hope to deceive such a master, and so continues to serve well.

There is one way for a prince to judge of a minister that never fails. When you notice that your minister is thinking more of himself than of you, and that everything he does serves his own interest, a man like this will never make a good minister; you cannot possibly trust him. The man who holds a prince's kingdom in his hand should think, not of himself, but of the prince; he should not even be aware of anything but his master's business. And on the other hand, the prince who wants to keep his minister obedient should think of his welfare, honor him, enrich him, load him with distinctions and offices. Thus the minister will not be able to stand without the prince, the many honors will keep him from looking elsewhere for more honor, the many riches will keep him from thinking of more riches, and the many offices will give him reason to fear changes. When the prince and his minister stand on these terms, they can have complete confidence in one another; when things are otherwise, they always turn out badly, either for one or the other.

XXIII

HOW TO AVOID FLATTERERS

I do not want to omit an important point on which princes find it hard to avoid error unless they are extremely prudent and choose their advisers very wisely. Courts are always full of flatterers; men take such pleasure in their own concerns, and are so easily deceived about them, that this plague of flattery is hard to escape. Besides, in defending against flattery, one runs the further risk of incurring contempt. For there is no way to protect yourself from flattery except by letting men know that you will not be offended at being told the truth. But when anyone can tell you the truth, you will not have much respect. Hence a prudent prince should adopt a third course, bringing wise men into his council and giving them alone free license to speak the truth—and only on those points where the prince asks for it, not on others. But he should ask them about everything, hear his advisers out, and make his decision after thinking things over, according to his own style. In dealing with his advisory councils and every member of them, he should make clear

3. The three sorts of mind are described in Livy 22.29, but the distinction was commonplace, even in Livy's day.

that the more freely they speak their minds, the better he will like it. But apart from these counselors he should not listen to anyone; he should go straight to the matter under discussion and stand firmly by his decision. Any prince who behaves differently will either be subject to the importunings of flatterers or will waver between different views of the subject, as a result of which he will be little respected.

In this connection, I'd like to propose a modern example. Father Luca, a servant of Maximilian, the present emperor,[4] in speaking of His Majesty, said that he never took counsel with anyone, and never did anything the way he wanted to. The reason for this was that he went about things in a way exactly contrary to that described above. The emperor is a secretive man, he communicates his plans to nobody, he accepts no advice; but when his plans become publicly known, as they start to be put into effect, then they start to be contradicted by his minsters; and the emperor, who does not stand firmly behind his ideas, gives up on them. Thus whatever he does one day he undoes the next; nobody understands what he really wants or plans to do; and there is no way of counting on his decisions even when they are made.

A prince should always take counsel, then, but when *he* wants advice, not when other people want to give it. On the contrary, he should prevent anyone from offering him uncalled-for advice. But he should also be a liberal questioner, and afterwards a patient hearer of the truth regarding whatever he has asked about. Many people think that a prince who is considered prudent gets that reputation, not on his own merits, but because he has good counselors around him. That is completely wrong. For this is a general and unfailing rule: that a prince who is not shrewd himself cannot get good counseling, unless he just happens to put himself in the hands of a single able man who makes all the decisions and is very knowing. In such a case, an ignorant prince might rule well, but he could not last, because in short order the counselor would take over supreme power. If he consults with several different advisers, a prince without wisdom will never get the different opinions coordinated, will never make a policy. Each of the ministers will think of his own interests, and the prince will not know how to recognize them for what they are, or how to make them pull together. Ministers are bound to act this way, because men will always turn out badly for you unless they are forced to be good. Hence I conclude that the prince's wisdom does not come from having good policies recommended to him; on the contrary, good policy, whoever suggests it, comes from the wisdom of the prince.

4. Pre' = Prete = Father Luca Raimondi was one of the chief agents of Maximilian I (1459–1519), the Holy Roman emperor. Machiavelli got to know Raimondi during his legation to the emperor in 1507–8; about this experience he wrote several reports, never failing to emphasize the way Maximilian's erratic and wavering conduct rendered ineffectual his many good qualities as soldier and statesman. A more remote influence may be that of Plutarch, who wrote a popular essay on flatterers; but Machiavelli did not have enough Greek to read the original.

XXIV
WHY THE PRINCES OF ITALY HAVE LOST THEIR DOMINIONS

The precepts given above, if properly observed, will help a new prince appear like an old one, and quickly make him more secure and better established on this throne than if it had been his for years. For the actions of a new prince are watched much more sharply than those of an hereditary prince; and when they are recognized as shrewd [*virtuose*], they do more to win men over and attract a deeper commitment than anything done by an established regime. Men are much more attracted by immediate than by remote events; when they find things going well in the here and now, they are pleased, and think of nothing else. Indeed, they will defend a new prince boldly as long as he himself does not let them down elsewhere. And so he will have double glory, from establishing a new state and then from having enriched and strengthened it with good laws, good armies, and good examples. Just so, the prince will suffer a double disgrace if he was born to the purple and then through his own lack of good sense lost it.

And if we consider those Italian lords who have lost their dominions in our day, like the king of Naples, the duke of Milan, and others, we shall find that they all made that first mistake which was described at length above,[5] of not maintaining their armed forces; and besides, some of them had the people against them, and others, who had the people on their side, could not protect themselves against the nobles. If a state has power enough to field an army, it can be lost only through errors like these. Philip of Macedon, not the father of Alexander, but the one who was defeated by Titus Quintius, had no great state, compared with the power of the Greeks and Romans who attacked him; but because he was a military man who knew how to win the favor of the people and keep the loyalty of the nobles, he held out against his enemies for several years, and even though in the end he lost a couple of cities, still he kept his kingdom.[6]

Thus these princes of ours, who, after holding power for many years, finally lose it, should not blame fortune, but rather their own sloth; they never thought, during quiet times, that things could change (and this

---

5. Though he mentions Frederick of Aragon (the king of Naples), and gestures at "others," Machiavelli has primarily in mind, throughout this brief chapter, Ludovico Sforza, duke of Milan. He was a luxurious, lazy, dissolute, deceitful prince, no warrior and no leader of men. It is a fair argument that if he had been half the soldier his father was, the French would never have taken Milan so easily or held it so long. But Frederick is a different case altogether. He was dispossessed through the collusion of the two greatest powers on the continent, France and Spain; the perfidy of his kinsman Ferdinand was a stab in the back that he had no reason to suspect; and no force that he could conceivably have mustered from his little kingdom would have sufficed against Ferdinand and Louis, combined.

6. Philip V of Macedon (221–179 B.C.) fought two wars against the Romans under Titus Quintius Flamininus. But though he struggled manfully, Machiavelli overstates the degree of his success. Livy tells us (33.30) that after his final defeat at Cynoscephalae (197 B.C.), he was practically wiped out as an independent prince.

is a common failing of men: they never think of storms so long as the sky is blue). Then when the tempest breaks, their first thought is to run away, not to defend themselves; they hope that the people, when they are tired of the arrogance of their conquerors, will call them back.[7] Maybe when there is no other recourse, this policy will work; but to abandon other remedies for this one is complete foolishness. There is never any point in falling simply in the hope of finding somebody else to pick you up. Whether this comes to pass or not, it never makes for your security, since it is a cowardly kind of defense that does not depend on your own efforts. The only good, safe, and dependable defenses are those that you control yourself with your own energy [*virtù*].

 XXV

THE INFLUENCE OF LUCK ON HUMAN AFFAIRS AND THE WAYS TO COUNTER IT

I realize that many people have thought, and still do think, that events are so governed in this world that the wisdom of men cannot possibly avail against them, indeed is altogether useless.[8] On this basis, you might say that there is no point in sweating over anything, we should simply leave all matters to fate. This opinion has been popular in our own times because of the tremendous change in public affairs during our lifetime, that actually is still going on today, beyond what anyone could have imagined. Indeed, sometimes when I think of it, I incline toward this opinion myself. Still, rather than give up on our free will altogether, I think it may be true that Fortune governs half of our actions, but that even so she leaves the other half more or less in our power to control. I would compare her to one of those torrential streams which, when they overflow, flood the plains, rip up trees and tear down buildings, wash the land away here and deposit it there; everyone flees before them, everyone yields to their onslaught, unable to stand up to them in any way. This is how they are; yet this does not mean that men cannot take countermeasures while the weather is still fine, shoring up dikes and dams, so that when the waters rise again, they are either carried off in a channel or confined where they do no harm. So with Fortune, who exerts all her power where there is no strength [*virtù*] prepared to oppose her, and turns to smashing things up wherever there are no dikes and restraining dams. And if you look at Italy, which is the seat of all these

7. Once again, Machiavelli glances at Ludovico Il Moro; after the first invasion he ran away, but was recalled, when the populace rose against the French; after he was deposed a second time, there was no question of recall; he died in a French jail. See chapter III, note 9, p. 5.

8. We today are likely to think this sort of loose, defeatist opinion could be held only by uneducated "popular" thinkers; but Fortuna was a very real force in Renaissance philosophy, with plenty of classical precedent; she was often identified with Nature, with Fate, with Nemesis, or (under the epithet Panthea) with all the other gods combined. Her omnipotence was a cliché, the variations on which are listed by Natale Conti in his *Mythologiae* (4.9).

tremendous changes, where they all began, you will see that she is an open country without any dikes or ditches. If she were protected by forces of proper valor [*virtù*], as are Germany, Spain, and France,[9] either this flood would never have wrought such destruction as it has, or it might not even have occurred at all. And let this much suffice on the general topic of opposing Fortune.

But coming now to the particulars, let me observe that we see a prince flourishing today and ruined tomorrow, and yet no change has taken place in his nature or any of his qualities. I think this happens, primarily, for the reasons discussed at length above, that is, that a prince who depends entirely on Fortune comes to grief immediately she changes. I believe further that a prince will be fortunate who adjusts his behavior to the temper of the times, and on the other hand will be unfortunate when his behavior is not well attuned to the times.[1] Anyone can see that men take different paths in their search for the common goals of glory and riches; one goes cautiously, another boldly; one by violence, another by stealth; one by patience, another in the contrary way; yet any one of these different methods may be successful. Of two cautious men, one will succeed in his design the other not; so too, a rash man and a cautious man may both succeed, though their approaches are so different. And this stems from nothing but the temper of the times, which does or does not accord with their method of operating. Hence two men proceeding in different ways may, as I have said, produce the same effect; while two men proceeding in the same way will vary in their effectiveness, one failing, one succeeding. This too explains the variation in what is good; for if a prince conducts himself with patience and caution, and the times and circumstances are favorable to those qualities, he will flourish; but if times and circumstances change, he will come to ruin unless he changes his method of proceeding. No man, however prudent, can adjust to such radical changes, not only because we cannot go against the inclination of nature, but also because when one has always prospered by following a particular course, he cannot be persuaded to leave it. Thus the cautious man, when it is time to act boldly, does not know how, and comes to grief; if he could only change his nature with times and circumstances, his fortune would not change.

In everything he undertook, Pope Julius proceeded boldly; and he found the times and circumstances of his life so favorable to this sort of procedure, that he always came off well. Consider his first campaign

---

9. Machiavelli had previously (chapter IV) described France as easy to take though hard to hold precisely because it was divided by political dikes and dams. What he seems to envisage as ideal is a political arrangement combining local loyalties and traditions with an overall central authority. It is interesting that he does not distinguish Germany, in this respect, from France and Spain—though, as late as the nineteenth century, Germany would be legendary for the divisions of its petty princedoms.

1. See *Discorsi* 3.8 (pp. 114–16) and the letter to Piero Soderini (pp. 124–26) for a further statement of Machiavelli's truly cynical view that success in government is a matter of adapting oneself to circumstances.

against Bologna, when Messer Giovanni Bentivogli was still alive.[2] The Venetians were unhappy with it, and so was the king of Spain; he held conversations about it with the French; but Julius, with his usual assurance and energy, directed the expedition in person. His activity kept the Spanish and the Venetians uneasy and inactive; the former were afraid, and the latter thought they saw a chance to recover the entire kingdom of Naples. Finally, the pope drew the king of France into his enterprise, because when the king saw what he was doing, and realized that he needed the pope's friendship to put down the Venetians, he judged that he could not deny the support of his troops without openly offending him.[3] Thus Julius carried off, in his rash and adventurous way, an enterprise that no other pope, even one who exercised the greatest human prudence, could successfully have performed. If he had waited before leaving Rome till all the diplomatic formalities were concluded, as any other pope would have done, he would never have succeeded. The king of France would have found a thousand excuses, and the other powers would have given him a thousand reasons to be afraid. His other actions can be omitted, as they were all like this one, and all turned out well. The shortness of his life prevented him from having the opposite experience; but in fact if circumstances had ever required him to act cautiously, he would have been ruined at once; he could never have varied from the style to which nature inclined him.

I conclude, then, that so long as Fortune varies and men stand still, they will prosper while they suit the times, and fail when they do not. But I do feel this: that is is better to be rash than timid, for Fortune is a woman, and the man who wants to hold her down must beat and bully her.[4] We see that she yields more often to men of this stripe than to those who come coldly toward her. Like a woman, too, she is always a friend of the young, because they are less timid, more brutal, and take charge of her more recklessly.

 XXVI

AN EXHORTATION TO RESTORE ITALY TO LIBERTY AND FREE HER FROM THE BARBARIANS

Considering, therefore, the matters discussed above, I ask myself whether at present the hour is ripe to hail a new prince in Italy, if there is material here that a careful, able [*virtuoso*] leader could mold into a

2. Writing at the time (1506), Machiavelli was very conscious of Pope Julius's rashness in gambling on French support. His reports from the field, collected as *Legazione seconda alla corte di Roma* compare well with his historical hindsight, as in *Discorsi* 3.44.

3. Pope Julius took to the field against the Baglioni of Perugia and the Bentivogli of Bologna, on August 26, 1506; he took Perugia on September 13, and Bologna on November 11.

During most of Julius's campaign, Machiavelli was with the papal court as Florentine legate, and could thus observe at first hand the diplomatic indecision of the Spaniards and Venetians.

4. The ninth story of Boccaccio's ninth day begins with a little lecture by the queen for the day; her theme is the ancient traditional theme of masculine "wisdom," "Good wife and bad wife both need the stick."

new form which might bring honor to him and benefits to all men; and I answer that all things now appear favorable to a new prince, so much so that I cannot think of any time more suitable than the present. And if, as I said above, it was necessary, to bring out the power [*virtù*] of Moses, that the children of Israel should be slaves in Egypt; and if, to know the magnanimity of Cyrus, it was necessary that the Persians be oppressed by the Medes; and for Theseus's merit to be known, that the Athenians should be scattered; then, at the present time, if the power [*virtù*] of an Italian spirit is to be manifested, it was necessary that Italy be reduced to her present state; and that she be more enslaved than the Hebrews, more abject than the Persians, more widely dispersed than the Athenians; headless, orderless, beaten, stripped, scarred, overrun, and plagued by every sort of disaster.[5]

And though one man recently showed certain gleams, such as made us think he was ordained by God for our salvation, still we saw how, at the very zenith of his career, he was deserted by Fortune.[6] Thus Italy, left almost lifeless, waits for a leader who will heal her wounds, stop the ravaging of Lombardy, end the looting of the Kingdom and of Tuscany, and minister to those sores of hers that have been festering so long. Behold how she implores God to send someone to free her from the cruel insolence of the barbarians; see how ready and eager she is to follow a banner joyously, if only someone will raise it up. There is no figure presently in sight in whom she can better place her trust than your illustrious house, which, with its fortune and its merits [*virtù*] favored by God and the Church of which it is now the head, can take the lead in this process of redemption.

The task will not be too hard if you keep your eye on the actions and lives of those leaders described above. Men of this sort are rare and wonderful, indeed, but they were nothing more than men, and each of them faced circumstances less promising than those of the present. Their cause was no more just than the present one, nor any easier, and God was no more favorable to them than to you. Your cause *is* just: "for war is justified when it is necessary, and arms are pious when without them there would be no hope at all."[7] Everyone is eager, and where there is such eagerness there can be no great difficulty, if you imitate the methods of those I have proposed as examples. Apart from this, we have experienced extraordinary, unexampled leadings from God in this matter; the sea has divided, a cloud has shown the way, a stone has yielded water, manna has rained from heaven.[8] All things point toward your

---

5. The reference is back to chapter VI.
6. The extraordinary bad luck of Cesare Borgia is detailed in chapter VII. It should be added that Machiavelli, though not without a romantic side, was not soft or eccentric in thinking that Cesare really did aspire to unify Italy; it was the common view of the time. "The

Kingdom," below, is the kingdom of Naples.
7. Livy uses these expressions in reporting a speech of Caius Pontius to the Samnites (9.1).
8. The Mosaic miracles are familiar enough; it is not clear by any means what recent prodigies Machiavelli would have cited if pressed for a modern parallel.

greatness. The rest is up to you. God will not do everything, lest he deprive us of our free will and a part of that glory which belongs to us.

There is nothing surprising in the fact that none of the Italians whom I have named was able to do what we hope for from your illustrious house; no reason even for wonder if, after so many revolutions in Italy and so many military campaigns, it seems as if military manhood [*virtù*] is quite extinct. The reason is simply that the old methods of warfare were not good, and no one has been able to find new ones. Nothing does so much honor to a man newly risen to power, as the new laws and rules that he discovers. When they are well-grounded and have in them the seeds of greatness, these institutions make him the object of awe and admiration. In Italy there is no lack of material to be given new forms; the limbs of the nation have great strength [*virtù*], so long as the heads are not deficient. Only look at the duels and tourneys where a few men are involved, and you will find that the Italians excel in strength, in dexterity, in mental agility;[9] but when it is a matter of armies, they don't stand the comparison. This all comes from the weakness of the heads; because those who know what they are doing cannot enforce obedience. Each one thinks he knows best, and there has not been anyone hitherto who has raised himself, by strength [*virtù*] or fortune to a point where the others would yield to him. This is the reason why for a long time, in all the wars waged over the last twenty years, whenever an army composed of Italians took the field, it showed up badly. Among the examples of this are, first, the Taro, then Alexandria, Capua, Genoa, Vailà, Bologna, and Mestre.[1]

If, then, your illustrious house is to follow the example of those excellent men who redeemed their native lands, you must first of all, before anything else, provide yourself with your own armies; that is the foundation stone of any enterprise, and you cannot possibly have more faithful, more reliable, or better soldiers than your own. And though each may be a good man individually, they will be even better as a group, when they see themselves united behind a prince of their own, who will support and reward them. It is necessary to build up an army of this sort, if you are to defend yourself with Italian valor [*virtù*] against foreigners. Doubtless the Swiss and Spanish infantry have fearful reputations, yet they are both deficient in ways that will allow a third force not only to withstand them, but to feel confident of overcoming them.

9. In a famous hand-to-hand fight on February 13, 1503, eleven Italian champions soundly defeated eleven French champions, to the immense delight of the Italian public. These were the days of Bayard and Gaston de la Foix—of a half-nostalgic, still animate chivalry. See J. S. Bridge, *History of France* (Oxford, 1929) 3.165–67.
1. Machiavelli's mournful roll call of Italian disasters is arranged in strict chronological or-

der, from the battle of Taro (July 5, 1495) when the French armies of Charles VIII first invaded Italy, to the devastation of Mestre near Venice by German and papal troops just before the battle of Vicenza (October 7, 1513). It is an impressionistic list, designed with skillful rhetorical intent to stir memories of Italian shame and disgrace in the mind of Lorenzo de' Medici, for whose special benefit (it seems likely) Machiavelli composed this final chapter.

The Spaniards cannot stand up against horsemen; and the Swiss are bound to crumble when they meet in battle enemies who are as stubborn as they are. We have seen this, and know by experience that the Spaniards could not hold up against French cavalrymen, and the Swiss were cut up by Spanish infantry. This last theory has not been completely tested, but we had a sample at the battle of Ravenna,[2] where the Spanish infantry came up against battalions of Germans, who are organized in the same way as the Swiss. The agile Spaniards, with the help of their spiked shields, got under the pikes of the Germans, or between them, and were able to stab at them without being in any danger themselves. If it had not been for the cavalry that charged them, the Spaniards would have eaten them all up. When you know the faults of these two infantries, you can set up a third sort, which will stand up to cavalry and not be afraid of infantry; this can be done by raising new armies and changing their formations. Such new inventions as these give a new prince the reputation of a great man.

The occasion must not be allowed to slip away; Italy has been waiting too long for a glimpse of her redeemer. I cannot describe the joy with which he will be greeted in all those districts which have suffered from the flood of foreigners; nor the thirst for vengeance, the deep devotion, the dedication, the tears, that will greet him. What doors would be closed to him? what people would deny him obedience? what envy could oppose him? what Italian would refuse allegiance? This barbarian occupation stinks in all our nostrils![3] Let your illustrious house, then, take up this task with that courage and with that hope which suit a just enterprise; so that, under your banner, our country may become noble again, and the verses of Petrarch may come true:

> Then virtue boldly shall engage
> And swiftly vanquish barbarous rage,
> Proving that ancient and heroic pride
> In true Italian hearts has never died.[4]

---

2. On the battle of Ravenna, one of the most desperately fought and technically innovative of the Italian wars, see chapter XIII, note 1, p. 38. A frequent opinion of modern historians is that the battle was decided by the artillery—a factor Machiavelli does not mention.

3. Machiavelli deliberately imitates the war cry of Julius II: "Fuori i barbari!" ("Out with the barbarians!") But one should not attribute to him the conception of a "nation" as it developed after the French Revolution. He wanted the Germans out, and to get them out he was even willing to call himself an Italian; but at heart he was a Florentine—and that is something else entirely.

4. Petrarch, canzone 128, "Italia mia, ben che'l parlar sia indarno," lines 93–96. The canzone is directed against "la tedesca rabbia," the German fury.

BACKGROUNDS

NORTH-CENTRAL
ITALY
in Machiavelli's Time

A.M. JAUSS

MILES

0   25   50

Machiavelli the Working Diplomat

NICCOLÒ MACHIAVELLI

[The Legation to Cesare Borgia]†

[Diplomacy in Renaissance Italy was no business for a man with weak nerves. Personal relations counted for a great deal, and decisions involving the life or death of a city had to be made, sometimes on the basis of nothing more than a smile or an innuendo. Communications were abominable. Even though he was only a few hundred miles from home, the ambassador could not ask a question and get an answer (during the winter, particularly, when the Apennine passes were sometimes closed and always perilous) in much less than a week. There was no systematic reporting of news throughout Italy, far less throughout Europe. News spread by word of mouth, with casual couriers, travelers, and merchants as its carriers, and often its garblers. Dealing with a man like Cesare Borgia, who was impatient of temper and quick to act, an ambassador had to be bold, decisive, and independent, yet careful to avoid overstepping the bounds of his commission.

For back in Florence Machiavelli had to deal not just with one commander in chief, but with a committee, the Dieci di Balia, or as we would say, the Council of Ten, though the Italian means the "Ten of Council." Under this neutral title they were in fact the Ministry of War. They commissioned numerous Florentine citizens, among them Machiavelli, to serve as their agents at the courts of various princes in Italy and abroad; and from these agents they received reports, more or less detailed, as circumstances required. Among these agents, Machiavelli, as a simple civil servant, a secretary, occupied a position of no great eminence. He was not, for example, a nobleman like his contemporary Count Baldassare Castiglione, who served several different princes; he was not a prelate or dignitary of the Church. During his first days in the service, he was generally associated with another ambassador, to whom he was junior if not directly subordinate. But as his talents became known, he was sent on more and more important missions, and assumed more authority over their conduct. In June of 1502, he was sent, with Francesco Soderini, bishop of Volterra and brother of Piero Soderini, the chief magistrate of Florence, to deal with Cesare Borgia, then in his ascendant. For a sketch of Cesare's circumstances and intentions, see the Historical Introduction, pp. xiv–xv. Machiavelli and Francesco Sod-

† Translated by the editor from Niccolò Machiavelli, *Legazione e commissaire*, ed. Sergio Bertelli (Milano: Feltrinelli, 1964), vol. 1 (vol. 3 of the Machiavelli *Opere*) 335–45, 502–10.

erini were much impressed with Cesare Borgia when they first saw him, as he was just setting out on his conquests. In a letter from Urbino, dated June 26, 1502, they summarized his character:

> This Lord is very splendid and magnificent and so fierce in battle that there's no great enterprise that he won't take lightly; in the pursuit of glory and reputation he never rests, and recognizes neither weariness nor danger; he has arrived at a new position before anyone understands that he has left the old one. He is well liked by his soldiers, and he has enrolled the best men in Italy. These qualities make him both victorious and dangerous for the future; added to which, he is always lucky.

The Florentines should, technically, have been natural allies of Cesare, since they were both allied to the king of France; but the connection was not one on which anybody could count. Cesare wanted the king's soldiers only until he could get together an army of his own; the Florentines, if they could only get back Pisa, wanted desperately to be left alone, so they could make their way by trading and manufacturing. But they were too fat a prize to live comfortably in the sea of sharks that was northern Italy. One of the fiercest and hungriest of these sharks was Cesare Borgia. Machiavelli's dealings with this up-and-coming tyrant (of which we can represent here only a small sample, culled from a second mission to Cesare in October–December 1502) show him hard at work on the daily business of diplomacy—playing for time, persuading, promising, calculating, observing, serving the best interests of his city in whatever way he could, under extremely difficult and trying circumstances. It was his long experience in this sort of work that tempered the mind of Machiavelli toward the writing of *The Prince*, after Cesare Borgia was dead and after the republic for which Machiavelli worked so faithfully had gone down the drain.

The translation of these documents has been made from Machiavelli's *Legazione e commissaire* (vol. 3 of his *Opere*). The translation aims at bald authenticity. Machiavelli's employers write committee-room prose at its worst; in Machiavelli's reports, the trivial rubs shoulders with the crucial; the spelling of names is very casual, and allusive formulas are everywhere. We are, as it were, in the workshop of sixteenth-century city-state diplomacy.]

1

Deliberations of the Signoria

October 5, 1502

The Magnificent Lords, etc., by special decree, have sent to the same illustrious Duke Valentino as their envoy Nicholas Malclavellus,[1] with

---

1. "Malclavellus" is a Latin secretary's instinctive effort to Latinize "Machiavelli" but it is etymologically correct; the name derives from the Latin for "bad keys," *mali clavelli*.

a salary which is stipulated elsewhere and with these instructions which are written below.

Departed, October 6.

Returned, January 23, 1503.

2

The Commission

Commission given to Niccolò Machiavelli, formulated by our esteemed masters on the fifth of October 1502.

Niccolò, we send you to Imola[2] to find His Excellency the Duke Valentino with credentials to him; you will proceed there on horse as fast as you can, and in your first conference with him you will explain that, in recent days, since his return into the Romagna, we've learned of the estrangement and departure of the Orsini from His Excellency, and the gathering and conclave of them and their adherents near La Magione in the neighborhood of Perugia, and the story has gone round that the duke of Urbino and Signor Bartolommeo d'Alviano will be there too, in order to plan and plot actions against His Excellency, actions which we consider to be directed against the Most Christian King,[3] and we too have been slyly requested to send our man to that meeting, and talk with them; but we continue to be of our old opinion, desirous of being good friends of Our Master and His Excellency, firmly committed against separating ourselves or abandoning our devotion to the king of France;[4] because, living in friendship with him, and under his protection, our city cannot fail to recall, when it's a question of the king's interests, and His Excellency's friends and dependents, everything which has been done and promised in our interests, and so reciprocate with all the good offices of good friends; and it's for this reason that we've sent you posthaste to His Excellency, since we think the importance of the business requires it; and you should tell him again that in these movements of our neighbors, we intend to preserve the greatest respect for his interests, and maintain the same esteem for him that we have always had, in view of the fact that we consider all the friends of France to be our friends, and where it's a question of their interests, there it's

2. Lying across the Apennines in the broad plain fronting the Adriatic Sea, Imola was only about fifty miles from Florence as the crow flies; but the actual distance was twice as much. As we learn below, one particularly urgent courier made the trip in about seventeen hours; most took longer. See the map of the area, p. 74.

3. The assembly at La Magione near Perugia, which did not actually convene till October 9 but was much talked of in advance, brought together local lords, soldiers, bravos, and family heads of the Romagna. Signor Bartolommeo d' Alviano was a Venetian soldier; his presence would greatly have strengthened the conspiracy. The plot was directed against Cesare, as captain of the Church, but also against his two chief supporters: his father, Pope Alexander VI, and the "Most Christian King," Louis XII of France.

4. "Our Master" is Louis XII, then with his army; "His Excellency" is Cesare.

also a question of ours. And this, it seems to us, ought to be enough for your first encounter, in which you will make it as clear as possible that we have great confidence and hope in His Excellency: and on this theme you can enlarge as much as you think proper, spelling out in your conversation all the details and circumstances of which the material allows, none of which need be expanded on here, as you're perfectly well acquainted with them: nor do we want you to talk of anything outside of this material, nor deal with it in any other way; and whenever His Excellency tries to push you further, we want you to tell us of it, and wait for our reply. And after this first opening statement, either in this first audience or later, will you thank His Excellency as warmly as you can for his good services to our merchants, which is a benefit we consider to be conferred on us, and a public benefaction; reminding him of the liberation of those goods which had been held up for some months past at Urbino, and about which we've just heard today from those merchants that they've been forwarded according to their instructions; with a great show of friendship, which will make clear that you have particular instructions to look into the matter; and then afterwards, when you think the occasion right, you can request of His Excellency in our name security and safe conduct through his states and territories for the goods of our merchants coming and going from the East; and this is a matter of considerable import, which you could call the very stomach of our city, and you must pay particular attention to it, and exercise all your diligence so that the outcome may be according to our desires.

3

Credentials Given to the Ambassador

October 5, 1502

To Duke Valentino.

Most Illustrious Lord, etc. We send to Your Excellency Niccolò Machiavelli, a citizen and our secretary, in order to acquaint you with various matters of great significance both to our friendship and present circumstances. We beg Your Lordship by our love to give this man the same trust that you would to ourselves.

4

Safe Conduct for Machiavelli

The Priors in the name of freedom and the Gonfalonier in the name of justice of the Florentine people, to all and sundry whom these letters may reach, greetings. We are sending Niccolò, son of Messer Bernardo Machiavelli, a very noble citizen and our secretary, to the most illustrious duke of Romagna, etc., on some of our business; and so we command all rectors, officials, subjects, and employees of ours, and we beg all you our friends and allies, to let pass the aforesaid Niccolò with all his goods and properties, without payment of any impost or excise; and if he should need any help or favor in order to arrive safely before the aforesaid lord, let him have it; and we will always be very ready to return a similar or greater favor, should need arise. Farewell.

From our palace, October 4, 1502.

Marcellus[5]

5

Machiavelli to the Ten

Magnificent and Distinguished Lords, my very particular masters. Since I found myself ill provided with horses at my departure, and it seemed to me that my duties required haste, I took post[6] at Scarperia and came to this place without any loss of time, where I arrived today around six o'clock; and because I had left behind my own horses and my servants, I presented myself immediately in traveling dress before His Excellency, who greeted me warmly; and as I presented my credentials, I explained to him the reason for my coming, and began to thank him for the restitution of our merchants' goods. Then I turned to the falling away of the Orsini and to the counsel they were holding with their adherents, and how Your Lordships had been secretly invited, and I reminded him of the views you hold regarding friendship with the king of France and your devotion to the Church; and I amplified on these topics with all the words that occurred to me, explaining that you felt bound to hold friendship with king and Church while avoiding complicity with their enemies. And I explained that in every action, Your Lordships are concerned to safeguard his particular interests, as befits the friendship you maintain with the king of France and the devotion you have always felt for his own power, since you consider all friends of France to be most faithful friends and allies of your own. His Excellency, on the matter of the restitutions, gave no answer at all; but, turning to the other particulars, he thanked Your Lordships for this kind and welcome demonstration: and then he said that he had always desired friendly relations with Your Lordships, and that any lapse in them should

5. Marcello Virgilio di Adriano Berti, secretary of the Florentine chancellery.
6. Instead of riding his own horse all the way, he rented successive horses from the post service. As each beast covered only a short stage of the journey, a man could travel faster by post than on his own animal. Scarperia is a little village about fifteen miles northnortheast of Florence on the road to Imola.

be laid to the malignity of others, not to his account; and he said he wanted to explain to me in particular what he had never told anyone else, regarding his coming with an army to Florence.[7] And he said that when Faenza had fallen and an attempt had been made on Bologna, the Orsini and Vitelli were on his back to get him to return to Rome by way of Florence; and when he said no, because the pope had ordered him to go another way, Vitellozzo threw himself at his feet in tears, begging him to go this way, and promising that he would do no harm either to the city or to the countryside. And he didn't want to grant even this much, until others came with similar requests that they be allowed to go there, but always with the proviso that the countryside should not be harmed and there should be no talk of the Medici. But since he was now going to Florence, he thought to profit by the occasion and reach a friendly agreement with Your Lordships: which shows that he had never in a business way talked at all or to any effect about the Medici, as the commissioners who treated with him know very well; nor did he ever want to have Pietro with him in his camp.[8] When they were at Campi, he says the Orsini and Vitelli often asked his permission to make a show of force before Florence or Pistoia, to show that those were feasible enterprises; but he never gave his consent, instead he gave them to understand with a thousand protests, that he would fight them. The agreement then followed,[9] but it seemed to the Orsini and Vitelli that he had had his will, and they hadn't had theirs, since the event had turned out to his advantage and their loss, so that they began secretly to sabotage it, and did all they could to make trouble for Your Lordships and upset the agreement. And he couldn't properly set things right, partly because he couldn't be everywhere at once, and partly because Your Lordships hadn't come through with the advance which had been agreed on, and which once seemed about to be paid. Things standing thus about the end of last June, the rebellion of Arezzo broke out at that time:[1] concerning which, he said, he had never had any foreknowledge, as he had already assured the bishop of Volterra; but he certainly welcomed it, supposing it offered him a chance to achieve recognition. Yet even then nothing was done, either through bad luck on both sides,

---

7. During the summer of 1501 Cesare Borgia, with his ragtag international army, had paid an ambiguous call on the Florentines. Cesare was much feared himself, and a chief captain in his army was Vitellozzo Vitelli, who bore a grudge against the Florentines because they had executed his brother Paolo. After some rather tense negotiations, Cesare was appointed "protector" of Florence, with an annual salary of thirty-six thousand ducats. Always a threat to the republic under such circumstances was the possibility that someone might try to reinstate the Medici, who had been driven from Florence in 1494.

8. Pietro de' Medici, deposed and disagreeable son of the Magnificent Lorenzo, who was al-

ways hanging around armies in the hope of being restored by them.

9. I.e., Cesare's agreement to "protect" Florence from enemies—including, in the first instance, himself. Technically, he took the city under his "condotta."

1. This was in June 1502. Arezzo, a city dependent on Florence, tried to break away; and Vitellozzo Vitelli, a neighbor who was always itching to get at the Florentines, came to the aid of the rebels. The "bishop of Volterra" was Francesco Soderini, brother of the Florentine gonfalonier, Piero Soderini, and a political associate of Machiavelli's in an earlier mission to Cesare.

or because your city was not then in a position to discuss and decide matters which would have been of great advantage to both; and yet he said that gave him no particular trouble, and being still disposed to do you good, in view of the king's good will, he wrote and sent men directly to Vitellozzo, telling him to clear out of Arezzo: and not content with this, he went off with his men toward Città di Castello, and could have taken Vitelli's own state from him, because the chief men of the countryside came forward to offer their help; and this, he said, was the prime source of Vitellozzo's discontent and ill humor. As for the Orsini, he said he didn't know what made them discontented in the French court, and couldn't tell without papal permission. But they perhaps resented that the French king had treated him more honorably than Cardinal Orsini, and given him special privileges;[2] and then rumor had said he was going to take their state away; so on that they broke away, and now found themselves in this convocation of bankrupts. And though he had received various messages from Signor Giulio Orsini, declaring that he was not going to oppose him, etc., and it wasn't reasonable to expect them to declare themselves openly, because they had taken his money:[3] still, when they did declare themselves, he expected they would prove crazier than people had thought, since they weren't even able to pick the right time to attack him—the king of France was in Italy, and His Holiness the pope was still living, and those two things lit such a fire under him that putting it out would require a different water than theirs. He didn't worry about the loss of Urbino, because he hadn't forgotten the way to get it back when he lost it.[4] And then he suggested that now was the time, if Your Lordships wanted to be his friends, to prove it; because he could now make friends with you without having to placate the Orsini, as he had always had to do before. But if Your Lordships delayed, and he meanwhile was reconciled with the Orsini, who are still dealing with him, then the same old problems would come back; and as the Orsini could scarcely be satisfied with any deal unless it replaced the Medici,[5] then Your Lordships would be back in the same old jealousies and troubles. Thus he thinks Your Lordships should declare yourselves at once to be his friends or theirs, one way or the other, because if you put it off, either the two parties will reach an agreement at your expense, or else one of them will be victorious, which in the hour of victory will be either hostile or else under no obligation to Your

---

2. This would have been four years before, in 1498, when Cesare was sent as papal legate to the court of France, bearing the order that annulled Louis's marriage with Jeanne of France and so enabled him to marry Anne of Brittany. Whatever the consequences for his domestic bliss, the shift of wives was a great political coup for Louis.

3. Cesare had made it his business to seem placatory and even generous toward the Orsini and Vitelli; it was by means of these soft words and lavish presents that he lured them into the trap at Sinigaglia; see below.

4. Only two days before (October 5) Urbino had revolted against Cesare as part of the general rising of the Romagna, which was coming to a head with the meeting at La Magione.

5. In Florence.

Lordships. And when you come to make your decision, he thinks you will see the necessity of it; he doesn't see how Your Lordships can take sides against the majesty of the king and the sanctity of the pope; and he adds that it would ease things for him if, when he moves Vitellozzo or others into one or another of his states, you would make a show with what forces you have in the direction of Borgo or those boundaries, in order to lend color to his actions.[6]

I listened very carefully as His Excellency went over the points given above: what he said was not just to the general effect that I report but in exactly the same words, which I have transcribed at length so that Your Lordships may better judge of the whole: I don't transcribe my own answers, as that isn't necessary: I tried very hard not to go beyond my commission, and in the matter of using your forces, I made no answer whatever; I simply said that I would write to Your Lordships, declaring his exact thoughts, in which I declared you would take extraordinary pleasure. And although His Excellency, as you see, showed a great desire to reach immediate agreement with you, still even when I pressed closely to draw him into some particulars, he always talked in large generalities, and I couldn't get anything out of him beyond what I've written. And since I'd mentioned in my opening remarks that there had been a certain turnaround in the state of Urbino, and His Excellency had said in his reply that he didn't much care what had happened in that dukedom, it occurred to me to ask in my reply how these things came about. To which His Excellency replied: My being too gentle, and taking too little care over the details, is what did me harm: I took that dukedom, as you know, in three days, and didn't ruffle a hair on anyone's head, except for Messer Dolce and two others, who had taken actions against His Holiness the pope; indeed, I went further, and appointed several of those leading citizens to offices in the state, one of them in charge of certain walls that I was having erected in the fort of San Leo. Two days ago, he conspired with some people of the countryside who made a show of bringing up a big beam for the work, and so they forced the gate, and the fortress was lost. Some say the cry that went up was Marco,[7] others Vitelli, others Orsini; but up to this point nobody has declared himself. Personally, I consider the dukedom was lost because it was a weak and sluggish state; the men were malcontents, whom I had overburdened with soldiery; but I expect to take care of it all. And you write to your lords that they should look to their own affairs here; because if the duke returns to Urbino and he comes from Venice,[8]

---

6. The suggestion is that the Florentines should mime an act of aggression so that Cesare could order Vitellozzo Vitelli, still technically in his service, into some disadvantageous position. "Borgo" is Borgo San Sepolcro.
7. "Marco" is San Marco, patron saint of Venice. "Overburdened with soldiery" means simply that there had been too many armies camped around Urbino, foraging off the countryside.
8. The Florentines had good reason to fear the Venetians, who as their commercial rivals had lent troops to the Pisans in their struggle against Florence.

it's not by any means our loss and your gain; which is one more reason why we should trust one another.

This is, in effect, all that I can write to Your Lordships at this time; and though it's part of my assignment to write you how many visitors are at this nobleman's court, where they are staying, and many other local particulars, still, since I just arrived today, I can't be sure of the truth of it, and thus I'll save it for another occasion: and I commend myself to Your Lordships.

Your servant, Nicolaus Machiavellus. At Imola.

October 7, 1502
E.V.D.[9]

Held over to the next day at four P.M., the horse supplier being completely out, and I haven't been able to find an animal up to now. And I can add that yesterday His Excellency in his talk with me said that the day before Pandolfo Petrucci[1] had sent a secret message, pledging that he would give no favors to anyone who opposed His Excellency, and went on to give more general pledges to this effect.

On my way here I encountered Messer Agapito some two miles out of town, with seven or eight horses; and when he recognized me, I told him where I was going and who sent me. He made me very welcome, and went forward only a little distance before turning back. This morning, I realized that the said Messer Agapito was on his way to Your Lordships as the emissary of this duke, and because of my coming he turned back.[2] Farewell again.

October 8, 1502

I have given the present horseman two ducats on the understanding that he will be there tomorrow morning before daybreak, which should be around nine A.M. Will you be good enough to reimburse Ser Agostino Vespucci.[3]

*   *   *

9. E.V.D. stands for Excellentissimae Vestrae Dominationis (Servitor), ("[Servant of] Your Most Excellent Lordship").

1. Pandolfo Petrucci was prince and tyrant of Siena.

2. The point being made is that Cesare had greater need of Florentine support than he let on; if the Florentines hadn't sent Machiavelli to him, he was on the point of sending Messer Agapito as an envoy to them.

3. Machiavelli asks that reimbursements for his expenses be paid to various of his friends, who would find ways to get the money to him.

77

Machiavelli to the Ten

Magnificent Lords, etc. By way of Bagno I wrote my latest to Your Lordships on the twenty-third, and since I wrote at length there of the departure of the French and the various opinions about it, there's no need for me now to say anything more of it, since there's nothing important to add.

The day before yesterday the boy of Ardingo, the courier, arrived, with two letters of Your Lordships' dated the twentieth and twenty-second, and though I made every effort after receiving them to talk with the duke, I could not do so, because my only chance was yesterday, and yesterday His Excellency was busy reviewing the infantry and in his other holiday pleasures, so I could not get to him; and this morning he rose early, and went off with the whole army to Santo Arcangelo, some fifteen miles from here and five miles from Rimini; so tomorrow I'll get up early and go to Rimini, since I can't lodge any closer because of the shortage of housing—it's very scant—even though people say we aren't to stop in this district for any time at all; but next day the army will move on to near Pesaro; nobody knows what's up; some think an attempt will be made on Sinigaglia, others say Ancona.[4] As for soldiers, he has those troops that I mentioned in my latest list, and in addition around thirty newly enrolled Albanian auxiliaries, in addition to 2,500 infantry from beyond the Alps, and about the same number of Italians, some of whom put on the show yesterday and the day before. You can figure that for every thousand infantry there are fifty horsemen capable of serving as cavalry; the artillery have moved at the same pace as the army's leader, with the necessary powder and shot. What sort of power the Orsini and the Vitelli have, nobody knows; we'll know better on the day when the armies get closer to one another; as I've often told Your Lordships, this duke is extremely secretive, and I don't think anyone but himself knows what he's about to do: even his chief secretaries have often told me that he never explains what he's going to do till he's already begun it, and he begins it when circumstances constrain him, and the situation is ripe, not otherwise; so I beg Your Lordships to excuse me, and don't think I'm negligent when I can't give Your Lordships exact information, since most of the time I can't even satisfy myself as to what is happening. Concerning San Leo and the deal he is making with Duke Guido there's no further news.[5] As for Camerino I wrote on another

4. Pesaro, Sinigaglia, and Ancona are stretched out along the Adriatic coast at intervals of about twenty to twenty-five miles; Cesare's interest wasn't in any of them, particularly, but in rounding up the conspirators of La Magione, who at the moment were desperately trying to pretend they were his best friends. When caught, they had taken Sinigaglia and proposed to present it to him as a peace offering. He took both it and them.

5. This deal clearly involved the fate of Urbino. "Duke Guido" is Guidobaldo da Montefeltro. Camerino, also captured by Cesare, was another city whose fate was up in the air.

occasion what the duke told me, who had been there on official duties, and afterwards I wrote as much as I had been able to get out of that secretary to Cardinal Farnese, who told me that there was little hope for it, and that mostly on the part of the French: yesterday I heard from the bishop of Euna that things were practically settled, but I'd better wait for the last word, in order not to be mistaken again.

This morning Messer Remirro was found in two pieces on the public square, where he still is: the whole city has been to see him: nobody is sure of the reason for his death, except that it was the will of the prince, who shows himself capable of making men and breaking them as he pleases, according to their merits.[6]

The courier I mentioned above brought me twenty-five golden ducats and sixteen yards of black damask. I thank Your Lordships for the one thing as well as the other.

Because the court is on the move, no man has been assigned to me to go and pick up the three horses that Your Lordships say are at Poppi; let me beg of Your Lordships to ensure that they are properly cared for till I can arrange for them to come here.

Messer Bartolommeo Marcelli of Bagno, for whom the baron of Bierra lately wrote to our exalted masters, asks nothing but that a little time be granted before his appearance, so that he can get there; he's writing on this point to Piero de Braccio Martelli, who is acting as his lawyer in the case; and I again recommend his request to Your Lordships' consideration; may all your affairs go well.

Your servant, Nicolaus Machiavellus, Secretary

From Cesena, December 26, 1502, at ten P.M.
E.V.D.

※　※　※

79

Machiavelli to the Ten

Magnificent Lords, etc. Day before yesterday I wrote from Pesaro to Your Lordships describing what I understood of Sinigaglia: yesterday I went to Fano, and this morning early the duke with his whole army came here to Sinigaglia where were assembled all the Orsini and Vitellozzo, who as I wrote before had taken possession of this area. They went into the city, he went in with them and as soon as he was near the center, he turned to his guard and took them all prisoner: and thus he has captured them all, and the district will be sacked everywhere; and it is now eleven P.M. I'm overwhelmed with business; I don't know

6. See *The Prince*, chapter VII.

if I'll be able to send this letter, for lack of anyone going that way. I'll write at length on another occasion; in my opinion, there won't be one of them alive tomorrow morning.

In Sinigaglia, the last day of December 1502.

All their people are in fact taken, and the papers which are being drawn up about them say that the traitors have been captured, etc.

I have given the present bearer three ducats, and Your Lordships will give him another three; for my share you will reimburse Biagio.[7]

Your servant, Nicolaus Machiavellus

8o

Machiavelli to the Ten

Magnificent Lords, etc. Yesterday I wrote two letters to Your Lordships about everything that happened after the arrival of His Excellence the Duke in Sinigaglia, and of how he captured Paolo Orsini, the duke of Gravina, Vitellozzo, and Oliverotto; in the first I simply gave you notice of the event, and in the second I described things in more detail, adding all the things that His Excellency told me, and an account of public opinion regarding this lord and his doings. I would repeat these letters in detail if I thought they had not reached you safely. But as I sent the first with all the force of six ducats and the second with the force of three, by picked men, one Florentine, the other from Urbino, I'm in good hopes. Still, I will summarize everything yet again for Your Lordships, out of an excess of caution, just in case my first letters don't reach you. This lord left Fano yesterday morning, and with his whole army came up to Sinigaglia, which had been occupied, except for the fortress, by the Orsini and Messer Liverotto da Fermo. The day before, Vitellozzo had arrived in the district from Castello; they went one after the other to meet with the duke, and then accompanied him into the town and into a house; and then when they were all together in one room, my lord had them made prisoner; then he had all their troops disarmed, who were in the suburbs around the city, and sent half his own army to disarm some other retainers, who had been placed in different castles six or seven miles around Sinigaglia. Afterwards he called me into his presence about two in the morning, and with the most cheerful expression in the world joked with me about these events, saying that he had spoken to me before about them, but hadn't explained his whole plan, which was true; then he added some wise and unusually affectionate words about our city, explaining all the reasons which made him eager

---

7. Biagio Buonaccorsi, Machiavelli's oldest and most intimate friend.

for your friendship, as long as you aren't found wanting. Indeed, he left
me in a state of astonishment, but I won't expand on this further, since
I described it at length in last night's letter. He concluded that I should
write three things to Your Lordships on his behalf. The first, that I was
delighted with his success in having destroyed those men who were most
bitterly hostile to the king, to himself, and to you; and in taking away
every seed of scandal and discord that could have disturbed Italy; for all
of which Your Lordships are much obliged to him. Next, that I should
earnestly request and beseech Your Lordships in his name, that in order
to make clear to the whole world that you have been his friends in this
matter, you should send some cavalry to Borgo, and assemble some
troops, so that you can move with him against Castello or Perugia,
which are the next orders of business. And he said he wanted to move
swiftly in this matter, and would have marched last night, if he hadn't
been afraid that when he left town Sinigaglia would be put to the sack.
And again he asked me to write that you should make every demonstration possible of being friendly to him, adding that for the present
there was no reason to fear or suspect anything, since he was well armed
and all your enemies were captured. *Finally*, he asked me to write Your
Lordships, in connection with the capture of Vitellozzo, that if Duke
Guido,[8] who is at Castello, should take refuge in your districts, he would
appreciate your holding him a prisoner. I said that giving up political
refugees didn't suit with the dignity of our city, and that you would
never do it; he answered that I talked very well, but it would be quite
adequate if Your Lordships simply held him in custody, and didn't let
him go without prior approval. I agreed to write everything; and he will
expect your answer.

I also wrote in my letter of yesterday that many men, well disposed
and friendly to our city, have suggested to me that this was a great
occasion for Your Lordships to place your city to advantage in the new
order of things. Everyone thinks that with regard to France, Your Lordships can safely trust them; and the feeling here is that you should send
one of your chief citizens to be ambassador there, particularly because
of this turn of events, and not postpone this action, because a man of
position who comes there with specific proposals to make, will find a
good response. This point has been made to me time and again by
people who wish well to our city; and I write it to Your Lordships with
the same sincerity that I have always observed toward you. And this is
in substance what I wrote in my second letter yesterday, perhaps even
spelled out in more detail.

As for recent developments, last night about ten o'clock this lord had
Vitellozzo and Oliverotto da Fermo put to death; the other two are still

8. Guidobaldo da Montefeltro, duke of Urbino, currently out of a job.

alive; it's thought they are waiting to see if the pope has his hands on the cardinal and the others at Rome. If he has, as they think, then they'll dispose of the whole parcel at once.

This morning early the fortress of Sinigaglia surrendered to the duke, and is now in his power; His Lordship left the same morning, and came here with his army; from here they will be heading toward Perugia or Castello for certain, and perhaps toward Siena; then they'll move down toward Rome, taking over all those strongholds of the Orsini, and the plan is to capture Bracciano, after which the others will go like a bonfire of straw. All this however is just popular conjecture. I'll remain here all day tomorrow, and the next day stay at Sassoferrato. You can imagine what sort of weather this is for making war, indeed you wouldn't believe it if I told you the hardships these troops are undergoing, as well as anyone who accompanies them, because it's a lucky man who has a roof over his head.

Messer Goro da Pistoia, an enemy of our city and rebel against it,[9] was with Vitellozzo, and is now being held here by certain Spaniards; I think for two hundred ducats, if Your Lordships wanted to spend that much, you could arrange for one of his present keepers to turn him over to one of your officials. Let Your Lordships consider this matter, and let me know what you think of it: I commend myself to Your Lordships; May all things go well with you.

Your servant, Nicholaus Machiavellus, Secretary

From Corinaldo, the first day of January 1503.
E.V.D.

*   *   *

---

9. Goro da Pistoia was an active agent of the Medici in their efforts to overthrow the republic, and so a declared enemy of Machiavelli's party.

Machiavelli the Democrat

NICCOLÒ MACHIAVELLI

From *Discourses on the First Ten Books of Titus Livius*†

[In chapter II of *The Prince* Machiavelli says that he will not discuss republics in this present treatise "because I've talked of them at length on another occasion." It is accepted that he is referring here to the *Discourses on Titus Livius*, or at least some of them—how much is still under earnest scholarly debate. Since we can be sure *The Prince* was written in 1513, it is clear also that after that date many of them were read to—and perhaps revised for— a group of intellectuals who made it a custom to meet from time to time informally in the Rucellai gardens known as the Orti Oricellari, off present via della Scala in Florence. Such clubs, academies, and informal gatherings were frequent in Renaissance Italy; not even the fact that the Medici were in power and many members of the group were known to share republican sentiments, limited the freedom of discussion. In the presence of people who shared his own interests, background, and social standing, Machiavelli was clearly free to speak at more liberty than in *The Prince*, and at greater length. Princes have short attention spans, and must be fed wisdom in capsule doses; people who live by ideas are more willing to hear them discussed fully. Without implying that Machiavelli was a hypocrite in *The Prince*, one can nevertheless sense that he must have expressed his mind more broadly in the *Discourses*.

The form of the book calls for some explanation. Titus Livius was a native of Padua and a contemporary of Augustus, who wrote his gigantic history of Rome from the first founding of the city; its customary title is just that: *Ab urbe condita* ("From the founding of the city"). It must have been an enormous book; what survives is only thirty-five books out of an original one hundred and forty-two, and this makes a substantial volume that we in English customarily refer to simply as "Livy." Machiavelli had a special feeling for Livy in the first place because the historian, though he had lived under the empire and had to deal with emperors, was a vigorous admirer of the Roman republic. In addition, Machiavelli's father had contributed

† The text is taken from *The Prince and the Discourses* (Modern Library, 1940); the translation, by Christian Edward Detmold, was originally published in Boston, in 1882. Footnotes are by the editor of this Norton Critical Edition, who has also made a few silent corrections in the Detmold translation.

an index to one of the very early printed editions of Livy and had been rewarded with a copy of the book; Machiavelli grew up with the volume, and imbibed from his early youth its strong assurance that practical lessons about human behavior could be learned by studying the historic past. Livy is the most warmly didactic of the Roman historians—more of the patrician than of the plebeian party, but above all an outspoken patriot, intent on learning from the glorious past what will help imperial Romans to deal with their dark present and even darker future.]

[Book I]

INTRODUCTION

Although the envious nature of men, so prompt to blame and so slow to praise, makes the discovery and introduction of any new principles and systems as dangerous almost as the exploration of unknown seas and continents, yet, animated by that natural desire which impels me to do what may prove for the common benefit of all, I have resolved to open a new route, which has not yet been followed by any one, and may prove difficult and troublesome, but may also bring me some reward in the approbation of those who will kindly consider the aim of my efforts.

And if my poor talents, my little experience of the present and insufficient study of the past, should make the result of my labors defective and of little utility, I shall at least have shown the way to others, who will carry out my views with greater ability, eloquence, and judgment, so that if I do not merit praise, I ought at least not to incur censure.

When we consider the general respect for antiquity, and how often —to say nothing of other examples—a great price is paid for some fragments of an antique statue, which we are anxious to possess to ornament our houses with, or to set before artists who strive to imitate them in their own works; and when we see, on the other hand, the wonderful examples which the history of ancient kingdoms and republics presents to us, the prodigies of virtue and of wisdom displayed by the kings, captains, citizens, and legislators who have sacrificed themselves for their country—when we see these, I say, more admired than imitated, or so much neglected that not the least trace of this ancient virtue remains, we cannot but be at the same time as much surprised as afflicted. The more so as in the differences which arise between citizens, or in the maladies to which they are subjected, we see these same people have recourse to the judgments and the remedies prescribed by the ancients. The civil laws are in fact nothing but decisions given by their jurisconsults, and which, reduced to a system, direct our modern jurists in their decisions. And what is the science of medicine, but the experience of ancient physicians, which their successors have taken for their guide? And yet to found a republic, maintain states, to govern a kingdom, organize an army, conduct a war, dispense justice, and extend empires, you will find neither prince, nor republic, nor captain, nor citizen, who has recourse to the examples of antiquity! This neglect, I am persuaded, is due less to the weakness to which the vices of our religion have reduced the world, than to the evils caused by the proud indolence which prevails in most of the Christian states, and to the lack of real knowledge of history, the true sense of which is not known, or the spirit of which they do not comprehend. Thus the majority of those who read it take pleasure only in the variety of the events which history relates, without ever thinking of imitating the noble actions, deeming that not only difficult, but impossible; as though heaven, the sun, the elements, and men had changed the order of their motions and power, and were different from what they were in ancient times.

Wishing, therefore, so far as in me lies, to draw mankind from this error, I have thought it proper to write upon those books of Titus Livius that have come to us entire despite the malice of time; touching upon all those matters which, after a comparison between the ancient and modern events, may seem to me necessary to facilitate their proper understanding. In this way those who read my remarks may derive those advantages which should be the aim of all study of history; and although the undertaking is difficult, yet, aided by those who have encouraged me in this attempt, I hope to carry it sufficiently far, so that but little may remain for others to carry it to its destined end.

* * *

[Book I, Chapter 2]

OF THE DIFFERENT KINDS OF REPUBLICS, AND OF WHAT KIND THE ROMAN REPUBLIC WAS

I will leave aside what might be said of cities which from their very birth have been subject to a foreign power, and will speak only of those whose origin has been independent, and which from the first governed themselves by their own laws, whether as republics or as principalities, and whose constitution and laws have differed as their origin. Some have had at the very beginning, or soon after, a legislator, who, like Lycurgus with the Lacedæmonians,[1] gave them by a single act all the laws they needed. Others have owed theirs to chance and to events, and have received their laws at different times, as Rome did. It is a great good fortune for a republic to have a legislator sufficiently wise to give her laws so regulated that, without the necessity of correcting them, they afford security to those who live under them. Sparta observed her laws for more than eight hundred years without altering them and without

1. Lycurgus, a semi-mythical figure whose "life" was written by Plutarch, is said to have given the Spartans (Lacedaemonians) a complete code of laws at a single stroke.

experiencing a single dangerous disturbance. Unhappy, on the contrary, is that republic which, not having at the beginning fallen into the hands of a sagacious and skillful legislator, is herself obliged to reform her laws. More unhappy still is that republic which from the first has diverged from a good constitution. And that republic is furthest from it whose vicious institutions impede her progress, and make her leave the right path that leads to a good end; for those who are in that condition can hardly ever be brought into the right road. Those republics, on the other hand, that started without having a perfect constitution, but made a fair beginning, and are capable of improvement,—such republics, I say, may perfect themselves by the aid of events. It is very true, however, that such reforms are never effected without danger, for the majority of men never willingly adopt any new law tending to change the constitution of the state, unless the necessity of the change is clearly demonstrated; and as such a necessity cannot make itself felt without being accompanied with danger, the republic may easily be destroyed before having perfected its constitution. That of Florence is a complete proof of this: reorganized after the revolt of Arezzo, in 1502, it was overthrown after the taking of Prato, in 1512.[2]

Having proposed to myself to treat of the kind of government established at Rome, and of the events that led to its perfection, I must at the beginning observe that some of the writers on politics distinguished three kinds of government, viz. the monarchical, the aristocratic, and the democratic; and maintain that the legislators of a people must choose from these three the one that seems to them most suitable. Other authors, wiser according to the opinion of many, count six kinds of governments, three of which are very bad, and three good in themselves, but so liable to be corrupted that they become absolutely bad. The three good ones are those which we have just named; the three bad ones result from the degradation of the other three, and each of them resembles its corresponding original, so that the transition from the one to the other is very easy. Thus monarchy becomes tyranny; aristocracy degenerates into oligarchy; and the popular government lapses readily into licentiousness. So that a legislator who gives to a state which he founds either of these three forms of government, constitutes it but for a brief time; for no precautions can prevent either one of the three that are reputed good, from degenerating into its opposite kind; so great are in these the attractions and resemblances between the good and the evil.

Chance has given birth to these different kinds of governments amongst men; for at the beginning of the world the inhabitants were few in number, and lived for a time dispersed, like beasts. As the human race increased, the necessity for uniting themselves for defence made itself felt; the better to attain this object, they chose the strongest and

2. Machiavelli speaks coolly and impassively of a failed experiment to which he had devoted his entire political life.

most courageous from amongst themselves and placed him at their head, promising to obey him. Thence they began to know the good and the honest, and to distinguish them from the bad and vicious; for seeing a man injure his benefactor aroused at once two sentiments in every heart, hatred against the ingrate and love for the benefactor. They blamed the first, and on the contrary honored those the more who showed themselves grateful, for each felt that he in turn might be subject to a like wrong; and to prevent similar evils, they set to work to make laws, and to institute punishments for those who contravened them. Such was the origin of justice. This caused them, when they had afterwards to choose a prince, neither to look to the strongest nor bravest, but to the wisest and most just. But when they began to make sovereignty hereditary and non-elective, the children quickly degenerated from their fathers; and, so far from trying to equal their virtues, they considered that a prince had nothing else to do than to excel all the rest in luxury, indulgence, and every other variety of pleasure. The prince consequently soon drew upon himself the general hatred. An object of hatred, he naturally felt fear; fear in turn dictated to him precautions and wrongs, and thus tyranny quickly developed itself. Such were the beginning and causes of disorders, conspiracies, and plots against the sovereigns, set on foot, not by the feeble and timid, but by those citizens who, surpassing the others in grandeur of soul, in wealth, and in courage, could not submit to the outrages and excesses of their princes.

Under such powerful leaders the masses armed themselves against the tyrant, and, after having rid themselves of him, submitted to these chiefs as their liberators. These, abhorring the very name of prince, constituted themselves a new government; and at first, bearing in mind the past tyranny, they governed in strict accordance with the laws which they had established themselves; preferring public interests to their own, and to administer and protect with greatest care both public and private affairs. The children succeeded their fathers, and ignorant of the changes of fortune, having never experienced its reverses, and indisposed to remain content with this civil equality, they in turn gave themselves up to cupidity, ambition, libertinage, and violence, and soon caused the aristocratic government to degenerate into an oligarchic tyranny, regardless of all civil rights. They soon, however, experienced the same fate as the first tyrant; the people, disgusted with their government, placed themselves at the command of whoever was willing to attack them, and this disposition soon produced an avenger, who was sufficiently well seconded to destroy them. The memory of the prince and the wrongs committed by him being still fresh in their minds, and having overthrown the oligarchy, the people were not willing to return to the government of a prince. A popular government was therefore resolved upon, and it was so organized that the authority should not again fall into the hands of a prince or a small number of nobles. And as all governments are at first looked up to with some degree of reverence, the popular state also maintained itself for a time, but not for long, lasting generally for about the lifetime of the generation that had established it; for it soon ran into that kind of license which inflicts injury upon public as well as private interests. Each individual only consulted his own passions, and a thousand acts of injustice were daily committed, so that, constrained by necessity, or directed by the counsels of some good man, or for the purpose of escaping from this anarchy, they returned anew to the government of a prince, and from this they generally lapsed again into anarchy, step by step, in the same manner and from the same causes as we have indicated.

Such is the circle which all republics are destined to run through. Seldom, however, do they come back to the original form of government, which results from the fact that their duration is not sufficiently long to be able to undergo these repeated changes and preserve their existence. But it may well happen that a republic lacking strength and good counsel in its difficulties becomes subject after a while to some neighboring state, that is better organized than itself; and if such is not the case, then they will be apt to revolve indefinitely in the circle of revolutions. I say, then, that all kinds of government are defective; those three which we have qualified as good because they are too short-lived, and the three bad ones because of their inherent viciousness. Thus sagacious legislators, knowing the vices of each of these systems of government by themselves, have chosen one that should partake of all of them, judging that to be the most stable and solid. In fact, when there is combined under the same constitution a prince, a nobility, and the power of the people, then these three powers will watch and keep each other reciprocally in check.

✻ ✻ ✻

[Book I, Chapter 6]

WHETHER IT WAS POSSIBLE TO ESTABLISH IN ROME A GOVERNMENT CAPABLE OF PUTTING AN END TO THE ENMITIES EXISTING BETWEEN THE NOBLES AND THE PEOPLE

We have discussed above the effects of the quarrels between the people and the senate. These same differences having continued to the time of the Gracchi,[3] when they became the cause of the loss of liberty, one might wish that Rome had done the great things we have admired, without bearing within her bosom such cause of discords. It seems to me therefore important to examine whether it was possible to establish

3. The Gracchi were popular Roman reformers of the second century B.C. See *The Prince*, chapter IX and note 3, page 29.

a government in Rome that could prevent all these misunderstandings; and to do this well, we must necessarily recur to those republics that have maintained their liberties without such enmities and disturbances; we must examine what the form of their goverment was, and whether that could have been introduced in Rome.

In Sparta we have an example amongst the ancients, and in Venice amongst the moderns; to both these states I have already referred above. Sparta had a king and a senate, few in number, to govern her; Venice did not admit these distinctions, and gave the name of gentlemen to all who were entitled to have a part in the administration of the government. It was chance rather than foresight which gave to the latter this form of government; for having taken refuge on those shallows where the city now is, for the reasons mentioned above, the inhabitants soon became sufficiently numerous to require a regular system of laws. They consequently established a government, and assembled frequently in council to discuss the interests of the city. When it seemed to them that they were sufficiently numerous to govern themselves, they barred the way to share in the government to the newly arrived who came to live amongst them; and finding in the course of time that the number of the latter increased sufficiently to give reputation to those who held the government in their hands, they designated the latter by the title of "gentlemen," and the others were called the popular class. This form of government had no difficulty in establishing and maintaining itself without disturbances; for at the moment of its origin all those who inhabited Venice had the right to participate in the government, so that no one had cause to complain. Those who afterwards came to live there, finding the government firmly established, had neither a pretext for, nor the means of, creating disturbances. They had no cause, for the reason that they had not been deprived of anything; and they lacked the means, because they were kept in check by those who held the government, and who did not employ them in any affairs that might tempt them to seize authority. Besides, the new-comers in Venice were not sufficiently numerous to have produced a disproportion between the governing and the governed, for the number of nobles equalled or exceeded that of the others; and thus for these reasons Venice could establish and preserve that form of government.

Sparta, as I have said, being governed by a king and a limited senate, could maintain itself also for a long time, because there were but few inhabitants, and strangers were not permitted to come in; besides, the laws of Lycurgus had obtained such influence that their observance prevented even the slightest pretext for trouble. It was also the easier for the citizens to live in union, as Lycurgus had established equality in fortunes and inequality in conditions; for an equal poverty prevailed there, and the people were the less ambitious, as the offices of the government were given but to a few citizens, the people being excluded

from them; and the nobles in the exercise of their functions did not treat
the people sufficiently ill to excite in them the desire of exercising them
themselves. This last advantage was due to the kings of Sparta; for being
placed in this government, as it were, between the two orders, and living
in the midst of the nobility, they had no better means of maintaining
their authority than to protect the people against all injustice; whence
these neither feared nor desired authority, and consequently there was
no motive for any differences between them and the nobles, nor any
cause for disturbances; and thus they could live for a long time united.
Two principal causes, however, cemented this union: first, the inhabitants of Sparta were few in number, and therefore could be governed
by a few; and the other was, that, by not permitting strangers to establish
themselves in the republic, they had neither opportunity of becoming
corrupt, nor of increasing their population to such a degree that the
burden of government became difficult to the few who were charged
with it.

In examining now all these circumstances, we see that the legislators
of Rome had to do one of two things to assure to their republic the same
quiet as that enjoyed by the two republics of which we have spoken;
namely, either not to employ the people in the armies, like the Venetians, or not to open the doors to strangers, as had been the case in
Sparta. But the Romans in both took just the opposite course, which
gave to the people greater power and infinite occasion for disturbances.
But if the republic had been more tranquil, it would necessarily have
resulted that she would have been more feeble, and that she would have
lost with her energy also the ability of achieving that high degree of
greatness to which she attained; so that to have removed the cause of
trouble from Rome would have been to deprive her of her power of
expansion. And thus it is seen in all human affairs, upon careful examination, that you cannot avoid one inconvenience without incurring
another. If therefore you wish to make a people numerous and warlike,
so as to create a great empire, you will have to constitute it in such
manner as will cause you more difficulty in managing it; and if you
keep it either small or unarmed, and you acquire other dominions, you
will not be able to hold them, or you will become so feeble that you
will fall a prey to whoever attacks you. And therefore in all our decisions
we must consider well what presents the least inconveniences, and take
that for the best, for we shall never find any course entirely free from
objections. Rome then might, like Sparta, have created a king for life,
and established a limited senate; but with her desire to become a great
empire, she could not, like Sparta, limit the number of her citizens;
and therefore a king for life and a limited senate would have been of
no benefit to her so far as union was concerned. If any one therefore
wishes to establish an entirely new republic, he will have to consider
whether he wishes to have her expand in power and dominion like

Rome, or whether he intends to confine her within narrow limits. In the first case, it will be necessary to organize her as Rome was, and submit to dissensions and troubles as best he may; for without a great number of men, and these well armed, no republic can ever increase or hold its new possessions. In the second case, he may organize her like Sparta and Venice; but as expansion is the poison of such republics, he must prevent her from making conquests, for such acquisitions by a feeble republic lead to ruin, as happened to both Sparta and Venice; the first of which, having subjected to her rule nearly all Greece, exposed its feeble foundations at the slightest accident, for when the rebellion of Thebes occurred, which was led by Pelopidas,[4] the other cities of Greece also rose up and almost ruined Sparta.

In like manner, Venice, having obtained possession of a great part of Italy, and the most of it not by war, but by means of money and fraud, when occasion came for her to give proof of her strength, she lost everything in a single battle.[5] I think, then, that to found a republic which should endure a long time it would be best to organize her internally like Sparta, or to locate her, like Venice, in some strong place; and to make her sufficiently powerful, so that no one could hope to overcome her readily, and yet on the other hand not so powerful as to make her formidable to her neighbors. In this wise she might long enjoy her independence. For there are but two motives for making war against a republic: one, the desire to subjugate her; the other, the apprehension of being subjugated by her. The two means which we have indicated remove, as it were, both these pretexts for war; for if the republic is difficult to be conquered, her defences being well organized, as I pre-suppose, then it will seldom or never happen that any one will venture upon the project of conquering her. If she remains quiet within her limits, and experience shows that she entertains no ambitious projects, the fear of her power will never prompt any one to attack her; and this would even be more certainly the case if her constitution and laws prohibited all aggrandizement. And I certainly think that if she could be kept in this equilibrium it would be the best political existence, and would insure to any state real tranquillity. But as all human things are kept in a perpetual movement, and can never remain stable, states naturally either rise or decline, and necessity compels them to many acts to which reason will not influence them; so that, having organized a republic competent to maintain herself without expanding, still, if forced by necessity to extend her territory, in such case we shall see her foundations give way and herself quickly brought to ruin. And thus, on the other hand, if Heaven favors her so as never to be involved in war, the continued tranquillity would enervate her, or provoke internal dis-

---

4. In 379 B.C. Pelopidas of Thebes led a successful revolt against the Spartans, who had conquered and occupied his city.

5. The battle of Vailà. See *The Prince*, chapter XII, note 7, page 36.

sensions, which together, or either of them separately, will be apt to prove her ruin. Seeing then the impossibility of establishing in this respect a perfect equilibrium, and that a precise middle course cannot be maintained, it is proper in the organization of a republic to select the most honorable course, and to constitute her so that, even if necessity should oblige her to expand, she may yet be able to preserve her acquisitions. To return now to our first argument, I believe it therefore necessary to take the constitution of Rome as a model rather than that of any other republic (for I do not believe that a middle course between the two can be found), and to tolerate the differences that will arise between the Senate and the people as an unavoidable inconvenience in achieving greatness like that of Rome.

∗   ∗   ∗

[Book I, Chapter 12]

THE IMPORTANCE OF GIVING RELIGION A PROMINENT INFLUENCE IN A STATE, AND HOW ITALY WAS RUINED BECAUSE SHE FAILED IN THIS RESPECT THROUGH THE CONDUCT OF THE CHURCH OF ROME.

Princes and republics who wish to maintain themselves free from corruption must above all things preserve the purity of all religious observances, and treat them with proper reverence; for there is no greater indication of the ruin of a country than to see religion contemned. And this is easily understood, when we know upon what the religion of a country is founded; for the essence of every religion is based upon some one main principle. The religion of the Gentiles had for its foundation the responses of the oracles, and the tenets of the augurs and aruspices; upon these alone depended all their ceremonies, rites, and sacrifices. For they readily believed that the Deity which could predict their future good or ill was also able to bestow it upon them. Thence arose their temples, their sacrifices, their supplications, and all the other ceremonies; for the oracle of Delos, the temple of Jupiter Ammon, and other celebrated oracles, kept the world in admiration and devoutness. But when these afterwards began to speak only in accordance with the wishes of the princes, and their falsity was discovered by the people, then men became incredulous, and disposed to disturb all good institutions. It is therefore the duty of princes and heads of republics to uphold the foundations of the religion of their countries, for then it is easy to keep their people religious, and consequently well conducted and united. And therefore everything that tends to favor religion (even though it were believed to be false) should be received and availed of to strengthen it; and this should be done the more, the wiser the rulers are, and the better they understand the natural course of things. Such was, in fact, the practice observed by sagacious men; which has given rise to the belief in the miracles that are celebrated in religions, however false they may be. For the sagacious rulers have given these miracles increased importance, no matter whence or how they originated; and their authority afterwards gave them credence with the people. Rome had many such miracles; and one of the most remarkable was that which occurred when the Roman soldiers sacked the city of Veii; some of them entered the temple of Juno, and, placing themselves in front of her statue, said to her, "Will you come to Rome?" Some imagined that they observed the statue make a sign of assent, and others pretended to have heard her reply, "Yes." Now these men, being very religious, as reported by Titus Livius, and having entered the temple quietly, they were filled with devotion and reverence, and might really have believed that they had heard a reply to their question, such as perhaps they could have presupposed. But this opinion and belief was favored and magnified by Camillus and the other Roman chiefs.[6]

And certainly, if the Christian religion had from the beginning been maintained according to the principles of its founder, the Christian states and republics would be much more united and happy than in fact they are. Nor can there be a greater proof of its decadence than to witness the fact that the nearer people are to the Church of Rome, which is the head of our religion, the less religious are they. And whoever examines the principles upon which that religion is founded, and sees how widely different from those principles its present practice and application are, will judge that her ruin or chastisement is near at hand. But as there are some of the opinion that the well-being of Italian affairs depends upon the Church of Rome, I will present such arguments against that opinion as occur to me; two of which are most important, and cannot according to my judgment be controverted. The first is, that the evil example of the court of Rome has destroyed all piety and religion in Italy, which brings in its train infinite improprieties and disorders; for as we may presuppose all good where religion prevails, so where it is wanting we have the right to suppose the very opposite. We Italians then owe to the Church of Rome and to her priests our having become irreligious and bad; but we owe her a still greater debt, and one that may cause our ruin, namely, that the Church has kept and still keeps our country divided. And certainly a country can never be united and happy, except when it obeys wholly one government, whether a republic or a monarchy, as is the case in France and in Spain; and the sole cause why Italy is not in the same condition, and is not governed by either one republic or one sovereign, is the Church; for having acquired and holding a temporal dominion, yet she has never had sufficient power or courage to enable her to seize the rest of the country and make herself

6. Livy, 5.22.

sole sovereign of all Italy. And on the other hand she has not been so feeble that the fear of losing her temporal power prevented her from calling in the aid of a foreign power to defend her against such others as had become too powerful in Italy; as was seen in former days by many sad experiences, when through the intervention of Charlemagne she drove out the Lombards, who were masters of nearly all Italy; and when in our times she crushed the power of the Venetians by the aid of France, and afterwards with the assistance of the Swiss drove out in turn the French.[7] The Church, then, not having been powerful enough to be able to master all Italy, nor having permitted any other power to do so, has been the cause why Italy has never been able to unite under one head, but has always remained under a number of princes and lords, which occasioned her so many dissensions and so much weakness that she became a prey not only to the powerful barbarians, but to whoever chose to assail her. This we other Italians owe to the Church of Rome, and to none other. And any one, to be promptly convinced by experiment of the truth of all this, should have the power to transport the court of Rome to reside, with all the power it has in Italy, in the midst of the Swiss, who of all the peoples nowadays live most according to their ancient customs so far as religion and their military system are concerned; and he would see in a very little while that the evil habits of that court would create more confusion in that country than anything else that could ever happen there.

*   *   *

[Book I, Chapter 27]

SHOWING THAT MEN ARE VERY RARELY EITHER ENTIRELY GOOD OR ENTIRELY BAD

When Pope Julius II went, in the year 1505, to Bologna to expel the Bentivogli from that state, the government of which they had held for a hundred years, he wanted also to remove Giovanpaolo Baglioni from Perugia, who had made himself the absolute master of that city; for it was the intention of Pope Julius to destroy all the petty tyrants that occupied the possessions of the Church. Having arrived at Perugia with that purpose, which was well known to everybody, he did not wait to enter the city with his army for protection, but went in almost alone, although Giovanpaolo had collected a large force within the city for his defense. And thus, with the customary impetuosity which characterized all his acts, Julius placed himself with only a small guard in the hands of his enemy Baglioni, whom he nevertheless carried off with him, leaving a governor in his stead to administer the state in the name of

7. In capsule form, these are the events of 1509–12.

the Church. Sagacious men who were with the pope observed his temerity and the cowardice of Baglioni, and could not understand why the latter had not by a single blow rid himself of his enemy, whereby he would have secured for himself eternal fame and rich booty, for the Pope was accompanied by all the cardinals with their valuables. Nor could they believe that he had refrained from doing this either from goodness or conscientious scruples; for no sentiment of piety or respect could enter the heart of a man of such vile character as Giovanpaolo, who had dishonored his sister, and murdered his nephews and cousins for the sake of obtaining possession of the state; but they concluded that mankind were neither utterly wicked nor perfectly good, and that when a crime has in itself some grandeur or magnanimity they will not know how to attempt it. Thus Giovanpaolo Baglioni, who did not mind open incest and parricide, knew not how to, or, more correctly speaking, dared not, attempt an act (although having a justifiable opportunity) for which everyone would have admired his courage, and which would have secured him eternal fame, as being the first to show these prelates how little esteem men merit who live and govern as they do. And he would have done an act the greatness of which would have overshadowed all the infamy and danger that could possibly result from it.

[Book I, Chapter 28]

WHY ROME WAS LESS UNGRATEFUL TO HER CITIZENS THAN ATHENS

In reading the history of republics we find in all of them a degree of ingratitude to their citizens; this, however, seems to have been the case to a less extent in Rome than in Athens, and perhaps less even than in any other republic. In seeking for the reason of this difference, so far as Rome and Athens are concerned, I believe it was because Rome had less cause for mistrusting her citizens than Athens. In fact, from the time of the expulsion of the kings until Sulla and Marius,[8] no Roman citizen ever attempted to deprive his country of her liberty; so that, there being no occasion to suspect her citizens, there was consequently no cause for offending them unnecessarily. The very contrary happened in Athens, for Pisistratus had by fraud robbed her of her liberty at the very time of her highest prosperity; so soon as she afterwards recovered her freedom, remembering the injuries received and her past servitude, she resented with the utmost harshness, not only all faults, but the mere semblance of faults, on the part of her citizens. It was this that gave rise to the exile and death of of so many of her illustrious men, and thence came the practice of ostracism and every other violence which that city exercised at various times against some of her noblest citizens. It is a very true saying of political writers, that those states which have recovered

8. From the sixth to the first century B.C.

their liberty treat their citizens with greater severity than such as have never lost it. A careful consideration of what has been said on this subject will show that Athens is neither to be blamed, nor Rome to be praised, for their respective conduct, and that it necessarily resulted entirely from the difference of the events that occured in those cities; for a penetrating observer will not fail to see that, if Rome had been deprived of her liberty in the manner Athens was, she would not have been more indulgent to her citizens than the latter. We may judge very correctly of this by her treatment of Collatinus and Publius Valerius after the expulsion of the kings; the first was exiled for no other reason than that he bore the name of the Tarquins, and the other was likewise sent into exile because he had excited suspicion by building a house on Mount Cœlius.[9] Seeing then how suspicious and severe Rome showed herself in these two cases, we may fairly judge that she would have been liable to the charge of ingratitude, the same as Athens, if she had been offended by her citizens in the beginning of her existence, before she had grown powerful. And so as not to be obliged to return to this subject of ingratitude, I shall continue what I have to say in relation to it in the next chapter.

[Book I, Chapter 29]

WHICH OF THE TWO IS MOST UNGRATEFUL, A PEOPLE OR A PRINCE

It seems to me proper here, in connection with the above subject, to examine whether the people or a prince is more liable to the charge of ingratitude; and by way of illustrating this question the better, I set out by saying that the vice of ingratitude springs either from avarice or fear. For when a people or a prince has sent a general on some important expedition where by his success he acquires great glory, the prince or people is in turn bound to reward him. But if instead of such reward they dishonor and wrong him, influenced thereto by avarice, then they are guilty of an inexcusable wrong, which will involve them in eternal infamy. And yet there are many princes who commit this wrong, for which fact Tacitus assigns the reason in the following sentence: "Men are more ready to repay an injury than a benefit, because gratitude is a burden and revenge a pleasure."[1] But when they fail to reward, or rather when they offend, not from avarice, but from suspicion and fear, then the people or the prince have some excuse for their ingratitude. We read of many instances of this kind; for the general who by his valor has conquered a state for his master, and won great glory for himself by his victory over the enemy, and has loaded his soldiers with rich booty, acquires necessarily with his own soldiers, as well as with those of the

9. Livy 2.2.6–8.   1. Tacitus, *History* 4.3.

enemy and with the subjects of the prince, so high a reputation, that his very victory may become distasteful and a cause for apprehension to his prince. For as the nature of men is ambitious as well as suspicious, and puts no limits to one's good fortune, it is not impossible that the suspicion that may suddenly be aroused in the mind of the prince by the victory of the general may have been aggravated by some haughty expressions or insolent acts on his part; so that the prince will naturally be made to think of securing himself against the ambition of the general. And to do this, the means that suggest themselves to him are either to have the general killed, or to deprive him of that reputation which he has acquired with the prince's army and the people, by using every means to prove that the general's victory was not due to his skill and courage, but to chance and the cowardice of the enemy, or to the sagacity of the other captains who were with him in that action.

After Vespasian, while in Judæa, had been declared Emperor by his army, Antonius Primus, who was at the head of another army in Illyria, took sides with him, and marched straight into Italy against Vitellius, then Emperor in Rome, and in the most gallant manner routed two Vitellian armies, and made himself master of Rome; so that Mutianus, who had been sent there by Vespasian, found everything achieved and all difficulties overcome. The reward which Antonius received for this service was that Mutianus deprived him of the command of the army, and gradually reduced his authority in Rome to nothing; so that Antonius, indignant, went to see Vespasian, who was still in Asia, who received him in such manner that, being soon after deprived of all rank, he died almost in despair. History is full of similar examples.[2]

We have seen in our own day with how much courage and perseverance Gonsalvo de Cordoba conducted the war in Naples for King Ferdinand of Aragon against the French; how he defeated them, and conquered the kingdom of Ferdinand; and how he was rewarded by his king, who left Spain and came to Naples, and first deprived Gonsalvo of his command of the army, and then took the control of the strong places from him, and finally carried him off with him to Spain, where Gonsalvo soon after died in obscurity.[3]

Fear and suspicion are so natural to princes that they cannot defend themselves against them, and thus it is impossible for them to show gratitude to those who, by victories achieved under their banners, have made important conquests for them. If then a prince cannot prevent himself from committing such wrongs, it is surely no wonder, nor matter worthy of more consideration, if a people acts in a similar manner. For as a free city is generally influenced by two principal objects, the one

2. Tacitus, *History* 3.4.
3. Gonsalvo de Cordoba (1453–1515) was known, because of his extraordinary record of victories, as the "Gran Capitan." A full account of his military triumphs, and of the pointed neglect that was their reward, can be collected from W. H. Prescott's creaky but vital *Ferdinand and Isabella* (1837).

to aggrandize herself, and the other to preserve her liberties, it is natural that she should occasionally be betrayed into faults by excessive eagerness in the pursuit of either of these objects. As to the faults that result from the desire for aggrandizement, we shall speak in another place; and those resulting from the desire to preserve her liberty are amongst others the following, namely, to injure those citizens whom she should reward, and to suspect those in whom she should place the most confidence. And although the effects of such conduct occasion great evils in a republic that is already corrupt, and which often lead to despotism,—as was seen under Cæsar in Rome, who took for himself by force what ingratitude had refused him,—still, in a republic not yet entirely corrupt, they may be productive of great good in preserving her freedom for a greater length of time; as the dread of punishment will keep men better, and less ambitious.

It is true that, of all the people who have ever possessed a great empire, the Romans were the least ungrateful; for it may be said that no other instance of their ingratitude can be cited than that of Scipio; for Coriolanus and Camillus were both exiled on account of the outrages which they had committed upon the people. The one was never pardoned, because he always preserved an implacable hatred against the people; but the other was not only recalled from exile, but was for the entire remainder of his life honored like a prince. The ingratitude to Scipio arose from jealousy such as never before had been felt towards any one else, and which resulted from the greatness of the enemy whom Scipio had conquered, from the great reputation which his victory after so long and perilous a war had given him, for the rapidity of his actions and the popular favor which his youth, his prudence, and other remarkable virtues had won for him. All of these were so great that everybody in Rome, even the magistrates, feared his influence and authority, which offended the intelligent men of Rome as an unheard of thing. And his manner of life was such that Cato the elder, who was reputed a man of the purest character, was the first to complain of him, saying that no city could call herself free where a citizen was feared by the magistrates. So that if in this case the people of Rome followed the opinion of Cato, they are entitled to that excuse which, as I have said above, those peoples and princes may claim who are ungrateful from suspicion and fear. In concluding, then, this dicourse, I say that, as the vice of ingratitude is usually the consequence of either avarice or fear, it will be seen that the people never fall into this error from avarice, and that fear also makes them less liable to it than princes, inasmuch as they have less reason for fear, as we shall show further on.

✳　✳　✳

[Book I, Chapter 37]

WHAT TROUBLES RESULTED IN ROME FROM THE ENACTMENT OF THE AGRARIAN LAW, AND HOW VERY WRONG IT IS TO MAKE LAWS THAT ARE RETROSPECTIVE AND CONTRARY TO OLD ESTABLISHED CUSTOMS

It was a saying of ancient writers, that men afflict themselves in evil, and become weary of the good, and that both these dispositions produce the same effects. For when men are no longer obliged to fight from necessity, they fight from ambition, which passion is so powerful in the hearts of men that it never leaves them, no matter to what height they may rise. The reason of this is that nature has created men so that they desire everything, but are unable to attain it; desire being thus always greater than the faculty of acquiring, discontent with what they have and dissatisfaction with themselves result from it. This causes the changes in their fortunes; for as some men desire to have more, whilst others fear to lose what they have, enmities and war are the consequences; and this brings about the ruin of one province and the elevation of another. I have made these remarks because the Roman people were not content with having secured themselves against the nobles by the creation of the Tribunes, to which they had been driven by necessity. Having obtained this, they soon began to fight from ambition, and wanted to divide with the nobles their honors and possessions, being those things which men value most. Thence the frenzy that occasioned the contentions about the agrarian law, which finally caused the destruction of the Roman republic. Now, as in well-regulated republics the state ought to be rich and the citizens poor, it was evident that the agrarian law was in some respects defective; it was either in the beginning so made that it required constant modifications; or the change in it had been so long deferred that it became most obnoxious because it was retrospective in its action; or perhaps it had been good in the beginning and had afterwards become corrupted in its application. But whichever it may have been, this law could never be discussed in Rome without causing the most violent excitement in the city. There were two principal points in this law; one provided that no citizen could possess more than a certain number of acres of land, and the other that all the lands taken from their enemies should be divided amongst the Roman people. This affected the nobles disadvantageously in two ways; for those who had more land than the law allowed (which was the case with the greater part of the nobles) had to be deprived of it; and by dividing amongst the people the lands taken from the enemy, it took from the nobles the chance of enriching themselves thereby, as they had previously done. Now, as it was a powerful class that had thus been affected, and who considered resistance to this law as a defence of the public good, whenever the subject was brought up, it occasioned, as we have said, the most violent disturbances. The nobles used all patience and every means in their power to gain time and delay action upon the subject, either by calling out an army, or by getting one tribune to oppose another who had proposed the law, or sometimes by yielding in part, or even by sending a colony to any place where lands were to be divided. This was done with the country of Antium, respecting which this law had caused a dispute; and therefore a colony drawn from amongst the citizens of Rome was sent there, to whom that country was assigned. In reference to this, Titus Livius makes the notable remark, that "it was difficult to find anyone in Rome willing to inscribe his name to go to that colony; so much more ready were the people to desire possessions in Rome than to go and have them in Antium."[4]

The troubles about this agrarian law continued to disturb Rome for some time, so that the Romans began to send their armies to the extreme ends of Italy, or even beyond; after which matters were seemingly calmed down, owing to the fact that the lands taken from the enemy were at at a great distance from Rome, and remote from the eyes of the people, and were situated where it was not easy to cultivate them, and consequently they were less desirable. Besides this, the Romans became less disposed to deprive their vanquished enemies of their lands, as they had done before; and when they did so deprive any of them of their possessions, they sent colonies to occupy them; so that from these several causes the agrarian law lay, as it were, dormant until the time of the Gracchi, who, after having revived it, wholly destroyed the Roman republic. For the power of the adversaries of the law had increased twofold in the mean time, and its revival excited such feelings of hatred between the people and the Senate, that it led to violence and bloodshed beyond all bounds or precedent. So that, the magistrates being unable to check these disturbances, and neither party having any confidence in the public authorities, they both resorted to private expedients, and each of the factions began to look for a chief capable of defending them against the other. In these extreme troubles and disorders the people began to cast their eyes on Marius, on account of his reputation, which was so great that they had made him Consul four times in succession, and with such short intervals between these several consulates that he was enabled to nominate himself three times more for that office. The nobility, seeing no other remedy against these abuses, gave their favor to Sulla, and made him chief of their party. Thus civil war was provoked, and after much bloodshed and varied fortunes the nobility retained the upper hand. In the time of Cæsar and Pompey these troubles were revived, Cæsar placing himself at the head of the party of Marius, and Pompey upholding that of Sulla; conflicts of arms ensued, and Cæsar

---

4. Antium is known today as Anzio; it lies on the coast about thirty miles south of Rome.

remained master and became the first tyrant of Rome, so that that city never afterwards recovered her liberty.

Such was the beginning and the end of the agrarian law. And as I have demonstrated elsewhere that the differences between the Senate and the people had been instrumental in preserving the liberty in Rome, because they had given rise to the enactment of laws favorable to liberty, therefore the results of this agrarian law may seem in contradiction with that previous conclusion. But I do not on that account change my opinion, for the ambition of the nobles is so great, that, if it is not repressed by various ways and means in any city, it will quickly bring that city to ruin. So that if the contentions about the agrarian law needed three hundred years to bring Rome to a state of servitude, she would have been brought there much quicker if the people, by these laws and other means, had not for so great a length of time kept the ambition of the nobles in check. This shows us how much more people value riches than honor; for the Roman nobility always yielded to the people without serious difficulties in the matter of honors, but when it came to a question of property, then they resisted with so much pertinacity that the people, to satisfy their thirst for riches, resorted to the above-described extraordinary proceedings. The chief promoters of these disorders were the Gracchi, whose intentions in this matter were more praiseworthy than their prudence. For to attempt to eradicate an abuse that has grown up in a republic by the enactment of retrospective laws, is a most inconsiderate proceeding, and (as we have amply discussed above) only serves to accelerate the fatal results which the abuse tends to bring about; but by temporizing, the end will either be delayed, or the evil will exhaust itself before it attains that end.

*   *   *

[Book I, Chapter 58]

THE PEOPLE ARE WISER AND MORE CONSTANT THAN PRINCES

Titus Livius as well as all other historians affirm that nothing is more uncertain and inconstant than the multitude; for it appears from what he relates of the actions of men, that in many instances the multitude, after having condemned a man to death, bitterly lamented it, and most earnestly wished him back. This was the case with the Roman people and Manlius Capitolinus, whom they had condemned to death and afterwards most earnestly desired him back, as our author says in the following words: "No sooner had they found out that they had nothing to fear from him, than they began to regret and wish him back." And elsewhere, when he relates the events that occured in Syracuse after the death of Hieronymus, nephew of Hiero, he says: "It is the nature of the multitude either humbly to serve or insolently to dominate."[5] I know not whether, in undertaking to defend a cause against the accusations of all writers, I do not assume a task so hard and so beset with difficulties as to oblige me to abandon it with shame, or to go on with it at the risk of being weighted down by it. Be that as it may, however, I think, and ever shall think, that it cannot be wrong to defend one's opinions with arguments founded upon reason, without employing force or authority.

I say, then, that individual men, and especially princes, may be charged with the same defects of which writers accuse the people; for whoever is not controlled by laws will commit the same errors as an unbridled multitude. This may easily be verified, for there have been and still are plenty of princes, and a few good and wise ones, such, I mean, as needed not the curb that controlled them. Amongst these, however, are not to be counted either the kings that lived in Egypt at that ancient period when that country was governed by laws, or those that arose in Sparta; neither such as are born in our day in France, for that country is more thoroughly regulated by laws than any other of which we have any knowledge in modern times. And those kings that arise under such constitutions are not to be classed amongst the number of those whose individual nature we have to consider, and see whether it resembles that of the people; but they should be compared with a people equally controlled by law as those kings were, and then we shall find in that multitude the same good qualities as in those kings, and we shall see that such a people neither obey with servility nor command with insolence. Such were the people of Rome, who, so long as that republic remained uncorrupted, neither obeyed basely nor ruled insolently, but rather held its rank honorably, supporting the laws and their magistrates. And when the unrighteous ambition of some noble made it necessary for them to rise up in self-defense, they did so, as in the case of Manlius, the Decemvirs, and others who attempted to oppress them; and so when the public good required them to obey the dictators and consuls, they promptly yielded obedience. And if the Roman people regretted Manlius Capitolinus after his death, it is not to be wondered at; for they regretted his virtues, which had been such that the remembrance of them filled every one with pity, and would have had the power to produce the same effect upon any prince; for all writers agree that virtue is to be admired and praised, even in one's enemies. And if intense desire could have restored Manlius to life, the Roman people would nevertheless have pronounced the same judgment against him as they did the first time, when they took him from prison and condemned him to death. And so we have seen princes that were esteemed wise, who have caused persons to be put to death and afterwards regretted it

5. Livy 6.20, and 24, 25.

deeply; such as Alexander the Great with regard to Clitus and other friends, and Herod with his wife Mariamne.[6] But what our historian says of the character of the multitude does not apply to a people regulated by laws, as the Romans were, but to an unbridled multitude, such as the Syracusans; who committed all the excesses to which infuriated and unbridled men abandon themselves, as did Alexander the Great and Herod in the above-mentioned cases.

Therefore, the character of the people is not to be blamed any more than that of princes, for both alike are liable to err when they are without any control. Besides the examples already given, I could adduce numerous others from amongst the Roman emperors and other tyrants and princes, who have displayed as much inconstancy and recklessness as any populace ever did. Contrary to the general opinion, then, which maintains that the people, when they govern, are inconsistent, unstable, and ungrateful, I conclude and affirm that that these defects are not more natural to the people than they are to princes. To charge the people and princes equally with them may be the truth, but to except princes from them would be a great mistake. For a people that governs and is well regulated by laws will be stable, prudent, and grateful, as much so, and even more, according to my opinion, than a prince, although he be esteemed wise; and, on the other hand, a prince, freed from the restraints of the law, will be more ungrateful, inconstant, and imprudent than a people similarly situated. The difference in their conduct is not due to any difference in their nature (for that is the same, and if there be any difference for good, it is on the side of the people); but to the greater or less respect they have for the laws under which they respectively live. And whoever studies the Roman people will see that for four hundred years they have been haters of royalty, and lovers of the glory and common good of their country; and he will find any number of examples that will prove both the one and the other. And should any one allege the ingratitude which the Roman people displayed toward Scipio, I shall reply the same as I have said in another place on this subject, where I have demonstrated that the people are less ungrateful than princes. But as regards prudence and stability, I say that the people are more prudent and stable, and have better judgment than a prince; and it is not without good reason that it is said, "The voice of the people is the voice of God"; for we see popular opinion prognosticate events in such a wonderful manner that it would almost seem as if the people had some occult virtue, which enables them to foresee the good and the evil. As to the people's capacity of judging things, it is exceedingly rare that, when they hear two orators of equal talents advocate different measures, they do not decide in favor of the best of the two; which proves their ability to discern the truth of what they hear. And if oc-

6. "Life of Alexander" by Plutarch 52; Josephus, *Antiquities* 15.7.4–7.

casionally they are misled in matters involving questions of courage or seeming utility, (as has been said above), so is a prince also many times misled by his own passions, which are much greater than those of the people. We also see that in the election of their magistrates they make far better choice than princes; and no people will ever be persuaded to elect a man of infamous character and corrupt habits to any post of dignity, to which a prince is easily influenced in a thousand different ways. When we see a people take an aversion to anything, they persist in it for many centuries, which we never find to be the case with princes. Upon both these points the Roman people shall serve me as proof, who in the many elections of consuls and tribunes had to regret only four times the choice they had made. The Roman people held the name of king in such detestation, as we have said, that no extent of services rendered by any of its citizens who attempted to usurp that title could save him from his merited punishment. We furthermore see the cities where the people are masters make the greatest progress in the least possible time, and much greater than such as have always been governed by princes; as was the case with Rome after the expulsion of the kings, and with Athens after they rid themselves of Pisistratus; and this can be attributed to no other cause than that the governments of the people are better than those of princes.[7]

It would be useless to object to my opinion by referring to what our historian has said in the passages quoted above, and elsewhere; for if we compare the faults of a people with those of princes, as well as their respective good qualities, we shall find the people vastly superior in all that is good and glorious. And if princes show themselves superior in making laws, and in the forming of civil institutions and new statutes and ordinances, the people are superior in maintaining those institutions, laws, and ordinances, which certainly places them on a par with those who established them.

And finally to sum up this matter, I say that both governments of princes and of the people have lasted a long time, but both required to be regulated by laws. For a prince who knows no other control but his own will is like a madman, and a people that can do as it pleases will hardly be wise. If now we compare a prince who is controlled by laws, and a people that is untrammelled by them, we shall find more virtue in the people than in the prince; and if we compare them when both are freed from such control, we shall see that the people are guilty of fewer excesses than the prince, and that the errors of the people are of less importance, and therefore more easily remedied. For a licentious and mutinous people may easily be brought back to good conduct by the influence and persuasion of a good man, but an evil-minded prince

7. Machiavelli's enthusiasm for popular government was very exceptional in his day, and contributed to his bad reputation almost down to the present, when it suddenly became an article to his credit.

is not amenable to such influences, and therefore there is no other remedy against him but cold steel. We may judge then from this of the relative defects of the one and the other; if words suffice to correct those of the people, whilst those of the prince can only be remedied by violence, no one can fail to see that where the greater remedy is required, there also the defects must be greater. The follies which a people commits at the moment of its greatest license are not what is most to be feared; it is not the immediate evil that may result from them that inspires apprehension, but the fact that such general confusion might afford the opportunity for a tyrant to seize the government. But with evil-disposed princes the contrary is the case; it is the immediate present that causes fear, and there is hope only in the future; for men will persuade themselves that the termination of his wicked life may give them a chance of liberty. Thus we see the difference between the one and the other to be, that the one touches the present and the other the future. The excesses of the people are directed against those whom they suspect of interfering with the public good; whilst those of princes are against apprehended interference with their individual interests. The general prejudice against the people results from the fact that everybody can freely and fearlessly speak ill of them in mass, even whilst they are at the height of their power; but a prince can only be spoken of with the greatest circumspection and apprehension. And as the subject leads me to it, I deem it not amiss to examine in the following chapter whether alliances with a republic or with a prince are most to be trusted.

[Book I, Chapter 59]

LEAGUES AND ALLIANCES WITH REPUBLICS ARE MORE TO BE TRUSTED THAN THOSE WITH PRINCES

As it is of daily occurrence that princes and republics contract leagues or friendships with each other, or that in like manner treaties and alliances are formed between a republic and a prince, it seems to me proper to examine whose faith is most constant and most to be relied upon, that of a republic or that of a prince. In examining the whole subject I believe that in many instances they are equal, but that in others there is a difference; and I believe, moreover, that agreements which are the result of force will no more be observed by a prince than by a republic, and where either the one or the other is apprehensive of losing their state, that to save it both will break their faith and be guilty of ingratitude. Demetrius, called the Conqueror of Cities, had conferred infinite benefits upon the Athenians. It happened that, having been defeated by his enemies, he took refuge in Athens as a city that was friendly to him, and which he had laid under obligations; but the Athenians refused to receive him, which gave Demetrius more pain than the loss of his men and the destruction of his army.[8] Pompey, after his defeat by Cæsar in Thessaly, took refuge in Egypt with Ptolemy, whom on a former occassion he had reinstated in his kingdom, but was treacherously put to death by him.[9] Both these instances are attributable to the same reasons; yet we see that the republic acted with more humanity and inflicted less injury than the prince. Wherever fear dominates, there we shall find equal want of faith in both, although the same influence may cause either a prince or a republic to keep faith at the risk of ruin. For it may well happen that the prince is the ally of some powerful potentate, who for the moment may not be able to assist him, but who, the prince may hope, will be able to reinstate him in his possessions; or he may believe that, having acted as his partisan, his powerful ally will make no treaties or alliances with his enemies. Such was the fate of those princes of the kingdom of Naples who adhered to the French party. And with regard to republics this occurred with Saguntum in Spain, which hazarded her own safety for the sake of adhering to the Roman party; and with Florence when in the year 1512 she followed the fortune of the French. Taking all things together now, I believe that in such cases which involve imminent peril there will be found somewhat more of stability in republics than in princes.

*　*　*

[Book II, Chapter 13]

CUNNING AND DECEIT WILL SERVE A MAN BETTER THAN FORCE TO RISE FROM A BASE CONDITION TO GREAT FORTUNE

I believe it to be most true that it seldom happens that men rise from low condition to high rank without employing either force or fraud, unless that rank should be attained either by gift or inheritance. Nor do I believe that force alone will ever be found to suffice, whilst it will often be the case that cunning alone serves the purpose; as is clearly seen by whoever reads the life of Philip of Macedon, or that of Agathocles the Sicilian, and many others, who from the lowest and most moderate condition have achieved thrones and great empires. Xenophon shows in his Life of Cyrus the necessity of deception to success: the first expedition of Cyrus against the king of Armenia is replete with fraud, and it was deceit alone, and not force, that enabled him to seize that kingdom. And Xenophon draws no other conclusion from it than that a prince who wishes to achieve great things must learn to deceive. Cyrus also practiced a variety of deceptions upon Cyaxares,[1] king of the Medes,

8. "Life of Demetrius" by Plutarch 30.
9. "Life of Pompey" by Plutarch, especially 77.
1. Xenophon's Cyropaedia, a kind of moral-izing romance, was translated into Latin by Poggio Bracciolini early in the fifteenth century. Machiavelli and his age still considered it historical.

his maternal uncle; and Xenophon shows that without these frauds Cyrus would never have achieved the greatness which he did attain. Nor do I believe that there was ever a man who from obscure condition arrived at great power by merely employing open force; but there are many who have succeeded by fraud alone, as, for instance, Giovanni Galeazzo Visconti in taking the state and sovereignty of Lombardy from his uncle, Messer Bernabò.[2] And that which princes are obliged to do in the beginning of their rise, republics are equally obliged to practice until they have become powerful enough so that force alone suffices them. And as Rome employed every means, by chance or choice, to promote her aggrandizement, so she also did not hesitate to employ fraud; nor could she have practised a greater fraud than by taking the course we have explained above of making other people her allies and associates, and under that title making them slaves, as she did with the Latins and other neighboring nations. For first she availed of their arms to subdue their mutual neighbors, and thus to increase her state and reputation; and after having subdued these, her power increased to the degree that she could subjugate each people separately in turn. The Latins never became aware that they were wholly slaves until they had witnessed two defeats of the Samnites, and saw them obliged to accept the terms of peace dictated to them. As this victory greatly increased the reputation of the Romans with the more distant princes, who felt the weight of their name before experiencing that of their arms, so it excited envy and apprehension in those who had seen and felt their arms, amongst whom were the Latins. And this jealousy and fear were so powerful that not only the Latins, but also the colonies which the Romans had established in Latium, together with the Campanians, whose defence the Romans had but a short time previously undertaken, conspired together against the Romans. The Latins began the war in the way we have shown that most wars are begun, not by attacking the Romans, but by defending the Sidicini from the Samnites, against whom the latter were making war with the permission of the Romans. And that it is true that the Latins began the war because they had at last become aware of the bad faith of the Romans is demonstrated by Titus Livius, when at an assembly of the Latin people he puts the following words into the mouth of Annius Setinus, a Latin Prætor: "For if now we can bear servitude under the specious name of equal confederates," &c.[3]

We see therefore that the Romans in the early beginning of their power already employed fraud, which it has ever been necessary for those to practice who from small beginnings wish to rise to the highest

2. Giangaleazzo Visconti deceived and then murdered his uncle, Messer Bernabò, in 1385; for a general account of the manners of the Italian despots, consult Burckhardt, *The Civilization of the Renaissance in Italy*, part 1.
3. Livy 8.4.

degree of power; and then it is the less censurable the more it is concealed, as was that practised by the Romans.

*   *   *

[Book III, Chapter 8]

WHOEVER WISHES TO CHANGE THE GOVERNMENT OF A REPUBLIC SHOULD FIRST CONSIDER WELL ITS EXISTING CONDITION

We have already shown that an evil-disposed citizen cannot effect
any changes for the worse in a republic, unless it be already corrupt.
Besides the reasons elsewhere given, this conclusion is confirmed by the
examples of Spurius Cassius and Manlius Capitolinus.[4] This Spurius,
being an ambitious man and wishing to obtain the supreme power in
Rome, endeavored to gain the favor of the people by numerous benefits,
such as selling to them the lands taken from the Hernici. This opened
the eyes of the senate to his ambitious projects, and he became suspected,
even by the people, to that point that when he offered them the proceeds
of the sale of the grain which the government had caused to be brought
from Sicily, the people refused it altogether; for it seemed to them as
though Spurius offered it as the price of their liberty. But if this people
had been corrupt, they would, so far from refusing this offer, have
accepted it, and thus have opened the way for Spurius to the tyranny
which now they closed against him.

The example of Manlius is even more forcible, and proves how this
evil ambition to rule cancels the noblest qualities of mind and body,
and the most important services rendered to a state. We see that this
ambition had its origin with Manlius in his jealousy of the honors
bestowed upon Camillus; and so blinded was he by it, that regardless of
the manners and customs of Rome, and without examining the condition
of the state, which was not yet prepared to accept a vicious form of
government, he set to work to stir up disturbances in Rome against the
senate and the institutions of his country. Here we recognize the perfection of the constitution of Rome, and the excellent character of its
population; for on the occasion of the fall of Manlius, not one of the
nobility (so ardent generally in their mutual support and defence) made
the slightest effort in his favor; nor did any of his relatives make any
attempt to support him. And whilst the families of others accused were
in the habit of showing themselves near them, all covered with dust and

---

4. For the story of Spurius Cassius, see Livy 2.33, 41, and for that of Manlius Capitolinus,
6.14–20.

in deep mourning and sadness, for the purpose of exciting the commiseration of the people for the accused, not one of the family of Manlius appeared near him. The tribunes of the people, so accustomed always to favor every measure that seemed for the advantage of the people, and the more so in proportion as it was adverse to the interests of the nobility, in this instance united with the nobles for the purpose of suppressing a common enemy. And finally the people of Rome, ever most jealous of its own interests, and eagerly in favor of everything that was adverse to the nobles, had at first shown themselves well disposed toward Manlius; but the moment the tribunes summoned him and brought his case before them, the same people, having now from defenders become judges, condemned him, without regard to his former services, to suffer the death penalty. I therefore think that there is no fact in history that more effectually shows the excellence of the Roman constitution than this example, where not a single person in the whole city stirred to defend a citizen gifted with the best qualities, and who had rendered the most signal services to the public, as well as to private individuals. For the love of country had more power over them than any other sentiment; and they thought so much more of its present dangers, to which the ambition of Manlius exposed them, than of his past services, that they saw no other way of relieving themselves of those dangers than by his death. And Titus Livius says: "Thus ended the career of this man, who would have been memorable had he not been born in a free community."

This brings us to two important considerations: the first, that the means of attaining glory are different in a republic that is corrupt from what they are in a republic that still preserves its institutions pure; and the second (which is in a measure comprised in the first), that men in their conduct, and especially in their most prominent actions, should well consider and conform to the times in which they live. And those who, from an evil choice or from natural inclination, do not conform to the times in which they live, will in most instances live unhappily, and their undertakings will come to a bad end; whilst, on the contrary, success attends those who conform to the times. And doubtless we may conclude from the words of our historian that, if Manlius had been born in the times of Marius and Sulla, when the people were already corrupt, and when he could have moulded them according to his ambition, he would have achieved the same results and successes as Marius and Sulla, and the others who after them aspired to the tyranny. And in the same way, if Sulla and Marius had lived in the times of Manlius, they would have been crushed in their first attempt. For a man may well by his conduct and evil ways begin to corrupt a people, but it is impossible for him to live long enough to enjoy the fruits of it. And even if it were possible that by length of time he should succeed, the natural impatience of the people, which cannot brook delay in the indulgence of their passion, would prove an obstacle to his success, so that by too much haste, or from error he would be led to engage in his attempt at the wrong time, and thus end in failure.

To usurp supreme and absolute authority, then, in a free state, and subject it to tyranny, the people must already have become corrupt by gradual steps from generation to generation. And all states necessarily come to this, unless (as we have shown above) they are frequently reinvigorated by good examples, and brought back by good laws to their first principles. Manlius thus would have been regarded as a rare and memorable man if he had lived in a corrupt republic. And therefore all such as desire to make a change in the government of a republic, whether in favor of liberty or in favor of tyranny, must well examine the condition of things, and from that judge of the difficulties of their undertaking. For it is as difficult to make a people free that is resolved to live in servitude, as it is to subject a people to servitude that is determined to be free. Having argued above that in many such attempts men should well consider the state of the times and govern themselves accordingly, I will develop this subject more fully in the next chapter.

*   *   *

[Book III, Chapter 9]

WHOEVER DESIRES CONSTANT SUCCESS MUST CHANGE HIS CONDUCT WITH THE TIMES

I have often reflected that the causes of the success or failure of men depend upon their manner of suiting their conduct to the times. We see one man proceed in his actions with passion, another warily; and as in both the one and the other case men are apt to exceed the proper limits, not being able always to observe the just middle course, they are apt to err in both. But he errs least and will be most favored by fortune who suits his proceedings to the times, as I have said above, and always follows the impulses of his nature. Every one knows how Fabius Maximus conducted the war against Hannibal with extreme caution and circumspection, and with an utter absence of all impetuosity or Roman audacity.[5] It was his good fortune that this mode of proceeding accorded perfectly with the times and circumstances. For Hannibal had arrived in Rome whilst still young and with his fortunes fresh; he had already

5. The tale of Fabius Cunctator and his part in the Second Punic War occupies Livy through much of books 20–30.

twice routed the Romans, so that the republic was as it were deprived of her best troops, and greatly discouraged by her reverses. Rome could not therefore have been more favored by fortune, than to have a commander who by his extreme caution and the slowness of his movements kept the enemy at bay. At the same time, Fabius could not have found circumstances more favorable for his character and genius, to which fact he was indebted for his success and glory. And that this mode of proceeding was the result of his character and nature, and not a matter of choice, was shown on the occasion when Scipio wanted to take the same troops to Africa for the purpose of promptly terminating the war. Fabius most earnestly opposed this, like a man incapable of breaking from his accustomed ways and habits; so that, if he had been master, Hannibal would have remained in Italy, because Fabius failed to perceive that the times were changed, and strategies would change as well. And if Fabius had been king of Rome, he might easily have lost the war, because he would never have been able to change his methods to suit the changing times. But Rome was a republic that produced citizens of various characters and dispositions, such as Fabius, who was excellent at the time when it was desirable to protract the war, and Scipio, when it became necessary to terminate it. It is this which assures to republics greater vitality and more enduring success than monarchies have; for the diversity of the genius of her citizens enables the republic better to accommodate herself to the changes of the times than can be done by a prince. For any man accustomed to a certain mode of proceeding will never change it, as we have said, and consequently when time and circumstances change, so that his ways are no longer in harmony with them, he must of necessity succumb. Piero Soderini, whom we have mentioned several times already, was in all his actions governed by humanity and patience. He and his country prospered so long as the times favored this mode of proceeding; but when afterwards circumstances arose that demanded a course of conduct the opposite to that of patience and humanity, he was unfit for the occasion, and his own and his country's ruin were the consequence. Pope Julius II acted throughout the whole period of his pontificate with the impetuosity and passion natural to his character; and as the times and circumstances well accorded with this, he was successful in all his undertakings. But if the times had changed so that different counsels would have been required, he would unquestionably have been ruined, for he could not have changed his character or mode of action.

That we cannot thus change at will is due to two causes; the one is the impossibility of resisting the natural bent of our characters; and the other is the difficulty of persuading ourselves, after having been accustomed to success by a certain mode of proceeding, that any other can succeed as well. It is this that causes the varying success of a man; for the times change, but he does not change his mode of proceeding. The ruin of states is caused in like manner, as we have fully shown above, because they do not modify their institutions to suit the changes of the times. And such changes are more difficult and tardy in republics; for necessarily circumstances will occur that will unsettle the whole state, and when the change of proceeding of one man will not suffice for the occasion.

*　*　*

Machiavelli the Moralist

NICCOLÒ MACHIAVELLI

The Exhortation to Penitence†

[There is no way to date the composition of "The Exhortation to Penitence," which survives in a single manuscript of Machiavelli's own handwriting. Florence had, and still has, a great many social and religious societies, before which their own members appear from time to time to deliver addresses. As early as 1495, Machiavelli became a member of the Company of Piety, but he need not have been restricted to preaching before it. Performances of this character did not necessarily imply an unusual measure of religious devotion in the speaker; they were part of the complex and long-continued initiation rituals by which a society in which money, family, and seniority counted overwhelmingly, prepared young men for formal positions of leadership and decision. Thus there is no reason to scan this discourse narrowly (as has often been done) for signs of irony or mental reservation. No such signs are to be found. Machiavelli we may be sure, made the sermon that was expected of him, received the commendations that were normal, and was set down as a serious and sensible young man, a thoroughly competent, reliable civil servant of the middle rank. Florentine society expected and wanted nothing more.]

De profundis clamavi ad te, Domine; Domine, exaudi vocem meam.[1] With your good will, honorable fathers and superior brothers, I am to talk to you this evening on the topic of penitence; and it seemed best to begin my talk with the words of that reader in the Holy Spirit, David the prophet, so that those of us who have sinned like him may gain from his words the hope of receiving at last, at the hands of the highest and most generous God, mercy; and never to despair of obtaining it, since this man obtained it, and there cannot possibly be united in any one person greater faults or greater penitence than in him, nor can there be conceived greater liberality on the part of God than was shown in pardoning him. And thus in the very words of the prophet let us say, "O Lord, I have called on you out of the depths of my sin, in a voice

† The text has been translated by the editor   Luigi Blasucci (Milano: Adelphi, 1964) 207–11.
from Niccolò Machiavelli, *Opere letteraire*, ed.   1. Psalm 130.

humbled and choked with tears. Mercy, O Lord; I beg it of you, and
implore you, in your infinite goodness to bestow it on me." Nor should
anyone despair of attaining it, if only, with tears in his eyes, with an
afflicted heart, and in a melancholy voice, he requests it. Oh, the
immense pity of God! His infinite goodness! God in his highest heavens
knew how easy it was for man to fall into sin; he saw that if he stood
strictly on his justice, it would be impossible for any man to gain salvation; nor could he provide a better remedy for human frailty than to
warn the human race that it is not sin, but perseverance in sin, that
will render him implacable. And thus he opened before mankind the
pathway of penitence, by which, even after losing the other way, we
may still get to heaven.

Penitence, then, is the only remedy that wipes out all the evils and
errors of men, who, though they are very numerous and go about their
business in many different ways, can still be divided very roughly into
two sorts: those who are ungrateful to God, and those who are hateful
to their neighbors.

But to understand our full ingratitude, it is necessary to consider what
are the great benefits we have received from God. Think, then, how all
things made and created were made and created for the benefit of man.
You observe in the first place the immense expanse of the earth which,
to make it habitable for man, he kept from being flooded everywhere
with water, but left part of it uncovered for human use. And on it he
caused to spring up all these many plants, animals, and grasses, and
everything which grows from the earth, all for man's benefit; and not
only did he order the earth to provide for man's existence, he ordered
the oceans also to breed an infinity of creatures, to serve for man's
nourishment. But, passing by these earthly thoughts, let us raise our
eyes to heaven and consider the beauty of the things we see there; part
of which he made for our service, and the other part so that, from
knowing the splendor and marvelous workmanship of it, we might feel
a deep and thirsty desire to know those other things which are hidden
even further beyond. Don't you see how much trouble the sun takes to
share his light with you, to generate by his power both ourselves and
all the different things created by God for our use? Thus everything is
created for the honor and benefit of man, and man is created only for
the benefit and honor of God. To man he gave the power of speech,
to praise him; he gave him features, not turned to earth like the other
beasts, but raised to the heavens, so that he might continually contemplate him; he gave him hands so that he might raise temples and make
sacrifices in his honor; he gave him reason and intellect so that he might
reflect and know the grandeur of God. You see then with what ingratitude
man presumes to rise against so great a benefactor! and how great is the
punishment he deserves when he perverts the use of these things, and
turns them to evil purposes! The tongue, which was made to honor

God, is turned to blaspheming him; the mouth, formed to nourish us, becomes a sewer, and a way to satisfy the gut with fancy, superflous foods; the eyes, which should be turned up to God, turn down to this earth; and the instinct to perpetuate the human race is turned to lust and other lascivious pastimes; and thus, through all these ugly actions, man tranforms himself from a rational creature to a brute beast. And when he shows this ingratitude to God, man also changes himself from angel to devil, from master to slave, and from human being to animal.

Those who are ungrateful to God can hardly fail to be hateful to their neighbors. A man is an enemy to his neighbor when he lacks charity. This it is, my fathers and brothers, only this is what raises our souls to heaven; this and this alone is worth all the other virtues of which men are capable; of this the Church speaks so broadly that she declares, The man who has no charity has nothing. Saint Paul speaks of this when he says, "Though I speak with the tongue of men and of angels, and have no charity, I am become as sounding brass."[2] On this one virtue is founded the faith of Christ. No man can be full of charity who is not also full of religion, because charity is patient and benign, without envy or perversity; it is never proud or contemptuous, it repents its misdeeds instead of rejoicing in them, it takes no pleasure in vanity, it endures all, believes all, hopes always. O divine virtue, happy are those who possess you! This is the celestial robe in which we must be dressed if we want to be admitted to the heavenly marriage of our ruler Jesus Christ in the kingdoms of heaven! and he who is not dressed in this robe will be driven from the marriage feast, and cast into perpetual fires! Anyone who lacks this virtue, it is obvious, must be an enemy to his neighbor: he does not help his neighbor, or comfort him in his weakness, or console him in his troubles; he neither teaches the ignorant nor counsels the erring; he neither helps the good, nor punishes the bad. These offenses against one's neighbor are serious, but ingratitude against God is the most serious of all; and because we often fall into these two vices, God the kindly creator has shown us the road of redemption, which is penitence. And he has made clear its power both by word and by deed: with words, when he told Peter to forgive his brother, not seven times, but seventy times seven.[3] And in deeds when he pardoned David for his adultery and homicide, and pardoned Saint Peter for having denied him, not just once but three times. For what crime will not God grant pardon, my brethren, if he pardoned these men for these crimes? For not only did he pardon them, he honored them among the elect and lofty spirits of Heaven. But only because David, prostrate on the earth, dissolved in tears and affliction, cried out: Lord, *have mercy on me*; only because Saint Peter *wept bitterly*; he bitterly bewailed his own fault, and David repented; both men deserved their pardon.

2. 1 Corinthians 13.1.   3. Matthew 18.21.

But because it's not enough to repent and bewail our faults, because we must prepare ourselves to work against sin, in order not to do evil again and to take away the very occasion of evil, it behooves us to imitate Saint Francis and Saint Jerome who undertook to mortify the flesh and so prevent it from forcing them into evildoing. And so the first of them sacrificed himself with thorns, and the other beat his breast with a rock. But with what rock or what thorns shall we repress our itch for usury, or for shameful pleasures, or for the tricks we delight in playing on our neighbors? The only way is with gifts of charity, by doing honor to our neighbor, by doing good to him. But we are tricked ourselves by lust, tangled in error, caught in the snares of sin; and so we find ourselves in the gripe of the devil. To escape, we must have recourse to penitence, we must cry with David, *Lord, have mercy on me*! and with Saint Peter we must weep bitterly, and repent of all the faults we have committed—

> Repent and tune ourselves to this one theme,
> That worldly pleasure is a short-lived dream.[4]

4. Petrarch, *Canzoniere*, 1.13–14. As noted in the first sentence of the headnote, there is no way to date the "Exhortation" accurately. After some hesitation the present editor introduced it as a work of Machiavelli's young manhood. But other scholars place it later, much later, in his career. A couple of interrogatories present food for thought. Would Machiavelli, with the scars and cynicisms of a lifetime on his conscience, have adressed unexceptionable moralities like these to a Company of Piety? Would the Company of Piety have chosen for a speaker a man known as the author of those rough-and-tumble sexual comedies *La Mandragola* and *La Clizia*? It's reason to read over the "Exhortation" from at least two points of view.

Machiavelli the Correspondent

NICCOLÒ MACHIAVELLI

From His Private Letters†

[Machiavelli was one of the great letter writers. He should have been; it was his business. What is remarkable, given his unpopularity and the chaos of Italy at the time, is that many of his letters were preserved. Originally there must have been thousands; several hundred survive. As a letter writer, Machiavelli is notable for his extraordinary mobility and variety. With every different correspondent, and sometimes within the same letter, he shifts character and changes tone. Now he is jocose, now ironic, now severely practical, now self-mocking, occasionally conspiratorial. Out of these riches we have selected just three letters. The first, written to his old boss Piero Soderini after the collapse of the Florentine republic, condenses even further the already condensed political lessons of *The Prince*. What he says here to Soderini (whom he always considered too gentle and kindly a man) confirms what he wrote after Soderini's death in *Discorsi* 3. 9 (above, p. 117). A second letter is addressed to Francesco Vettori, the closest friend of Machiavelli's later years. Vettori was a cautious, cynical Florentine functionary at the papal court in Rome; with this wise, tough old bird, Machiavelli felt free to joke, complain, talk international politics, or compare wenching experiences. His letter describing the circumstances under which *The Prince* was composed is surely the most famous letter in Italian literature. Finally, a letter to Francesco Guicciardini, the famous historian of Florence, was written from a monastery to which Machiavelli (then in his fifties and long since removed from major public office) had been sent to select a special preacher for an upcoming religious festival in Florence. With Guicciardini, who fancied himself a joker and a cynic, Machiavelli is even more earthy than with Vettori. The scene that results is worthy of one of Machiavelli's stage comedies—*La Clizia* or *La Mandragola*—from which, alas, the present volume has no room even to excerpt.]

† The text of the letters is from Allan Gilbert, trans. and ed., *Machiavelli, the Chief Works and Others* (Durham, N.C.: Duke University Press, 1965) volume 2. Unless otherwise noted, the footnotes are by Gilbert.

1

January 1512 (1513), Florence
To Piero Soderini, in Ragusa[1]

A letter of yours came to me in a hood,[2] yet after ten words I recognized it. I am sure the crowds at Piombino will recognize you, and of your hindrances and Filippo's I am certain, because I know one is harmed by a little light, the other by too much. January does not trouble me, if only February supports me with his hands. I am sorry about Filippo's suspicions, and in suspense wait for its end. [*He who does not know how to fence overcomes him who knows fencing.*]

Your letter was short but I by rereading it made it long. It was pleasing to me because it gave me a chance to do what I feared to do and what you remind me that I should not do; and this part alone I have observed in it as without application. At this I would wonder, if my fate had not shown me so many and such varied things that I am obliged to wonder but little, or to confess that I have not comprehended while reading and experiencing the actions of men and their methods of procedure.

I understand you and the compass by which you navigate; and if it could be condemned, which it cannot, I would not condemn it, seeing to what port it has taken you and with what hope it can feed you. Consequently, I see, not with your mirror, where nothing is seen but prudence, but with that of the many, which is obliged in political affairs to judge the result when they are finished, and not the management while they are going on. Each man according to his own imagination guides himself. And I see various kinds of conduct bringing about the same thing, as by various roads one comes to the same place, and many who work differently attaining the same end. The actions of this pontiff[3] and their results have furnished anything needed to confirm this opinion.

Hannibal and Scipio were equally excellent in their military attainments; one of them with cruelty, treachery and lack of religion kept his armies united in Italy and made himself admired by the people, who to follow him rebelled against the Romans; the other, with mercy, loyalty and religion, in Spain got from those people the same effect; both of them won countless victories. But because it is not usual to bring up the Romans, Lorenzo de'Medici disarmed the people to hold Florence; Messer Giovanni Bentivoglio in order to hold Bologna armed them; the Vitelli in Città de Castello and the present duke of Urbino in his territory

---

1. This letter is apparently a rough draft, with notes (bracketed and italicized by Gilbert) for possible expansions. Piero Soderini, gonfalonier of the Florentine Republic, had been driven into exile by the return of the Medici. The letter, addressed to him at Ragusa, would have to go to the southernmost tip of Sicily to find him. The "crowds at Piombino" are therefore, like "January," "February," and almost certainly "Filippo," part of a secret code [*Editor*].

2. In a hood: as an enclosure within another letter, mailed from a different address.

3. Julius II, who was always surprising Machiavelli by coming to unexpected ends by unexpected paths. He added one more surprise to the list about a month after this letter was written by dying unexpectedly, February 20, 1513 [*Editor*].

destroyed the fortresses in order to retain those states; Count Francesco Sforza and many others built them in their states to make themselves sure of those states. [*To test Fortune, who is the friend of young men, and to change according to what you find. But it is not possible to have fortresses and not to have them, to be cruel and compassionate.*] Titus the Emperor believed he would lose his position on any day when he did not benefit somebody; some others might believe they would lose theirs on the day when they did anybody a favor. To many, weighing and measuring everything, success comes in their undertakings. [*As Fortune gets tired, anything is ruined. The family, the city, every man has his Fortune founded on his way of proceeding, and each Fortune gets tired, and when she is tired, she must be got back in another way. Comparison of the horse and the bridle about fortress.*] This Pope Julius, who hasn't a pair of scales or a yardstick in his house, gains through chance—although unarmed—what through organization and arms he scarcely could attain.

We have seen and see every day those I have mentioned, and countless others who could be used as instances, gaining kingdoms and sovereignties or falling, according to circumstances; and a man who was praised while he was gaining is reviled when he is losing; and frequently after long prosperity a man who finally loses does not in any way blame himself but accuses the heavens and the action of the Fates. But the reason why different ways of working are sometimes equally effective and equally damaging I do not know, but I should much like to know. So in order to get your opinion I shall be so presuming as to give mine.

I believe that as Nature has given each man an individual face, so she has given him an individual disposition and an individual imagination. From this it results that each man conducts himself according to his disposition and his imagination. On the other hand, because times vary and affairs are of varied types, one man's desires come out as he had prayed they would; he is fortunate who harmonizes his procedure with his time, but on the contrary he is not forturnate who in his actions is out of harmony with his time and with the type of its affairs. Hence it can well happen that two men working differently come to the same end, because each of them adapts himself to what he encounters, for affairs are of as many types as there are provinces and states. Thus, because times and affairs in general and individually change often, and men do not change their imaginings and their procedures, it happens that a man at one time has good fortune and at another time bad.

And certainly anybody wise enough to understand the times and the types of affairs and to adapt himself to them would have always good fortune, or he would protect himself always from bad, and it would come to be true that the wise man would rule the stars and the Fates. But because there never are such wise men, since men in the first place are shortsighted and in the second place cannot command their natures, it follows that Fortune varies and commands men and holds them under her yoke. And to verify this opinion, I think the instances given above, on which I have based it, are enough, and so I expect one to support the other.

To give reputation to a new ruler, cruelty, treachery and irreligion are enough in a province where humanity, loyalty and religion have for a long time been common. Yet in the same way humanity, loyalty and religion are sufficient where cruelty, treachery and irreligion have dominated for a time, because, as bitter things disturb the taste and sweet ones cloy it, so men get bored with good and complain of ill. These causes, among others, opened Italy to Hannibal and Spain to Scipio; thus both of them found times and things suited to their way of proceeding. At that very time a man like Scipio would not have been so successful in Italy, or one like Hannibal so successful in Spain, as they both were in the provinces where they acted.

Niccolò Machiavelli

2

10 December 1513, Florence
To Francesco Vettori, his benefactor, in Rome

Magnificent Ambassador:
"Never late were favors divine."[4] I say this because I seemed to have lost—no, rather mislaid—your good will; you had not written to me for a long time, and I was wondering what the reason could be. And of all those that came into my mind I took little account, except of one only when I feared that you had stopped writing because somebody had written to you that I was not a good guardian of your letters, and I knew that, except Filippo and Pagolo,[5] nobody by my doing had seen them. I have found it again through your last one of the twenty-third of the past month, from which I learn with pleasure how regularly and quietly you carry on this public office, and I encourage you to continue so, because he who gives up his own convenience for the convenience of others, only loses his own and from them gets no gratitude. And since Fortune wants to do everything, she wishes us to let her do it, to be quiet, and not to give her trouble, and to wait for a time when she will allow something to be done by men; and then will be the time for you to work harder, to stir things up more, and for me to leave my farm and say: "Here I am." I cannot however, wishing to return equal favors, tell you in this letter anything else than what my life is; and if you judge it is to be swapped for yours, I shall be glad to change it.

I am living on my farm, and since I had my last bad luck, I have not

4. Petrarch, *Triumph of Eternity* 13.
5. Filippo Casavecchia and Pagolo Vettori, brother of the recipient of the letter.

spent twenty days, putting them all together, in Florence. I have until now been snaring thrushes with my own hands. I got up before day, prepared birdlime, went out with a bundle of cages on my back, so that I looked like Geta when he was returning from the harbor with Amphitryo's books.[6] I caught at least two thrushes and at most six. And so I did all September. Later this pastime, pitiful and strange as it is, gave out, to my displeasure. And of what sort my life is, I shall tell you.

I get up in the morning with the sun and go into a grove I am having cut down, where I remain two hours to look over the work of the past day and kill some time with the cutters, who have always some bad-luck story ready, about either themselves or their neighbors. And as to this grove I could tell you a thousand fine things that have happened to me, in dealing with Frosino da Panzano and others who wanted some of this firewood. And Frosino especially sent for a number of cords without saying a thing to me, and on payment he wanted to keep back from me ten lire, which he says he should have had from me four years ago, when he beat me at *cricca* at Antonio Guicciardini's. I raised the devil, and was going to prosecute as a thief the waggoner who came for the wood, but Giovanni Machiavelli came between us and got us to agree. Battista Guicciardini, Filippo Ginori, Tommaso del Bene and some other citizens, when that north wind was blowing, each ordered a cord from me. I made promises to all and sent one to Tommaso, which at Florence changed to half a cord, because it was piled up again by himself, his wife, his servant, his children, so that he looked like Gabburra when on Thursday with all his servants he cudgels an ox.[7] Hence, having seen for whom there was profit, I told the others I had no more wood, and all of them were angry about it, and especially Battista, who counts this along with his misfortunes at Prato.[8]

Leaving the grove, I go to a spring, and thence to my aviary. I have a book in my pocket, either Dante or Petrarch, or one of the lesser poets, such as Tibullus, Ovid, and the like. I read of their tender passions and their loves, remember mine, enjoy myself a while in that sort of dreaming. Then I move along the road to the inn; I speak with those who pass, ask news of their villages, learn various things, and note the various tastes and different fancies of men. In the course of these things comes the hour for dinner, where with my family I eat such food as this poor farm of mine and my tiny property allow. Having eaten, I go back to the inn; there is the host, usually a butcher, a miller, two furnace tenders. With these I sink into vulgarity for the whole day, playing at *cricca* and at trichtrach, and then these games bring on a thousand disputes and countless insults with offensive words, and usually we are fighting over

---

6. A reference to a story founded on the *Amphitryo* of Plautus.

7. Gabburra, apparently a butcher, is unknown.

8. Battista Guicciardini was podestà (mayor) of Prato when it was taken by the Spanish forces in 1512; as an immediate result the Medici were restored to Florence. It is remarkable that Machiavelli could use the fall of Prato in a jest.

a penny, and nevertheless we are heard shouting as far as San Casciano. So, mixed up with these lice, I keep my brain from growing mouldy, and satisfy the malice of this fate of mine, being glad to have her drive me along this road, to see if she will be ashamed of it.

On the coming of evening, I return to my house and enter my study; and at the door I take off the day's clothing, covered with mud and dust, and put on garments regal and courtly; and reclothed appropriately, I enter the ancient courts of ancient men, where, received by them with affection, I feed on that food which only is mine and which I was born for, where I am not ashamed to speak with them and to ask them the reason for their actions; and they in their kindness answer me; and for four hours of time I do not feel boredom, I forget every trouble, I do not dread poverty, I am not frightened by death; entirely I give myself over to them.

And because Dante says it does not produce knowledge when we hear but do not remember, I have noted everything in their conversation which has profited me,[9] and have composed a little work *On Princedoms*, where I go as deeply as I can into considerations on this subject, debating what a princedom is, of what kinds they are, how they are gained, how they are kept, why they are lost. If ever you can find any of my fantasies pleasing, this one should not displease you; and by a prince, and especially by a new prince, it ought to be welcomed. Hence I am dedicating it to His Magnificence Giuliano.[1] Filippo Casavecchia has seen it; he can give you some account in part of thing in itself and of the discussions I have had with him, though I am still enlarging and revising it.

You wish, Magnificent Ambassador, that I leave this life and come to enjoy yours with you. I shall do it in any case, but what tempts me now are certain affairs that within six weeks I shall finish. What makes me doubtful is that the Soderini we know so well are in the city, whom I should be obliged, on coming there, to visit and talk with. I should fear that on my return I could not hope to dismount at my house but should dismount at the Bargello, because though this government has mighty foundations and great security, yet it is new and therefore suspicious, and there is no lack of wiseacres who, to make a figure, like Pagolo Bertini, would place others at the dinner table and leave the reckoning to me.[2] I beg you to rid me of this fear, and then I shall come within the time mentioned to visit you in any case.

I have talked with Filippo about this little work of mine that I have spoken of, whether it is good to give it or not to give it; and if it is good

9. This seems to be Machiavelli making notes on Livy's *History* for his own *Discourses*, out of which rose *The Prince*.

1. Giuliano de' Medici, later duke of Nemours, son of Lorenzo the Magnificent. He resided in Florence after the restoration of the Medici in 1512, but in 1513 withdrew to Rome.

2. Pagolo Bertini is unknown and the meaning of the sentence is uncertain. [But "dismounting at the Bargello" is very clear; it means being called before the central police authority on suspicion of conspiring with Soderini against the Medici—*Editor*.]

to give it, whether it would be good to take it myself, or whether I should send it there.[3] Not giving it would make me fear that at the least Giuliano will not read it and that this rascal Ardinghelli will get himself honor from this latest work of mine.[4] The giving of it is forced on me by the necessity that drives me, because I am using up my money, and I cannot remain as I am a long time without becoming despised through poverty. In addition, there is my wish that our present Medici lords will make use of me, even if they begin by making me roll a stone; because then if I could not gain their favor, I should complain of myself; and through this thing, if it were read, they would see that for the fifteen years while I have been studying the art of the state, I have not slept or been playing, and well may anybody be glad to get the services of one who at the expense of others has become full of experience. Of my honesty there should be no doubt, because having always preserved my honesty, I shall hardly now learn to break it; he who has been honest and good for forty-three years, as I have, cannot change his nature; as a witness to my honesty and goodness I have my poverty.

I should like, then, to have you also write me what you think best on this matter, and I give you my regards. Be happy.

Niccolò Machiavelli, in Florence.

17 May 1521, Carpi
To his Magnificent Master Francesco Guicciardini, J.U.D.,[5] Governor of Modena and Reggio, most worthy and especially to be most honored
* * *

Magnificent Sir, Ruler to be Most Respected:

I was on the privy seat when your messenger came, and just then I was thinking of the absurdities of this world, and I was giving all my attention to imagining for myself a preacher after my mind for the place at Florence, and he would be just what would please me, because in this I intend to be as obstinate as in my other opinions. And because I never failed that city by not benefiting her when I could—if not with deeds, with words, if not with words, with gestures—I do not intend to fail her this time either. It is true that I know I am opposed, as in many other things, to the opinion of the citizens there: they would like a preacher who would show them the road to Paradise, and I should like to find one who would teach them the way to go to the house of the Devil; they would like, besides, that he should be a man prudent, blameless and true; and I should like to find one crazier than Ponzo,

---

3. There is a story that Machiavelli did give Giuliano the book, but that someone else at the same time gave him a brace of fine greyhounds, so the book was set aside [Editor].

4. Piero Ardinghelli was secretary to Pope Leo X. Machiavelli seems to have feared that [if] Giuliano had not read The Prince, Ardinghelli

would steal ideas from it and offer them as his own.

5. J.U.D. means "Juris Utrisque Doctor," i.e., "Doctor of Both Laws" (canon and civil). All these formalities are burlesque, as is the letter [Editor].

more crafty than Fra Girolamo, more of a hypocrite than Frate Alberto,[6] because it would seem to me a fine thing, worthy of the goodness of these times, that all we have experienced in many friars should be experienced in one, because I believe the true way of going to Paradise would be to learn the road to Hell in order to avoid it. Seeing, besides this, how much credit a bad man has who conceals himself under the cloak of religion, I can easily conjecture how much of it a good man would have who in truth and not in pretense continued to tread muddy places like St. Francis. So since my fancy seemed to me good, I have planned to take Rovaio,[7] and I believe that if he is like his brothers and sisters, he will be just right. I should be glad if, next time you write, you will give me your opinion.

I continue in idleness here because I cannot carry out my commission until the general and the assessors are chosen, and I keep ruminating on how I can sow so much discord among them that either here or elsewhere they may go to hitting each other with their sandals; and if I do not lose my wits, I believe I am going to succeed; and I believe that the advice and help of Your Lordship would assist greatly. So if you would come as far as this with the excuse of a pleasure jaunt, it would not be a bad thing, or at least by writing give me some master strokes. If you once every day would send me a servant just for this purpose, as you have today, you would do several good things: for one, you would give me light on some things quite to my purpose; for another, you would make me more esteemed by those in the house, seeing the messages come thick. And I can tell you that on the arrival of this arbalester with the letter, making a bow down to the earth, and with his saying that he was sent specially and in haste, everybody rose up with so many signs of respect and such a noise that everything was turned upside down, and I was asked by several about the news. I, that its reputation might grow, said that the emperor was expected at Trent, and that the Swiss had summoned new diets, and that the king of France wanted to go in person to speak with that king, but that his councilors advised him against it; so that they all stood with open mouths and with their caps in their hands; and while I write I have a circle of them around me, and seeing me write at length they are astonished, and look on me as inspired; and I, to make them wonder more, sometimes hold my pen still and swell up, and then they slaver at the mouth, but if they could see what I am writing, they would marvel at it more. Your Lordship knows that these friars say that when one is confirmed in grace, the Devil has no more power to tempt him. So I have no more fear that these friars will make me a hypocrite, because I believe I am very well confirmed.

As to the lies of the Carpigiani, I should like a contest in that matter

6. Ponzo is obscure; Fra Girolamo is Savonarola; Frate Alberto is from the *Decameron* 4.2.   7. Giovan Gualberto, a Florentine, and a Franciscan.

with all of them, because quite a while ago I trained myself in such a way that I do not need Francesco Martelli[8] for a servant, because for a long time I have not said what I believed, nor do I ever believe what I say, and if indeed sometimes I do happen to tell the truth, I hide it among so many lies that it is hard to find.

To that governor I did not speak, because having found lodgings, I thought speaking to him useless. It is true that this morning in church I stared at him a bit while he was standing to look at some paintings. He did seem to me well set up, and I can believe that the whole corresponds to the part, and that he is what he seems, and that his crooked back is not a liar;[9] hence that if I had your letter with me, I should have made an attempt at drawing a bucketful out of him. At any rate, no damage has been done, and I expect tomorrow some advice from you on my affairs and that you will send one of the same arbalesters and that he will hurry and get here all sweaty, so that the household will be amazed; for by so doing you will bring me honor, and at the same time your arbalaster will get a little exercise, which for the horses on these spring days is very wholesome.

I might write to you also some other things, if I were willing to weary my fancy, but I wish tomorrow to keep it as fresh as I can. I send my regards to Your Lordship, and may you ever prosper as you desire.

Your faithful Niccolò Machiavelli,
Ambassador to the Minor Friars.

8. Unknown.
9. The original of this sentence is not clear. [But the general implication is plain that the man's crooked back is a good index to his crooked mind—*Editor.*]

Machiavelli the Poet

NICCOLÒ MACHIAVELLI

From *Carnival Songs*†

[Carnival songs were a special phenomenon of the Florentine Renaissance; they were part of that rich ceremonial life so eloquently celebrated by Burckhardt in his *Civilization of the Renaissance in Italy*. The biggest carnival fiestas used to be held in Rome, the next most elaborate in Venice, but the Florentines made most of the songs. *Canti Carnaschialesci* were written by poets and princes (including the Magnificent Lorenzo), by monks and tailors and tosspots, by the artisan in his shop and the tripe seller on the street corner. Because carnival is a time of license and misrule, frankly related to the old pagan festival of Saturnalia, many of these songs (which can be read in the still classic edition of Professor Singleton) were comic or bawdy or both. All the more surprising is a sequence of songs from the pen of Machiavelli, probably composed for some sort of pageant or masquerade. Groups of costumed perfomers evidently came onto a stage or into a cleared space, and explained in song their plight or their desires. Ladies debated with their lovers the consequences of kindness or severity; hermits chorused the praises of the contemplative life; and a choir of blessed spirits appeared, to sing in passionate accents the praises of peace. And in this particular poem, just as in *The Prince*, when Machiavelli wishes to express the highest reach of his patriotic enthusiasm, he begins to echo unmistakably the poetry of Petrarch, especially the great patriotic *canzone*, "Italia mia" (*Rime* 128).]

HYMN OF THE BLESSED SPIRITS

Blessed spirits are we,
Who from those seats on high
Have come down here to earth's low floor
Because indeed we see
In what distress the peoples lie,
And what slight reasons stir men up to war;
We want to show

† Translated by the editor from Machiavelli, *Opere letterarie*, ed. Luigi Blasucci (Milano: Adelphi, 1964) 331–33.

To him who strays from Truth's bright star,
That nothing here below
Brings to Our Lord such heartfelt ease
As when men lay down arms and live in peace.

The life on earth of humankind
Is martyrdom, bitter and cruel and long;
Hateful their pains, and no cure can they find
For their disease; and so their constant song
Is but of endless grief and pain,
Of which all day and night they must complain,
Lamenting, wailing every wrong,
Sobbing aloud and calling out their grief,
And each man asking mercy and relief.

This is for God a bitter pain,
As it must be for any living heart
Where traces of humanity remain;
And so he told us to impart,
And to you people here below explain,
How fierce his anger is and his disdain
At seeing how his kingdom disappears.
His flock grows ever fewer with the years—
Unless new ways come in with the new swain.[1]

So deep is the fierce thirst to lay
This ancient country waste
Which once gave laws to all of humankind,
That you are wholly blind
And don't see how your quarrels pave the way
For enemies who press you thick and fast.
The Turkish sultan, day by day,
Sharpens his sword, and rubs his bloody hands,
Ready to burst upon your peaceful lands.[2]

Raise, then, your weapons high
Against a cruel foe;
But to your own, bring healing remedy.
Lay down that old hostility
Fostered between you since long, long ago.
Turn on the real foe your common strength,
Else heaven will at length
Deny to you the right to any force,
Seeing that pious zeal in you has run its course.

1. The "new swain" is Leo X, elected to the papacy early in 1513; the allusion thus places composition of this song very close indeed to the period when *The Prince* was being written.
2. The Turkish sultan is Selim I, who ruled from 1512 to 1521. He was in fact a voracious conqueror, who is said to have complained at one point that the whole world was not big enough to satisfy his imperial ambitions. Whether he ever actually contemplated a descent on Italy is doubtful; but his constant thrashing about upset the entire Mediterranean.

Dismiss, then, all fears,
All hatreds and rancorous jeers,
All cruelty, avarice, pride:
Bring back honor and trust,
The love of the true and the just,
And turn back the world to the ages of gold:
The heavenly gates will then open wide
To let the blessed people inside,
And the fire of virtue [*virtù*] will never grow cold.

NICCOLÒ MACHIAVELLI

On Occasion†

[Machiavelli's little poem on "Occasion"—or, perhaps, we should say "Opportunity"—is not really Machiavelli's poem; it is not-very-faithful translation of the twelfth epigram of Ausonius, a grammarian of the fourth century A.D., who lived near Bordeaux, and wrote a number of poems, including a description of the Moselle River and a Cento Nuptialis, consisting of verses and half-verses of Virgil, rearranged with incredible virtuosity to produce a poem of incredible obscenity.

Whatever he thought of Ausonius, Machiavelli was always interested in Opportunity; and he revealed some of his thoughts by dedicating this translation to Filippo de' Nerli, whom there is reason to think he knew through the *conversazione* at the Orti Oricellari, where Machiavelli read many parts, if not all, of the *Discorsi*. Filippo was sixteen years younger than Machiavelli; in 1512—when the Republic fell, the Medici returned to Florence, and Machiavelli's active political career lay in ruins—Filippo was barely twenty-seven years old, and he was a partisan of the Medici. Opportunity was advancing to meet him, just as she was turning her back on Machiavelli. In addressing his young friend on the topic of Lady Luck, Machiavelli's basic advice was, "Don't let her get away!" and it's not beyond thinking that he hoped some of his friend's timely fortune might rub off on himself. He was always a hopeful man.]

—Who are you, lady of no mortal mien,
Endowed by heaven with such a lofty air?
Why wingèd feet? Why are you never seen
At rest?—I am Occasion: sparse and rare
Are my acquaintance, and I'm ill at ease
From standing with one foot upon a sphere.
My flight is swift as any fitful breeze;
Wings on my feet sustain me in the air,
So when I pass, nobody really sees.

† Translated by the editor from Machiavelli, *Opere letterarie*, ed. Luigi Blasucci (Milano: Adelphi, 1964) 325.

Low on my brow before me spreads my hair,
So that it covers all my breast and face;
Thus, no one knows me, coming, till I'm there.
Of hair behind my head there's not a trace,
Hence, one I've turned against, or hurried by,
Can never catch me: it's no good to try.

—Tell me, then: who's this person by your side?
—She's Penitence; and this you'd better note,
Who misses me, gets her to be his bride.
    And you who stand here talking, you who dote
On idle chatter, while the hour lingers,
Wise up a bit, you klutz, you've missed the boat,
And I've already slipped between your fingers!

NICCOLÒ MACHIAVELLI

The Death of Piero Soderini †

The night that Piero Soderini died,
He left for Hell via the common stair.
But "Not for your sort!" was what Pluto cried;
"We have a Hell for little boys. Go there!"

† Piero Soderini was gonfaloniere (chief magistrate) of Florence from 1502 to 1512. He was a moderate and intelligent statesman; Machiavelli was one of his close counsellors. But throughout his term of office, supporters of the exiled Medici were scheming to undermine Soderini's republic and bring back a princely form of government. Soderini, like Machiavelli, knew what they were up to, but could not bring himself to take decisive action agianst them. After the republic collapsed, Machiavelli refused to turn against his old boss. But, as he said directly in *Discorsi* 3.9, he judged Soderini severely from a political point of view; he had been too nice a person to do the dirty work required by politics. Hence this bitter little epigram.

INTERPRETATIONS

J. R. HALE

The Setting of *The Prince*: 1513–1514†

Life at Sant' Andrea[1] had its own mild distractions. Machiavelli's house was beside the inn, and he owned a little woodland, some olives, and vines. He took pleasure in rural occupations, like bird-snaring, and in passing the afternoons in gossip and cards over a glass of wine, but these occupations could give pleasure only when part of a daily routine that was ballasted with something more weighty and absorbing. When in August he began to spend the evenings working at a treatise *De principatibus*[2] they fell into place, but in the spring and early summer the burnt countryside must have seemed to him the *Stinche*[3] where men were punished for being unemployed. From a career of often hectic industry, long journeys, and meetings with men whose levers moved the world, his horizon had shrunk to idleness and the chatter of a rural hamlet. Before leaving for Sant' Andrea he had told Vettori in a letter of 9 April that "fortune has decreed that, knowing nothing of silk manufacture nor the wool business, nor of profit or loss, I must talk politics, and unless I take a vow of silence I must discuss them." And the politics he wished to talk was present politics. Dead politics, history, was to satisfy him later, as it had intrigued him before, but his instinct now was to discuss the political struggles of which he was himself a casualty—an instinct he determined to resist.

During the weeks after his release from prison there had been puzzling and threatening moves among the great powers. On 23 March Louis[4] had arranged a truce with Venice and on 1 April with Spain, which left him free to repair his fortunes in Italy. In Italy this gave rise to widespread bewilderment. Why had Ferdinand[5] given his enemy a free hand? "If this truce between France and Spain is true," Vettori wrote to Machiavelli on 19 April,

> either the Catholic King is not that astute and prudent man he is thought be to, or some mischief is brewing, and what has often been mooted has got into these princes' heads, and Spain, France, and the Emperor[6] intend to divide up our poor Italy.

† From *Machiavelli and Renaissance Italy* by J. R. Hale (London, 1961, 1972), chapter 7. Footnotes are by the editor of this Norton Critical Edition.
1. Machiavelli's country house, at Sant' Andrea in Percussina, near San Casciano.
2. "On princely governments."
3. Dungeons.
4. Louis XII of France.
5. Ferdinand V of Castile, and Leon II of Aragon, best known as "The Catholic."
6. Maximilian, the Holy Roman emperor.

And returning to the subject two days later, he wrote: "Since this truce is assured, I wish we could walk together from the Ponte Vecchio along via de' Bardi and on to Castello, and discuss what fancy has got into Spain's head." And he ended: "I would be glad of your opinion, because to tell you the truth without flattery, I have found you to be sounder in these matters than any other man I have spoken to."

This was an invitation that Machiavelli could not resist. It broke his resolve to forget current affairs and held him from finding solace in books. He replied from Sant' Andrea with a commentary on the political scene which ran to between two and three thousand words. "While I read your letter," he wrote on 29 April,

> which I have read many times, I quite forgot my miserable state, and thought myself back in those activities which cost me—all for nothing—so much fatigue and time. And although I have sworn neither to think of nor discuss politics— my coming to stay in the country bears witness to that—all the same, to reply to your request, I am forced to break my vow.

The next shift in the pattern of international relations was given by the battle of Novara on 6 June. Louis and the Venetians had attempted to take the Milanese[7] from its duke, Massimiliano Sforza, but at this battle the French were completely routed by the Swiss, who, in their own interest, had constituted themselves the duke's somewhat proprietary guardians. On 20 June Machiavelli gave his opinion in a letter dated from Florence, for he did not take his self-exile too literally, and escaped from time to time from the dullness of Sant' Andrea to the news, the women, and the drinking companions of the city. Though he was no longer concerned with political affairs, he said, he could not resist discussing them. Novara had been a great victory for the papal, anti-French party, and when Machiavelli referred to it as one of the events "among the other great good fortunes, which have befallen His Holiness the pope and that illustrious family," he was probably hoping that matters were more auspicious for his obtaining some favor from Leo,[8] if Vettori should take up his suit again. He went on to survey the situation especially from Leo's point of view: what moves should the pope take next?

The correspondence continued through July and into August as a sort of political game. Each proposed a settlement that would bring peace to Italy and invited the other to criticize it. Their letters were full of reference to "my peace" and "your peace." Machiavelli was prepared to make great concessions. France should have Milan and thus be satisfied; Spain should have Naples; the pope the States of the Church;

---

7. I.e., the city of Milan.   8. Leo X, the Medici pope.

Venice should keep the bulk of her mainland possessions. The parties aggrieved by this arrangement would be the duke of Milan (but he was an unimportant cipher) and Germany and the Swiss—but France would keep them in check. This "peace" correspondence began from a suggestion from Vettori, but it was Machiavelli to whom it meant most. For Vettori it was largely a recreation, and, seeking a solution less passionately than Machiavelli, he was, in an off-hand way, less doctrinaire and more realistic, hoping less for a panacea than a stop-gap. For Machiavelli, with nothing else to do, the correspondence was a central preoccupation and, besides, there was always the hope that what he wrote would find its way to the eyes of the Medici.

In a letter of 12 July Vettori had said that Leo wanted to maintain the Church in all the possessions he found her endowed with "unless to make over some to his relations Giuliano [his younger brother] or Lorenzo [his nephew], to whom he is eager to give states." It seemed that there would soon be new jobs for men of experience who could commend themselve to the Medici. Machiavelli did not represent himself as a man of glibly encouraging counsels. Vettori has seen Milan, Venice, and Ferrara as uniting to contain France and the Swiss. Machivelli's answer was downright. Milan would always be a danger spot, with its weak duke and Swiss tutelage, he pointed out on 10 August.

> As for the union of the other Italians—you make me laugh. First, because there never will be any union that will do any good, and even if the leaders were united it would not be enough, for they have no arms worth a halfpenny. . . . In the second place, because the tails are not united to the heads— if this generation takes a step to further any cause, they fall to squabbling amongst themselves.

Vettori, on the 20th, attempted to defend the morale of Italian armies, pointing out that even the French were not uniformly effective. In 1494 they had promenaded through the peninsula, but Novara had seen them defeated, and now they were frightened by—of all countries—England, who had hardly known how to tell one end of a sword from another for twenty-five years. [9]

Machiavelli replied on the 26th in a letter dated from Florence. The Italians, as at present organized in mercenary bands, would never change and become good soldiers. The best armies are those composed of native troops—it was so amongst the Romans and is true today of the Swiss. If the French could be victors one day and be vanquished another, can the Italians become victors in their turn? No. The French won against divided and mixed armies, and when they lost it was to national forces,

9. Henry VIII of England and Francis I of France were truculent antagonists, and Henry was especially aggressive.

like those of the Swiss (at Novara) and English (at the battle of the Spurs).[1] He reviews the international situation, starting with a scathing description of the heads of states. Significantly, the only one who is flatteringly described is the pope.

> We have a pope who is wise, prudent and respected; an unstable and fickle emperor, a haughty and timid king of France; a king of Spain who is miserly and close-fisted; a king of England who is rich, wrathful and thirsty for glory; the Swiss—brutal, victorious, and insolent, and we Italians—poor, ambitious, and craven.

With this mixture any peace—either "yours" or "mine"—is difficult, and none likely. Nor can one be framed by reason alone. Monarchs behave so irrationally—as the emperor with the Swiss, whom he should fear but does not—"that I hesitate to judge anything." He confessed himself terrified by the situation. If France does not protect Italy (once given Lombardy, a condition of Machiavelli's "peace") he sombrely concludes his letter, "then I see no other remedy, and will now begin to mourn with you our ruin and slavery, which, if it does not happen today, or tomorrow, will come in our time." This was the last letter he wrote to Vettori before telling him, on 10 December, that he had almost finished a short treatise *De principatibus*.

The Prince, as this work came to be known, is a natural outcome of Machiavelli's interest in external affairs, and in a sense is a continuation of the "peace" correspondence in treatise form. He had not yet shown (as he was to show later in the *Discourses*) much interest in internal, constitutional affairs. His work for the Ten had led him to think primarily of Florence's impact on other states. He was concerned with Italian resistance to France and Spain, not with the balance of classes within his own city. He accepted the fact of Medicean domination. The Florentines had shown in their welcome of Giovanni and their rapture over his being made Pope that they endorsed the family's return. Machiavelli was still hopeful of employment. The Medici had as yet done nothing within Florence so threatening to the republican constitution as to divert his attention from the enthralling and tragic scenes in Italy and Europe as a whole. When he ceased to write to Vettori in August he continued to think about how to give strength to states which had no armies and little desire to unite against their common enemies. His diplomatic career had shown him some of the factors that led to power in the modern world, in Cesare Borgia he had seen an enthralling attempt to knock a new state together. Preoccupied with the need for drastic action in external affairs, it was natural for Machiavelli, though a republican in

1. The battle of Guinegatte (1513), in which Henry VIII, with the Emperor Maximilian, defeated the French.

sympathy—was not the state which canalized the energies of all sections of the community potentially the strongest?—to think in terms of princes. To reason *de principatibus* was, besides, the most dynamic way of relieving his own nostalgia for action in diplomacy and war.

The work was a release, too, from personal distress. Writing to his nephew Gionvanni Vernaccia on 4 August, Machiavelli tells him of the death of a three-day-old daughter, and says towards the end of the letter: "I am well in body—but ill in every other way. And I see no hope save from God." The letter of 10 December, perhaps the most famous letter ever written by an Italian, shows how the hours spent each day in his study helped to bring a measure of balance and even exhilaration into his life as a whole.[2]

At this important moment, then, the documents do not fail us. In the spring and summer the "peace" correspondence showed his all-consuming interest in the international political scene. In the autumn, as this letter proves, he drew on his experience and his reading to add —though in a profoundly personal way—to the popular class of books *de regimine principum*, "On Princely Rule." And when it was drafted he began to see it as a possible means of getting employment and to think of dedicating it to the pope's older brother, who was rumored to be on the point of obtaining a principality of his own from the territories of the Church. How far *De principatibus* resembled the final *Il Principe* at this unplumped and unpolished stage is not known, but probably the only major change was the addition some time afterwards of the dedication and the last chapter, the exhortation to the dedicatee to liberate Italy from the barbarians.

The book was a discussion of princedoms, with special emphasis on new ones—the result of recent conqest, the products of change and themselves liable to change—and on how to render them stable through the exercise of special qualities by the prince himself, by his choice of agents and his use of a national army. Finally, Machiavelli justifies the book by showing that politics is a science from which men can learn, not just a learned recreation to be indulged in while Fortune dictates what is done; Fortune, he emphasizes, can, and must, be made to serve the deft and resolute prince. It was written to satisfy a need, but the impulse was a personal rather than a specific political one; the energy with which it was written imposed a unity of mood rather than of content. So far as is known, it was never subjected to final revision nor actually presented to Giuliano or his nephew Lorenzo, to whom Machiavelli dedicated it when Giuliano died in 1516.

The Prince reflects Machiavelli's fifteen years' experience in the chancery service. They had been years of war or of an uneasy peace that was scarcely distinct from war. The consistent good faith he vaunted in

2. See the full letter, pages 126–29.

himself as an employee could be folly or treachery if practiced by statesmen, under cover of whose purely pragmatic use of truth and falsehood ordinary citizens could indulge their own harmless rectitude. "Everyone realizes how praiseworthy it is for a prince to honor his word and to be straightforward rather than crafty in his dealings; nonetheless contemporary experience shows that princes who have achieved great things have been those who have given their word lightly." Machiavelli does not simply endorse the use of bad faith in case of necessity—the lie that diverts the killer from his victim—but as a natural part of statecraft. He had seen and admired the success of princes like Louis XII, Ferdinand, Cesare Borgia, Alexander VI and Julius II, and seen that all had depended at times on deception. As an amateur of war he was familiar with the need for strategem and deceit, and had read the praise of these devices in ancient writers on military matters. As a diplomatist he had combated men who were professionally committed to outwit and deceive him; as Soderini's *mannerino*[3] he had been the victim of malice and intrigue. He had, besides, a relish for cleverness, whatever form it took. All these factors, together with the dramatic form in which he couched his arguments, help to push his observations on good faith and bad faith to an extreme. If men were good, then one should be good in return, "but because men are wretched creatures, who would not keep their word to you, you need not keep your word to them." Machiavelli could not observe without exhorting. It is the "go thou and do likewise" tone that has caused offense, not the evidence from which this advice is deduced. His impatience of observation for its own sake, without it being stripped, as it were, for action, led him to omit saving clauses which might otherwise humanize his statements. "Men will always be false to you unless they are compelled by necessity to be true" is not a statement to be literally maintained by a man in the circle of his family and friends, but in the form "A statesman in time of crisis should act as though men will always be false," it is less open to criticism. Moreover, his assumption that craft and cruelty are necessary is accompanied by an acceptance that they stain a prince's noblest attribute—his glory.

There is hardly a year from Machiavelli's career in the chancery that cannot be shown to have provided some evidence, or reflection on events, that helped to shape *The Prince*. A clear reference to his French experience that justice and reason are but subsidiary weapons—that the unarmed man is "Ser Nihilo"[4]—is to be found in Chapter 14, which is about the need for a national army. "Among other evils caused by being disarmed, it renders you contemptible." *The Prince* contains three chapters on soldiers. The worst sort are mercenary—and he instances Vitelli. Only slightly better are friendlies, auxiliaries—and he describes the perils that threatened Florence owing to her use of French troops

---

3. "Little man."   4. "Mr. Nothing."

against Pisa. Then, "I shall never hesitate to cite Cesare Borgia and his conduct as an example," Machiavelli wrote, and went on to describe how, after experimenting with mercenary and auxiliary troops, Cesare came to rely upon his own subjects. The lessons of the mission to Cesare and the advice of the tract *Remarks on the raising of money* recur here in extended form: negotiation must be based on strength; neutrality is fatal. And the warning he gives there that the Florentines have a baneful optimism which sees a day's sunshine as lasting for ever is echoed in a warning to princes not to be taken unawares by war "as it is a common fault of men not to reckon on storms during fair weather." The judicial murder of Ramiro Lorqua, brusquely reported in the dispatch of 26 December 1502, now becomes a symbol of wisely resolute political action. In Chapter 12 when Machiavelli states that "the main foundations of every state, new states as well as ancient or composite ones, are good laws and good arms," we hear an echo from the infantry ordinance, and his reflections in Chapter 6 on the problems facing a reformer, whose own side only supports him halfheartedly while his opponents fight *à l'outrance*,[5] reflect his own teething troubles with the militia. The chapter "How much human affairs are governed by fortune, and how fortune may be opposed" is almost all extended from passages in the letter to Soderini in Ragusa; so, too, the musing on the phenomenon of different means producing identical ends, the conclusion that "the successful man is he whose mode of procedure accords with the needs of the times." In Chapter 3 of *The Prince*, about states that absorb new territories, the tone of the argument—concise, intense, and personal— and the matter itself (the problem is illustrated by the recent behavior of the French in Italy) make it seem like a continuation of the "peace" correspondence. This chapter epitomizes the way in which Machiavelli called on his past experience. The point that "men must be either pampered or crushed" was made in 1503 in the pamphlet on the Val di Chiana rebellion. His scorn of those who play for time instead of taking active precautions was confirmed, as we have seen, by his earliest diplomatic encounters. He goes on to elaborate the argument he had had with d'Amboise in 1500 about the errors of French policy in Italy. D'Amboise had defended French support of the Borgia by referring to promises made by Louis to Alexander VI. Machiavelli's comment in *The Prince* is fortified by the behavior of Julius II in cancelling papal promises to the Bolognese. "A prudent ruler," he says, "cannot, and should not, honor his word when it places him at a disadvantage, and when the reasons for which he made his promise no longer exist."

This dour conclusion was the result of his own observation, and this is true of all the conclusions in *The Prince*. Conversations with the illustrious shades of antiquity play a much smaller part than the letter

5. "To the bitter end."

of 10 December might have led Vettori to believe, and he illustrates all his important points by quoting contemporary instances. He repeats his double indebtedness in the dedication.

> I have not found among my belongings anything as dear to me or that I value as much as my understanding of the deeds of great men, won for me from a long acquaintance with contemporary affairs and a continual study of the ancient world.

But this statement, though it increased the fashionableness and respectability of the work, conceals the dependence in raw contemporary experience.

His use of historical illustrations was rhetorical and arbitrary. In the last years of his life, when writing the *History of Florence*), he arranged his evidence, and sometimes warped it, to drive home general principles. He does this even more in the earlier work, where he was not concerned with the past, even the immediate past, as such. He cuts the film to obtain significant stills: Cesare Borgia's shoddy decline becomes irrelevant; "I know of no better precepts to give a new prince than ones derived from Cesare's actions," he writes in Chapter 7. He is not concerned to re-create. His aim is to expose in history the nerve of resolute actions. He is not concerned to qualify his conclusions. The hesitations, the exceptions, the safeguards could be shaded in when they were applied to particular situations. When he comes to a subject which cannot be reduced to black and white, he moves aside. "There are many ways in which a prince can win [the people] over. These vary according to circumstances, so no definite rule can be given and I shall not deal with them here." The style he uses shows a similar scorn of sinuosities. There are few literary flowers: a handful of metaphors and analogies, most of these being pithy, familiar, and racy, and one parable in which David is shown refusing Saul's arms when he goes out against Goliath: "arms belonging to someone else either fall from your back [mercenaries], or weigh you down [auxiliaries], or impede your movements [a mixture of both]."

Machiavelli was not seeking in *The Prince* to give specific advice for the present situation, but the book is vibrant, nevertheless, with the conviction that advice is needed and that he is the one to give it. "The wish to acquire more," he remarks in Chapter 3, "is admittedly a very natural and common thing." It followed that change and flux should be taken as a norm, and that rulers should never relax their vigilance. There was a danger, especially when disasters were coming thick and fast, that men would throw up their hands and declare themselves the playthings, not the master, of events. The book stresses man's responsibility to act; fortune—the pattern of events—can be directed by the self-reliant man. It is true that, in one sense, Cesare's own downfall "was not his fault but arose from the extraordinary and inordinate malice of fortune," but in another sense he fell because, at a moment of crisis, he wavered; though ill at the time of Pius III's election, on that pope's death he should not have supported Giuliano della Rovere, who, as Julius II, remembered all too clearly the injuries that Cesare had formerly done him. "So the duke's choice was a mistaken one, and it was the cause of his ultimate ruin." Men should never blame fate for their disasters; "the only sound, sure, and durable methods of defense are those based on your own actions and prowess."

The importance of his work, and its novelty, Machiavelli claimed, resided in the fact that he was concerned only with *il vero*,[6] the true picture of what actually happened, and that he only talked about politics in terms directly deduced from the way in which men had behaved and did behave. To have a private morality up one's sleeve and put it to one's nose when the stench of political morality became too great was sheer hypocrisy. Referring to the extreme cruelty of Hannibal, he noted that "the historians, having given little thought to this, on the one hand admire what Hannibal achieved, and on the other condemn what made his achievements possible." But you cannot have it both ways—admire the end and deplore the means. Machiavelli emphasized that his approach (familiar enough in discussion and dispatch) was something new in a work of political theory. Writing for statemen, he will do them the service of writing in terms that they can apply directly to the problems of the real world. "Since my intention is to say something that will prove of practical use to the inquirer," he emphasized in Chapter 15,

> I have thought it proper to represent things as they are in real truth, rather than as they are imagined . . . the gulf between how one should live and how one does live is so wide that a man who neglects what is actually done for what should be done learns the way to self-destruction rather than self-preservation. The fact is that a man who wants to act virtuously in every way necessarily comes to grief among so many who are not virtuous. . . . If a person wants to maintain his rule he must learn how not to be virtuous, and to make use of this or not according to need.

Quixotry, in fact, is one of the worst foibles a statesmen can indulge in.

There was naturally an embarrassment in talking so frankly even in a manuscript not intended, so far as we know, for the press, but this insistence on a double standard of morality, a sense of private right and wrong from which the responsible ruler must diverge as necessity dictates,

6. "The truth."

is made to play a surprisingly emphatic role in *The Prince*. One more example will suffice to show how Machiavelli labored the point. "You have to understand this, that a prince, and especially a new prince," he wrote in Chapter 18, "cannot observe all those things which give men a reputation for virtue, because, in order to maintain his state, he is often compelled to act in defiance of good faith, of charity, of human courtesy, of religion." The point about this remark is not that it is shocking but that it is obvious. The lessons of *The Prince* do not require the anxious moral glosses with which Machiavelli surrounds them. Statesmen had been functioning efficiently on Machiavellian lines for centuries, and by begging them to be self-conscious about the motives for their actions, Machiavelli was not aiding but embarrassing their freedom of action.

If Machiavelli had been born to the ruling class, he would not have been concerned to defend its acceptance of expediency. As it was, he could not identify himself with the prince without bringing with him the conscience of a subject. For all its dogmatic force there is a tentative, apologetic note in *The Prince*. This is what I would do, Machiavelli seems to be saying, and this is why it would be allowable for me to do it. The streak of republican high-mindedness, which was never far beneath the surface in Florence, forced Machiavelli to make those explanations which blackened his reputation with posterity. There were complex motives which helped him identify himself with the interests of his Prince: confidence in his own powers, frustration at the bungling of others, a sense of urgency, the glamour of power; but none of these lifted him clear of the standards of his family and his class. Princes, especially new princes, must use cruelty and fraud to secure themselves, he wrote, and princes all over Europe would have greeted this dictum with an acquiescent and unalarmed nod. But Machiavelli could not leave the matter there. He elaborated, saying of cruelties: "We can say that cruelty is used well (if it is permissible to talk in this way of what is evil) when it is employed once for all, and one's safety depends on it, and then it is not persisted in." It is as though Machiavelli's Prince had started life as an honest bourgeois, and needed constant reassurance that he need act no longer as a private citizen. The assumption that political action would be based on expediency was part of Machiavelli's novel approach to his subject; the laboring of this assumption a reminder that he brought to it a not altogether unconventional state of mind.

[After writing *The Prince*, Machiavelli sent the manuscript to Vettori, in the hope that Vettori, through his connections at the papal court, might be able to arrange a post of some sort. But Vettori either couldn't or wouldn't help his old friend, so their correspondence turned to other topics, mostly girl chasing. Toward the end of 1514, however, politics came up again, and events turned Machiavelli back to a reconsideration of his manuscript.]

It is possible that it was at this point that Machiavelli took up *The Prince* and on rereading it gained the impetus to crown it with the "Exhortation to Liberate Italy from the Barbarians." Here at last, through Paolo's patronage,[7] was the longed-for chance of employment with the Medici. Here was a concrete proposal which would call for talents such as his, and a situation to which much of the subject-matter of *The Prince* was directly relevant. Italy now stood in even greater peril of invasion than at the end of 1513. He began by dwelling on the urgency of the situation. In his letter of 10 December 1514, he had urged a French alliance; now, in this last chapter, with an optimism of which there had been no trace in his correspondence in 1513, he urged that the opposing Swiss and Spanish armies were not invincible. He referred again, as he had in the recent letter of 31 January, to Duke Valentino—"a gleam of hope has appeared before now which gave hope that some individual might be appointed by God for her redemption, yet at the highest summit of his career he was thrown aside by fortune." Now there was a second chance to save Italy. But salvation must come from strength—and Machiavelli, the creator of the militia, and identified with it as with no other aspect of his career, spent more than a third of his space stressing the need for an indigenous army trained on lines superior to the recently reconstituted militia forces, damaging the literary shape of the chapter for the sake of an emphasis that would direct attention to his own qualifications for employment.

This personal plea, and the note of passionate faith that Italy's salvation could be at hand which occurs in two paragraphs of this exhortation, were vain. Cardinal dei Medici, who had known of Machiavelli's ideas through Francesco Vettori, had not been softened by them. On hearing of Paolo's interest in Machiavelli he wrote to Giuliano to forbid his employment. Once more Machiavelli had to turn from thoughts of an active life to one of reflection; from an absorption with external relations and the actions of princes to a growing concern with internal relations and constitutional expedients. He was not to write to Vettori again for twelve years. Modern events had no place for him. He turned instead to the study of the past.

7. Vettori's brother Paolo was in the service of Giuliano de' Medici.

FELIX GILBERT

[Fortune, Necessity, *Virtù*]†

* * *

According to Machiavelli, actions, whether they were those of an individual or those of a collective group, could be the result of motivations which could be rationally explained, but they could also be instinctive. Of this there is testimony in Machiavelli's strange description of the pagan "sacrificial acts in which there was much shedding of blood and much ferocity, and in them great numbers of animals were killed. Such spectacles, because terrible, caused men to become like them."[1] The ideal at which Machiavelli aimed in his recommendations for a perfect republic was the creation of a unified body, which, by acting instinctively, generated the strength, single-minded will power, and vitality necessary for political success. Such a republic possessed *virtù*.

Although there was nothing new in Machiavelli's use of the Roman republic as a pattern for imitation, he differed from his contemporaries in what he believed the Roman example taught. Machiavelli's views made it easier than his contemporaries thought—as well as more difficult—to imitate Rome. To Machiavelli, political revival could not be achieved only by imitating Roman institutions or just by effecting a moral reeducation of individuals in order to produce obedience and self-sacrifice. But they were accompaniments and consequences of what was essential for a political renaissance. To Machiavelli, the imitation of Rome meant a return to a life according to man's inherent natural instincts.

To Machiavelli, man is one of the forces of nature and man's strength emerges in accepting this fate. This conception of man gave Machiavelli's political utopia its unique character. For Machiavelli *was* the creator of an utopia; with his image of Roman politics he made his contribution to the body of literature in which perfect societies are constructed. But whereas the architects of other utopias place man outside history in a social world free of political conflicts and tensions so that he can live in permanent harmony and peace, Machiavelli's ideal political order was one in which man lives in time and is subject to its ravages. It was the test of a good political order to grow, to expand and to absorb other political societies, even to ward off decline for a

† From *Machiavelli and Guicciardini* (Princeton: Princeton UP, 1965) 191–200. Reprinted by permission.

1. *Discorsi* II, 2. See also the famous passage in *The Prince*, chap. 18; or see *Discorsi* I, chap. 18.

while as Rome had been able to do. But decline was inevitable; everything on earth has to undergo the natural cycle of birth, flowering,
decline and death.[2] Man's action remains tied to the specific, steadily
changing circumstances of the situation in which he finds himself at
the moment. It was of little relevance to consider man's qualities ab-
stractly and in isolation; the interaction of man and his surroundings
was the sensitive point at which the potentialities of man for political
action were revealed.

The crucial significance of this idea becomes evident when we go
beyond a discussion of Machiavelli's political views and analyze the
assumptions on which they were based. Machiavelli was not a philosopher. He intended neither to outline a philosophical system nor to
introduce new philosophical terms. Here again what is characteristic is
the particular turn which he gave to the commonly used concepts dealing
with the problems of human existence. The great images through which
Machiavelli tried to define the strength and weakness of man's position
in the universe were the same as those used by his contemporaries:
Fortuna, *virtù*, and *Necessità*. But a precise reading of Machiavelli's
works reveals distinctive variations. Like others who wrote before him,
Machiavelli recognized *Necessità* as a factor determining actions but
outside man's control. However, in Machiavelli's view *Necessità* is not
just a hostile force which makes man's actions purely automatic.[3] *Necessità* may coerce man to take an action which reason demands; *Necessità* may create opportunities. In whatever situation man finds himself
the final outcome depends on his response to the conditions which
Necessità has produced. Thus, according to Machiavelli, rarely is there
a situation which ought to be regarded as entirely desperate. At most
times there are possibilities for men to turn circumstances to their advantage. As long as man uses all the capacities with which nature has
endowed him he is not helpless in the face of external pressures.

The view that man has the possibility of controlling events also shaped
Machiavelli's idea of the relation between *virtù* and *Fortuna*. In general
Machiavelli's ideas on this topic were again those commonly held in
his time: he believed that man can exert a certain counterweight against
Fortuna, and that there is a certain balance between *virtù* and *Fortuna*:
"I think it may be true that *Fortuna* is the ruler of half of our actions,
but that she allows the other half or thereabouts to be governed by us,"
he writes in the twenty-fifth chapter of the *Prince* on "How much *Fortuna*
can do in human affairs and how it may be opposed."[4] At the end of
the same chapter he wrote the famous statement that "*Fortuna* is a
woman, and it is necessary, if you wish to master her, to conquer her

---

2. *Discorsi* III, 1 or 6, or at many other places.

3. See particularly *Discorsi* III, 12, but also I,

3 or 6.

4. *The Prince*, chap. 25.

by force; and it can be seen that she lets herself be overcome by the bold rather than by those who proceed coldly."[5] Others before Machiavelli had said that *Fortuna* was capricious and smiled only on those who were her favorites. The assumption of *Fortuna's* preference for the bold re-echoed the Latin adage that *"fortes fortuna adjuvat."* However Machiavelli's formulation modified these common views. In contrast to the static quality inherent in the belief in the existence of *Fortuna's* elect, Machiavelli's formulation presumed the dynamism of a constantly changing scene in which sudden action can bring about the assistance of *Fortuna*.

A further implication in Machiavelli's simile of the relation between *virtù* and *Fortuna* also expressed his belief that this constant change takes the form of a struggle; continuous strife is an abiding condition of political life. His insistence on the decisive importance of power in politics can be regarded as the counterpart of this fundamental attitude to the nature of politics. His image pitting *virtù* and *Fortuna* against each other in a struggle for superiority indicates that he believed that the chance of controlling external events is offered to man only in brief, fleeting moments. Therefore man must make use of a singular conjuncture in which there must be a meeting of circumstances and invyduality.[6]

This demand for coincidence of individual *virtù* with favorable circumstances pointed to the most striking and revolutionary feature of Machiavelli's political thought. No special human quality will guarantee success in politics; the qualities by which man can control events vary according to the circumstances. The impetuosity with which Julius II conducted his policy was appropriate to the situation in which the Church State found itself in the time of his reign. In less turbulent years the careful, almost timid rationalism of Soderini might have prevailed and saved Florence.[7] This kind of relativism pervades all the chapters of the *Prince* in which Machiavelli discussed the qualities required for political leadership.

These chapters of the *Prince* contain the essence of Machiavelli's thought in the sense that they exhibit most strongly his view that political action cannot be kept within the limits of morality. Although he indicated that amoral action might frequently be the most effective measure which can be taken in any situation, he never showed a preference for amoral actions over moral actions. He was not a conscious advocate of evil; he did not want to upset all moral values. But it is equally misleading to maintain the opposite: that Machiavelli wanted to replace Christian morality by another morality and that he encouraged politicians to dis-

5. *Ibid.* For an application of this view to the course of history, see *Discorsi* II, 1, but also 29, 30, and III, 31.

6. See *The Prince*, chap. 26, and *Discorsi* III, 9.

7. *Discorsi* III, 9.

regard customary morality because their motives for acting ought to be the good of the political society which represented the highest ethical value. Just as Machiavelli admitted that it might be possible to found political societies which could exist in peaceful isolation, he also believed that men could arrange their lives in such a manner that they could follow Christian morality.[8] But when men joined the game of politics they had to follow its rules; and these rules did not contain a distinction between moral and amoral actions.

Because Machiavelli felt that Christian morality frequently formed an obstacle to actions dictated by the rules of politics, he criticized Christian morality and the Church. On the other hand, because he realized the usefulness of religion for disciplining the members of society, he envisaged a religion, perhaps even a true Christianity, which broadened the concept of morality in such a way that it would encompass not only the virtues of suffering and humility, but also that of political activism.[9] But such observations were incidental rather than basic to Machiavelli's thinking. The central point of his political philosophy was that man must choose: he could live aside from the stream of politics and follow the dictates of Christian morality; but if man entered upon the *vita activa* of politics, he must act according to its laws.[1]

Finally Machiavelli's image of man's need to conquer *Fortuna* by force—corresponding to man's sexual drive—suggests the tension which Machiavelli regarded as a necessary accompaniment of political action. The need to concentrate on a brief moment, the need to use all possible weapons, and the need to choose from a variety of methods the one best suited to the given situation—all this implied that political action demanded not only awareness of one's aim but also intensity in pursuing it. Similar to the passage in the *Discourses* in which he saw men becoming animals, he suggested in the *Prince* that the ruler should be a lion or a fox, or best, both.[2] He did not refer to animals because they symbolize human qualities; to Machiavelli, animals possess the pristine genuineness which, in men, is weakened by reason. Man's control over his world depends on his attaining a level of instinctiveness where he becomes part of the forces surrounding him. This identification is prerequisite for man's mastery of political life.

Machiavelli believed in the creative power of man in the world of

8. "Doubtless these means are cruel and destructive of all civilized life, and neither Christian nor even human, and should be avoided by everyone. In fact the life of a private citizen would be preferable to that of a king at the expense of the ruin of so many human beings. Nevertheless, whoever is unwilling to adopt the first and humane course must, if he wishes to maintain his power, follow the latter evil course," *Discorsi* I, 26. On the issue of political isolation, see *Discorsi* I, 6 and 19; Machiavelli was skeptical about the possibility of keeping a state permanently out of power competition.

9. "Men have interpreted our religion according to the promptings of indolence rather than those of virtue," *Discorsi* II, 2.

1. See above, note 3.

2. "A prince being thus obliged to know well how to act as a beast, must imitate the fox and the lion," *The Prince*, chap. 18.

politics. Man's political potentialities comprised two aspects. Like many of his contemporaries Machiavelli believed in the rational nature of man; to him man was an instrument which had a rationally definable purpose and he could be employed in a calculable way. But at the same time, Machiavelli also saw man as an animal, driven by instincts which made him disregard obstacles and rational interests and which enabled him to exploit incalculable forces. But the opportunity when man could exert his power was rare, the moment brief and fleeting. Man was placed in a constantly changing world in which new forces and new situations were thrown up at any moment.

This recognition of the supreme challenge inherent in the ceaseless movement of history was a reflection of what Machiavelli had seen happening in Italy and all over Europe. And what had happened was becoming increasingly evident to greater numbers of Italians. Although Machiavelli's political proposals were aimed at answering questions raised by specific problems of the Florentine city-state, he was aware—and because of his experience as a diplomat he was certainly quite as well aware as anyone—of the relation of the Florentine crisis to the appearance of foreign armies on Italian soil. Since the French invasion of 1494, whatever happened in Italy was dependent on the struggles among the great powers beyond the Alps. The Italians had lost control of their fate, and every order, every peace was put in jeopardy again and again by new waves of invaders. The crises which had been shaking the Italian states since 1494 made it clear that every political action in Italy was circumscribed by forces originating at great distances. It was natural for Machiavelli to draw the conclusion that the dimension in which politics worked was history and that every political action had to be fitted into the context of historical change.

If, as we set forth at the beginning of this chapter, it was Machiavelli's intention to startle his readers with novel and contrary statements, his success was greater than ever he could have expected. To the religious of his age and of the following centuries his teachings—especially his proposition that man must choose between the rules of political activism and the precepts of Christian morality—were thought to be machinations of the devil. For his insistence on struggle and force as the quintessence of politics he was anathematized by those who believed in the harmony existing between enlightened self-interest and the common good. In more recent times he has been called the prophet of the national state and he has been credited with the discovery of the role of the ruling group in politics. There has been no generation since the time of the Renaissance which has not found some aspect of Machiavelli's writings repulsive or prophetic, puzzling or revealing. But the individual theses which he propounded would hardly have provoked such a furor had they not formed parts of a vision of politics, relevant and valid. Machiavelli expressed what men were slowly coming to realize: it is impossible to establish one permanent social order which mirrors the will of God or in which justice is distributed in such a way that it fulfills all human needs. Machiavelli clung to the idea that politics had its own laws and therefore it was, or ought to be, a science; its purpose was to keep society alive in the ever-moving stream of history. The consequences of this view—a recognition of the need for political cohesion and the proposition of the autonomy of politics which later developed into the concept of the state—have made Machiavelli's writings a landmark in the history of political thought. We can never return to concepts of politics which existed before Machiavelli wrote.

But Machiavelli is not merely a figure who contributed to the evolution of modern Western political thought. When we read his works we find that they still speak to us directly, immediately, in a strangely compelling way. Many of his examples are antiquated, many of his proposals exaggerated and unreal. But there are insights which disclose an opposite truth, there are passages which touch us like an electric shock. In placing politics in the stream of history, in demonstrating that every situation is unique and requires man to use all his forces to probe all the potentialities of the moment, Machiavelli has revealed—more than anyone before or after him—that, at any time, politics is choice and decision. Tanto nomini nullum par elogium.[3]

ERNST CASSIRER

Implications of the New Theory of the State†

The Isolation of the State and Its Dangers

The whole argument of Machiavelli is clear and coherent. His logic is impeccable. If we accept his premises we cannot avoid his conclusions. With Machiavelli we stand at the gateway of the modern world. The desired end is attained; the state has won its full autonomy. Yet his result has had to be bought dearly. The state is entirely independent; but at the same time it is completely isolated. The sharp knife of Machiavelli's thought has cut off all the threads by which in former generations the state was fastened to the organic whole of human existence. The political

3. The phrase is engraved on Machiavelli's tomb in Santa Croce: "For such a name no praise is adequate."
† From *The Myth of the State* by Ernst Cassirer (New Haven: Yale UP, 1973) chapter 12. Reprinted by permission of Yale University Press. Professor Cassirer's notes have been trimmed a little here and augmented a bit there, in view of the special circumstances of this edition.

world has lost its connection not only with religion or metaphysics but also with all the other forms of man's ethical and cultural life. It stands alone—in an empty space.

That this complete isolation was pregnant with the most dangerous consequences should not be denied. There is no point in overlooking or minimizing these consequences. We must see them face to face. I do not mean to say that Machiavelli was fully aware of all the implications of his political theory. In the history of ideas it is by no means unusual that a thinker develops a theory, the full purport and significance of which is still hidden to himself. In this regard we must, indeed, make a sharp distinction between Machiavelli and Machiavellism. There are many things in the latter that could not be foreseen by Machiavelli. He spoke and judged from his own personal experience, the experience of a secretary of the state of Florence. He had studied with the keenest interest the rise and fall of the "new principalities." But what were the small Italian tyrannies of the Cinquecento when compared to the absolute monarchies of the seventeenth century and with our modern forms of dictatorship? Machiavelli highly admired the methods used by Cesare Borgia to liquidate his adversaries. Yet in comparison with the later much more developed technique of political crimes these methods appear to be only child's play. Machiavellism showed its true face and its real danger when its principles were later applied to a larger scene and to entirely new political conditions. In this sense we may say that the consequences of Machiavelli's theory were not brought to light until our own age. Now we can, as it were, study Machiavellism in a magnifying glass.

There was still another circumstance that prevented Machiavellism from coming to its full maturity. In the centuries that followed, in the seventeenth and eighteenth centuries, his doctrine played an important role in practical political life; but, theoretically speaking, there were still great intellectual and ethical forces which counterbalanced its influence. The political thinkers of this period, with the single exception of Hobbes, were all partisans of the "Natural Right theory of the state." Grotius, Pufendorf,[1] Rousseau, Locke looked upon the state as a means, not as an end in itself. The concept of a "totalitarian" state was unknown to these thinkers. There was always a certain sphere of individual life and individual freedom which remained inaccessible to the state. The state and the sovereign in general were *legibus solutus* (released from the laws). But this meant only that they were free from legal coercion; it did not mean that they were exempt from moral obligations. After the beginning of the nineteenth century, however, all this was suddenly called in question. Romanticism launched a violent attack against the theory of natural rights. The romantic writers and philosophers spoke

1. Hugo Grotius and Samuel Pufendorf were distinguished jurists of the seventeenth century—the first Dutch, the second German [*Editor*].

as resolute "spiritualists." But it was precisely this metaphysical spiritualism that paved the way for the most uncouth and uncompromising materialism in political life. In this regard it is a highly interesting and remarkable fact that the "idealistic" thinkers of the nineteenth century, Fichte and Hegel, became the advocates of Machiavelli and the defenders of Machiavellism. After the collapse of the theory of natural rights the last barrier to its triumph was removed. There was no longer any great intellectual or moral power to check and counterbalance Machiavellism; its victory was complete and seemed to be beyond challenge.

That Machiavelli's *Prince* contains the most immoral things and that Machiavelli has no scruples about recommending to the ruler all sorts of deceptions, of perfidy, and cruelty is incontestable. There are, however, not a few modern writers who deliberately shut their eyes to this obvious fact. Instead of explaining it they make the greatest efforts to deny it. They tell us that the measures recommended by Machiavelli, however objectionable in themselves, are only meant for the "common good." The ruler has to respect this common good. But where do we find this mental reservation? *The Prince* speaks in quite a different, in an entirely uncompromising way. The book describes, with complete indifference, the ways and means by which political power is to be acquired and to be maintained. About the *right use* of this power it does not say a word. It does not restrict this use to any consideration for the commonwealth. It was only centuries later that the Italian patriots began to read into Machiavelli's book all their own political and national idealism. In any word of Machiavelli, declared Alfieri, we find the same spirit, a spirit of justice, of passionate love for freedom, of magnanimity and truth. He who understands Machiavelli's work in the right way must become an ardent enthusiast for liberty and an enlightened lover of all political virtues.

This is, however, only a rhetorical answer to our question, not a theoretical one. To regard Machiavelli's *Prince* as a sort of ethical treatise or a manual of political virtues is impossible. We need not enter here into a discussion of the vexed problem whether the last chapter of *The Prince*, the famous exhortation to deliver Italy out of the bonds of barbarians, is an integral part of the book or a later addition. Many modern students of Machiavelli have spoken of *The Prince* as if the whole book were nothing but a preparation for this closing chapter, as if this chapter were not only the climax but also the quintessence of Machiavelli's political thought. I think this view to be erroneous, and, as far as I see, the *onus probandi*[2] rests in this case with the advocates of the thesis. For there are obvious differences between the book taken as a whole and the last chapter, differences of thought and differences of style. In the book itself Machiavelli speaks with an entirely detached mind. Every-

---

2. "Burden of proof" [*Editor*].

one may hear him and make what use he will of his advice which is
available not only to the Italians but also to the most dangerous enemies
of Italy. In the third chapter Machiavelli discusses at great length all
the errors committed by Louis XII in his invasion of Italy. Without
these errors, he declares, Louis XII would have had no difficulty in
attaining his end, which was to subjugate the whole of Italy. In his
analysis of political actions Machiavelli never gives vent to any personal
feeling of sympathy or antipathy. To put it in the words of Spinoza he
speaks of these things as if they were lines, planes, or solids. He did not
attack the principles of morality; but he could find no use for these
principles when engrossed in problems of political life. Machivelli looked
at political combats as if they were a game of chess. He had studied the
rules of the game very thoroughly. But he had not the slightest intention
of changing or criticizing these rules. His political experience had taught
him that the political game never had been played without fraud, deception, treachery, and felony. He neither blamed nor recommended
these things. His only concern was to find the best move—the move
that wins the game. When a chess champion engages in a bold combination, or when he tries to deceive his partner by all sorts of ruses and
strategems, we are delighted and admire his skill. That was exactly
Machiavelli's attitude when he looked upon the shifting scenes of the
great political drama that was played before his eyes. He was not only
deeply interested; he was fascinated. He could not help giving his opinion. Sometimes he shook his head at a bad move; sometimes he burst
out with admiration and applause. It never occurred to him to ask by
whom the game was played. The players may be aristocrats or republicans, barbarians, or Italians, legitimate princes or usurpers. Obviously
that makes no difference for the man who is interested in the game
itself—and in nothing but the game. In his theory Machiavelli is apt
to forget that the political game is not played with chessmen, but with
real men, with human beings of flesh and blood; and that the weal and
woe of these beings is at stake.

It is true that in the last chapter his cool and detached attitude gives
way to an entirely new note. Machiavelli suddenly shakes off the burden
of his logical method. His style is no longer analytical but rhetorical.
Not without reason has that last chapter been compared to Isocrates'
exhortation to Philip.[3] Personally we may prefer the emotional note of
the last chapter to the cold and indifferent note of the rest of the book.
Yet it would be wrong to assume that in the book Machiavelli has
concealed his thoughts; that what is said there was only a sham. Machiavelli's book was sincere and honest; but it was dictated by his conception of the meaning and task of a *theory* of politics. Such a theory
must describe and analyze; it cannot blame or praise.

3. See L. A. Burd's notes in his edition of *"Il Principe,"* p. 366.

No one has ever doubted the patriotism of Machiavelli. But we should not confuse the philosopher with the patriot. *The Prince* was the work of a political thinker—and a very radical thinker. Many modern scholars are liable to forget or, at least, to underrate this radicalism of Machiavelli's theory. In their efforts to purge his name from all blame they have obscured his work. They have portrayed a harmless and innocuous but at the same time a rather trivial Machiavelli. The real Machiavelli was much more dangerous—dangerous in his thoughts, not in his character. To mitigate his theory means to falsify it. The picture of a mild or lukewarm Machiavelli is not a true historical portrait. It is a "fable convenue"[4] just as much opposed to the historical truth as the conception of the "diabolic" Machiavelli. The man himself was loath to compromise. In his judgments about political actions he warned over and over again against irresolution and hesitation. It was the greatness and the glory of Rome that in Roman political life all half measures were avoided.[5] Only weak states are always dubious in their resolves, and tardy resolves are always hateful.[6] It is true that men, in general, seldom know how to be wholly good or wholly bad. Yet it is precisely this point in which the real politician, the great statesman, differs from the average man. He will not shrink from such crimes as are stamped with an inherent greatness. He may perform many good actions, but when circumstances require a different course he will be "splendidly wicked."[7] Here we hear the voice of the real Machiavelli, not of the conventional one. And even if it were true that all the advice of Machiavelli was destined only for the "common good," who is the judge of this common good? Obviously no one but the prince himself. And he will always be likely to identify it with his private interest: he will act according to the maxim: *L'état c'est moi.*[8] Moreover, if the common good could justify all those things that are recommended in Machiavelli's book, if it could be used as an excuse for fraud and deception, felony, and cruelty, it would hardly be distinguished from the common evil.

It remains, however, one of the great puzzles in the history of human civilization how a man like Machiavelli, a great and noble mind, could become the advocate of "splendid wickedness." And this puzzle becomes the more bewildering if we compare *The Prince* with Machiavelli's other writings. There are many things in these other writings that seem to be in flagrant contradiction with views exposed in *The Prince*. In his *Discourses* Machiavelli speaks as a resolute republican. In the struggles between the Roman aristocracy and the plebeians his sympathy is clearly on the side of the people. He defends the people against the reproach

4. A "made-up story" [*Editor*].
5. *Discourses*, Book II, chap. 23.
6. Idem, Book II, chap. 15; Book I, chap. 38.
7. Idem, Book I, chap. 27. [See pp. 100–101 of this Norton Critical Edition—*Editor*].
8. "The state is me." Attributed to Louis XIV [*Editor*].

of inconstancy and fickleness;[9] he declares that the guardianship of public freedom is safer in the hands of the commons than those of the patricians.[1] He speaks in a very disparaging tone of the *gentiluomini*, of those men who lived in opulence and idleness on the revenues of their estates. Such persons, he declares, are very mischievous in every republic or country. But even more mischievous are those who are lords of strongholds and castles besides their estates, and who have vassals and retainers who render them obedience. Of these two classes of men the Kingdom of Naples, the Romagna and Lombardy were full; and hence it happened that in these provinces no commonwealth or free form of government ever existed; because men of this sort are the sworn foes to all free institutions.[2] Taking everything into consideration, declares Machiavelli, the people are wiser and more constant than a prince.[3]

In *The Prince* we hear very little of these convictions. Here the fascination of Cesare Borgia is so strong that it seems completely to eclipse all republican ideals. The methods of Cesare Borgia become the hidden center of Machiavelli's political reflections. His thought is irresistibly attracted to this center. "Upon a thorough review of the duke's conduct and actions," says Machiavelli,

> I see nothing worthy of reprehension in them; on the contrary, I have proposed them and here propose them again as a pattern for the imitation of all such as arrive at dominion by the arms or fortune of others. For as he had a great spirit and vast designs, he could not well have acted otherwise in his circumstances: and if he miscarried in them, it was entirely owing to the sudden death of his father, and the desperate conditions in which he happened to lie himself at that critical juncture.[4]

If Machiavelli reprehends anything in Cesare it is not his character; it is not his ruthlessness, his cruelty, his treachery and rapacity. For all this he has no word of blame. What he blames in him is the only grave error in his political career: the fact that he allowed Julius II, his sworn enemy, to be elected pope after the death of Alexander VI.

There is a story according to which Talleyrand,[5] after the execution of the Duke of Enghien by Napoleon Bonaparte, exclaimed: "C'est plus qu'un crime, c'est une faute!"[6] If this anecdote be true then we must

---

9. Idem, Book I, chap. 58. [See pp. 107–11 of this Norton Critical Edition—*Editor.*]
1. Idem, Book I, chaps. 4, 5.
2. Idem, Book I, chap. 55.
3. Idem, Book I, chap. 58. [See pp. 107–11 of this Norton Critical Edition—*Editor.*]

4. *The Prince*, chap. 7.
5. Charles Maurice de Talleyrand-Périgord (1754–1838), the subtlest and most devious diplomat of his day [*Editor*].
6. "It is more than a crime, it is a mistake" [*Editor*].

say that Talleyrand spoke as a true disciple of Machiavelli's *Prince*. All judgments of Machiavelli are political and moral judgments. What he thinks to be objectionable and unpardonable in a politician are not his crimes but his mistakes.

That a republican could make the Duca Valentino his hero and model seems to be very strange: for what would have become of the Italian Republics and all their free institutions under a ruler like Cesare Borgia? There are however two reasons that account for this seeming discrepancy in Machiavelli's thought: a general and a particular one. Machiavelli was convinced that all his political thoughts were entirely realistic. Yet when studying his republicanism we find very little of this political realism. His republicanism is much more "academic" than practical; more contemplative than active. Machiavelli had served, sincerely and faithfully, the cause of the city-state of Florence. As a secretary of the state he had combatted the Medici. But when the power of the Medici was restored he hoped to retain his post; he made the greatest efforts to make his peace with the new rulers. That is easily understandable. Machiavelli did not swear by the words of any political program. His was not a stern unyielding and uncompromising republicanism. He could readily accept an aristocratic government; for he had never recommended an ochlocracy, a dominion of the populace. It is not without reason, he declares, that the voice of the people has been likened to the voice of God.[7] But on the other hand he is convinced to give new institutions to a commonwealth, or to reconstruct old institutions on an entirely new basis, must be the work of one man.[8] The multitude is helpless without a head.[9]

Yet if Machiavelli admired the Roman plebs, he had not the same belief in the power of the citizens of a modern state to rule themselves. Unlike many other thinkers of the Renaissance he did not cherish the hope of restoring the life of the ancients. The Roman Republic was founded upon the Roman virtù—and this virtù is lost, once for all. The attempts to resuscitate ancient political life appeared to Machiavelli as idle dreams. His was a sharp, clear, and cool mind; not the mind of a fanatic and enthusiast like Cola di Rienzi. In Italian life of the fifteenth century Machiavelli saw nothing to encourage his republican ideals. As a patriot he felt the strongest sympathies for his fellow citizens, but as a philosopher he judged them very severely; his feeling bordered on contempt. Only in the North he was still able to find some traces of love of freedom and the ancient virtù. The nations of the North, he says, have to a certain degree been saved because they did not learn the manners of the French, the Italians, or the Spaniards—this corruption

7. *Discourses*, Book I, chap. 58. [See pp. 107–   8. Idem, Book I, chap. 9.
11 of this Norton Critical Edition—*Editor.*]   9. Idem, Book I, chap. 44.

of the world.[1] This judgment about his own times was irrevocable.
Machiavelli did not even admit that it could be questioned by anyone.
"I know not," he says,

> whether I may not deserve to be reckoned in the number of
> those who deceive themselves, if, in these discourses of mine,
> I render excessive praise to the ancient times of the Romans
> while I censure our own. And, indeed, were not the excellence
> which then prevailed and the corruption which prevails now
> clearer than the sun, I should proceed more guardedly in what
> I have to say. . . . But since the thing is so plain that everyone
> sees it, I shall be bold to speak freely all I think, both of old
> times and of new, in order that the minds of the young who
> happen to read these my writings may be led to shun modern
> examples, and be prepared to follow those set by antiquity
> whenever chance affords the opportunity.[2]

Machiavelli was by no means especially fond of the *principati nuovi*,
of the modern tyrannies. He could not fail to see all their defects and
evils. Yet under the circumstances and conditions of modern life these
evils seemed to him to be unavoidable. There is no doubt that Machiavelli personally would have abhorred most of the measures he recommended to the rulers of the new states. He tells us in so many words
that these measures are most cruel expedients, repugnant not merely to
every Christian, but to every civilized rule of conduct and such as every
man should shun, choosing rather to lead a private life than to be a
king on terms so hurtful to mankind. But, as he adds very characteristically, whoever will not keep to the fair path of virtue, must, to maintain
himself, enter the path of evil.[3] *Aut Caesar aut nihil*[4]—either to lead
a private, harmless and innocuous life, or to enter the political arena,
struggle for power, and maintain it by the most ruthless and radical
means. There is no choice between these two alternatives.

When speaking of Machiavelli's "immoralism" we must, however,
not understand this term in our modern sense. Machiavelli did not judge
human actions from a standpoint "beyond good and evil." He had no
contempt for morality; but he had very little esteem for men. If he was
a skeptic, his skepticism was a human rather than a philosophical skepticism. The best proof of this ineradicable skepticism, of this deep mistrust of human nature, is to be found in his comedy *Mandragola*. This
masterpiece of comic literature reveals perhaps more of Machiavelli's

---

1. Idem, Book I, chap. 55. "Perchè non hanno
possuto pigliare i costumi nè franciosi, nè spag-
nuoli, nè italiani; le quali nazioni tutte insieme
sono la corruttela del mondo." [Translated
loosely in the text—*Editor.*]
2. Idem, Book II, Preface.
3. Idem, Book I, chap. 26.
4. "Either Caesar or nothing" [*Editor*].

judgment about his contemporaries than all his political and historical writings. For his own generation and his own country he saw no hope. And in his *Prince* he tried to inculcate the same conviction of the deep moral perversion of men upon the minds of the rulers of states. This was an integral part of his political wisdom. The first condition for ruling men is to understand man. And we shall never understand him as long as we are suffering from the illusion of his "original goodness." Such a conception may be very humane and benevolent; but in political life it proves to be an absurdity. Those that have written upon civil government lay it down as first principle, says Machiavelli, and all historians demonstrate the same, that whoever would found a state, and make proper laws for the government of it, must presuppose that all men are bad by nature, and that they will not fail to show that natural depravity of heart, whenever they have a fair opportunity.[5]

This depravity cannot be cured by laws; it must be cured by force. Laws are, indeed, indispensable for every commonwealth—but a ruler should use other and more convincing arguments. The best foundations of all states, whether new, old, or mixed, says Machiavelli, are good laws and good arms. But since good laws are ineffective without arms, and since, on the other hand, good arms will always give due weight to such laws, I shall here no longer argue about laws but speak about arms.[6] Even the "saints," the religious prophets have always acted according to this principle as soon as they became rulers of states. Without this they were lost from the very beginning. Savonarola failed to attain his end, because he had neither power to keep those steady in their persuasion who acknowledged his mission nor to make others believe who denied it. Hence it comes that all the prophets who were supported by an armed force succeeded in their undertakings, whereas those that had not such a force to rely on were defeated and destroyed.[7]

Of course Machiavelli prefers by far the good, the wise, and noble rulers to the bad and cruel ones; he prefers a Marcus Aurelius to a Nero. Yet if you write a book that is destined solely for these good and just rulers, the book itself may be excellent but it will not find many readers. Princes of this kind are the exception, not the rule. Everyone admits how praiseworthy it is in a prince to keep faith, and to live with integrity. Nevertheless, as matters stand, a prince has also to learn the opposite art: the art of craft and treachery.

> A prince ought to know how to resemble a beast as well as a man, upon occasion: and this is obscurely hinted to us by ancient writers who relate that Achilles and several other princes in former times were sent to be educated by Chiron

5. Idem, Book I, chap. 3.

6. *The Prince*, chap. 12.

7. Idem, chap. 6.

the Centaur; that as their preceptor was half-man and half-beast, they might be taught to imitate both natures since one cannot long support itself without the other. Now, because it is so necessary for a prince to learn how to act the part of a beast sometimes, he should make the lion and the fox his patterns: for the lion has not cunning enough of himself to keep out of snares and toils; nor the fox sufficient strength to cope with a wolf: so that he must be a fox to enable him to find out the snares, and a lion in order to terrify the wolves.[8]

This famous simile is highly characteristic and illuminating. Machiavelli did not mean to say that a teacher of princes should be a brute. Yet he has to do with brutal things and must not recoil from seeing them eye to eye and from calling them by their right names. Humanity alone will never do in politics. Even at its best politics still remains an intermediary between humanity and bestiality. The teacher of politics must therefore understand both things: he must be half man, half beast.

No political writer before Machiavelli had ever spoken in this way. Here we find the clear, the unmistakable and ineffaceable difference between his theory and that of all his precursors—the classical as well as the medieval authors. Pascal says that there are certain words which, suddenly and unexpectedly, make clear the sense of a whole book. Once we meet with these words we no longer can have any doubt about the character of the book: all ambiguity is removed. Machiavelli's saying that a teacher of princes must be *un mezzo bestia e mezzo uomo*[9] is of such a kind: it reveals, as in a sudden flash, the nature and purpose of his political theory. No one had ever doubted that political *life*, as matters stand, is full of crimes, treacheries, and felonies. But no thinker before Machiavelli had undertaken to teach the *art* of these crimes. These things were done, but they were not taught. That Machiavelli promised to become a teacher in the art of craft, perfidy, and cruelty was a thing unheard of. And he was very thorough in his teaching. He did not hesitate or compromise. He tells the ruler that since cruelties are necessary they should be done quickly and mercilessly. In this case, and in this case alone, they will have the desired effect: they will prove to be *crudeltà bene usate*.[1] It is no use postponing or mitigating a cruel measure; it must be done at one blow and regardless of all human feelings. A usurper who has won the throne must not allow any other man or woman to stand in his way; he must extirpate the whole family of the legitimate ruler.[2] All these things may be called shameful; but in political

---

8. Idem, chap. 18.
9. "Half beast, half man" [*Editor*].
1. "Cruelties well used" [*Editor*].
2. *Discourses*, Bk. III, chaps. 4, 30; cf. *The Prince*, chap. 3: "a possederli sicuramente basta avere spenta la linea del principe che li dominava." ["To hold them securely it suffices to have wiped out the line of the prince who used to rule them"—*Editor*.]

life we cannot draw a sharp line between "virtue" and "vice." The two things often change places: if everything is considered we shall find that some things that seem to be very virtuous, if they are turned into actions, will be ruinous to the prince, whereas others that are regarded as vicious are beneficial.[3] In politics all things change their place: fair is foul, and foul is fair.

It is true that there are some modern students of Machiavelli who see his work in quite a different light. They tell us that this work was by no means a radical innovation. It was, after all, a rather commonplace thing; it belonged to a familiar literary type. *The Prince*, these writers assure us, is only one of the innumerable books that, under various titles, had been written for the instruction of kings. Medieval and Renaissance literatures were full of these treatises. Between the years 800 and 1700 there were accessible some thousand books telling the king how to conduct himself so that he may be "clear in his great office." Everyone knew and read these works: *De officio regis*, *De institutione principum*, *De regimine principum*. Machiavelli simply added a new link to this long list. His book is by no means *sui generis*;[4] it was rather a typical book. There is no real novelty in *The Prince*—neither a novelty of thought nor a novelty of style.[5]

Against this judgment we can, however, appeal to two witnesses: to the witness of Machiavelli himself and to that of his readers. Machiavelli was deeply convinced of the originality of his political views. "Prompted by that desire which nature has implanted in me fearlessly to undertake whatsoever I think offers a common benefit to all," he wrote in the Preface to his *Discourses*, "I enter on a path which, being untrodden by any though it involve me in trouble, may yet win me thanks from those who judge my efforts in a friendly spirit."[6] This hope was not disappointed: Machiavelli's readers judged likewise. His work was read not only by scholars or by students of politics. It had a much wider circulation. There is hardly one of the great modern politicians who did not know Machiavelli's book and who was not fascinated by it. Among its readers and admirers we find the names of Catarina de' Medici, Charles V, Richelieu, Queen Christina of Sweden, Napoleon Bonaparte. To those readers the book was much more than a book; it was a guide and lodestar in their political actions. Such a deep and permanent influence of *The Prince* would hardly be understandable if the book were only a specimen of a well-known literary type. Napoleon Bonaparte declared that of all political works those of Machiavelli were the only ones worth reading. Can we think of a Richelieu, a Catarina de' Medici, a Napoleon Bonaparte as enthusiastic students of works such as Thomas

3. *The Prince*, chap. 15.
4. "Unique" [*Editor*].
5. See Allan H. Gilbert, *Machiavelli's "Prince" and Its Forerunners. "The Prince" as a Typical Book "de Regimine Principum"* (Duke University Press, 1938).
6. See above, p. 90 [*Editor*].

Aquinas' *De regimine principum*, Erasmus' *Institutio principis Christiani*
or Fénélon's *Télémaque?*

In order to show the striking contrast between *The Prince* and all the
other works *De regimine principum* we need, however, not rely on
personal judgments. There are other and better reasons to prove that
there is a real gulf between Machiavelli's views and those of all previous
political writers. Of course *The Prince* had its forerunners; what book
has not? We may find in it many parallels to other writers. In Burd's
edition most of these parallels have been carefully collected and annotated. But literary parallels do not necesarily prove parallels of thought.
The Prince belongs to a "climate of opinion" quite different from that
of previous writers on the subject. The difference may be described in
two words. The traditional treatises *De rege et regimine*, *De institutione
regis*, *De regno et regis institutione* were *pedagogical* treatises. They were
destined for the education of princes. Machiavelli had neither the ambition nor the hope of being equal to this task. His book was concerned
with quite different problems. It only tells the prince how to acquire his
power and how, under difficult circumstances, to maintain it. Machiavelli was not naïve enough to assume that the rulers of the *principati
nuovi*, that men like Cesare Borgia, were apt subjects for "education."
In earlier and later books that called themselves *The King's Mirror* the
monarch was supposed to see, as in a mirror, his fundamental duties
and obligations. But where do we find such a thing in Machiavelli's
Prince? The very term "duty" seems to be missing in his book.

The Technique of Politics

Yet if *The Prince* is anything but a moral or pedagogical treatise, it
does not follow that, for this reason, it is an immoral book. Both judgments are equally wrong. *The Prince* is neither a moral nor an immoral
book: it is simply a technical book. In a technical book we do not seek
for rules of ethical conduct, of good and evil. It is enough if we are told
what is useful or useless. Every word in *The Prince* must be read and
interpreted in this way. The book contains no moral prescripts for the
ruler nor does it invite him to commit crimes and villainies. It is especially concerned with and destined for the "new principalities." It tries
to give them all the advice necessary for protecting themselves from all
danger. These dangers are obviously much greater than those which
threaten the ordinary states—the ecclesiastic principalities or the hereditary monarchies. In order to avoid them the ruler must take recourse
to extraordinary means. But it is too late to seek for remedies after the
evil has already attacked the body politic. Machiavelli likes to compare
the art of the politician with that of a skilled physician. Medical art
contains three parts: diagnosis, prognosis, and therapy. Of these a sound
diagnosis is the most important task. The principal thing is to recognize

the illness at the right moment in order to be able to make provision against its consequences. If this attempt fails the case becomes hopeless. "The physician," says Machiavelli,

> say of hectic fevers, that it is no hard task to get the better of them in their beginning, but difficult to discover them: yet in course of time, when they have not been properly treated and distinguished, they are easily discovered, but difficult to be subdued. So it happens in political bodies; for when the evils and disturbances that may probably arise in any government are foreseen, which yet can only be done by a sagacious and provident man, it is easy to ward them off; but if they are suffered to sprout up and grow to such a height that their malignity is obvious to every one, there is seldom any remedy to be found of sufficient efficacy to repress them.[7]

All the advice of Machiavelli is to be interpreted in this spirit. He foresees the possible dangers that threaten the different forms of government and provides for them. He tells the ruler what he has to do in order to establish and to maintain his power, to avoid inner discords, to foresee and prevent conspiracies. All these counsels are "hypothetical imperatives," or to put it in the words of Kant, "imperatives of skill." "Here," says Kant, "there is no question whether the end is rational and good, but only what one must do in order to attain it. The precepts for the physician to make his patient thoroughly healthy, and for a poisoner to ensure certain death, are of equal value in this respect, that each serves to effect its purpose perfectly."[8] These words describe exactly the attitude and method of Machiavelli. He never blames or praises political actions; he simply gives a descriptive analysis of them—in the same way in which a physician describes the symptoms of a certain illness. In such an analysis we are only concerned with the truth of the description not with the things spoken of. Even of the worst things a correct and excellent description can be given. Machiavelli studied political actions in the same way as a chemist studies chemical reactions. Assuredly a chemist who prepares in his laboratory a strong poison is not responsible for its effects. In the hands of a skilled physician the poison may save the life of man—in the hands of a murderer it may kill. In both cases we cannot praise or blame the chemist. He has done enough if he has taught us all the processes that are required for preparing the poison and if he has given us its chemical formula. Machiavelli's *Prince* contains many dangerous and poisonous things, but he looks at them with the coolness

---

7. *The Prince*, chap. 3.
8. See Kant, *Fundamental Principles of the Metaphysics of Morals*. English trans. by T. K. Abbott, *Kant's Critique of Practical Reason and Other Works on the Theory of Ethics* (6th ed. New York and London, Longmans, Green & Co., 1927), p. 32.

and indifference of a scientist. He gives his political prescriptions. By whom these prescriptions will be used and whether they will be used for a good or evil purpose is no concern of his.

What Machiavelli wished to introduce was not only a new science but a new *art* of politics. He was the first modern author who spoke of the "art of the state." It is true that the idea of such an art was very old. But Machiavelli gave to this old idea an entirely new interpretation. From the times of Plato all great political thinkers had emphasized that politics cannot be regarded as mere routine work. There must be definite rules to guide our political actions; there must be an art (*technē*) of politics. In his dialogue *Gorgias* Plato opposed his own theory of the state to the views of the sophists—of Protagoras, Prodikos, Gorgias. These men, he declared, have given us many rules for our political conduct. But all these rules have no philosopical purport and value because they fail to see the principal point. They are abstracted from special cases and concerned with particular purposes. They lack the essential character of a technē—the character of universality. Here we grasp the essential and ineradicable difference between Plato's technē and Machiavelli's *arte dello Stato*.[9] Plato's technē is not "art" in Machiavelli's sense; it is knowledge (*epistēmē*) based on universal principles. These principles are not only theoretical but practical, not only logical but ethical. Without an insight into these principles no one can be a true statesman. A man may think himself to be an expert in all problems of political life, because he has, by long experience, formed right opinions about political things. But this does not make him a real ruler; and it does not enable him to give a firm judgment, because he has no "understanding of the cause."[1]

Plato and his followers had tried to give a theory of the *Legal* State; Machiavelli was the first to introduce a theory that suppressed or minimized this specific feature. His art of politics was destined and equally fit for the illegal and for the legal state. The sun of his political wisdom shines upon both legitimate princes and usurpers or tyrants, on just and unjust rulers. He gave his counsel in affairs of state to all of them, liberally and profusely. We need not blame him for this attitude. If we wish to compress *The Prince* into a short formula we could perhaps do no better than to point to the words of a great historian of the nineteenth century. In the introduction to his *History of English Literature* Hippolyte Taine declares that the historian should speak of human actions in the same way as a chemist speaks of different chemical compounds. Vice and virtue are products like vitriol or sugar and we should deal with them in the same cool and detached scientific spirit. That was exactly the method of Machiavelli. To be sure he had his personal feelings, his political ideals, his national aspirations. But he did not allow these things to affect his political judgment. His judgment was

9. "Art of the State" [*Editor*].   1. See Plato, *Republic*, 533B.

that of a scientist and a technician of political life. If we read *The Prince* otherwise, if we regard it as the work of a political propagandist, we lose the gist of the whole matter.

SHELDON S. WOLIN

[The Economy of Violence]†

While there had been few political theorists before Machiavelli who would have contested the elementary proposition that "security for man is impossible unless it be conjoined with power,"[1] there had been still fewer prepared to declare power the dominant mark of the state. Indeed, it has been and remains one of the abiding concerns of the Western political theorist to weave ingenious veils of euphemism to conceal the ugly fact of violence. At times he has talked too sonorously of "authority," "justice," and "law," as though these honorific expressions alone could transform coercion into simple restraint. True, the psychological impact of power is softened and depersonalized if it is made to appear the agent of an objective good. True, too, there are numerous and subtle forms of coercion that shade off from the extreme of violence. That the application of violence is regarded as abnormal represents a significant achievement of the Western political tradition, yet if it is accepted too casually it may lead to neglect of the primordial fact that the hard core of power is violence and to exercise power is often to bring violence to bear on someone else's person or possessions. Writers before Machiavelli cannot be accused of having ignored power. The classical and mediaeval theorists had spoken long and eloquently of its brutalizing and corrupting effects on those who were called to exercise it. They rarely faced up, however, to the problem of the cumulative effect on society of the consistent application of coercion and the not infrequent use of violence. This evasion had come about largely because attention to power had arisen primarily in connection with the establishment or reform of a political system. It had been assumed that once affairs were set in motion along the prescribed paths, once proper education, the spread of knowledge or of faith, the improvement of social morality, and all of the other pressures flowing from a rightly ordered environment had begun to operate, there would be progressively less need for the systematic application of force. Nor is it easy to see in what ways the modern political theorist has illuminated the problem by the focal concepts of "decision-making," "the political process," and "who gets what, when, and how."

† From *The Politics of Vision* by Sheldon S. Wolin (Boston: Little, Brown, 1960) 220–35. Some of Professor Wolin's copious and informative notes have been omitted or curtailed.

1. *Discourses*, I, 1; *History*, II, 2. [Throughout Professor Wolin's notes, "*History*" refers to Machiavelli's *Florentine History—Editor.*]

All that can be said with confidence is that euphemisms for power and violence have not been dispelled by positivism.

With Machiavelli the euphemisms were cast aside and the state was directly confronted as an aggregate of power. Its profile was that of violence. Machiavelli believed that the vitalities of politics could not be controlled and directed without the application of force and the threat at least of violence. This conclusion was sustained partly by a certain scepticism about what Yeats once called "the profane perfection of mankind." It was also the outcome of a conviction about the inherent instability of the political world which could be combated, and then only partially, by resolute action. Equally important, however, in making power and violence urgent matters was the nature of the context in which power was exerted: the tightly-packed condition of political space which mocked any merely verbal attempt at translating power into simple direction or supervision of the affairs of society. Inevitably the role of the political actor was to dispense violence. This was most sharply defined in the case of the ruler who, after seizing power, was compelled "to organize everything in that state afresh."[2] "The new prince, above all other princes, cannot possibly avoid the name of cruel."[3] Even when the political actor was not faced with the task of creating a *tabula rasa*, he could not avoid inflicting injuries on some one. He must act while hemmed in by vested interests and expectations, privileges and rights, ambitions and hopes, all demanding preferential access to a limited number of goods.

If this were the nature of political action, what has been called an obsession with power on Machiavelli's part might be better described as his conviction that the "new way" could make no greater contribution than to create an economy of violence, a science of the controlled application of force. The task of such a science would be to preserve the distinguishing line between political creativity and destruction. "For it is the man who uses violence to spoil things, not the man who uses it to mend them, that is blameworthy."[4] The control of violence was dependent upon the new science's being able to administer the precise dosage appropriate to specific situations. In corrupt societies, for example, violence represented the only means of arresting decadence, a brief but severe shock treatment to restore the civic consciousness of the citizenry.[5] In other situations there might well be a diminishing need for extreme actions; men could be managed by playing on their fears, by using the threat rather than the actuality of coercion. But every application had to be considered judiciously, because the indiscriminate exercise of force and the constant revival of fear could provoke the greatest

---

2. *Discourses*, I, 26.
3. *Prince*, XVII.
4. *Discourses*, I, 9.
5. Ibid., III, 22. Yet there were also societies

which had become so corrupt as to be beyond redemption. Here power was unavailing. *Discourses*, I, 16.

of all dangers for any government, the kind of widespread apprehension and hatred which drove men to desperation. The true test of whether violence had been rightly used was whether cruelties increased or decreased over time.[6]

This preoccupation with economy was manifest also in Machiavelli's discussion of the external forms of violence—war, imperialism, and colonialism. One of the basic aims of the *Art of War* was to demonstrate that, while military action remained an unavoidable fact of the political condition, its costliness could be reduced by proper attention to strategy, discipline, and organization. *The Prince* and *The Discourses* followed the same theme of economy with counsels like these: a prince ought carefully to consider his resources, because, while a war may be started out of whim, it could not be as easily stopped; an unreliable army was an inefficient instrument of violence because it multiplied devastation without any of the compensations of victory; to avoid a necessary war was costly, but to prolong it was equally prodigal; a prince who found his position weakened by a victory had overestimated his power resources.[7]

In the matter of imperialism Machiavelli's adverted to the example of Rome for the significant reason that Roman imperial policy had sought to preserve the wealth of the subject populations and their native institutions, thereby limiting the cost in devastation for both conqueror and conquered. If imperialism were handled efficiently the destructive consequences could be minimized, and the whole transaction reduced to a mere change in power.[8] In contrast to Rome's controlled use of violence were those destructive wars which had been compelled by necessities, such as hunger, plague, or overpopulation.[9] Necessity was the enemy of calculated violence.

While Machiavelli's economy of violence subsumed both domestic and external actions, it never seriously entertained the proposition that the incidence of force could be appreciably lessened in international politics. The effects of violence might be controlled, but the resort to it would not diminish. He saw quite clearly that the absence of arbitrating arrangements, such as law and institutional procedure, left the international field more exposed than the domestic to conflicts of interest and the drives of ambition.[1] On the other hand, he believed that the internal politics of society could be structured by a variety of methods aimed at minimizing the need for extreme acts of repression. The im-

6. *Prince*, VIII; *Discourses*, I, 45; III, 6. In *Prince* XIX there was a significant contrast drawn between the degree and kind of violence needed to establish a new state, as exemplified by Severus, with that needed to maintain a state, as in the case of Marcus. Only the latter is called truly glorious by Machiavelli.

7. *Discourses*, II, 10; III, 32; *History*, VI, I.
8. *Discourses*, II, 6, 21, 32.
9. Ibid., II, 7.
1. See the working-paper of Machiavelli reproduced in Machiavel, *Toutes les lettres*, ed. E. Barincou, 2 vols., 6th ed. (Paris: Gallimard, 1955), Vol. I, p. 311.

portance of law, political institutions, and habits of civility was that in regularizing human behavior they helped to reduce the number of instances in which force and fear had to be applied.

Machiavelli's most important insight into the problem of internal power politics came when he began to explore the implications of a political system based on the active support of its members. He grasped the fact that popular consent represented a form of social power which, if properly exploited, reduced the amount of violence directed at society as a whole. One reason for the superiority of the republican system consisted in its being maintained by the force of the populace, rather than by force over the populace.[2] The economy of force which resulted from the people's feeling a sense of common involvement with the political order made it in the interests of the prince to cultivate their support. Lacking this, he would have to draw on his own fund of violence and the eventual result would be "abnormal measures" of repression. "The greater his cruelty, the weaker does his regime become."[3] Far from limiting his initiative, popular approval could be utilized to depreciate the great cost in violence of radical reforms. In a revolution by consent (*commune consenso*), only the few had to be harmed.[4]

In evaluating Machiavelli's economy of violence it is easy to criticize it as being the product of a technician's admiration for efficient means. A century like ours, which has witnesed the unparalleled efficiency displayed by totalitarian regimes in the use of terror and coercion, experiences difficulty in being tolerant on the subject. Yet to see Machiavelli as the philosopher of Himmlerism would be quite misleading; and the basic reason is not alone that Machiavelli regarded the science of violence as the means for reducing the amount of suffering in the political condition, but that he was clearly aware of the dangers of entrusting its use to the morally obtuse. What he hoped to further by his economy of violence was the "pure" use of power, undefiled by pride, ambition, or motives of petty revenge.[5] A more meaningful contrast to Machiavelli would be the great modern theoretician of violence, Georges Sorel. Here is a true example of the irresponsible political intellectual, fired by romantic notions of heroism, preaching the use of violence for ends which are deliberately and proudly clothed in the vague outline of the irrational "myth," contemptuous of the cost, blinded by a vision of virile proletarian barbarians who would revitalize the decadent West.[6] In contrast, there was no hint of child-like delight when Machiavelli contemplated the barbarous and savage destructiveness of the new prince, sweeping away the settled arrangements of society and "leaving nothing intact." There was, however, the laconic remark that

2. *Discourses* I, 9.
3. Ibid., I, 16.
4. Ibid., III, 7.

5. Ibid., II, 20; III, 8.
6. *Réflexions sur la violence*, 10th ed. (Paris, 1946), pp. 120–122, 168, 173–174, 202, 273.

is was better to be a private citizen than to embark on a career which involved the ruin of men.[7] This suggests that the theorist like Machiavelli, who was aware of the limited efficacy of force and who devoted himself to showing how its technique could be used more efficiently, was far more sensitive to the moral dilemmas of politics and far more committed to the preservation of man than those theorists who, saturated with moral indignation and eager for heroic regeneration, preach purification by the holy flame of violence.

* * * In most commentaries, Machiavelli's prince has emerged as the heroic ego incarnate, exhilarated by the challenges of political combat, unencumbered by moral scruples, and utterly devoid of any tragic sense of the impermanence of his own mission. In the preceding pages we have deliberately used the term "political actor" instead of "prince" or "ruler" to suggest that if the prince is looked upon as a kind of actor, playing many roles and wearing many masks, we may then better see that Machiavelli has given us something more than a single-dimensional portrait of a power-hungry figure. What we have is a portrait of modern political man drawn with dramatic intensity: if there was heroism, there was also anguish; if there was creativity, there was also loneliness and uncertainty.

These overtones were part of the new setting in which political action occurred. Machiavelli's actor was, to borrow a phrase from Merleau-Ponty, *"l'expression d'un monde disloqué."*[8] He performed in a universe hushed in moral stillness: there were no prefigured meanings, no implicit teleology—"it looks as if the world were become effeminate and as if heaven were powerless"[9]—and no comforting backdrop of a political cosmos, ruled by a divine monarch and offering a pattern for earthly rulers. Yet by his vocation, political man was compelled to act, to affirm his existence as a thoroughly politicized creature. To be committed to political action meant surrendering the multiple dimensions of life, and concentrating exclusively on the single dimension of politics.

By the nature of his situation political man must be an actor, for he addresses himself not to a single political condition, but to a variety of political conditions. Circumstances change, the conjunction of political factors follows a shifting pattern, hence the successful political actor cannot afford a consistent and uniform character. He must constantly rediscover his identity in the role cast for him by the changing times.[1] The mercurial quality of Machiavelli's political actor stands in sharp contrast to the classical and mediaeval conception of the character of

7. *Discourses*, I, 26.
8. "The expression of a dislocated world" [*Editor*]. Maurice Merleau-Ponty, *Humanisme et terreur*, 8th ed. (Paris: Gallimard, 1947), p. 205.

9. *Discourses*, II, 2.
1. *Prince*, XV; XVIII; *Discourses*, III, 9; Letter to Soderini (1513?), *Toutes les lettres*, vol. II, 327.

the good ruler. The older writers had viewed political knowledge as enabling men to establish stable situations, points of fixity within which ethical behavior became possible. Towards this end, they emphasized the importance of training men's characters so that virtue, for example, would be an habitual disposition towards the good.[2] For this reason classical and mediaeval writers tended to be suspicious of "prudence" and rarely ranked it among the supreme virtues.[3] Prudence implied a character which reacted too glibly to changing conditions.

Machiavelli's criticism of traditional moral theory was not, as has often been supposed, founded on cynicism or amorality. Nor is the more valid contention, that he was intent on divorcing the norms of political conduct from those governing private relationships, fully correct. Instead his concern was, first, to indicate the situations where political action ought to conform to the standards commonly applied to private conduct. Thus when a government operated within a stable, secure environment it ought to follow the accepted virtues such as compassion, good faith, honesty, humaneness and religion. Under these circumstances public and private ethics were identical.[4] But Machiavelli's second concern was to point out that, because most political situations were unstable and subject to flux, "a commonwealth and a people is governed in a different way from a private individual."[5] To adopt the rules of accepted morality was to bind one's behavior by a set of consistent habits. But rigidities in behavior were not suited to the vagaries of an inconsistent world. Moreover, to act uniformly merely armed one's opponents with a foreknowledge of your probable reactions to a given situation.[6] There was the further difficulty that one must act in a world where the other actors did not follow the same code.[7] To be sure, a similar issue arose in private relationships when other men did not honor the same moral usages, yet the cases were different because the responsibilities were different: in the one the individual suffered for being a moral man in an immoral society, while in the other a whole society might be injured because of the moral scruples of the ruler.[8]

But if politics posed issues for which common morality was inadequate, it did not follow that there was no connection between political action and traditional moral dictates. In the first place, it was difficult to govern a society and gain support if all of the ruler's actions violated the moral usages cherished by society. As a political actor, the ruler

---

2. Aristotle, *Politics*, 1332 b; 1337 a 11; see Aquinas: "Justice is a habit (*habitus*), whereby a man renders to each one his due with constant and perpetual will." *Summa Theologiae*, II, II, Q. 58, art. 1.

3. An important exception is the recognition by Aquinas of a distinctively political form of prudence.

4. *Prince*, XV; XVIII.

5. Cited in *Il Principe* by Burd, p. 290 fn.

6. *Prince*, XV.

7. Ibid., XVIII.

8. *Discourses*, II, 12.

must be a "skilful pretender and dissembler," he must "seem" to have
the virtues of good faith, charity, humanity, and religion. This was part
of his mastery in the art of illusions. "Men are so simple and so subject
to present needs that he who deceives in this way will always find those
who will let themselves be deceived."[9]

The basic question, however, was whether Machiavelli believed morality to be nothing more than a useful factor in political manipulation.
Did morality constitute a set of restraints or merely a datum for successful
action? Machiavelli's own words are so crucial that they deserve to be
quoted at length:

> I will even venture to say that [the virtues] damage a prince
> who *possesses them and always observes them*, but if he seems
> to have them they are useful. I mean that he should seem
> compassionate, trustworthy, humane, honest, and religious,
> and *actually be so*; but yet he should have his mind so trained
> that, when it is necessary not to practice these virtues, he can
> change to the opposite and do it skilfully. It is to be understood
> that a prince, especially a new prince, cannot observe all the
> things because of which men are considered good, because he
> is often obliged, if he wishes to maintain his government, to
> act contrary to faith, contrary to charity, contrary to humanity,
> contrary to religion. It is therefore necessary that he have a
> mind capable of turning in whatever direction the winds of
> Fortune and the variations of affairs require, and . . . that *he*
> *should not depart from what is morally right, if he can observe*
> *it*, but should know how to adopt what is bad, when he is
> obliged to.[1]

This passage suggests that instead of belaboring Machiavelli for pointing out the limitations of private ethics, attention ought to be directed
instead at the dual role which is thus created for the political actor. He
is made to perform in an atmosphere of tensions where accepted moral
values limit his behavior in normal circumstances, while a distinctively
political ethic, accompanied by the new knowledge, comes into play
when circumstances of necessity appear. By itself each form of ethic is
inadequate. The normally bad acts justified by the political ethic would,
if unrestrained by the inhibiting pressure of common morality, encourage unlimited ambition and all of its destructive consequences. On
the other hand, if common morality were to be extended to situations
for which it had not been designed, the consequences would be destructive of the order and power which made private morality possible. It was
the anguishing situation of the political actor that he must decide which

9. *Prince*, XVIII.   1. Ibid.

form of ethic should govern, but while the new science could facilitate his choice it could not compensate for the fact that he must partially dwell outside the realm of what is usually considered goodness. This means, in effect, that Machiavelli broke with classical theory which had approached the problems of political action with the question of how men could develop their moral potentialities through a life devoted to political office. But for Machiavelli the problem became more acute, for the issue no longer involved the statesman's quest for a moral perfection which, by its very moral quality, would benefit the community; it involved instead the political actor who was driven to break the moral law in order to preserve his society.

There was still another reason why politics could not satisfy the aspiration towards moral fulfillment. Traditional ethical notions operated on the assumption that the result of ethical conduct would be the creation of a desirable or more desirable state of affairs; that, for example, to act honestly or in good faith would produce situations which would be characterized by honesty and good faith. But Machiavelli rejected this notion of the literal translation of ethical acts into ethical situations and substituted instead a notion of the irony of the political condition. "Some things seem to be virtuous, but if they are put into practice will be ruinous . . . other things seem to be vices, yet if put into practice will bring the prince security and well-being."[2] Thus there was a kind of alchemy in the political condition whereby good was transmuted into evil, and evil into good.[3] Take, for example, the classical virtue of liberality which prescribed that acts of generosity should be done in a restrained manner. For Machiavelli's political actor such advice would be absurd; he was not a private donor, but a public figure whose actions, to be significant, needed a well-publicized flourish, even a vulgar display. But even with this amendment, it was doubtful that liberality qualified as a political virtue at all. The political actor usually expended not his private resources but public revenues. In a political setting liberality was translated into taxes, and these, in turn, were certain to breed popular resentments. Hence the vice of niggardliness became a political virtue; it was transformed, in fact, into liberality because it gave the subject a greater share of his own property.[4] Again, take the case of the trusting ruler who refused to believe that most men were vicious and ready to deceive at every turn. If a ruler of this type were to govern according to the virtue of clemency, he would soon be driven to adopt increasingly more severe and cruel measures in order to retain power. On the other hand, the contradictions of politics were such that a ruler who applied rational cruelty at the proper time would be more truly humane. Cruelty, when used economically, was more merciful than clemency, for where

2. Ibid., XV.
3. Ibid., XV; *History*, V, I.

4. *Prince*, XV–XVI.

the first injured only the few and the rest were restrained by apprehension, the second bred disorders which injured the *una universalità intera*. Nevertheless, the justification of cruel measures was not meant to imply that any method of retaining power was equal in moral worth to any other method. Cruelty might be useful in attaining certain ends, such as security, but it could not bring true glory.[5]

Machiavelli's concern with the shortcomings of traditional ethics and his quest for a suitable political ethic stemmed from a profound belief in the discontinuities of human existence. This was expressed in his view of history. History was conceived not as a smoothly flowing continuum, but as a process which irrupted in destructive frenzy, obliterating the achievements and memory of the past and condemning man to a perpetual labor of recovery.[6] Equally important, there were discontinuities between the forms of existence at a particular time. Religion, art, economic activity, private life and public seemed to be carried on according to special logics of their own, unconnected by any overarching heteronomous principle.[7] Thus man dwelt in a fragmentized universe and his special anguish came from being condemned to live in several alien worlds at once. If political existence was to be lived in a world of its own, it was imperative that there be relevant criteria for ordering existence. Relevancy, in turn, was conceived by Machiavelli in terms of the conditions to which the criteria appertained; that is, to the particular world of politics. This was expressed in his frequent use of the word *necessità* in describing political situations. By *necessità* he did not mean a form of determinism, but rather a set of factors challenging a man's political creativity, manageable only if man treated them as strictly political, excluding all else from his span of attention.[8]

In terms of ethics this did not mean that politics was to be conducted without ethical criteria, but that the criteria could not be imported from the "outside." The failure to appreciate this has led many modern critics of Machiavelli into false dilemmas. It does not follow, as one modern writer would have it, that because politics demands an ethic different from private life that "moral imperatives do not have absolute value." This is to put the issue badly, for the real questions are, what morals? what is meant by "absolute"? The whole point of Machiavelli's argument was to urge that precisely because of the unescapably autonomous nature of politics, it was all the more compelling that criteria for action be established and that appropriate means be fashioned for their implementation. In brief, the denial of heteronomy need not entail a denial of morality in politics, any more than the impossibility of ethical criteria follows from the denial of ethical absolutes.

5. *Prince*, VIII.
6. *Discourses*, II, 5.

7. Ibid., II, Preface; II, 5.
8. Ibid., I, 1; 3; 28; II, 12; III, 12.

FEDERICO CHABOD

Machiavelli's Method and Style†

During the summer and autumn of 1500 Niccolò Machiavelli was at the Court of France, undergoing his first great experience of European politics. Together with Francesco della Casa, he had been sent by the Government of Florence on a mission to Louis XII, 'the master of the shop', in other words the contemporary arbiter of Italian affairs, his object being to try to solve the disastrous problem of Pisa. As a first 'lesson' of this experience Machiavelli was forced to take due account of the miseries of an inadequate salary, inferior 'beyond all reason, human or divine', to Della Casa's. At the very outset he had to draw upon his capital to the extent of forty ducats, so that he was left 'without a halfpenny'. As a result he threatened to return home at once, since it was better to lie 'at the mercy of fortune' in Italy than in France.

Henceforth, in fact, he had to think and act amid daily difficulties and privations. Yet he was by nature an openhanded man, incapable of 'doing anything without spending money'—a sociable man, fated nevertheless 'to lead a life of hardship rather than one of gaiety'. Later on, in the far harsher circumstances of 1513, he would be forced to 'turn his face to fortune', to seek relief from 'the malignity of fate' by gambling at the inn near his house at S. Andrea in Percussina, squabbling over a farthing, brawling and arguing with the landlord, the butcher or the miller, and finding an outlet in letters to friends for his desire to do something, if only to 'roll a stone' because by continuing as at present 'I am wearing myself out, and if I go on like this for long my poverty will make me an object of contempt'.

And yet, in the evenings of those summer and autumn days of 1513, Machiavelli would take off his every-day attire, 'steeped in mud and filth', and, putting on 'regal and curial robes', would enter the 'ancient courts of the men of old, where, being received with solicitude, I nourish myself with that food which is mine alone, and which I was born to eat . . . and for four hours I am conscious of no boredom, I forget all my troubles, I cease to fear poverty, I have no terror of death. I give myself up entirely to them'. These were the days during which, with a single sustained effort, he composed *The Prince*.

Now, in the summer and autumn of 1500, at the time of his first great political experience, just as he was already deploring his privations and troubles, so too he suddenly succeeded in translating himself to another, loftier world—the world of political understanding. And if the great reflections and the powerful pages of *The Prince* were as yet a thing

† Reprinted by permission of the publisher from *Machiavelli and the Renaissance* by Federico Chabod, translated by David Moore, Cambridge, Mass.: Harvard University Press, Copyright © 1958 by Federico Chabod.

of the future, his thoughts, his notes, even his literary style already presaged his masterpiece.

For the letters which he wrote from the Court of France contain opinions later repeated and fully elaborated in his great works—as when he advises Cardinal Georges d'Amboise about the policy which Louis XII should pursue in Italy—namely, to follow 'the method of those who have in the past sought to acquire a foreign province, which is to diminish the numbers of the strong, to cajole the subject population, to keep one's friends, and to fight shy of would-be 'colleagues', i.e. of those who wish to have equal authority in the region'. Here we have the essence of Chapter III of *The Prince*.

Far more important, the Machiavelli of this period affords us a glimpse of the real Machiavelli, with his characteristic way of looking at political problems, and in particular his dilemmatic technique of invariably putting forward the two extreme and antithetical solutions, disregarding half-measures and compromise solutions, and employing a disjunctive style: for example, the people of Florence think they can no longer hope for anything '*either* because of the malignancy of their fate *or* because they have so many enemies', while the French only respect '*either* those who are strongly armed *or* those who are ready to give'. This method constantly recurs in Machiavelli's prose. He is so rigorous in his use of it that it seems at times too obvious—I would venture to say too ingenuous—as when, in the *Arte della Guerra* (IV) we are confronted with the sentence 'I say, then, that pitched battles are either lost or won'. It is, on the other hand, a perfect formal expression of a mode of thought which is always based upon the precept that 'virtue' in a politician consists entirely in making prompt and firm decisions, and that in public life nothing is more pernicious than obscure or slow and tardy deliberation—a fault which results 'either from weakness of mind and body or from the malevolence of those who have to deliberate' (*Discorsi*, II, xv). Machiavelli is always emphasizing that no State should delude itself that it can always adopt a 'safe course of action; rather should it realize that its policy will always be attended by risk: for we find that, in the nature of things, if we seek to avoid one difficulty we always come up against another; but prudence consists in knowing how to recognize the character of difficulties and preferring to face the one that is least serious' (*The Prince*, Chapter XXI; *Discorsi*, I, vi). He is always resolute in regarding 'half-measures' as ruinous; indeed, they were always avoided by 'his' Romans, who invariably went to 'extremes' (*Discorsi*, II, xxiii). Men adopt ruinous half-measures, says Machiavelli, because they are lazy and incompetent, because they do not know 'either how to be wholly bad or how to be wholly good' (*Discorsi*, I, xxvi).

There are signs that this technique, which is characteristic of Machiavelli in his maturity, was already employed by the author during his early years of political rumination, during the period of the legations.

Most important of all, even at this early stage he is never satisfied with the mere analysis, however lucid, of a specific political situation. Instead, he is impelled—I would say by instinct—to proceed straight from facts to considerations of a general nature and to regard the concrete episode as one of the innumerable changing manifestations of something which does not change, because it is perennial—the struggle for power, in other words politics. In the reflections of this by no means front-rank civil servant about the events of the day, and in his official reports to his Government, we can already see the mighty Machiavellian 'imagination' at work—the sudden flash of intuition, identical with that of the great poet, who in any single event detects the ever-recurring workings of a universal process that is part and parcel of the human story. Hence the advice imparted to the all-powerful prime minister of Louis XII on the way in which the King ought to conduct himself in Italy, 'following the method of those who have in the past sought to acquire a foreign province'. Here he is already holding up the example of 'his' Romans and recommending the constant study of antiquity. As an assessment of the policy which France should adopt towards Italy it is far more comprehensive than one would expect, coming as it does from a Florentine envoy whose mission was limited to the affairs of Pisa.

Many years later, in 1522, Machiavelli was to offer advice to his friend Raffaello Girolami, who was going to Spain as Ambassador to Charles V. It was useful advice, in which he explained the method by which an envoy should set about winning friends at Court so that he might be well informed concerning matters which it was essential for him to understand and so on. But as for expressing opinions in his reports to Florence, it was better to never speak in the first person. 'To put your opinion into your own mouth would be odious', notes Machiavelli. Let Girolami therefore make use of such devices as this: 'Cautious men here think that the effect is likely to be such-and-such.' Admirably prudent advice for a professional diplomat—a rule for the avoidance of personal embarrassment which might well be termed universal in its application. But when Machiavelli had had to write of 'conjectures' and 'opinions' himself, though sometimes employing such devices, he had often used the first person, openly admonishing his Government: 'I wish to warn you, lest you persuade yourselves that you are likely to be ready every time' (Legation to Valentino, letter dated 9 October 1502); and sometimes he had apologized for having written 'disrespectfully and frankly', at the cost of being proved wrong, because he preferred to injure himself 'by writing and being proved wrong' rather than to harm Florence by not doing so (first Legation to France, letter dated 3 September 1500), or because it seemed to him that he was not exceeding his 'duty' by reporting what he heard at the Court of Louis XII (third Legation to France, letter dated 26 July 1510). But subsequently he had begun once more to offer opinions and advice, and to

write 'I consider . . . '. Sometimes he had even ventured to entreat the
Dieci di Balià to accept his opinion, 'as they accept the Gospel' (third
Legation to France, letter dated 9 August 1510)—his opinion being that,
if war broke out between the Pope and the King of France, Florence
would have to come out openly on side of one or another of the con-
testants: let them therefore think immediately, 'without waiting until the
time came', of the advantages that would accrue from an alliance with
France; 'and, since opportunities are short-lived, you had better decide
quickly'—yes or no, but quickly.

Such was not the procedure which he later recommended to Girolami;
nor could he have recommended it to anyone, for this was in truth the
food 'which is mine alone', and no one else's. To others he might be
generous in his advice regarding what we may call diplomatic technique;
but he could not tell them what he felt to be wholly personal, and
incommunicable.

Henceforth, then, we find him interspersing his accounts of audiences
or his descriptions of certain intrigues with maxims of a general nature.
The method is similar to that which he employs in his last great work,
the *Florentine Histories*. Here, too, before resuming his discussion of
Cosimo de' Medici and Neri Capponi, he says that he desires, 'in accordance with our usual method of exposition, to explain at some length
how those who hope that a republic can be unified greatly delude themselves' (VII, i). Again, when describing the conspiracy of the Pazzi he
says that he would like 'to follow our custom' and speak of the different
kinds of conspiracies and their significance, if he had not already discussed the matter elsewhere or if it were a subject that could be speedily
disposed of (VIII, i). Finally, he apologizes if he, a historian of Florentine
affairs, has described events in Lombardy and Naples at undue length.
The reason is that had he not done so 'our own history would be less
intelligible and less agreeable reading' (VII, i), just as, in former days,
had he not expressed his opinions and conjectures the Government of
Florence would have had a less precise and complete idea of the way
in which matters were proceeding in France or in Rome or at the Court
of the Emperor Maximilian.

The Machiavelli who emerges from the Legations is a youthful Machiavelli, one who had certainly not yet acquired the comprehensiveness
of vision, the incisiveness of phrase, the plasticity of imagination which
he was to reveal in the years subsequent to 1512; yet the manner of this
Machiavelli is distinctive, precise and confident. We note the frequent
intrusion of popular expressions, as when he speaks of his 'horsy' appearance in the presence of Caesar Borgia, of 'tapping sources', 'steering
clear' or 'fighting shy' of people or 'giving them a wide berth' in order
to pick up information and to avoid compromising himself. We note,
too, his way of expressing an opinion by means of a graphic image. And
certain syntactical constructions, all subject and verb and therefore con-

cise and vigorous, adumbrate, albeit vaguely, images and syntactical constructions that occur in his most perfect prose, that of *The Prince*.

Moreover, even in these years he contrives in a few writings apart from official reports to express his true nature, which, as he himself said, was that of a man intended by fate to apply his powers of reasoning not to the silk-trade or the wool-trade or to questions of profit and loss, but to politics and politics alone.

In the *Discorso fatto al Magistrato dei Dieci sopra le cose di Pisa*, in the essay *Del modo di trattare i popoli della Val di Chiana ribellati*, as also in the more famous *Descrizione del modo tenuto dal duca Valentino nello ammazzare Vitellozzo Vitelli, Oliverotto da Fermo, il signor Pagolo e il duca di Gravina Orsini*—in other words, in those of Machiavelli's works which were written between 1499 and 1503—the idiosyncrasies of thought and style already perceptible even in the early Legations naturally emerge far more clearly. Hence, what is most striking about the author's lucid and laconic method of exposition is his unequivocal determination to infer from particular events a lesson in the art of politics, or as he himself would say, those 'general rules' which are infallible. This determination is clearly expressed in the discussion on the peoples of Val di Chiana, that early, minor work which nevertheless contains the whole essence of Machiavelli and already has the approach and the stamp of a chapter of the *Discorsi*;[1] and it is now justified for the first time by the reference to the immutablity of human passions—a theme which will later inspire some famous passages in the *Discorsi sopra la prima deca di Tito Livio* (I, Preface and xi, xxxix, and xliii): 'I have heard it said that history is the teacher who determines our actions, and above all our principles, and that the world has been inhabited in all ages alike by men who have always been subject to the same passions, and that there have always been those who serve and those who command, those who serve unwillingly and those who serve willingly, and those who rebel and are reconquered. . . . Therefore, if it is true that history is the teacher who determines our actions, it would not have been a bad thing if those whose duty it was to punish and judge the peoples of Valdichiana had modelled themselves upon, and emulated, those have been masters of the world.' But the Florentines did not do this: 'And if the judgment of the Romans is worthy of commendation, yours is equally worthy of blame.' Here too begins the great polemic which Machiavelli will carry on to the end of his writings. It is directed against the men of his time, whom he appraises and judges in the light of the experience of ancient Rome, and rightly so, for every man can accomplish what others have accomplished in the past, 'because men are born, and live, and die in accordance with an unvarying order' (*Discorsi*, I, xi). And once again the basic controversy finds an immediate and highly effective

1. Where, moreover, we find the same theme and the same method of development (*Discorsi*, II, xxiii).

echo in the style, with the polemical exchanges between Machiavelli and his imaginary antagonists and the cut-and-thrust—'And if you were to say . . . I should say . . .'—which makes the dilemmatic technique already noticed in the letters from the Court of France appear even more effective. This has by now become the typical dialectical method employed by Machiavelli. We shall find an example of it in the polemical denunciation of mercenaries in Chapter XII of *The Prince*: 'I want to demonstrate more clearly the disadvantage of such troops. Mercenary captains are either excellent soldiers or not. If they are, you cannot rely on them, because they will always seek their own advancement, either by oppressing you, who are their master, or by oppressing others, contrary to your intention. But if your captain is without virtue he will generally destroy you. And if the reply is given that anyone who is put in possession of arms will do this, whether he be a mercenary or not, I would answer that the use of arms should be controlled either by a prince or by a republic.'

Thus, around the years 1500–1503 Machiavelli's personality was already emerging in ever more emphatic detail, with its characteristic bias towards politics. And in the course of these early experiences (as indeed of those which followed) at Florence or during missions to foreign courts—as when he returned to France, or when he was accredited to the Roman Curia and Pope Julius II or to the Emperor Maximilian—particular thoughts which were later to constitute the ever-recurring theme of his great works steadily acquired clearer definition. From now on we find him laying special emphasis on opportunity, which is short-lived, so that men must understand its nature and know how to put it to good use; on the small value which can to-day be attached to 'faith', promises and even solemn pledges; or on the tendency of men, and even of princes, to take account of present advantage without heeding possible eventualities. Again, invocations of 'reason', of what is 'reasonable', alternate in his disquistions with appeals to 'nature', i.e. physical nature. Machiavelli readily falls back on 'nature' when he wants to pass judgment on the French or Germans, who are 'by nature' such-and-such. He also draws a parallel between nature and incidents of human existence, borrowing from the language of natural and medical science terms and images which he applies to political events and to the life of the community. So we now find him likening the politician to the doctor who by his skill expels bad 'humours' from the body. His partiality for this metaphor will later inspire the celebrated image of States that spring up overnight and, 'like everything else in nature that springs up without warning and grows quickly, must lack the fibres and the limbs that are appropriate to them', i.e. cannot have deep roots (*Prince*, VII).

A continual accumulation of experience and a progressive strengthening and development of his critical faculty—such was the fruit of

Machiavelli's fifteen years (1498–1512) of public service. This experience led him more and more to pass negative judgments on the Italian States of the time and on the political capacity of their rulers. He became more and more convinced that Italy's great political crisis, the collapse of States like Milan and Naples, and the invasion of the peninsula by 'barbarians' who became 'masters of the shop' had certain quite definite and recognizable causes. As he says in the second *Decennale,* these misfortunes were the fault of arrogant men, 'who possess sceptres and crowns, but have not an inkling of the future!' They are the fault of princes who lack not only prudence and virtue but, especially, their own military forces. 'The road would be short and easy if you were to reopen the Temple of Mars', he had told the Florentines in the first *Decennale,* written in 1504. But it was above all in the *Parole da dirle sopra la provisione del danaio* (1503) that Machiavelli had given expression to what was from that time forth both the criterion by which he interpreted recent Italian history and the chief plank in the new political system of which he dreamed so fondly: '. . . those who have watched the changes that have come about in kingdoms and the ruin of provinces and cities have seen that these things were caused solely by the lack of armed strength or of sagacity.' Without military forces no State can survive, especially as, if the good faith of private citizens is guaranteed by 'laws, written documents and agreements', that of princes is guaranteed 'solely by force of arms'. Therefore the Prince must arm or perish; and if he meets with disaster it will be his own fault, for the gods are neither willing nor able 'to sustain something that is bound to fail'.

These and similar opinions were the starting-point of Machiavelli's meditations when the 'ruin' was complete, that is after 1512. The collapse of the Florentine Republic of Soderini and the return of the Medici spelt the 'ruin' of a political experiment in which he had played an active part. 29 August, 1512 saw the 'ruin' at Prato of that military 'formation' (*ordinanza*) which Machiavelli had sponsored and created and which had represented his own great effort to give his city 'an army of its own' in place of 'cowardly' mercenary troops. And he, Messer Niccolò, had now been completely excluded from public office, confined for a year to State territory, and even, after Boscoli's conspiracy in February, 1513, imprisoned and subjected to torture. Eventually, he had taken refuge in his house near San Casciano, shunning, as he says in a letter to Vettori, the 'conversation' and the company even of his friends.

And yet it is enough for Vettori to write him a letter, telling him that he would like to be with him so that they could see 'whether we might be able to put this world to rights', and asking him to draft the terms of peace between the King of France, the King of Spain, the Pope, the Emperor and the Swiss. It is enough, then, for someone to breathe into his ear the word 'politics' ('cose di stato') and he, forgetting his present circumstances and imagining that he is occupied once more 'with those activities on which I have expended so much effort and so much time in vain', plunges once more into political discussion.

In his exchange of letters with his friend Francesco Vettori he discusses the immediate and urgent problem of what is going to happen in Europe and Italy. It is *to-day*, then, that first demands attention. But *to-day* has never offered sufficient scope for the powerful political imagination of Machiavelli. When he was still a mere civil servant he had sought escape from the present, even when writing his official reports to his Government, in those parentheses and comments which raised an account of certain specific happenings to the level of a general assessment of the political situation. All the more completely does he escape from it now, when he is condemned to official idleness and silence, with no outlet save that of making 'capital' out of his conversation with the 'men of old' and the experience gained during fifteen years 'which I have spent studying the statesman's art'—compelled either to keep quiet or to discourse only upon that which is his special province, to wit, politics and statesmanship. Thus, 'in this verminous atmosphere', he does in truth scrape the 'mould' from his brain. But now it is a brain that comprehends and observes with a lucidity and a discernment worthy of the great moment of creation, which has come at last.

Between *to-day*, i.e. the passing moment with its particular problems, and *the eternal*, i.e. the great and ever-valid laws of politics, there certainly remains a continuing connection, we might even say a reciprocity. For Machiavelli's determination to find a remedy for the present ills of Florence and Italy and his abiding faith in the possibility that such a remedy exists are always bringing him back to these general laws. He derives his faith—that faith which inspires the last chapter of *The Prince* and the exhortation—from his diagnosis of the causes of Italy's present woes. As we have already observed, this diagnosis traces the fact that Italy is 'enslaved and reviled' to the political 'sins' of princes, and indicates that the absence of its own army and the cowardice of the Italian *condottieri* are responsible for Italy's having been 'overrun by Charles, plundered by Louis, violated by Ferrando and reviled by the Swiss.'

Hence his abiding faith in the possibility of a revival, brought about through the virtue of a great prince—a faith which induces him to put aside his first notes for the *Discorsi sopra la prima deca di Tito Livio*— a quieter but at the same time a more comprehensive work—and, with a single sustained effort, to throw off *The Prince* between July and December, 1513.

The diagnosis was false. Machiavelli lived at a time when the crisis in Italy's history was at its height, and in reviewing and basing theories upon the outcome of two hundred years of that history he exalted the

'virtue' of an individual, the 'virtue' of a prince, to the dignity of the
supreme controlling factor of life. As a result, he attributed Italy's ruin
wholly to the 'sins' of her princes. Inevitably, he failed to pin-point the
origin and development of that crisis and, in concentrating principally
on the 'cowardice' of mercenary troops, he passed outside the realm of
truth. He was mistaken, then; his appeal to the prince-redeemer was
bound to fall on deaf ears, and it was in the nature of things that the
faith which inspires the last chapter of *The Prince* should have given
way to the melancholy resignation which characterizes the beginning
and the end of *L'Arte della Guerra*.

But it was a fortunate mistake, because it prompted Machiavelli once
again to admonish rulers and ruled alike and so led him to discontinue
his joint commentary with Vettori on the events of the day and to search
for those 'general rules' which would enable him at last to open the eyes
of the blind and make the true nature of politics intelligible to all. From
a polemic directed against the Italian princes he proceeds to a polemic
of a more general character whose theme is the contrast between 'my'
Romans and all, or nearly all, the men of modern times in whom 'not
a vestige of that ancient virtue remains' (*Discorsi*, I Preface and lv). From
the realm of Italian affairs in particular he ascends to the realm of
universal history, from advice on how to prevent the Swiss from becoming the arbiters of Italy he proceeds to the enumeration of rules that
never fail. In other words, from a simple commentary on events in the
Italy and the Europe of his day he proceeds to that great commentary
which reveals and proclaims the necessity of regarding politics as an end
in itself, i.e. as something beyond the realm of good and evil, unconditioned by any assumptions or aims that are not purely and simply
political. In short, his watchwords are 'action' and 'power'.

Now he can give full rein to his political 'imagination', by which is
meant the capacity to proceed without hesitation from a point of detail
to a problem of a general order, to grasp at once the connection—which
is eternal, not contingent—between two political occurrences. For different occurrences are mere moments in the eternal activity of man—
in his political activity, which is unvarying in its motives, in its aims,
and above all in its fundamental postulate, namely that politics is politics,
and must be conceived and practised in the light of purely political
criteria, without regard to considerations of a different order, whether
moral or religious.

Let us read again those monumental periods in Chapter XV of *The
Prince*, in which we are conscious of the writer's full realization that he
is throwing open to men the portals of a new world: 'Since it is my
purpose to write what may be useful to those who heed it, I have thought
it more fitting to concern myself with the effective reality of things than
with speculation. And many have imagined republics and principates

which have never been seen or known to exist in reality; for there is such a difference between life as it is and life as it ought to be that he who neglects what is done for what ought to be done will ensure his ruin rather than his preservation. For a man who desires to appear good in every respect must surely come to grief among so many who are evil. Wherefore it is essential for a prince, if he wishes to maintain his position, to learn the ways of evil, and to use his knowledge or to refrain from using it as the need arises.'

He is fully aware of the novelty of his ideas, and emphasizes the fact in the Preface to Book I of the *Discorsi*: 'I have resolved to enter upon a road which, not having been trodden by any man before, may lead me into trouble and difficulty, but may also be paved with gold.'

Men are 'wicked', and as a rule 'ungrateful, fickle, prone to simulation and dissimulation, afraid of danger, greedy of gain' (*The Prince*, XVII); and the affairs of the world are 'carried on by men, who are, and always have been, governed by the same passions' (*Discorsi*, III, xliii). Among these passions the two most powerful incentives are love of power, i.e. ambition, and love of 'substance' ('roba'), i.e. greed, because ambition has 'such power over the hearts of men that, no matter to what heights they rise, they never renounce it' (*Discorsi*, I xxxvii), and also 'because a man sooner forgets the death of his father than the loss of his inheritance' (*The Prince*, XVII). Therefore the Prince, whose supreme task it is to maintain and so far as possible to expand his State, cannot possess nor altogether respect the 'good qualities' demanded for private individuals, 'because human conditions do not allow it'. Therefore 'let him not scruple to incur the infamy attaching to those vices without which he can hardly preserve his State; for if we consider the whole matter carefully we shall discover qualities which resemble virtue but which, if he cultivated them, would be the ruin of him, and others which resemble vice but which, if he cultivates them, will ensure his safety and prosperity' (*The Prince*, XV). Men—he will make Cosimo the Old say in the *Florentine Histories*—do not rule States 'with paternosters in their hands' (VII, vi).

Thus Machiavelli came to affirm the principle of 'politics for politics' sake', or, as has justly been said, to recognize the 'autonomy' of politics, regarded as a form of human activity existing *per se* and unconditioned by any assumptions or aims of a theological or moral character.

This, however, is the point on which it is most essential to be definite, especially if we bear in mind certain trends which have become apparent in some of the recent essays on Machiavelli. The writers of these essays strive fruitlessly to saddle Machiavelli with the mentality and the problems of a modern doctrinarian, philosophical or juridical in bias. They try to make him out to be a rigid, over-logical, stereotyped advocate of principles and laws which, being strictly interrelated, conjure up a picture of a State that is 'systematized' down to the smallest detail; or else—and this is an even graver misconception—a prophet of the ethical State in the tradition of Hegel; or, finally, simply the creator of a new moral consciousness.

At the basis of these attempts there is also the supposition that Machiavelli was a pure logician, a logician of an ultra-modern kind, well aware of the various forms of mental activity and therefore concerned to co-ordinate one with another, for example economy with ethics, in a well-ordered 'system'.

All this is quite wrong. Machiavelli knows perfectly well that he exceeds the bounds of ethics—traditional ethics, which in itself he does not question, but indeed accepts; and his reflections sometimes give the impression that it almost pains him to have to disregard moral principles: 'And if all men were good, this precept would not be good; but since they are wicked' the Prince need not keep faith when 'such observance would be to his disadvantage' (*The Prince*, XVIII). Note the distinction between the acquisition of glory and the acquisition of authority: 'Moreover, it cannot be called virtuous to slay one's fellow-citizens, to betray one's friends, to spurn good faith, pity and religion. Such conduct may help a Prince to acquire authority, but not glory' (*The Prince*, VIII). Note too how he 'blames' Caesar and the founders of tyrannies, and his 'intense longing' for 'good' times (*Discorsi*, I, x); or, again, the emphasis which he lays on men who 'never do anything good except from necessity'—hence, he who establishes a republic must assume that all men are wicked (*Discorsi*, I, iii).

But he has explained his intention. He is entering upon a new road, never trodden by any man, and he will reveal the reality of things— that is to say, the nature of politics—even at the cost of putting moral precepts behind him. He is discussing the actions of princes, not of private individuals. Private life is different from public life; he admits the distinction and, since he is only capable of discussing affairs of State, he will speak to us only about public life. 'And forced promises which concern the public will always be broken when the strength to enforce them is lacking, and this will be no reflection on those who break them.' It is worthy of note that this passage is taken not from the celebrated eighteenth chapter of *The Prince*—the so-called 'tyrants' blue-print— but from Chapter XLII of the third book of the *Discorsi*.

Nor is it any more true to say that the Machiavellian ethic is embodied in his concept of patriotism; for he too he makes a clear distinction, both when he speaks for himself—'I love my native city (*patria*) more than my soul' (Letter to Vettori, dated 16 April 1527, *Lettere Familiari*, CCXXV)—or for the Florentines of the Trecento, who 'had a higher regard for their native city (*patria*) than for their souls' (*Florentine Histories*, III, vii), and, especially, when he declares that whenever men are taking thought above all else for the safety of their country, 'they should disregard questions of justice or injustice, of pity or cruelty, of glory or ignominy; rather, setting aside all other considerations, they should follow in everything that party which will preserve their country's existence and maintain its liberty' (*Discorsi*, III, xli). It is only proper that a man should sacrifice his soul for his country; but his country is not synonymous with his soul, that is to say, it cannot take the place of those moral and religious values of which a 'soul' consists. It can and should inspire men to sacrifice even what is just and laudable; but, even when it has been sacrificed in the interest of the safety of the State, *justice* is still *justice*. Nothing is further from Machiavelli's mind than to undermine common morality, replacing it with a new ethic; instead, he says that in public affairs the only thing that counts is the political criterion, by which he abides: let those who wish to remain faithful to the precepts of morality concern themselves with other things, not with politics. In the same way, he does not even think of substituting patriotism for the Christian moral ideal, and thereby creating a new civil ethic.

The truth is that Machiavelli leaves the moral ideal intact, and he does so because it need not concern him. Since he is wholly and exclusively preoccupied with his inner 'demon', his *furor politicus*, his inability to talk of anything but affairs of State—or else he must be silent—and since he is completely absorbed by what is the beginning and end of his inner life, his political fixation, everything else remains outside his range of vision. Above all he possesses *imagination*—that is, an intuition similar to that of the great poet or the great artist, to whom the world presents itself in such and such a light, the only light that he can see. Others see only shapes and colours, and some will say that they *must* express all they feel, that they can only express it, in the form of musical notes. As for him—he frankly admits it—once he has cast off his mud-stained, filthy garments all his thoughts and feelings take on a political character.

He is not, then, primarily a logician, working from principles from which, by a continuous process of reasoning, rigorous and slavish, he deduces a complete 'system'. He is first and foremost a man of imagination, who sees *his* truth in a flash, with blinding clarity, and only afterwards trusts to reason to enable him to comment on that truth. His 'truth' is politics, revealed in all its savage nakedness. Machiavelli bequeathed the problem of co-ordinating this new truth with others previously recognized, and in particular with moral 'truth', to posterity, so that for four hundred years of European thought he has remained in the thick of the bitter and agonizing struggle that has constantly been waged between *kratos* and *ethos* (strength and right).

Supreme among the political thinkers of all time, Machiavelli, in common with the greatest politicians—who, like him, so resemble the artist in that their logic and their dogma are completely subordinate to their intuition—has what may literally be termed initial inner 'illuminations', immediate, intuitive visions of events and their significance. Only afterwards does he pass on to what we may call 'application by reasoning'. Certainly, in Machiavelli's prose there is frequent repetition of phrases like 'it is reasonable' or 'it is not reasonable that this should be'; but the reasonableness or otherwise consists in the application (it might be termed the 'tactic'), in the particular comment which follows the great moment of intuition and creation and is, comparatively speaking, of secondary importance.

A typical example of the absolute predominance of Machiavelli's intuition, which is concentrated exclusively on the problem in question, first apprehending it, then analysing it and, by a process of reasoning, presenting it in its various aspects, is the way in which he expounds his doctrines. Even at the outset, in the dedications of *The Prince* and the *Discorsi*, he adduces only his 'long experience of modern affairs and . . . (his) continual reading of ancient history.' There is not the faintest suggestion of the excessive logicality which, two centuries later, will prompt another great man, Montesquieu, to make in the *Preface* to *L' Esprit des Lois* another lofty but very different assertion: 'I have stated the principles, and I have observed that particular cases seem to conform to those principles automatically. I have seen that the history of every nation is merely the consequence of this process, and that each individual law is linked to another law or is dependent on a more general law.' Machiavelli, on the other hand, will say that in many cases it is impossible to lay down any 'inflexible rule' because modes of action 'vary according to circumstances'; or else that it is impossible to formulate a 'definite precept without coming down to details'. Therefore he will discuss these cases 'in that general way which is permissible in the nature of things . . .' (*The Prince*, IX and XX; cf. *Discorsi*, I, xviii). Thus, on the one hand we have the general rules that always hold good, on the other those cases for which it is impossible to lay down any definite rule.

When he gets down to his subject in earnest, Machiavelli employs a characteristic method, one that is peculiar to himself. He does not enquire, either on his own behalf or on the reader's, as to the nature of the State, its origin and its aims. Hence, we find no hint of the traditional arguments, prevalent both before and since, about the origins of human society and the 'why and wherefore' of the State. He would regard all this as idle digression. The political activity of man is an eternal reality. The State, in which this activity finds concrete expression, is also a reality. To discuss these things would be like discussing the reasons why a man breathes or why his heart beats. And so he deals straight away with precise and definite problems: 'All those States and Empires which have had, and have, authority over men have been and are either republics or principates. Principates are either hereditary or newly-established.' So begins *The Prince*; and in the first chapter of the first book of the *Discorsi* we read: 'I say that all cities are built either by men who are natives of the district or by foreigners.'

This form of introduction is as clear and incisive as the dilemmatic sentence-structure itself. Think of the *Politics* of Aristotle and the *De Regimine Principum* of St. Thomas, with their preambles on the nature and motivation of society; think of Locke's lengthy discussions on the state of nature and the origin of the political society, or of the first book of Montesquieu's *L' Esprit des Lois*, or of the early chapters of Rousseau's *Contract Social*—to cite only a few examples—and you will at once perceive the essential difference between Machiavelli's approach to the problem, which is unique, and that of the other major political thinkers.

But in recognizing the predominance of intuition over pure logic we must also bear in mind not so much the lack of symmetry which is here and there perceptible even in the exposition of the *Discorsi* as certain hesitations and vacillations even in the handling of problems—above all that of the relationship between virtue and fortune—which to Machiavelli are of fundamental importance. It is useless to look for an absolute uniformity of outlook on this question in all his works, from *The Prince* to the *Florentine Histories*, for the simple reason that it is not there. Instead, affirmations of complete confidence in human 'virtue', which is said to be capable even of subduing fortune, alternate with affirmations of the 'power of heaven over human affairs' (*Discorsi*, II, xxix), which reach their climax in the disconsolate assertion (*Vita di Castruccio*): '. . . since Fortune wishes to demonstrate to the world that it is she who makes men great, not prudence.'

Such fluctuations of opinion apart, what greater contrast could there be than that between the pessimistic judgments pronounced by Machiavelli on the Italy of his time, which is 'rotten to the core', and his act of faith in the coming of the Prince who is to be the redeemer of Italy? Again, consider his opinion of men, who in his judgment are for the most part wicked and wholly intent on pursuing their own ends, ready, before the need is urgent, to pledge themselves and their possessions and then, when they find themselves faced with danger and the necessity to fight, forgetful of all their promises and offers (*The Prince*, IX and XVII). Yet in the last chapter of *The Prince* he imagines them waiting with great eagerness for the coming of the Prince-redeemer— waiting for him 'with what a thirst for vengeance, with what unshakable faith, with what reverence, with what tears of joy! What gates would not be open to him? What peoples would refuse him obedience? What envy would bar his way? What Italian would not defer to him?' Not a shred remains here of Machiavelli's pessimistic judgment of mankind.

Exalted by his passion, Machiavelli imagines and can already see almost physically the redeemer of the Italians, a nation 'more servile than the Hebrews, more slavish than the Persians, more scattered than the Athenians, leaderless and unorganized; a vanquished, despoiled, devastated land.' He forgets all his past judgments, for he is dazzled by a new prospect—the prospect of an Italy liberated from the barbarian yoke. And yet the exhortation with which *The Prince* closes is not a subsequent addition, as has sometimes been said, nor is it a piece of oratory tacked on as if to justify by means of a noble invocation the sorry facts affirmed in all the other chapters of the treatise. It is even in its style an integral part of the underlying conception of *The Prince*.

For Machiavelli's prose is, in short, a complete expression of the predominance of imagination over pure logic.

In place of the precise and carefully-weighed opinion we find, just when a solution seems farthest away, the plastic image that resolves the doubt through imagination, not through logic. For example, in Chapter XXV of *The Prince* we have this necessary premise to the final exhortation to Italians to open the way to the Prince-redeemer: 'I firmly believe that it is better to be impetuous than cautious; for Fortune is a woman, and if you wish to subdue her you must beat her and chastise her . . . and being a woman, she is always friendly-disposed towards the young, because they are fiercer and less cautious, and use bolder methods to keep her in subjection.'

So we have the plastic image of the woman beaten into submission, and the powerful climax that dispels all doubts—by forceful imagery, however, and not by logic. When the author's enthusiasm runs high, the dilemmatic method, the method of syllogism and disputation gives way, even in the matter of style, to a violent upsurging of emotion in which logic is replaced by imagery. And in the final exhortation at the end of *The Prince* we find the writer suddenly adopting an exalted, Biblical tone and recalling miracles decreed of God: 'The sea has opened; a cloud has accompanied you on your way; water has flowed from a stone; manna has rained down from the heavens.' This is the imagery of one whose emotion is still tempered by faith. At the end of *L' Arte della Guerra* the emotion is that of a man who is disheartened and disappointed: 'Of what can I make them feel ashamed who were born and bred without sense of shame? Why should they heed me who do not know me? By what God or by what saints should I make them swear? By those whom they adore, or by those whom they blaspheme?'

Such, then, is the genius of Machiavelli—a potent genius, peerless in the realm of political thought, consisting entirely of sudden, immediate flashes of insight, coupled with an almost miraculous natural dynamism and the manner and the imagery of a great poet. And the miracle of Machiavelli is a miracle that has never been repeated throughout the course of modern history.

During his early years of public life Machiavelli's genius was still kept within bounds, yet it was already clearly perceptible. Becoming fully conscious and certain both of itself and of its novelty and grandeur during the greatest creative period, that of *The Prince* and the *Discorsi*, his political imagination, in other words his political creativeness, remained until the last at once his glory and his torment. Weary, embittered, disappointed both with himself and with others, imbued with a sense of inward disillusionment of which we catch glimpses in the *Vita di Castruccio* and in the *Florentine Histories*, he rediscovered, two months before he died, the old pugnacity which in his youth had prompted him to express even in official letters his scarcely-veiled disapproval of the policy of Florence. Sent on a mission to Francesco Guicciardini, lieutenant-general of Pope Clement VII, between February and April 1527, he resumed his old habit of offering information and even advice. In one of his last letters, written at Forli on 11 April 1527, he resorts once more to the dilemmatic method: 'Accordingly, matters have come to such a pass that it is necessary either to revive the war or to conclude peace.' On the very eve of the 'utter ruin' which he felt instinctively lay in store for Florence and on the eve of his own death, which he did not anticipate, Niccolò Machiavelli once again adopts his characteristic tone—the imperious, comprehensive tone which typifies all his thought.

J. H. WHITFIELD

[Big Words, Exact Meanings]†

The coupling of Machiavelli's name with that of Savonarola led, as we saw, to a surprising close, in which the former sighs, or seems to sigh, for someone who should be more generally good than Savonarola. But had Machiavelli the right to think in such a way? Has he not pinned his faith to something different, something that has seemed indissolubly attached to his name and writings: to a doctrine of *virtú*? Now in English we have reduced the word *virtue* to one main sense, and to this sense of conformity to moral principles all other senses are subordinate (as when we say *by virtue of . . .*), or else are obsolescent. This simplicity of use, which is not affected by differences between abstract and concrete, makes us perhaps a little insensitive to the possibility of other employment for the word. We can distinguish with ease between virtue and virtuosity, because the words no longer seem connected. Nor do objects of vertu (a monopoly of sale catalogues) disturb us. But the spectacle of the word *virtue* with an obviously divergent sense from our own is enough to cause misgiving. And, indeed, no word in Machiavelli's vocabulary has aroused more excitement, or more indignation, than the simple word *virtú*. For those who have known no more of this author than his reputation, the notion that he abandoned virtue to put in its

† From *Machiavelli* by J. H. Whitfield (1947 New York, 1965). Reprinted by permission of the author.

place some pagan conception of *virtú* has replaced the need for documentation on his qualities as a writer: it has represented concrete, and detailed, proof of his wickedness. An author who has no concern for virtue must be immoral or amoral (the former being the old-fashioned, the latter the modern, view of Machiavelli). And for many there has seemed no need to consider the case of Machiavelli more closely when he had revealed his colours so clearly. There have been, of course, excuses for such an attitude. Although many have written on Machiavelli, few have examined the values he attaches to words; and in consequence some traps have lain ready for the unwary. Benoist, who was ready to find some excuse for Machiavelli in his patriotism, remarked on a sentence in the *Legations*, 'Le grand mot y est en toutes lettres: *la patria.*'[1] It was there indeed, but it was not, and never became, a *grand mot* for Machiavelli. It was one's birthplace, therefore, one's native city: it never expanded in his use, or in his mind, to reach the concept of patriotism. Machiavelli never has the nineteenth-century Risorgimento idea of the unity of Italy, any more than anyone else of his own time. That is why we have seen the ambiguous term *provincia* as his use for a whole country. And if Benoist caught a crab with *patria*, anyone who jumped at *nazione* in Machiavelli's pages and tried to link it with its reappearance in France at the end of the eighteenth century would simply go astray: *nazione*, and it is the regular Florentine use, is the identification of where one is born, so that a man may be of the Florentine, though he cannot be of the Italian, nation.

There are, then, snags; and Ercole, who (apart from the useful, though not impeccable annotations of editors such as Lisio) stands almost alone in this examination of terms, has shown that there is much to learn on Machiavelli's vocabulary generally. But his work is fairly recent, and in the matter of *virtú* it does not offer much help. As a basis of consideration for this latter word perhaps Ercole's conclusions of the Machiavellian use of *stato* are the most helpful. *Stato* has a whole gamut of meanings, ranging from the Latin one of *state, condition*, to something very near the modern conception of the *State*; but with a general tendency to convey something less than this last *power, those that hold it, government* rather than *territory*—though this last is not absent.[2] In any given passage the word *stato*—such is the uncertainty of Machiavelli's use of it—may have any one of this range of shades. And this unscientific use of terms is not untypical of Machiavelli. He is so much more concerned with things than with words that his symbols may be inadequate. His vision of things is, as has been generally recognized, astonishingly sharp; and even as a consequence of that very sharpness, his notation of them is at times misleading.

1. Charles Benoist, *La Machiavelisme* (Paris, 1907) 129. "The big word is there, spelled out in full: *la patria*."

2. Ercole, *La Politica di Machiavelli*. 65.

Such a point of departure for the consideration of the word *virtú* would not seem to lead to a doctrine based on this word. Yet it has been a fairly general belief that such a doctrine existed, and that to the exclusion of the meaning *virtue*. Even, this certainty as to the existence of a blind spot in Machiavelli's make-up (and, by one of those inviting side-steps, in the Renaissance as well. Is it not the Age of Machiavelli, or of Peter Aretine?) has seemed sufficiently well known to need only a passing allusion to it. Lanson expresses, and dismisses, it in a bare sentence which may give us clearly the usual definition of it: 'The theory of virtú, from which every notion of morality is excluded, makes of the individual himself the work of art, within which the artist works to realize the fullness of his own force and beauty.'[3] And a trail of others, more or less authoritative, but all unanimous, keep Lanson company. Thus Woodward, in his novel about Caesar Borgia, wrote: 'For what in the days of the Borgia was legitimacy in comparison with force, with personal distinction, with *virtú*?'[4] It is clear, from such a question, that the individuality of the word is taken for granted, and felt as giving a dubious air not only to its author, but to his times as well. One does not call the Renascence 'the days of the Borgia' without conveying a slur of some sort; and this slur spreads from the conception of *virtú*. *Elena* was the unsuccessful divagation of a scholar; but other scholars than Lanson have said the same in their own field. Einstein remarked on Elizabethan borrowing from Machiavelli, noting it as often from the pseudo-Machiavelli: 'Nevertheless, it can scarcely be doubted that Machiavelli's doctrine of *virtú* fitted in with the ideas of the age.'[5] Praz wrote of 'that pagan doctrine of *virtú*.'[6] Gentile quoted Burckhardt's definition of the Machiavellian *virtú* as a union of force and ability, something that can be summed up in force alone, if by force one means human, not mechanical, force: will, and therefore force of ability.[7] Ercole himself, in spite of his habit of examining the variations in Machiavelli's use of words, talked of the rise of 'the concept of machiavellian virtú'.[8] so strongly was this current flowing; and in a later work, where his criticism of Machiavelli has been wholly overlaid by a Fascist gloss (was not Mussolini's so-called thesis on Machiavelli merely a crib from Ercole's earlier work?), he presents the definition of the word in two stages. I have already made my comment on the swollen idiom which has passed for literary criticism in Italy in recent times, and I leave Ercole's definition to stand in the words he used himself. Basically, *virtú* is the 'concrete exercise of his own freedoms by the man of energetic and conscious will, not just to hold his position or to turn as he will the

3. Lanson, 224.
4. Woodward, *Elena* (1929) 18
5. Lewis Einstein, *Italian Renaissance in England* (New York, 1902) 368.
6. Mario Praz, *Studi di litteratura inglesa* (Firenze, 1937) 61.
7. Gentile, *Studi sull Rinascimento*, 2nd ed. (Firenze, 1936) 108.
8. Francesco Ercole, *La Politica di Machiavelli* (1926) 20.

course of reality within which he exists and which surrounds him, but to bend it in such a way as to impose on it the mark of his own action—not just to form a wish but to act in such a way as to transform it into reality.'[9] This, then, is purely utilitarian if it is made to serve private ends, the good of the individual; it becomes moral, at least for Machiavelli, when it serves something transcending this, not for mere 'personal freedom, but for a duty which cancels all liberty'—that is, for one's country. Hence *virtú* is either good or bad according to its application; but in any case it is the privilege of the very few.[1] Such language is more ambitious, it presupposes the existence of a modern conception of patriotism in Machiavelli, and it has the vice of building a general theory on a particular statement of his; but it is only in this rider that it modifies accepted ideas.

I do not know of anyone after Ercole who has seen fit to examine the problem. The first necessary step is to dismiss the casual statements which imply a doctrine or theory of *virtú* individual to Machiavelli, and seek to characterize him, or even the Renascence, thereby. There is no doctrine of *virtú* in Machiavelli. If there were it would be easy to discover in his works; but Machiavelli was not given to such theorizing, and he himself would have been the first to be surprised at the stir the word has caused. The second point is that even if Machiavelli were always to use *virtú* as something poles apart from *virtue* that particular would not, in itself, permit the deduction that he was oblivious of the claims, or ignorant of the existence, of virtue. To say that Machiavelli uses *virtú* always in an odd sense of his own is a linguistic observation only, unless it is accompanied by a certificate that he has no other word for virtue. Then we should have a surprising, and an incriminating, omission. But it is quite clear that Machiavelli is not short of words, and normally *buono, onesto* with their opposites *cattivo, tristo* replace *virtuous* and *vicious*. They are adjectives which accord straitly with contemporary Florentine usage, so that Landucci remarks on the fate of Savonarola that 'the bad (tristi) had more power than the good (buoni).'[2] One can hardly be preoccupied with goodness and badness without having some conception of virtue; and there is no moral case that can be based against Machiavelli on the use he makes of *virtú*.

But one can go further than this: Machiavelli has not only other words for virtue, he does not even exclusively reserve *virtú* for a pagan (*scilicet*, a Latin) sense. It is exactly here as it was with *stato*: his use of terms is imprecise, and he employs them as they come to cover any of their several acceptations—beginning with what he found in his Latin authors, and ending with current meanings. Tommasini, in noting the influence of Galen on Machiavelli, with a consequent tendency to use

9. Francesco Ercole, *Pensatori* etc. 169.   2. L. Landucci, *Diaries* 124.
1. Francesco Ercole, *Politica* 170–71.

medical metaphors, observed that his use of *virtú* was medical also, and that it represented a 'certain power of bringing something about.'[3] That I believe to be a more helpful annotation than the elaborated theorizing of Ercole. But it is only a single facet of the word, and Tommasini probably exaggerated this medical connection. Machiavelli was only using the metaphors that the historians and moralists of Rome had found to hand. And for *virtú* itself, there are passages, and by no means solitary ones, in which its acceptation must perforce be that of virtue. To begin with the *Prince*, and with a passage which we have met already, it is plain that here there is no twist to virtue: 'For if you look at the matter carefully, you will see that something resembling virtue, if you follow it, may be your ruin, while something else resembling vice will lead, if you follow it, to your security and well-being.'[4] Equally plain are two examples from the *Discorsi*. In the passage contrasting the Roman Empire under a good and a bad emperor Machiavelli sees in the first state of things 'nobility and virtue exalted'; in the second he sees innumerable cruelties in Rome '(and on the other hand) nobility, riches, honor, and above all vitue (*virtú*) accounted capital crimes.'[5] Later on, in demonstrating that good laws may become bad in changed conditions, he notes that originally in Rome those who deserved magistratures demanded them; but with the passage of time, and the growth of effrontery, the good stood on one side, the bad grasped out for office: 'It was no longer the most virtuous and deserving, but the most powerful who asked for official positions; and the least powerful, often the most virtuous, abstained from candidacy out of fear.'[6] This observation is worth noting, because it completely precludes any interpretation of *virtú* in terms of force, energy of the will, or what-have-you. It is unmistakably plain virtue that Machiavelli means.

I do not put forward those few quotations as all in which *virtú* and virtue are synonymous; but as sufficient in themselves to show incontrovertibly that Machiavelli, apart from other words which have the same meaning (as *bontà*), is not ignorant of virtue under its own label. Nor, naturally, do I put them forward either as preventing him from using the word elsewhere (even in close proximity) in a different sense. Just as he juxtaposes verb-forms from the stem *poss*- by others from the stem *pot*-, so that *posseva* follows *poteva*, etc., with no concern for the discrepancy, so it is with the senses of *stato*, or of *virtú*. Indeed, it is quite obvious that the idea of a theory of *virtú* could not have arisen were there not conspicuous examples in which *virtú* has a sense akin to, or derived from, that of Galen. Nor are other Latin senses unrepresented. Thus in 'It is astonishing that an army so constructed should

3. O. Tommasini, *Vita e scritti di N.M.* II. 39.
4. *Principe* XV.
5. *Discorsi* I, 10.
6. *Discorsi* I, 18.

have sufficient energy (*virtú*) to obtain the victory, or that any should be found so imbecile as to allow such a disorderly rabble to vanquish them.'[7] the word is defined by its opposite to give the sense of valor and bravery which Machiavelli found most frequently given to it in his author, Livy. And the *surprise* over a victory by 'disordinate genti' shows that Machiavelli had in mind as well the contrast between barbaric *furor* and Latin *virtus*. Other opposites, beside *vizio* and *viltà*, stand with *virtú*, and give relief to it in specific passages. Thus *ozio* gives a sharp definition in a passage of the *Discorsi*.[8] Perhaps more frequent still is the opposition with *fortuna*, a pair which Machiavelli had obviously learnt from the Latin historians, from whom so much of his idiom comes. Quintus Curtius, for example, had discussed the question whether Alexander the Great owed more to *virtus* or to *fortuna*;[9] a question which Machiavelli repeats for Caesar Borgia in Chapter VII of the *Prince*. And it is the same Quintus Curtius, if it is not Sallust, who defined the word most sharply in the sense that has been proclaimed essentially Machiavellian. When Alexander's soldiers quail before their leader's appetite for conquests, and for jungle penetration, their spokesman says, 'Your virtue is always on the increase, but our energy is already exhausted.'[1] And Sallust makes that quite explicit by debating whether military success depends more on the *vis* of the body, or on the *virtus* of the mind.[2] We may see once more a comparable use a few pages earlier in Quintus Curtius, where Porus uses his last weapon to transfix his brother Taxilis (who had urged on him surrender to Alexander): The force of his mind being spent, he turned to the force of his legs.[3] In cases such as these virtue is already an energy of the will, transcending mere force. It is a regular Latin sense, and one which is surely implicit still in Cicero's contribution of virtue as moral perfection;[4] it represents, that is to say, one avenue of development towards a perfection. Where Machiavelli is so often indebted to his Latin authors for construction and vocabulary there is nothing odd in his taking also the various Latin uses of *virtus*, and leaving them concurrent, as he did with the senses of *stato*.

In the case of *virtú* there is a further check on the process. I do not think the dictionary recognizes it quite explicitly, but there is in Latin a gap between *virtus* and *virtutes*. It is the first one only that admits the sense of energy of the will, or bravery; the second is already concerned only with good actions, or good qualities. In Valerius Maximus there is *virtus* in the anecdote of Xenophon's continuing his sacrifice, and

7. *Istorie Fiorentine* V, 34.
8. *Discorsi* II, 2.
9. Quintus Curtius X, 5.
1. *Ibid.*, IX, 3.

2. Sallust, *The War with Catiline* 1.
3. Q. Curtius VIII, 14.
4. Cicero, *De Legibus* I, 8, 25.

replacing of his wreath, when learning that his son had died in battle, but had died with valour.[5] But Valerius Maximus uses the plural *virtutes* differently. Marcus Brutus is 'suarum prius virtutum, quam patriae parentis parricida'.[6] The ancient Roman who killed his wife because she had drunk wine found no accuser, for the use of wine for women shuts the door to all the virtues, and opens it to all the vices—'et virtutibus omnibus ianuam claudit et delictis aperit.'[7] We could trace this opposition between singular and plural in other Latin authors, who may be, perhaps, closer to Machiavelli, as in Tacitus, or in Suetonius (who, for Domitian, talks of a mixture of *virtutes* and *vitia*, which makes it quite clear).[8] But probably this illustration is already sufficient. Machiavelli retains this plural when, for instance, he speaks of the prince's duty to show himself 'lover of the virtues'.[9] And this coincidence with the Latin use is sufficient to resolve the ambiguity which Lisio recognized—though he spoke for the good interpretation—in the passage on Hannibal in the *Prince*. When Machiavelli writes of 'his inhuman cruelty, which along with his countless other talents (*virtù*) made him an object of awe and terror to his soldiers,'[1] there is implied a contrast between the qualities, as there is explicit one between the epithets resulting from them. Hannibal is not venerable because of his inhuman cruelty, or terrible because of his virtues. This plural is, I think, rarely used by Machiavelli: there is at least one case where he has replaced a Latin plural by the singular, with the sense of virtue, and this in the passage I quoted on Rome under the bad emperors.[2] But if it is a rare use, at least it is stable in sense, as it was in Latin.[3] The singular is more volatile. This ambiguity, however, which leaves the reader with the task of fitting one of the several Latin senses, the medical one, that of energy of the will, of bravery, of Ciceronian virtue, or the post-classical sense of Christian virtue, can involve no reflection on Machiavelli. Rather, it is clear, as it was in our consideration of the *Prince*, that there are other elements to Machiavelli's theory of the prince, or of the republic, than mere go-getting; and it is not profitable to consider him as a writer without taking them fully into account. Machiavelli is no more the standard-bearer of *virtù* than the Renascence is the age of the Borgias.

That does not mean, of course, that we should neglect consideration of this particular aspect of the word when Machiavelli uses it. Not only does it appear to me that Machiavelli cannot easily be dismissed from the moral field, in that he did not only know this sense, but that he finds himself in irreproachable company at this point precisely where

---

5. Valerius Maximus V, 10, 5.
6. *Ibid.*, VI, 4, 8.
7. *Ibid.*, VI, 3, 10.
8. Tacitus, *Historiae* II, 269; Suetonius, *Domit.* V.

9. *Principe* XXI.
1. *Principe* XVII.
2. *Discorsi* I, 10, 47.
3. Cf. the end of *Prince* 11.

he has been most vilified. Let us go back to this *virtú* which records respect of some sort for the energy of achievement without regard to the moral nature of the achievement. It is this that has stuck in people's throats; it is this that had least right to do so. For Machiavelli is, I imagine, merely treading here on the same ground as Dante; and Dante at this point speaks the same language as does either Cicero before him, or La Rochefoucauld after him. One could, by looking harder, probably see more; but I hope that such citation will be enough to put Machiavelli, on this point at least, in better light. While before in this chapter I have been concerned to show that there is no consistent doctrine of *virtú* in Machiavelli's writings, it is my purpose now to prove that where he touches some such doctrine fleetingly it is a common (and I would add, a common-sense) inheritance.

Let us begin with Dante. Quite palpably Dante hesitates at the outset of his journey. He stands in danger of showing pusillanimity, and in the effort of separating himself from this *viltà* (the recurrences of the word itself are worth noting in the first few cantos of the *Inferno*) he writes the finely savage episode of the nameless crew who rush for ever naked after a blank banner, with the admirable biting lines against the nameless pope who runs with them. As soon, says Dante, as I saw him there, *at once* I knew the nature of the throng. They do not speak (what could they have to say?), there is no name given to their category; and Dante looks away. So far, by this tremendous scorn, is he himself removed from the *viltà* with which Virgil had reproached him at the beginning of the canto.[4] And these sinners, whether originally angels who took no part as between God and Lucifer, or men who had the courage neither for good nor ill, are outside hell, and yet, by Dante's scorn for them, beneath its lowest depths:

> 'Heaven cast them forth; their presence there would dim
> The light; deep Hell rejects so base a herd
> Lest sin should boast itself because of them.'
> *Inferno* III. 40 ff. (tr. Dorothy Sayers)

That is theologically wrong, and psychologically right. These are the vile, the spineless, the aimless; and even those below,

> "Who dared conceive enormous ill, and even carried it out,"

have some claim on our regard which these have not.

This attitude of Dante, and its relation to his temperament, is sufficiently known for there to be no point in my labouring it; but surprisingly enough it has not been related (perhaps because of this fact that it has

4. *Inferno* III, 15.

its roots in Dante's nature) to a passage in a work which Dante knew well, the *De Officiis* of Cicero. At least, I do not find the connection made by Dr. Edward Moore, nor have I noted it elsewhere. Yet this passage in Cicero is germain to Dante's conception of *ignavia*, and is not uninteresting for Machiavelli—who also, as we have seen, was well acquainted with his *De Officiis*. I give it *in extenso* because of its importance as a link between the three of them: 'For men generally admire all those things which they observe as great, and outside their expectation; separately in individuals if they see some unexpected good quality. And thus they exalt with the highest praises those men in whom they think they see certain excellent and outstanding virtues. But they despise and condemn those in whom they think there is no capacity (*nihil virtutis*), no spirit, and no vigour. For they do not despise everyone of whom they think ill. They think ill of those who are wicked, slanderous, fraudulent, ready to commit injustices, without indeed despising them. Wherefore, as I said, those are despised who, as the saying goes, are of no use either to themselves or others, in whom there is no exertion, no activity, no care for anything.'[5] That text is abundantly clear: one may say, if one likes, that Dante's view of *ignavia* derives from it; or that it does not need to. The identity, at any rate, will remain a constant.

Similarly, if we look beyond Machiavelli to La Rochefoucauld, we shall find that this very natural idea has occured to him as well. Two or three maxims are worth quoting, and they will not take up the room of Cicero: 'Weakness is more contrary to virtue than is vice.' 'One doesn't despise those who have vices, just those who have no virtue.'—that is almost literally Ciceronian. 'No man deserves the name of good if he has not the grit and determination to be bad. Most other virtue is generally laziness or weakness of will.'—which we may relate to the *alcuna gloria* of Dante's text. And finally, to clinch the series, 'There are heroes in evil as in good.' Now, although many have labelled La Rochefoucauld as a cynic (a little rashly, perhaps—but that is none of our business here), no one would care to maintain that he intended equal applause for both sorts of *heroes*. He implies approval for those who do good, and disapproval for those who do bad (you cannot, after all, use the words *good* and *bad* in more than one way); and there remains contempt for those who are in between, who are without the means to do either. Despise Alexander, or Napoleon? No, but condemn them if you like.

Now let us think of Machiavelli, and his so-called admiration for *virtú*. I think we may do so suitably in terms of one of the most telling shafts of Pascal in his third *Lettre Provinciale*. What is most orthodox in others became heresy in M. Arnauld's use, and could only become orthodox again if others took it over from him. How so? 'It is not the

5. Cicero, *De officiis* II, 10.

opinions of M. Arnauld that are heretical; it is simply his person. His is a personal heresy. He is not a heretic because of anything he has said or written, but simply through being M. Arnauld.' And in precisely the same way, we know how wicked Machiavelli is, so therefore what was righteous indignation in Dante, or moral analysis in Cicero, or social reflection in La Rochefoucauld, becomes repulsive cynicism in Machiavelli. One cannot, it seems, bear a name like his with impunity. If we need an instance, first, of the label, let us turn to Professor Toffanin, whose chapter in his survey *Il Cinquecento* can be taken as one stopping-point for modern views of Machiavelli. The episode for use as a touchstone is obviously that on the conduct of G.-P. Baglioni at Perugia on the occasion of Julius II's imprudent putting of himself at the mercy of this petty tyrant whom he had come to oust. It is an episode that inspired, says Toffanin, 'one of the most cynically stupendous pages in the *Discorsi*.[6] Those are strong words; but usual ones, for, as we may expect, this page is also one of those black-listed by the estimable Burd as worthy of perusal by those who might wish to convince themselves that the 'methods suggested in the *Discorsi* are quite as thorough and as unscrupulous and quite as little determined by moral considerations as those of the *Prince*.'[7]

When we are just about to turn to the *Discorsi* for their contribution to Machiavelli's general attitude, it is very good that we should have the opportunity of a preliminary investigation at an incriminated point. But alas! it looks as if poor Machiavelli must have given himself badly away; and after such advertisement as Burd and Toffanin supply we may expect the worst. What, if we turn now to *Discorsi* I, Chapter XXVII, do we find? As the particulars of this expedition of Julius II are well known I may legitimately limit myself to quoting the comments of Machiavelli. First, there is his judgment on (that is, against) Julius II. The fall of Julius, at any hands, would serve for Machiavelli as a moral lesson to the Church, showing what estimate one should have of those who live and reign like Julius.[8] One cannot easily retain a flair for moral lessons when one has washed one's hands entirely of moral considerations. And in this case we have very excellent corroboration for Machiavelli's judgment on Julius in two blunt passages in the *Legations*. They both date from 1510, and they both think of Julius (with admirable cause) as one who may bring Italy to ruin. 'Everyone here is upset with this action of the Pope, since they think he's trying to ruin Christianity and reduce Italy to ashes,' so Machiavelli wrote from Blois on the 26th July; and only a few days later he confirmed this with a statement of 'that diabolical spirit' which was reported to have entered into Julius, so that he might

6. Toffanin, *Il Cinquecento* 302.
7. Burd, 42, note 1.

8. *Discorsi* I, 27.

well 'cause Florence to be trampled on, and bring himself to the grave'.[9] If there was reason for such views, can one doubt whether Machiavelli was justified in passing condemnation on Julius? Perhaps, however, it is the comment on Giovampagolo Baglioni which betrays the cloven hoof? 'All the prudent men accompanying the Pope took note of his temerity and of Giovampagolo's weakness of spirit. . . . Nor could they believe that he had refrained from doing this either from goodness or conscientous scruples . . . but they concluded that men do not know how to be honorably bad or perfectly good, and that when a crime has in itself some grandeur or magnanimity, they will not know how to attempt it.'[1] If we reduce that to its essential elements we find G.-P. Baglioni despised for his pusillanimity (and Machiavelli uses Dante's word—*viltà*), his badness being stated as beyond question; while the matter itself is stated in terms of a Machiavellian *aut-aut* (be *honorably wicked*, that is, qualify for the *alcuna gloria*, be a Capaneus or a Mahomet; or else, be perfectly good—a Trajan, shall we say?). And in between remains that condemnation of most men who have the energy for neither course, a condemnation by contempt. 'There are heroes in evil as well as in good.' No doubt there are: but Giovampagolo is in no danger of belonging with them.

If we are just to Machiavelli we must admit, I think, that there is an absolute identity here of views with Cicero, Dante, and La Rochefoucauld. We do not imagine that Dante liked Mahomet because he despised Celestine V. We only imagine that Machiavelli would have approved more highly of a more wicked Baglioni because we have been told by responsible historians like Villari that such was Machiavelli's strange attitude of mind. And there have always been the Maritains to offer their assent absolutely *a priori* to Villari's words on Machiavelli's supposed admiration for brigand chiefs who upset a country and his lack of alarm at 'any sanguinary and cruel action'. 'For I assure you that Machiavelli didn't believe in God! nor in the church of Rome either!' as an unkind reviewer summed up Maritain's expostulations.[2] But if we look honestly at the two texts I quoted from the *Legations* on Julius II whose policy is feared as one calculated to bring ruin on Christendom and to consummate the downfall of Italy, on Julius whom Machiavelli sees as possessed with a diabolical spirit, then the situation wears a different air. M. Maritain appeals to the idea of what the papacy ought to be, and therefore must have been; so Machiavelli's revolt from it can only have been occasioned by his own wickedness. Machiavelli looked at what it was, which does not happen to have been identical with what

---

9. Opp. P. M. VI, 30 and 71.
1. *Discorsi*, I, 27.
2. Quoted from the South American review

Lettres françaises fév. 1943, in a *compte rendu* of Jacques Maritain, *La fin du machiavelisme*, 1941.

it must have been. And perhaps it is the place here to refer the reader
to the words of Laurent which Tommasini rescued from that author's
short section on machiavellianism. 'What has harmed the repute of
Machiavelli are illusions about Christianity and chivalry. Men imagine
that in the middle ages there was a Christian politics of which the popes
were the agents; and what could these politics be if not an expression
of the pure morality of the Gospels? Again, men imagine that chivalry
introduced into human relations only the most lofty and delicate of
sentiments, thanks to Christianity again. And then they suppose that
Machiavelli replaced the Christian ideal with the vile doctrine of self-
interest. These illusions contain about as many errors as they have
words.'[3] Not everything that Laurent says on Machiavelli in his section
is still acceptable, but could one more genially bring back M. Maritain
to consider what Machiavelli's attitude should have been to the *diabolical*
policy of Julius II? Here we have a Machiavelli taking alarm at sanguinary
action. It is the Machiavelli whose distress at the plight of Italy in the
first quarter of the sixteenth century led him to pen, a year before his
death, that anguished phrase to Guicciardini.[4] This is the man who has,
to use the frivolous words of Toffanin, the Renascence admiration for
the *facinus* ('crime').[5]

It is well to remember too that this whole chapter of Julius II and
Baglioni is introduced as an illustration to a theme stated in the previous
chapter; and the second half of this Chapter XXVI is very pertinent to
us here. Machiavelli mentions as a model Philip of Macedon, and quotes
on him the bitter words of Justin.[6] Here surely, if the Villaris are to
have any justification for their language, will be the brigand chief whose
virtú Machiavelli is bound to admire: this man who made himself, from
being a petty ruler, monarch of all Greece! This man who, in the words
of Justin and Machiavelli himself, transferred whole peoples as herdsmen
do their cattle. Here is the *facinus* in this forerunner of Hitler: where
is the admiration for it? Alas! Machiavelli turns away from the model
he has proposed, as he did before from Agathocles. 'Doubtless these
means are cruel and destructive of all civilized life, and neither Christian
nor even human, and should be avoided by everyone. In fact the life
of a private citizen would be preferable to that of a king at the expense
of the ruin of so many human beings.'[7] That is a most revealing sentence
for the mentality of Machiavelli; only it does not reveal anything we
might have expected from the statements of Villari or Toffanin; or from
any acquaintance with Maritain and machiavellianism. But in this case
Philip of Macedon is not a *model*? No, the word is misleading—he is

3. Laurent, *Etudes sur l'humanité* X, 387. Cf.
Tommasini, II, 727.
4. VIII, 202. "Free Italy from her constant
cares, exterminate these fearful beasts who
though they have human faces and voices, have

no other attribute of humanity."
5. Toffanin, 376 etc.
6. Justin, VIII, 5.
7. *Discorsi* I, 26.

a *pattern* which conduct will assume if it goes one way, and which needs stating for completeness (just as Dante states hell, while he desires paradise). Again, you must be one thing or the other, or something in between; and Machiavelli states the problem starkly, and in terms of good and ill: 'Nevertheless, whoever is unwilling to adopt the first and humane course must, if he wishes to maintain his power, follow the latter evil course. But men generally decide upon a middle course, which is most hazardous; for they know neither how to be entirely good or entirely bad, as we shall illustrate by examples in the next chapter.' (The example of Julius and Baglioni follows.)[8] That makes Machiavelli's attitude to G.-P. Baglioni perfectly plain before he is introduced: he is a bad man, and having started on a bad course he could maintain himself by being wholly bad (and parenthetically, his badness might even prove of benefit if it cancelled that of Julius II); but he ends by being merely despicable because he has not personality to do that. Is it not clear that he stands condemned by Machiavelli in any case? And that Machiavelli's objectivity does not mean cutting himself adrift from moral considerations?

Nor does it make the matter different that Machiavelli has both Livy and Tacitus behind him in this objection to the 'middle way.' It was a phrase that first came under his pen in that short discourse of 1503 on the rebellion a year before in the Valdichiana. That was Machiavelli's initiation to the idea of a full eradication of one's troubles. It was enthusiastic and unrealistic, and we cannot take it as anything final. Rather, his Livian connection is one to be examined next when we turn to its main expression in the *Discourses*. For the moment, let us content ourselves with looking at Tacitus, who also concurs with Machiavelli and with the other authors who have expressed contempt for spinelessness. Thus Tacitus wrote of Fabius Valens, who dallied, wasting in consultation the time for action, that in the end he rejected both counsels and did what is the worst of things, he followed an ambiguous course, 'he compromised.'[9] Here also then the middle way is rejected. But Tacitus is not indifferent to which side a person takes, and his comment a little later on another similar case makes his position clear. Claudius Apollinaris was 'neither constant in faith, nor strenuous in perfidy'.[1] It is, I hope, visible that *strenuous in perfidy* is not a term of approval. The attitude of Tacitus is the same one that Machiavelli adopts towards G.-P. Baglioni. Machiavelli is in reasonable company, and we may conclude: firstly, that it never occurred to him that there was a theory of *virtú*, so that he is innocent of any systematic use of the word itself, as of any systematic exclusion of the idea of virtue; and secondly, that in following Dante and the rest who prefer energy to the lack of it, he still, with them, prefers a good use of it to a bad one. Have we not

8. *Ibid*.
9. Tacitus, *Historiae* III, 40.

1. *Ibid*. III, 57.

already seen the statements of the *Prince,* and do we not know from it
that if one turns wholly with Philip of Macedon to the left, not to the
right, one will not maintain oneself for long? Once we have realized
that this matter of *virtú* rests largely on prejudice, and not on reason,
we are ready to approach Machiavelli's main statement of his political
ideas in his commentary to Livy.

ISAIAH BERLIN

The Question of Machiavelli†

I

There is something surprising about the sheer number of interpretations
of Machiavelli's political opinions. There exist, even now, over a score of
leading theories of how to interpret *The Prince* and *The Discourses*—apart
from a cloud of subsidiary views and glosses. The bibliography of this
is vast and growing faster than ever. While there may exist no more than
the normal extent of disagreement about the meaning of particular terms
or theses contained in these works, there is a startling degree of divergence
about the central view, the basic political attitude of Machiavelli.

This phenomenon is easier to understand in the case of other thinkers
whose opinions have continued to puzzle or agitate mankind—Plato,
for example, or Rousseau or Hegel or Marx. But then it might be said
that Plato wrote in a world and in a language that we cannot be sure
we understand; that Rousseau, Hegel, Marx were prolific theorists and
that their works are scarcely models of clarity and consistency. But *The
Prince* is a short book: its style is usually described as being singularly
lucid, succinct, and pungent—a model of clear Renaissance prose. *The
Discourses* are not, as treatises on politics go, of undue length and they
are equally clear and definite. Yet there is no consensus about the
significance of either; they have not been absorbed into the texture of
traditional political theory; they continue to arouse passionate feelings;
The Prince has evidently excited the interest and admiration of some of
the most formidable men of action of the last four centuries, especially
our own, men not normally addicted to reading classical texts.

† "The Question of Machiavelli" by Isaiah
Berlin was first published in *New York Review
of Books,* November 4, 1971 and is extracted
from "The Originality of Machiavelli" which
was first published in Myron P. Gilmore (ed.),
Studies on Machiavelli (Florence, 1972: Sansoni) and printed with corrections in *Against*
the Current: Essays in the History of Ideas by
Isaiah Berlin, edited by Henry Hardy (London,
1979: Hogarth Press and New York, 1980, Viking). "The Question of Machiavelli" by Isaiah
Berlin is reprinted by kind permission of Curtis
Brown Group Ltd., London, and of the author.
Copyright © Isaiah Berlin, 1971.

There is evidently something peculiarly disturbing about what Machiavelli said or implied, something that has caused profound and lasting uneasiness. Modern scholars have pointed out certain real or apparent inconsistencies between the (for the most part) republican sentiment of *The Discourses* (and *The Histories*) and the advice to absolute rulers in *The Prince*. Indeed there is a great difference of tone between the two treatises, as well as chronological puzzles: this raises problems about Machiavelli's character, motives, and convictions which for three hundred years and more have formed a rich field of investigation and speculation for literary and linguistic scholars, psychologists, and historians.

But it is not this that has shocked Western feeling. Nor can it be only Machiavelli's "realism" or his advocacy of brutal or unscrupulous or ruthless politics that has so deeply upset so many later thinkers and driven some of them to explain or explain away his advocacy of force and fraud. The fact that the wicked are seen to flourish or that wicked courses appear to pay has never been very remote from the consciousness of mankind. The Bible, Herodotus, Thucydides, Plato, Aristotle—to take only some of the fundamental works of Western culture—the characters of Jacob or Joshua, Samuel's advice to Saul, Thucydides' Melian dialogue or his account of at least one ferocious but rescinded Athenian resolution, the philosophies of Thrasymachus and Callicles, Aristotle's more cynical advice in *The Politics*, and, after these, Carneades' speeches to the Roman Senate as described by Cicero, Augustine's view of the secular state from one vantage point, and Marsilio's from another—all these had cast enough light on political realities to shock the credulous and naïve out of uncritical idealism.

The explanation can scarcely lie in Machiavelli's tough-mindedness alone, even though he did perhaps dot the i's and cross the t's more sharply than anyone before him. Even if the initial shock—the reactions of, say, Pole or Gentillet—is to be so explained, this does not account for the reactions of one who had read or even heard about the opinions of Hobbes or Spinoza or Hegel or the Jacobins and their heirs. Something else is surely needed to account both for the continuing horror and for the differences among the commentators. The two phenomena may not be unconnected. To indicate the nature of the latter phenomenon one may cite only the best known interpretations of Machiavelli's political views produced since the sixteenth century.

According to Alberico Gentili and the late Professor Garrett Mattingly, the author of *The Prince* wrote a satire—for he certainly cannot literally have meant what he said. For Spinoza, Rousseau, Ugo Foscolo, Signor Ricci (who introduces *The Prince* to the readers of the Oxford Classics), it is a cautionary tale; for whatever else he was, Machiavelli was a passionate patriot, a democrat, a believer in liberty, and *The Prince* must have been intended (Spinoza is particularly clear on this) to warn men of what tyrants could be and do, the better to resist them. Perhaps the author could not write openly with the two rival powers—those of the Church and of the Medici—eying him with equal (and not unjustified) suspicion. *The Prince* is therefore a satire (though no work seems to me to read less like one).

For Professor A. H. Gilbert it is anything but this—it is a typical piece of its period, a mirror for princes, a genre exercise common enough in the Renaissance and before (and after) it, with very obvious borrowings and "echoes"; more gifted than most of these, and certainly more hard-boiled (and influential), but not so very different in style, content, or intention.

Professors Giuseppe Prezzolini and Hiram Haydn, more plausibly, regard it as an anti-Christian piece (in this following Fichte and others) and see it as an attack on the Church and all her principles, a defense of the pagan view of life. Professor Toffanin, however, thinks Machiavelli was a Christian, though a somewhat peculiar one, a view from which Marchese Ridolfi, his most distinguished living biographer, and Father Leslie Walker (in his English edition of *The Discourses*) do not wholly dissent. Alderisio, indeed, regards him as a passionate and sincere Catholic, although he does not go quite so far as the anonymous nineteenth-century compiler of *Religious Maxims faithfully extracted from the works of Niccolò Machiavelli* (referred to by Ridolfi in the last chapter of his biography).

For Benedetto Croce and all the many scholars who have followed him, Machiavelli is an anguished humanist, and one who, so far from seeking to soften the impression made by the crimes that he describes, laments the vices of men which make such wicked courses politically unavoidable—a moralist who wrings his hands over a world in which political ends can only be achieved by means that are morally evil, and therefore the man who divorced the province of politics from that of ethics. But for the Swiss scholars Wälder, Kaegi, and von Muralt, he is a peace-loving humanist, who believed in order, stability, pleasure in life, in the disciplining of the aggressive elements of our nature into the kind of civilized harmony that he found in its finest form among the well-armed Swiss democracies of his own time.

For the great sixteenth-century neo-Stoic Justus Lipsius and later for Algarotti (in 1759) and Alfieri (in 1796), he was a passionate patriot who saw in Cesare Borgia the man who, if he had lived, might have liberated Italy from the barbarous French and Spaniards and Austrians who were trampling on her and had reduced her to misery and poverty, decadence and chaos. The late Professor Mattingly could not credit this because it was obvious to him, and he did not doubt that it must have been no

less obvious to Machiavelli, that Cesare was incompetent, a mounte-
bank, a squalid failure; while Professor Vögelin seems to suggest that it
is not Cesare, but (of all men) Tamerlane who was hovering before
Machiavelli's fancy-laden gaze.

For Cassirer, Renaudet, Olschki, and Sir Keith Hancock, Machiavelli
is a cold technician, ethically and politically uncommitted, an objective
analyst of politics, a morally neutral scientist, who (K. Schmid tells us)
anticipated Galileo in applying inductive methods to social and historical
material, and had no moral interest in the use made of his technical
discoveries—being equally ready to place them at the disposal of liberators and despots, good men and scoundrels. Renaudet describes his
method as "purely positivist," Cassirer, as concerned with "political
statics." But for Federico Chabod he is not coldly calculating at all, but
passionate to the point of unrealism. Ridolfi, too, speaks of *il grande
appassionato* and De Caprariis thinks him positively visionary.

For Herder he is, above all, a marvelous mirror of his age, a man
sensitive to the contours of his time, who faithfully described what others
did not admit or recognize, an inexhaustible mine of acute contemporary
observation; and this is accepted by Ranke and Macaulay, Burd, and,
in our day, Gennaro Sasso. For Fichte he is a man of deep insight into
the real historical (or super-historical) forces that mold men and transform their morality—in particular, a man who rejected Christian principles for those of reason, political unity, and centralization. For Hegel
he is the man of genius who saw the need for uniting a chaotic collection
of small and feeble principalities into a coherent whole. His specific
nostrums may excite disgust, but they are accidents due to the conditions
of their own time, now long past. Yet, however obsolete his precepts,
he understood something more important—the demands of his own
age—that the hour had struck for the birth of the modern, centralized,
political state, for the formation of which he "established the truly necessary fundamental principles."

The thesis that Machiavelli was above all an Italian and a patriot, speaking above all to his own generation, and if not solely to Florentines, at
any rate only to Italians, and that he must be judged solely, or at least
mainly, in terms of his historical context is a position common to Herder
and Hegel, Macaulay and Burd.[1] Yet for Professors Butterfield and

---

1. Ernst Cassirer makes the valid and relevant
point that to value—or justify—Machiavelli's
opinions solely as a mirror of their times is one
thing; to maintain that he was himself con-
sciously addressing only his own countrymen,
and, if Burd is to be believed, not even all of
them, is a very different one, and entails a false
view of him and the civilization to which he
belonged. The Renaissance did not view itself
in historical perspective. Machiavelli was looking for—and thought that he had found—
timeless, universal laws of social behavior.
  It is no service either to him or to the truth
to deny or ignore the unhistorical assumptions
which he shared with all his comtemporaries
and predecessors. The praise lavished upon
him by the German historical school from Herder onward, including the Marxist Antonio
Gramsci, for the gifts in which they saw his
strength—his realistic sense of his own times,

Ramat he suffers from an equal lack of scientific and historical sense. Obsessed by classical authors, his gaze is on a imaginary past; he deduces his political maxims in an unhistorical and a priori manner from dogmatic axioms (according to Professor Huovinen)—a method that was already becoming obsolete at the time at which he was writing. In this respect his slavish imitation of antiquity is judged to be inferior to the historical sense and sagacious judgment of his friend Guicciardini (so much for the discovery in him of inklings of modern scientific method).

For Bacon (as for Spinoza, and later for Lassalle) he is above all the supreme realist and avoider of utopian fantasies. Boccalini is shocked by him, but cannot deny the accuracy or importance of his observations; so is Meinecke for whom he is the father of *Staatsraison*, with which he plunged a dagger into the body politic of the West, inflicting a wound which only Hegel would know how to heal. (This is Meinecke's optimistic verdict half a century ago, implicitly withdrawn after the Second World War.)

But for Koenig he is not a tough-minded cynic at all, but an aesthete seeking to escape from the chaotic and squalid world of the decadent Italy of his time into a dream of pure art, a man not interested in practice who painted an ideal political landscape much (if I understand this view correctly) as Piero della Francesca painted an ideal city. *The Prince* is to be read as an idyl in the best neoclassical, neo-pastoral, Renaissance style. Yet De Sanctis in the second volume of his *History of Italian Literature* denies *The Prince* a place in the humanist tradition on account of Machiavelli's hostility to imaginative visions.

For Renzo Sereni it is a fantasy indeed but of a bitterly frustrated man, and its dedication is the "desperate plea" of a victim of "severe and constant misfortune." A psychoanalytic interpretation of one queer episode in Machiavelli's life is offered in support of this thesis.

For Macaulay he is a political pragmatist and a patriot who cared most of all for the independence of Florence, and acclaimed any form of rule that would ensure it. Marx calls *The Discourses* a "genuine masterpiece," and Engels (in the *Dialectics of Nature*) speaks of Machiavelli as "one of the giants of the Enlightenment," a man "free

---

his insight into the rapidly changing social and political conditions of Italy and Europe in his time, the collapse of feudalism, the rise of the national state, the altering power relationships within the Italian principalities, and the like—would have been galling to a man who believed he had discovered eternal truths.

He may, like his countryman Columbus, have mistaken the nature of his own achievement. If the historical school (including the Marxist) is right, Machiavelli did not and could not have done what he set out to do. But nothing is gained by supposing he did not set out to do it; and plenty of witnesses from his day to ours would deny Herder's assertion, and maintain that Machiavelli's goal—the discovery of the permanent principles of a political science—was anything but utopian; and that he came nearer than most to attaining them.

from *petit-bourgeois* out-look . . . ." Soviet criticism is more am-
bivalent.[2]

For the restorers of the short-lived Florentine republic he was evidently
nothing but a venal and treacherous toady, anxious to serve any master,
who had unsuccessfully tried to flatter the Medici in the hope of gaining
their favor. Professor Sabine in his well-known textbook views him as
an anti-metaphysical empiricist, a Hume or Popper before his time, free
from obscurantist, theological, and metaphysical preconceptions. For
Antonio Gramsci he is above all a revolutionary innovator who directs
his shafts against the obsolescent feudal aristocracy and Papacy and their
mercenaries. His *Prince* is a myth which signifies the dictatorship of
new, progressive forces: ultimately of the coming role of the masses and
of the need for the emergence of new politically realistic leaders—*The
Prince* is "an anthropomorphic symbol" of the hegemony of the "collective will."

Like Jakob Burckhardt and Friedrich Meinecke, Professors C. J. Friedrich and Charles Singleton maintain that he has a developed conception
of the state as a work of art. The great men who had founded or maintain
human associations are conceived as analogous to artists whose aim is
beauty, and whose essential qualification is understanding of their
material—they are molders of men, as sculptors are molders of marble
or clay. Politics, in this view, leaves the realm of ethics and approaches
that of aesthetics. Singleton argues that Machiavelli's originality consists
in his view of political action as a form of what Aristotle called
"making"—the goal of which is a non-moral artifact, an object of beauty
or use external to man (in this case a particular arrangement of human
affairs)—and not of "doing" (where Aristotle and Aquinas had placed
it), the goal of which is internal and moral, not the creation of an object,
but a particular kind—the right way—of living or being.

This position is not distant from that of Villari, Croce, and others,
inasmuch as it ascribes to Machiavelli the divorce of politics from ethics.
Professor Singleton transfers Machiavelli's conception of politics to the
region of art, which is conceived as being amoral. Croce gives it an
independent status of its own: of politics for politics' sake.

2. The only extended treatment of Machiavelli
by a prominent Bolshevik intellectual known
to me is in Kamenev's short-lived introduction
to the Russian translation of *The Prince* (Aka-
demia, Moscow, 1934). This unswervingly follows the full historicist-sociological approach
criticized by Cassirer. Machiavelli is described
as an active publicist, preoccupied by the
"mechanism of the struggles for power" within
and between the Italian principalities, a soci-
ologist who gave a masterly analysis of the "sociological" jungle that preceded the formation
of "a powerful, national, essentially bourgeois"
Italian state. His almost "dialectical" grasp of
the realities of power and freedom from metaphysical and theological fantasies establish
him as a worthy forerunner of Marx, Engels,
Lenin, and Stalin.

These opinions were brought up and pillo-
ried by Vyshinsky, the prosecutor at Kamenev's
trial. See on this, "Kamenev's Last Essay" by
Ch. Abramsky in *New Left Review*, London,
June, 1962, pp. 34–42.

But the commonest view of him, at least as a political thinker, is still that of most Elizabethans, dramatists and scholars alike, for whom he is a man inspired by the Devil to lead good men to their doom, the great subverter, the teacher of evil, *le docteur de la scélératesse*, the inspirer of St. Bartholomew's Eve, the original of Iago. This is the "murderous Machiavel" of the famous 400 references in Elizabethan literature.

His name adds a new ingredient to the more ancient figure of Old Nick. For the Jesuits he is "the devil's partner in crime," "a dishonorable writer and an unbeliever," and *The Prince* is, in Bertrand Russell's words, "a handbook for gangsters" (compare with this Mussolini's description of it as a *"vade mecum* for statesmen," a view tacitly shared, perhaps, by other heads of state). This is the view common to Protestants and Catholics, Gentillet and François Hotman, Cardinal Pole, Bodin, and Frederick the Great, followed by the authors of all the many anti-Machiavels, the latest of whom are Jacques Maritain and Professor Leo Strauss.

There is prima facie something strange about so violent a disparity of judgments. What other thinker has presented so many facets to the students of his ideas? What other writer—and he not even a recognized philosopher—has caused his readers to disagree about his purposes so deeply and so widely? Yet I must repeat, Machiavelli does not write obscurely; nearly all his interpreters praise him for his terse, dry, clear prose.

What is it that has proved so arresting to so many?

II

Machiavelli, we are often told, was not concerned with morals. The most influential of all modern interpretations—that of Benedetto Croce, followed to some extent by Chabod, Russo, and others—is that Machiavelli, in E. W. Cochrane's words, "did not deny the validity of Christian morality, and did not pretend that a crime required by political necessity was any the less a crime. Rather he discovered . . . that this morality simply did not hold in political affairs, and that any policy based on the assumption that it did, would end in disaster. His factual objective description of contemporary practices is a sign not of cynicism or detachment but of anguish."

This account, it seems to me, contains two basic misinterpretations. The first is that the clash is one between "this [i.e., Christian] morality" and "political necessity." The implication is that there is an incompatibility between, on the one hand, morality—the region of ultimate values sought after for their own sakes, values recognition of which alone enables us to speak of "crimes" or morally to justify and condemn anything; and on the other, politics—the art of adapting means to ends, the region of technical skills, of what Kant was to call "hypothetical imperatives," which take the form "If you want to achieve x, do y" (e.g., betray a friend, kill an innocent man) without necessarily asking whether x is itself intrinsically desirable or not. This is the heart of the divorce of politics from ethics which Croce and many others attribute to Machiavelli. But this seems to me to rest on a mistake.

If ethics is confined to, let us say, Stoic or Christian or Kantian, or even some type of utilitarian ethics, where the source and criterion of value are the word of God, or eternal reason, or some inner sense or knowledge of good and evil, of right and wrong, voices which speak directly to the individual consciousness with absolute authority, this might have been tenable. But there exists an equally time-honored ethics, that of the Greek *polis*, of which Aristotle provided the clearest exposition. Since men are beings made by nature to live in communities, their communal purposes are the ultimate values from which the rest are derived, or with which their ends as individuals are identified. Politics—the art of living in a *polis*—is not an activity that can be dispensed with by those who prefer private life: it is not like seafaring or sculpture which those who do not wish to do so need not undertake. Political conduct is intrinsic to being a human being at a certain stage of civilization, and what it demands is intrinsic to living a successful human life.

Ethics so conceived—the code of conduct or the ideal to be pursued by the individual—cannot be known save by understanding the purpose and character of his *polis*; still less be capable of being divorced from it, even in thought. This is the kind of pre-Christian morality that Machiavelli takes for granted. "It is well-known," says Benedetto Croce, "that Machiavelli discovered the necessity and autonomy of politcs, which is beyond moral good and evil, which has its own laws against which it is useless to rebel, which cannot be exorcised and made to vanish by holy water." Beyond good and evil in some non-Aristotelian, religious, or liberal-Kantian sense; but not beyond the good and evil of those communities, ancient or modern, whose sacred values are social through and through. The arts of colonization or of mass murder (let us say) may also have their "own laws against which it is useless to rebel" for those who wish to practice them successfully. But if or when these laws collide with those of morality, it is possible, and indeed morally imperative, to abandon such activities.

But if Aristotle and Machiavelli are right about what men are (and should be—and Machiavelli's ideal is, particularly in *The Discourses*, drawn in vivid colors), political activity is intrinsic to human nature, and while individuals here and there may opt out, the mass of mankind cannot do so; and its communal life determines the moral duties of its members. Hence in opposing the "laws of politics" to "good and evil" Machiavelli is not contrasting two "autonomous" spheres of acting—the "political" and the "moral": he is contrasting his own "political" ethics with another ethical conception which governs the lives of persons who are of no interest to him. He is indeed rejecting one morality—the Christian—but not in favor of something that is not a morality at all but a game of skill, an activity called political, which is not concerned with ultimate human ends and is therefore not ethical at all.

He is indeed rejecting Christian ethics, but in favor of another system, another moral universe—the world of Pericles or of Scipio, or even of the Duke Valentino, a society geared to ends just as ultimate as the Christian faith, a society in which men fight and are ready to die for (public) ends which they pursue for their own sakes. They are choosing not a realm of means (called politics) as opposed to a realm of ends (called morals), but opt for a rival (Roman or classical) morality, an alternative realm of ends. In other words the conflict is between two moralities, Christian and pagan (or as some wish to call it, aesthetic), not between autonomous realms of morals and politics.

Nor is this a mere question of nomenclature, unless politics is conceived as being concerned (as it usually is) not with means, skills, methods, technique, "knowhow" (whether or not governed by unbreakable rules of its own), but with an independent kingdom of ends of its own, sought for their own sake; unless politics is conceived as a substitute for ethics. When Machiavelli said (in a letter to Guicciardini) that he loved his country more than his soul, he revealed his basic moral beliefs—a position with which Croce does not credit him.

The second implausible hypothesis in this connection is the idea that Machiavelli viewed the crimes of his society with anguish. (Chabod in his excellent study, unlike Croce and some Croceans, does not insist on this.) This entails that he accepts the dire necessities of the *raison d'état* with reluctance, because he sees no alternative. But there is no evidence for this: there is no trace of agony in his political works, any more than in his plays or letters.

The pagan world that Machiavelli prefers is built on recognition of the need for systematic guile and force by rulers, and he seems to think it natural and not at all exceptional or morally agonizing that they should employ these weapons wherever they are needed. Nor does he seem to think exceptional the distinction he draws between the rulers and the ruled. The subjects or citizens must be Romans too: they do not need the *virtù* of the rulers, but if they also cheat, Machiavelli's maxims will not work; they must be poor, militarized, honest, and obedient; if they lead Christian lives, they will accept too uncomplainingly the rule of mere bullies and scoundrels. No sound republic can be built of such materials as these. Theseus and Romulus, Moses and Cyrus did not preach humility or a view of this world as but a temporary resting place for their subjects.

But it is the first misinterpretation that goes deepest, that which represents Machiavelli as caring little or nothing for moral issues. This is surely not borne out by his own language. Anyone whose thought revolves round central concepts such as the good and the bad, the corrupt and the pure, has an ethical scale in mind in terms of which he gives moral praise and blame. Machiavelli's values are not Christian, but they are moral values.

On this crucial point Professor Hans Baron's criticism of the Croce-Russo thesis seems to me correct. Against the view that for Machiavelli politics were beyond moral criticism Professor Baron cites some of the passionately patriotic, republican, and libertarian passages in *The Discourses* in which the (moral) qualities of the citizens of a republic are favorably compared with those of the subjects of a despotic prince. The last chapter of *The Prince* is scarcely the work of a detached, morally neutral observer, or of a self-absorbed man, preoccupied with his own inner personal problems, who looks on public life "with anguish" as the graveyard of moral principles. Like Aristotle's or Cicero's, Machiavelli's morality was social and not individual: but it was a morality no less than there, not an amoral region, beyond good or evil.

It does not, of course, follow that he was not often fascinated by the techniques of political life as such. The advice given equally to conspirators and their enemies, the professional appraisal of the methods of Oliverotto or Sforza or Baglioni spring from typical humanist curiosity, the search for an applied science of politics, fascination by knowledge for its own sake, whatever the implications. But the moral ideal, that of the citizen of the Roman Republic, is never far away. Political skills are valued solely as means—for their effectiveness in re-creating conditions in which sick men recover their health and can flourish. And this is precisely what Aristotle would have called the moral end proper to man.

This leaves still with us the thorny problem of the relation of *The Prince* to *The Discourses*. But whatever the disparities, the central strain which runs through both is one and the same. The vision, the dream—typical of many writers who see themselves as tough-minded realists—of the strong, united, effective, morally regenerated, splendid, and victorious *patria*, whether it is saved by the *virtù* of one man or many, remains central and constant. Political judgments, attitudes toward individuals or states, toward *Fortuna* and *necessità*, evaluation of methods, degree of optimism, the fundamental mood—these vary between one work and another, perhaps within the same exposition. But the basic values, the ultimate end—Machiavelli's beatific vision—does not vary.

His vision is social and political. Hence the traditional view of him as simply a specialist in how to get the better of others, a vulgar cynic who says that Sunday school precepts are all very well, but in a world full of evil men, a man must lie, kill, and betray if he is to get somewhere, is incorrect. The philosophy summarized by "eat or be eaten, beat or be beaten"—the kind of worldly wisdom to be found in, say, Lappo Mazzei or Giovanni Morelli, with whom he has been compared, is not what is central in him. Machiavelli is not specially concerned with the opportunism of ambitious individuals; the ideal before his eyes is a shining vision of Florence or of Italy. In this respect he is a typically impassioned humanist of the Renaissance, save that his ideal is not artistic or cultural but political, unless the state—or regenerated Italy —is considered, in Burckhardt's sense, as an artistic goal. This is very different from mere advocacy of tough-mindedness as such, or of a realism irrespective of its goal.

Machiavelli's values, I should like to repeat, are not instrumental but moral and ultimate, and he calls for great sacrifices in their name. For them he rejects the rival scale—the Christian principles of *ozio* and meekness, not, indeed, as being defective in themselves, but as inapplicable to the conditions of real life; and real life for him means not merely (as is sometimes alleged) life as it was lived around him in Italy—the crimes, hypocrisies, brutalities, follies of Florence, Rome, Venice, Milan. This is not the touchstone of reality. His purpose is not to leave unchanged or to reproduce this kind of life, but to lift it to a new plane, to rescue Italy from squalor and slavery, to restore her to health and sanity.

The moral ideal for which he thinks no sacrifice too great—the welfare of the *patria*—is for him the highest form of social existence attainable by man; but attainable, not unattainable; not a world outside the limits of human capacity, given human beings as we know them, that is, creatures compounded out of those emotional, intellectual, and physical properties of which history and observation provide examples. He asks for men improved but not transfigured, not superhuman; not for a world of angelic beings unknown on this earth, who, even if they could be created, could not be called human.

If you object to the political methods recommended because they seem to you morally detestable, if you refuse to embark upon them because they are, to use Ritter's word, *"erschreckend,"* too frightening, Machiavelli has no answer, no argument. In that case you are perfectly entitled to lead a morally good life, be a private citizen (or a monk), seek some corner of your own. But, in that event, you must not make yourself responsible for the lives of others or expect good fortune; in a material sense you must expect to be ignored or destroyed.

In other words you can opt out of the public world, but in that case he has nothing to say to you, for it is to the public world and to the men in it that he addresses himself. This is expressed most clearly in his notorious advice to the victor who has to hold down a conquered province. He advises a clean sweep: new governors, new titles, new powers, and new men; "He should make the poor rich and the rich poor, as David did when he became king . . . who heaped riches on the needy and dismissed the wealthy empty-handed." Besides this, he should destroy the old cities and build new ones, and transfer the inhabitants from one place to another. In short, he should leave nothing unchanged in that province, so that there should be "neither rank, nor grade, nor honor, nor wealth that would not be recognized as coming from him." He should take Philip of Macedon as his model, who "by proceeding in that manner became . . . master of all Greece."

Now Philip's historian informs us—Machiavelli goes on to say—that he transferred the inhabitants from one province to another "as shepherds move their flocks" from one place to another. "Doubtless," Machiavelli continues, "these means are cruel and destructive of all civilized life, and neither Christian nor even human, and should be avoided by everyone. In fact, the life of a private citizen would be preferable to that of a king at the expense of the ruin of so many human beings. Nevertheless, whoever is unwilling to adopt the first and humane course must, if he wishes to maintain his power, follow the latter evil course. But men generally decide upon a middle course which is most hazardous; for they know neither how to be wholly good nor wholly bad, and so lose both worlds."

This is plain enough. There are two worlds, that of personal morality and that of public organization. There are two ethical codes, both ultimate; not two "autonomous" regions, one of "ethics," another of "politics," but two (for him) exhaustive alternatives between two conflicting systems of value. If a man chooses the "first, humane course," he must presumably give up all hope of Athens and Rome, of a noble and glorious society in which human beings can thrive and grow strong, proud, wise, and productive. Indeed, he must abandon all hope of a tolerable life on earth: for men cannot live outside society; they will not survive collectively if they are led by men who (like Soderini) are influenced by the first, "private" morality; they will not be able to realize their minimal goals as men; they will end in a state of moral, not merely political, degradation. But if a man chooses, as Machiavelli himself has done, the second course, then he must suppress his private qualms, if he has any, for it is certain that those who are too squeamish during the remaking of a society or even during its pursuit and maintenance of its power and glory, will go the wall. Whoever has chosen to make an omelette cannot do so without breaking eggs.

Machiavelli is sometimes accused of too much relish at the prospect of breaking eggs—almost for its own sake. This is unjust. He thinks these ruthless methods are necessary—necessary as means to provide good results, good in terms not of a Christian, but of a secular, humanistic, naturalistic morality. His most shocking examples show this. The most famous, perhaps, is that of Giovanpaolo Baglioni, who caught Julius II during one of his campaigns, and let him escape, when in Machiavelli's view he might have destroyed him and his cardinals and thereby committed a crime "the greatness of which would have overshadowed the infamy and all the danger that could possibly result from it."

Like Frederick the Great (who called Machiavelli "the enemy of mankind" and followed his advice),[3] Machiavelli is, in effect, saying *"Le vin est tiré: il faut le boire."* Once you embark on a plan for the transformation of a society you must carry it through no matter at what cost: to fumble, to retreat, to be overcome by scruples is to betray your chosen cause. To be a physician is to be a professional, ready to burn, to cauterize, to amputate; if that is what the disease requires, then to stop halfway because of personal qualms, or some rule unrelated to your art and its technique, is a sign of muddle and weakness, and will always give you the worst of both worlds. And there are at least two worlds: each of them has much, indeed everything, to be said for it; but they are two and not one. One must learn to choose between them and, having chosen, not look back.

There is more than one world, and more than one set of virtues: confusion between them is disastrous. One of the chief illusions caused by ignoring this is the Platonic-Hebraic-Christian view that virtuous rulers create virtuous men. This, according to Machiavelli, is not true. Generosity is a virtue, but not in princes. A generous prince will ruin the citizens by taxing them too heavily, a mean prince (and Machiavelli does not say that meanness is a good quality in private men) will save the purses of the citizens and so add to public welfare. A kind ruler—and kindness is a virtue—may let intriguers and stronger characters dominate him, and so cause chaos and corruption.

Other writers of "Mirrors for Princes" are also rich in such maxims, but they do not draw the implications. Machiavelli's use of such generalizations is not theirs; he is not moralizing at large, but illustrating a specific thesis: that the nature of men dictates a public morality that is different from, and may come into collision with, the virtues of men who profess to believe in, and try to act by, Christian precepts. These may not be wholly unrealizable in quiet times, in private life, but they lead to ruin outside this. The analogy between a state and people and an individual is a fallacy: "The state and people are governed in a different

---

3. It is still not clear how much of this Frederick owed to his mentor Voltaire.

way from an individual." "It is not the well-being of individuals that makes cities great, but of the community."

One may disagree with this. One may argue that the greatness, glory, and wealth of a state are hollow ideals, or detestable, if the citizens are oppressed and treated as mere means to the grandeur of the whole. Like Christian thinkers, or like Constant and the liberals, or like Sismondi and the theorists of the welfare state, one may prefer a state in which citizens are prosperous even though the public treasury is poor, in which government is neither centralized nor omnipotent, nor, perhaps, sovereign at all, but the citizens enjoy a wide degree of individual freedom; one may contrast this favorably with the great authoritarian conceptions of power built by Alexander or Frederick the Great or Napoleon, or the great autocrats of the twentieth century.

If so, one is simply contradicting Machiavelli's thesis: he sees no merit in such loose political textures. They cannot last. Men cannot long survive in such conditions. He is convinced that states that have lost the appetite for power are doomed to decadence and are likely to be destroyed by their more vigorous and better armed neighbors; and Vico and modern "realistic" thinkers have echoed this.

III

Machiavelli is possessed by a clear, intense, narrow vision of a society in which human talents can be made to contribute to a powerful and splendid whole. He prefers republican rule in which the interests of the rulers do not conflict with those of the ruled. But (as Macaulay perceived) he prefers a well-governed principate to a decadent republic, and the qualities he admires and thinks capable of being welded into—indeed, indispensable to—a durable society are not different in *The Prince* and *The Discourses*: energy, boldness, practical skills, imagination, vitality, self-discipline, shrewdness, public spirit, good fortune, *antiqua virtus*, *virtù*—firmness in adversity, strength of character, as celebrated by Xenophon or Livy. All his more shocking maxims—those responsible for the "murderous Machiavel" of the Elizabethan stage—are descriptions of methods of realizing this single end: the classical, humanistic, and patriotic vision that dominates him.

Let me cite the best known of his most notoriously wicked pieces of advice to princes. One must employ terrorism or kindness, as the case dictates. Severity is usually more effective, but humanity, in some situations, brings better fruit. You may excite fear but not hatred, for hatred will destroy you in the end. It is best to keep men poor and on a permanent war footing, for this will be an antidote to the two great enemies of obedience—ambition and boredom—and the ruled will then feel in constant need of great men to lead them (the twentieth century offers us only too much evidence for this sharp insight.) Competition —divisions between classes—in a society is desirable, for it generates energy and ambition in the right degree.

Religion must be promoted even though it may be false, provided it is a kind that preserves social solidarity and promotes manly virtues, as Christianity has historically failed to do. When you confer benefits (he says, following Aristotle), do so yourself; but if dirty work is to be done, let others do it, for then they, not the prince, will be blamed and the prince can gain favor by duly cutting off their heads: for men prefer vengeance and security to liberty. Do what you must do in any case, but try to represent it as a special favor to the people. If you must commit a crime do not advertise it beforehand, since otherwise your enemies may destroy you before you destroy them. If your action must be drastic, do it in one fell swoop, not in agonizing stages. Do not be surrounded by over-powerful servants—victorious generals are best got rid of, otherwise they may get rid of you.

You may be violent and use your power to overawe, but you must not break your own laws, for that destroys confidence and disintegrates the social texture. Men should either be caressed or annihilated; appeasement and neutralism are always fatal. Excellent plans without arms are not enough or else Florence would still be a republic. Rulers must live in the constant expectation of war. Success creates more devotion than an amiable character; remember the fate of Pertinax, Savonarola, Soderini. Severus was unscrupulous and cruel, Ferdinand of Spain is treacherous and crafty: but by practicing the arts of both the lion and the fox they escaped both snares and wolves. Men will be false to you unless you compel them to be true by creating circumstances in which falsehoods will not pay. And so on.

These examples are typical of "the devil's partner." Now and then doubts assail our author: he wonders whether a man high-minded enough to labor to create a state admirable by Roman standards will be tough enough to use the violent and wicked means prescribed; and, conversely, whether a sufficiently ruthless and brutal man will be disinterested enough to compass the public good which alone justifies the evil means. Yet Moses and Theseus, Romulus, and Cyrus combined these properties.[4] What has been once can be again: the implication is optimistic.

These maxims have one property in common: they are designed to create or resurrect or maintain an order that will satisfy what the author conceives as men's most permanent interests. Machiavelli's values may be erroneous, dangerous, odious; but he is in earnest. He is not cynical.

4. Professor H. L. Trevor-Roper has drawn my attention to the irony of the fact that the heroes of this supreme realist are all, wholly or in part, mythical.

The end is always the same: a state conceived after the analogy of Periclean Athens, or Sparta, but above all the Roman Republic. Such an end, for which men naturally crave (of this he thinks that history and observation provide conclusive evidence), "excuses" any means. In judging means, look only to the end: if the state goes under, all is lost. Hence the famous paragraph in the forty-first chapter of the third book of *The Discourses* where he says:

> When the very safety of the country depends upon the resolution to be taken, no considerations of justice or injustice, humanity or cruelty, not of glory or of infamy, should be allowed to prevail. But putting all other considerations aside, the only question should be "What course will save the life and liberty of the country?"

The French have reasoned thus, and the "majesty of their King and the greatness of France" have come from it. Romulus could not have founded Rome without killing Remus. Brutus would not have preserved the republic if he did not kill his sons. Moses and Theseus, Romulus, Cyrus, and the liberators of Athens had to destroy in order to build. Such conduct, so far from being condemned, is held up to admiration by the classical historians and the Bible. Machiavelli is their admirer and faithful spokesman.

What is there, then, about his words, about his tone, which has caused such tremors among his readers? Not, indeed, in his own lifetime—there was a delayed reaction of some quarter of a century. But after that it is one of continuous and mounting horror. Fichte, Hegel, Treitschke "reinterpreted" his doctrines and assimilated them to their own views. But the sense of horror was not thereby greatly mitigated. It is evident that the effect of the shock that he administered was not a temporary one: it has lasted almost into our own day.

Leaving aside the historical problem of why there was no immediate contemporary criticism, let us consider the continuous discomfort caused to its readers during the four centuries that have passed since *The Prince* was placed upon the Index. The great originality, the tragic implications of Machiavelli's theses seem to me to reside in their relation to a Christian civilization. It was all very well to live by the light of pagan ideals in pagan times; but to preach paganism more than a thousand years after the triumph of Christianity was to do so after the loss of innocence— and to be forcing men to make a conscious choice. The choice is painful because it is a choice between two entire worlds. Men have lived in both, and fought and died to preserve them against each other. Machiavelli has opted for one of them, and he is prepared to commit crimes for its sake.

In killing, deceiving, betraying, Machiavelli's princes and republicans are doing evil things not condonable in terms of common morality. It is Machiavelli's great merit that he does not deny this. Marsilio, Hobbes, Spinoza, and, in their own fashion, Hegel and Marx did try to deny it. So did many a defender of the *raison d'état*, Imperialist and Populist, Catholic and Protestant. These thinkers argue for a single moral system, and seek to show that the morality which justifies, and indeed demands, such deeds is continous with, and a more rational form of, the confused ethical beliefs of the uninstructed morality which forbids them absolutely.

From the vantage point of the great social objectives in the name of which these (*prima facie* wicked) acts are to be performed, they will be seen (so the argument goes) as no longer wicked, but as rational— demanded by the very nature of things, by the common good, or man's true ends, or the dialectic of history—condemned only by those who cannot or will not see a large enough segment of the logical or theological or metaphysical or historical pattern; misjudged, denounced only by the spiritually blind or short-sighted. At worst, these "crimes" are discords demanded by the larger harmony, and therefore, to those who hear this harmony, no longer discordant.

Machiavelli is not a defender of any such abstract theory. It does not occur to him to employ such casuistry. He is transparently honest and clear. In choosing the life of a statesman, or even the life of a citizen with enough civic sense to want his state to be as successful and splendid as possible, a man commits himself to rejection of Christian behavior.[5] It may be that Christians are right about the well-being of the individual soul, taken outside the social or political context. But the well-being of the state is not the same as the well-being of the individual—"they cannot be governed in the same way." You have made your choice: the only crimes are weakness, cowardice, stupidity which may cause you to draw back in midstream and fail.

Compromise with current morality leads to bungling, which is always despicable, and when practiced by statesmen involves men in ruin. The end "excuses" the means, however horrible these may be in terms of even pagan ethics, if it is (in terms of the ideal of Thucydides or Polybius, Cicero or Livy) lofty enough. Brutus was right to kill his children: he saved Rome. Soderini did not have the stomach to perpetrate such deeds, and ruined Florence. Savonarola, who had sound ideas about austerity and moral strength and corruption, perished because he did not realize that an unarmed prophet will always go to the gallows.

---

5. At the risk of exhausting the patience of the reader, I must repeat that this is a conflict not of pagan statecraft with Christian morals, but of pagan morals (indissolubly connected with social life and inconceivable without it) with Christian ethics which, whatever its implication for politics, can be stated independently of it, as, e.g., Aristotle's or Hegel's ethics cannot.

If one can produce the right result by using the devotion and affection of men, let this be done by all means. There is no value in causing suffering as such. But if one cannot, then Moses, Romulus, Theseus, Cyrus are the exemplars, and fear must be employed. There is no sinister satanism in Machiavelli, nothing of Dostoevsky's great sinner, pursuing evil for evil's sake. To Dostoevsky's famous question "Is everything permitted?" Machiavelli, who for Dostoevsky would surely have been an atheist, answers, "Yes, if the end—that is, the pursuit of a society's basic interests in a specific situation—cannot be realized in any other way."

This position has not been properly understood by some of those who claim to be not unsympathetic to Machiavelli. Figgis, for example, thinks that he "permanently suspended the *habeas corpus* of the human race," that is to say, that he advocated methods of terrorism because for him the situation was always critical, always desperate, so that he confused ordinary political principles with rules needed, if at all, only in extreme cases.

Others—perhaps the majority of his interpreters—look on him as the originator, or at least a defender, of what later came to be called "*raison d'état*," "*Staatsraison*," "*Ragion di Stato*"—the justification of immoral acts when undertaken on behalf of the state in exceptional circumstances. More than one scholar has pointed out, reasonably enough, that the notion that desperate cases require desperate remedies—that "necessity knows no law"—is to be found not only in antiquity but equally in Aquinas and Dante and other medieval writers long before Bellarmine or Machiavelli.

These parallels seem to me to rest on a deep but characteristic misunderstanding of Machiavelli's thesis. He is not saying that while in normal situations current morality—that is, the Christian or semi-Christian code of ethics—should prevail, yet abnormal conditions can occur, in which the entire social structure in which alone this code can function becomes jeopardized, and that in emergencies of this kind acts that are usually regarded as wicked and rightly forbidden are justified.

This is the position of, among others, those who think that all morality ultimately rests on the existence of certain institutions—say, Roman Catholics who regard the existence of the Church and the Papacy as indispensable to Christianity, or nationalists who see in the political power of a nation the sole source of spiritual life. Such persons maintain that extreme and "frightful" measures needed for protecting the state or the Church or the national culture in moments of acute crisis may be justified, since the ruin of these institutions may fatally damage the indispensable framework of all other values. This is a doctrine in terms of which both Catholics and Protestants, both conservatives and communists have defended enormities which freeze the blood of ordinary men.

But it is not Machiavelli's position. For the defenders of the *raison d'état*, the sole justification of these measures is that they are exceptional—that they are needed to preserve a system the purpose of which is precisely to preclude the need for such odious measures, so that the sole justification of such steps is that they will end the situations that render them necessary. But for Machiavelli these measures are, in a sense, themselves quite normal. No doubt they are called for only by extreme need; yet political life tends to generate a good many such needs, of varying degrees of "extremity"; hence Baglioni, who shied from the logical consequences of his own policies, was clearly unfit to rule.

The notion of *raison d'état* entails a conflict of values which may be agonizing to morally good and sensitive men. For Machiavelli there is no conflict. Public life has its own morality, to which Christian principles (or any absolute personal values) tend to be a gratuitous obstacle. This life has its own standards: it does not require perpetual terror, but it approves, or at least permits, the use of force where it is needed to promote the ends of political society.

Professor Sheldon Wolin[6] seems to me right in insisting that Machiavelli believes in a permanent "economy of violence"—the need for a consistent reserve of force always in the background to keep things going in such a way that the virtues admired by him, and by the classical thinkers to whom he appeals, can be protected and allowed to flower. Men brought up within a community in which such force, or its possibility, is used rightly will live the happy lives of Greeks or Romans during their finest hours. They will be characterized by vitality, genius, variety, pride, power, success (Machiavelli scarcely ever speaks of arts or sciences); but it will not, in any clear sense, be a Christian commonwealth. The moral conflict which this situation raises will trouble only those who are not prepared to abandon either course: those who assume that the two incompatible lives are, in fact, reconcilable.

But to Machiavelli the claims of the official morality are scarcely worth discussing: they are not translatable into social practice. "If men were good . . ." but he feels sure that they can never by improved beyond the point at which power considerations are relevant. If morals relate to human conduct, and men are by nature social, Christian morality cannot be a guide for normal social existence. It remained for someone to state this. Machiavelli did so.

One is obliged to choose: and in choosing one form of life, give up the other. That is the central point. If Machiavelli is right, if it is in principle (or in fact: the frontier seems dim) impossible to be morally good and do one's duty as this was conceived by common European, and especially Christian, ethics, and at the same time build Sparta or

---

6. In his book *Politics and Vision* (Little, Brown, 1960). [Cf. above, pp. 169–77—*Editor.*]

Periclean Athens or the Rome of the Republic or even of the Antonines, then a conclusion of the first importance follows: that the belief that the correct, objectively valid solution to the question of how men should live can in principle be discovered is itself, in principle, not true. This was a truly *erschreckend* proposition. Let me try to put it in its proper context.

One of the deepest assumptions of Western political thought is the doctrine, scarcely questioned during its long ascendancy, that there exists some single principle that not only regulates the course of the sun and the stars, but prescribes their proper behavior to all animate creatures. Animals and subrational beings of all kinds follow it by instinct; higher beings attain to consciousness of it, and are free to abandon it, but only to their doom. This doctrine in one version or another has dominated European thought since Plato; it has appeared in many forms and has generated many similes and allegories. At its center is the vision of an impersonal Nature or Reason or cosmic purpose, or of a divine Creator whose power has endowed all things and creatures each with a specific function; these functions are elements in a single harmonious whole, and are intelligible in terms of it alone.

This was often expressed by images taken from architecture: of a great edifice of which each part fits uniquely in the total structure; or from the human body as an all-embracing organic whole; or from the life of society as a great hierarchy, with God as the *ens realissimum* at the summit of two parallel systems—the feudal order and the natural order—stretching downward from Him, and reaching upward to Him, obedient to His will. Or it is seen as the Great Chain of Being, the Platonic-Christian analogue of the world-tree Ygdrasil, which links time and space and all that they contain. Or it has been represented by an analogy drawn from music, as an orchestra in which each instrument or group of instruments has its own tune to play in the infinitely rich polyphonic score. When, after the seventeenth century, harmonic metaphors replaced polyphonic images, the instruments were no longer conceived as playing specific melodies, but as producing sounds which, although they might not be wholly intelligible to any given group of players (and even sound discordant or superfluous if taken in isolation), yet contributed to the total pattern perceptible only from a loftier standpoint.

The idea of the world and of human society as a single intelligible structure is at the root of all the many various versions of Natural Law—the mathematical harmonies of the Pythagoreans, the logical ladder of Platonic Forms, the genetic-logical pattern of Aristotle, the divine *logos* of the Stoics and the Christian churches and of their secularized offshoots. The advance of the natural sciences generated more empirically conceived versions of this image as well as anthropomorphic similes: of Dame Nature as an adjuster of conflicting tendencies (as in Hume or Adam Smith), of Mistress Nature as the teacher of the best way to happiness (as in the works of some French Encyclopaedists), of Nature as embodied in the actual customs or habits of organized social wholes; biological, aesthetic, psychological similes have reflected the dominant ideas of an age.

This unifying monistic pattern is at the very heart of traditional rationalism, religious and atheistic, metaphysical and scientific, transcendental and naturalistic, which has been characteristic of Western civilization. It is this rock, upon which Western beliefs and lives had been founded, that Machiavelli seems, in effect, to have split open. So great a reversal cannot, of course, be due to the acts of a single individual. It could scarcely have taken place in a stable social and moral order; many besides him, ancient Skeptics, medieval nominalists and secularists, Renaissance humanists, doubtless supplied their share of the dynamite. The purpose of this paper is to suggest that it was Machiavelli who lit the fatal fuse.

If to ask what are the ends of life is to ask a real question, it must be capable of being correctly answered. To claim rationality in matters of conduct was to claim that correct and final solutions to such questions can in principle be found.

When such solutions were discussed in earlier periods, it was normally assumed that the perfect society could be conceived, at least in outline; for otherwise what standard could one use to condemn existing arrangements as imperfect? It might not be realizable here, below. Men were too ignorant or too weak or too vicious to create it. Or it was said (by some materialistic thinkers in the centuries following *The Prince*) that it was technical means that were lacking, that no one had yet discovered methods of overcoming the material obstacles to the golden age; that we were not technologically or educationally or morally sufficiently advanced. But it was never said that there was something incoherent in the very notion itself.

Plato and the Stoics, the Hebrew prophets and Christian medieval thinkers, and the writers of utopias from More onward had a vision of what it was that men fell short of; they claimed, as it were, to be able to measure the gap between the reality and the ideal. But if Machiavelli is right, this entire tradition—the central current of Western thought—is fallacious. For if his position is valid then it is impossible to construct even the notion of such a perfect society, for there exist at least two sets of virtues—let us call them the Christian and the pagan—which are not merely in practice, but in principle, incompatible.

If men practice Christian humility, they cannot also be inspired by the burning ambitions of the great classical founders of cultures and religions; if their gaze is centered upon the world beyond—if their ideas are infected by even lip-service to such an outlook—they will not be likely to give all that they have to an attempt to build a perfect city. If suffering and sacrifice and martyrdom are not always evil and inescapable necessities, but may be of supreme value in themselves, then the glorious victories over fortune, which go to the bold, the impetuous, and the young, might neither be won nor thought worth winning. If spiritual goods alone are worth striving for, then of how much value is the study of *necessita*—of the laws that govern nature and human lives—by the manipulation of which men might accomplish unheard-of things in the arts and the sciences and the organization of social lives?

To abandon the pursuit of secular goals may lead to disintegration and a new barbarism; but even if this is so, is this the worst that could happen? Whatever the differences between Plato and Aristotle, or of either of these thinkers from the Sophists or Epicureans or the other Greek schools of the fourth and later centuries, they and their disciples, the European rationalists and empiricists of the modern age, were agreed that the study of reality by minds undeluded by appearances could reveal the correct ends to be pursued by men—that which would make men free and happy, strong and rational.

Some thought that there was a single end for all men in all circumstances, or different ends for men of different kinds or in dissimilar historical environments. Objectivists and universalists were opposed by relativists and subjectivists, metaphysicians by empiricists, theists by atheists. There was profound disagreement about moral issues; but what none of these thinkers, not even the Skeptics, had suggested was that there might exist ends—ends in themselves in terms of which alone everything else was justified—which were equally ultimate, but incompatible with one another, that there might exist no single universal over-arching standard that would enable a man to choose rationally between them.

This was indeed a profoundly upsetting conclusion. It entailed that if men wished to live and act consistently, and understand what goals they were pursuing, they were obliged to examine their moral values. What if they found that they were compelled to make a choice between two incommensurable systems? To choose as they did without the aid of an infallible measuring rod which certified one form of life as being superior to all others and which could be used to demonstrate this to the satisfaction of all rational men? Is it, perhaps, this awful truth, implicit in Machiavelli's exposition, that has upset the moral conscious-ness of men, and has haunted their minds so permanently and obsessively ever since?

Machiavelli did not himself propound it. There was no problem and no agony for him; he shows no trace of skepticism or relativism; he chose his side, and took little interest in the values that this choice ignored or flouted. The conflict between his scale of values and that of conventional morality clearly did not (*pace* Croce and the other defenders of the "anguished humanist" interpretation) seem to worry Machiavelli himself. It upset only those who came after him, and were not prepared, on the one hand, to abandon their own moral values (Christian or humanist) together with the entire way of thought and action of which these were a part; nor, on the other, to deny the validity of, at any rate, much of Machiavelli's analysis of the political facts, and the (largely pagan) values and outlook that went with it, embodied in the social structure which he painted so brilliantly and convincingly.

Whenever a thinker, however distant from us in time or culture, still stirs passion, enthusiasm, or indignation, any kind of intense debate, it is generally the case that he has propounded a thesis that upsets some deeply established *idée reçue*, a thesis that those who wish to cling to the old conviction nevertheless find it hard or impossible to dismiss or refute. This is the case with Plato, Hobbes, Rousseau, Marx.

I should like to suggest that it is Machiavelli's juxtaposition of the two outlooks—the two incompatible moral worlds, as it were—in the minds of his readers, and the collision and acute discomfort that follow that, over the years, has been responsible for the desperate efforts to interpret his doctrines away, to represent him as a cynical and therefore ultimately shallow defender of power politics; or as a diabolist; or as a patriot prescribing for particularly desperate situations which seldom arise; or as a mere time server; or as an embittered political failure; or as a mere mouthpiece of truths we have always known but did not like to utter; or again as the enlightened translator of universally accepted ancient social principles into empirical terms; or as a crypto-republican satirist (a descendant of Juvenal, a forerunner of Orwell); or as a cold scientist, a mere political technologist free from moral implications; or as a typical Renaissance publicist practicing a now obsolete genre; or in any of the numerous other roles that have been and are still being cast for him.

Machiavelli may have possessed some of these attributes, but concentration on one or other of them as constituting his essential, "true" character seems to me to stem from reluctance to face and, still more, discuss the uncomfortable truth that Machiavelli had, unintentionally, almost casually, uncovered: namely, that not all ultimate values are necessarily compatible with one another—that there might be a conceptual (what used to be called "philosophical"), and not merely a material, obstacle to the notion of the single ultimate solution which, if it were only realized, would establish the perfect society.

IV

Yet if no such solution can, even in principle, be formulated, then all political and, indeed, moral problems are thereby transformed. This is not a division of politics from ethics. It is the uncovering of the possibility of more than one system of values, with no criterion common to the systems whereby a rational choice can be made between them. This is not the rejection of Christianity for paganism (although Machiavelli clearly prefers the latter), nor of paganism for Christianity (which, at least in its historical form, he thought incompatible with the basic needs of normal men), but the setting of them side by side with the implicit invitation to men to choose either a good, virtuous private life or a good, successful social existence, but not both.

What has been shown by Machiavelli, who is often (like Nietzsche) congratulated for tearing off hypocritical masks, brutally revealing the truth, and so on, is not that men profess one thing and do another (although no doubt he shows this too) but that when they assume that the two ideals are compatible, or perhaps are even one and the same ideal, and do not allow this assumption to be questioned, they are guilty of bad faith (as the existentialists call it, or of "false consciousness," to use a Marxist formula) which their actual behavior exhibits. Machiavelli calls the bluff not just of official morality—the hypocrisies of ordinary life—but of one of the foundations of the central Western philosophical tradition, the belief in the ultimate compatibility of all genuine values. His own withers are unwrung. He has made his choice. He seems wholly unworried by, indeed scarcely aware of, parting company with traditional Western morality.

But the question that his writings have dramatized, if not for himself, then for others in the centuries that followed, is this: what reason have we for supposing that justice and mercy, humility and *virtù*, happiness and knowledge, glory and liberty, magnificence and sanctity will always coincide, or indeed be compatible at all? Poetic justice is, after all, so called not because it does, but because it does not, as a rule, occur in the prose of ordinary life, where, *ex hypothesi*, a very different kind of justice operates. "States and people are governed in a different way from an individual." Hence what talk can there be of indestructible rights, either in the medieval or the liberal sense? The wise man must eliminate fantasies from his own head, and should seek to dispel them from the heads of others; or, if they are too resistant, he should at least, as Pareto or Dostoevsky's Grand Inquisitor recommended, exploit them as a means to a visible society.

"The march of world history stands outside virtue, vice and justice," said Hegel. If for the march of history you substitute "a well governed *patria*," and interpret Hegel's notion of virtue as it is understood by Christians or ordinary men, then Machiavelli is one of the earliest proponents of this doctrine. Like all great innovators, he is not without ancestry. But the names of Palmieri and Pontano, and even of Carneades and Sextus Empiricus, have left little mark on European thought.

Croce has rightly insisted that Machiavelli is not detached nor cynical nor irresponsible. His patriotism, his republicanism, his commitment are not in doubt. He suffered for his convictions. He thought continually about Florence and Italy, and of how to save them. Yet it is not his character, nor his plays, his poetry, his histories, his diplomatic or political activities that have gained him his unique fame.[7] Nor can this be due only to his psychological or sociological imagination. His psychology is often excessively primitive. He scarcely seems to allow for the bare possibility of sustained and genuine altruism, he refuses to consider the motives of men who are prepared to fight against enormous odds, who ignore *necessità* and are prepared to lose their lives in a hopeless cause.

His distrust of unworldly attitudes, absolute principle divorced from empirical observation, is fanatically strong—almost romantic in its violence; the vision of the great prince playing upon human beings like an instrument intoxicates him. He assumes that different societies must always be at war with each other, since they have conflicting purposes. He sees history as one endless process of cutthroat competition, in which the only goal that rational men can have is to succeed in the eyes of their contemporaries and of posterity. He is good at bringing fantasies down to earth, but he assumes, as Mill was to complain about Bentham, that this is enough. He allows too little to the ideal impulses of men. He has no historical sense and little sense of economics. He has no inkling of the technological progress that is about to transform political and social life, and in particular the art of war. He does not understand how either individuals, communities, or cultures develop and transform themselves. Like Hobbes, he assumes that the argument or motive for self-preservation automatically outweighs all others.

He tells men above all not to be fools: to follow a principle when this may involve you in ruin is absurd, at least if judged by worldly standards; other standards he mentions respectfully, but takes no interest in them: those who adopt them are not likely to create anything that will perpetuate their name. His Romans are no more real than the stylized figures in his brilliant comedies. His human beings have so little inner life or capacity for cooperation or social solidarity that, as in the case of

7. The moral of his best comedy, *Mandragola*, seems to me close to that of the political tracts: that the ethical doctrines professed by the characters are wholly at variance with what they do to attain their various ends. Virtually every one of them in the end obtains what he wants; if Callimaco had resisted temptation, or the lady he seduces had been smitten with remorse, or Fra Timoteo attempted to practice the maxims of the Fathers and the Schoolmen with which he liberally seasons his speeches, this could not have occurred. But all turns out for the best, though not from the point of view of accepted morality. If the play castigates hypocrisy and stupidity, the standpoint is not that of virtue but of candid hedonism. The notion that Callimaco is a kind of Prince in private life, successful in creating and maintaining his own world by the correct use of guile and fraud, the exercise of *virtù* and a bold challenge to *fortuna*, appears highly plausible. For this, see Henry Paolucci, Introduction to *Mandragola* (Library of Liberal Arts, 1957).

Hobbes's not dissimilar creatures, it is difficult to see how they could develop enough reciprocal confidence to create a lasting social whole, even under the perpetual shadow of carefully regulated violence.

Few would deny that Machiavelli's writings, more particularly *The Prince*, have scandalized mankind more deeply and continuously than any other political treatise. The reason for this, let me say again, is not the discovery that politics is the play of power—that political relationships between and within independent communities involve the use of force and fraud, and are unrelated to the principles professed by the players. That knowledge is as old as conscious thought about politics—certainly as old as Thucydides and Plato. Nor is it merely caused by the examples that he offers of success in acquiring or holding power—the descriptions of the massacre at Sinigaglia or the behavior of Agathocles or Oliverotto da Fermo are no more or less horrifying than similar stories in Tacitus or Guicciardini. The proposition that crime can pay is nothing new in Western historiography.

Nor is it merely his recommendation of ruthless measures that so upsets his readers. Aristotle had long ago allowed that exceptional situations might arise, that principles and rules could not be rigidly applied to all situations; the advice to rulers in *The Politics* is tough-minded enough. Cicero is aware that critical situations demand exceptional measures; *ratio publicae utilitatis, ratio status* were familiar in the thought of the Middle Ages. "Necessity is not subject to law" is a Thomist sentiment; Pierre d'Auvergne says much the same. Harrington said this in the following century, and Hume applauded him.

These opinions were not thought original by these, or perhaps any, thinkers. Machiavelli did not originate nor did he make much use of the notion of *raison d'état*. He stressed will, boldness, address, at the expense of the rules laid down by the calm *ragione*, to which his colleagues in the *Pratiche Fiorentine*, and perhaps the Oricellari Gardens, may have appealed. So did Leon Battista Alberti when he declared that *fortuna* crushes only the weak and propertyless; so did contemporary poets; so, too, in his own fashion, did Pico della Mirandola in his great apostrophe to the powers of man the creator, who, unlike the angels, can transform himself into any shape—the ardent image that lies at the heart of European humanism in the North as well as the Mediterranean.

Far more original, as has often been noted, is Machiavelli's divorce of political behavior as a field of study from the theological world picture in terms of which this topic was discussed before him (even by Marsilio) and after him. Yet it is not his secularism, however audacious in his own day, that could have disturbed the contemporaries of Voltaire or Bentham or their successors. What shocked them is something different.

Machiavelli's cardinal achievement is his uncovering of an insoluble dilemma, the planting of a permanent question mark in the path of posterity. It stems from his *de facto* recognition that ends equally ulti-mate, equally sacred, may contradict each other, that entire systems of value may come into collision without possibility of rational arbitration, and that not merely in exceptional circumstances, as a result of abnor-mality or accident or error—the clash of Antigone and Creon or in the story of Tristan—but (this was surely new) as part of the normal human situation.

For those who look on such collisions as rare, exceptional, and disas-trous, the choice to be made is necessarily an agonizing experience for which, as a rational being, one cannot prepare (since no rules apply). But for Machiavelli, at least in *The Prince, The Discourses, Mandragola*, there is no agony. One chooses as one chooses because one knows what one wants, and is ready to pay the price. One chooses classical civilization rather than the Theban desert, Rome and not Jerusalem, whatever the priests may say, because such is one's nature, and—he is no existentialist or romantic individualist *avant la parole*—because it is that of men in general, at all times, everywhere. If others prefer solitude or martyrdom, he shrugs his shoulders. Such men are not for him. He has nothing to say to them, nothing to argue with them about. All that matters to him and those who agree with him is that such men be not allowed to meddle with politics or education or any of the cardinal factors in human life; their outlook unfits them for such tasks.

I do not mean that Machiavelli explicitly asserts that there is a plu-ralism or even a dualism of values between which conscious choices must be made. But this follows from the contrasts he draws between the conduct he admires and that which he condemns. He seems to take for granted the obvious superiority of classical civic virtue and brushes aside Christian values, as well as conventional morality, with a disparaging or patronizing sentence or two, or smooth words about the misinter-pretation of Christianity.[8] This worries or infuriates those who disagree

---

8. E.g., in the passages from *The Discourses* cited above, or as when he says, "I believe that the greatest good that can be done, and the most pleasing to God, is that which is done to one's country." My thanks are due to Professor Myron Gilmore for this reference to *The Discourses on Reforming Florence*. This sentiment is by no means unique in Machiavelli's works: but, leaving aside his wish to flatter Leo X, or the liability of all authors to fall into the clichés of their own time, are we to suppose that Ma-chiavelli means us to think that when Philip of Macedon transplanted populations in a man-ner that (unavoidable as it is said to have been) caused even Machiavelli a qualm, what Philip did, provided it was good for Macedon, was pleasing to God, and, *per contra*, that Gio-vanpaolo Baglioni's failure to kill the Pope and the Curia were displeasing to Him? Such a notion of the deity is, to say the least, remote from that of the New Testament. Are the needs of the *patria* automatically identical with the will of the Almighty? Are those who permit themselves to doubt this in danger of heresy?

Machiavelli may at times have been repre-sented as too Machiavellian; but to suppose that he believed that the claims of God and of Cae-sar were perfectly reconcilable reduces his cen-tral thesis to absurdity. Yet of course this does not prove that he lacked all Christian senti-ment: the *Esortanzione alla pentitenza* com-posed in the last year of his life (if it genuine and not a later forgery) may well be wholly sincere, as Ridolfi and Alderisio believe; Cap-poni may have exaggerated the extent to which he "drove religion from his heart," even though

with him the more because it goes against their convictions without seeming to be aware of doing so—and recommends wicked courses as obviously the most sensible, something that only fools or visionaries will reject.

If what Machiavelli believed is true, this undermines one major assumption of Western thought: namely, that somewhere in the past or the future, in this world or the next, in the church or the laboratory, in the speculations of the metaphysician or the findings of the social scientist or in the uncorrupted heart of the simple good man, there is to be found the final solution of the question of how men should live. If this is false (and if more than one equally valid answer to the question can be returned, then it is false) the idea of the sole true, objective, universal human ideal crumbles. The very search for it becomes not merely utopian in practice, but conceptually incoherent.

One can surely see how this might seem unfaceable to men, believers or atheists, empiricist or apriorists, brought up on the opposite assumption. Nothing could well be more upsetting to those brought up in a monistic religious or, at any rate, moral, social, or political system than a breach in it. This is the dagger of which Meinecke speaks, with which Machiavelli inflicted the wound that has never healed; even though Professor Felix Gilbert is right in thinking that he did not bear the scars of it himself. For he remained a monist, albeit a pagan one.

Machiavelli was doubtless guilty of much confusion and exaggeration. He confused the proposition that ultimate ideals may be incompatible with the very different proposition that the more conventional human ideals—founded on ideas of Natural Law, brotherly love, and human goodness—were unrealizable and that those who acted on the opposite assumption were fools, and at times dangerous ones; and he attributed this dubious proposition to antiquity and believed that it was verified by history.

The first of these assertions strikes at the root of all doctrines committed to the possibility of attaining, or at least formulating, final solutions; the second is empirical, commonplace, and not self-evident. The two propositions are not, in any case, identical or logically connected. Moreover he exaggerated wildly: the idealized types of the Periclean Greek or the Roman of the old Republic may be irreconcilable with the ideal citizen of a Christian commonwealth (supposing such were conceivable), but in practice—above all in history, to which our author went for illustrations if not for evidence—pure types seldom obtain: mixtures and com-

---

"it was not wholly extinct in his thought." The point is that there is scarcely any trace of such états d'âme in his political writings with which alone we are concerned. There is an excellent discussion of that by Giuseppe Prezzolini in his article, "The Christian Roots of Machiavelli's

Moral Pessimism," pp. 26–7 (*Review of National Literatures*, Vol. I, No. I, New York, 1970) in which this attitude is traced to Augustine, and Croce's thesis is, by implication, controverted.

pounds and compromises and forms of communal life that do not fit into easy classifications, but which neither Christians nor liberal humanists nor Machiavelli would be compelled by their beliefs to reject, can be conceived without too much intellectual difficulty. Still, to attack and inflict lasting damage on a central assumption of an entire civilization is an achievement of the first order.

He does not affirm this dualism. He merely takes for granted the superiority of Roman *antiqua virtus* (which may be maddening to those who do not) over the Christian life as taught by the Church. He utters a few casual words about what Christianity might have become, but does not expect it to change its actual character. There he leaves the matter. Anyone who believes in Christian morality, regards the Christian Commonwealth as its embodiment, but at the same time largely accepts the validity of Machiavelli's political and psychological analysis and does not reject the secular heritage of Rome—a man in this predicament is faced with a dilemma which, if Machiavelli is right, is not merely unsolved, but insoluble. This is the Gordian knot which, according to Vanini and Leibniz, the author of *The Prince* had tied, a knot which can only be cut, not untied. Hence the efforts to dilute his doctrines, or interpret them in such a way as to remove their sting.

After Machiavelli, doubt is liable to infect all monistic constructions. The sense of certainty that there is somewhere a hidden treasure—the final solution to our ills—and that some path must lead to it (for, in principle, it must be discoverable); or else, to alter the image, the conviction that the fragments constituted by our beliefs and habits are all pieces of a jigsaw puzzle, which (since there is an a priori guarantee for this) can, in principle, be solved; so that it is only because of the lack of skill or stupidity or bad fortune that we have not so far succeeded in discovering the solution whereby all interests will be brought into harmony—this fundamental belief of Western political thought has been severely shaken. Surely in an age that looks for certainties, this is sufficient to account for the unending efforts, more numerous today than ever, to explain *The Prince* and *The Discourses*, or to explain them away?

This is the negative implication. There is also one that is positive, and might have surprised and perhaps displeased Machiavelli. So long as only one ideal is the true goal, it will always seem to men that no means can be too difficult, no price too high, to do whatever is required to realize the ultimate goal. Such certainty is one of the great justifications of fanaticism, compulsion, persecution. But if not all values are compatible with one another, and choices must be made for no better reason than that each value is what it is, and we choose it for what it is and not because it can be shown on some single scale to be higher than another—if we choose forms of life because we believe in them, because we take them for granted, or, upon examination, find that we are morally unprepared to live in any other way (although others choose differently); if rationality and calculation can be applied only to means or subordinate ends, but never to ultimate ends; then a picture emerges different from that constructed round the ancient principle that there is only one good for men.

If there is only one solution to the puzzle, then the only problems are first how to find it, then how to realize it, and finally how to convert others to the solution by persuasion or by force. But if this is not so (Machiavelli contrasts two ways of life, but there could be, and, save for fanatical monists, there obviously are, more than two), then the path is open to empiricism, pluralism, toleration, compromise. Toleration is historically the product of the realization of the irreconcilability of equally dogmatic faiths, and the practical improbability of complete victory of one over the other. Those who wished to survive realized that they had to tolerate error. They gradually came to see merits in diversity, and so became skeptical about definitive solutions in human affairs.

But it is one thing to accept something in practice, another to justify it rationally. Machiavelli's "scandalous" writings begin the latter process. This was a major turning point, and its intellectual consequences, wholly unintended by its originator, were, by a fortunate irony of history (which some call its dialectic), the basis of the very liberalism that Machiavelli would surely have condemned as feeble and characterless, lacking in single-minded pursuit of power, in splendor, in organization, in *virtù*, in power to discipline unruly men against huge odds into one energetic whole. Yet he is, in spite of himself, one of the makers of pluralism, and of its—to him—perilous acceptance of toleration.

By breaking the original unity he helped to cause men to become aware of the necessity of making agonizing choices between incompatible alternatives, incompatible in practice or, worse still, for logical reasons, in public and private life (for the two could not, it became obvious, be genuinely kept distinct). His achievement is of the first order, if only because the dilemma has never given men peace since it came to light (it remains unsolved, but we have learned to live with it). Men had, no doubt, in practice, often enough experienced the conflict that Machiavelli made explicit. He converted its expression from a paradox into something approaching a commonplace.

The sword of which Meinecke spoke has not lost its edge: the wound has not healed. To know the worst is not always to be liberated from its consequences; nevertheless it is preferable to ignorance. It is this painful truth that Machiavelli forced on our attention, not by formulating it explicitly, but perhaps the more effectively by relegating much uncriticized traditional morality to the realm of utopia. This is what, at any rate, I should like to suggest. Where more than twenty interpretations hold the field, the addition of one more cannot be deemed an impertinence. At worst it will be no more than yet another attempt to solve the problem, now more than four centuries old, of which Croce at the end of his long life spoke as *"una questione che forse non si chiuderà mai: la questione de Machiavelli"* ["A question that perhaps will never be closed; the question of Machiavelli"].

ROBERT M. ADAMS

The Rise, Proliferation, and Degradation of Machiavellism: An Outline

The history of Machiavellism, it has been well said, is a history of misunderstandings. The word has stood, in its time, not only for trickery, equivocation, and unscrupulous cruelty, but also for utter honesty and surgical accuracy of thought. It has stood for audacious republicanism, craven support of tyranny, and unscrupulous tyrannicide; for fanatical Catholicism and for religious toleration; for national liberation and enslavement to the devil; for cynical opportunism and the highest of moral principles. Not all these interpretations can be right, and the current popular use of the word is less right than most. Still, at this late date, there's no use protesting; *Machiavellism* is set in the language to describe unscrupulous political behavior.

But to write an account of unscrupulous political behavior (ambition, greed, falsehood, cruelty) would take us far and wide, back into the mists of antiquity, around the globe, and down to the present day—in a reasonable assurance that the future won't be much different. With most of this wickedness the Florentine secretary had absolutely nothing to do, and we can therefore cheerfully discard it to the historians of infamy. The present outline is more modest; it aims to present in capsule form the elements of a chronology tracing some specific ways in which Machiavelli's reputation and influence developed and at the same time diffused across three centuries. A severely practical way to begin this story is with a bald summary of the publishing history of *The Prince*.

I. *Manuscripts, editions, translations*

1513: *The Prince* was written under circumstances described in Machiavelli's famous letter to Vettori. Some time between 1516 and 1519 he changed the dedication, but without trying very actively to press the book or his own fortunes with Lorenzo, duke of Urbino (see the Medici family tree, p. x). Handwritten copies circulated for nearly twenty years, how widely we don't know. In 1523, nine years before *The Prince* was published and four years before Machiavelli's death, a rascal named Agostino Nifo cribbed wholesale from one of these manuscripts, and after translating his pickings into Latin, published a treatise on government that in substance was pure Machiavelli. Cardinal Reginald Pole said that in 1529 Thomas Cromwell, one of Henry VIII's most hard-bitten agents, recommended to him a new Italian book on politics. It may or may not have been *The Prince*. Pole, writing ten years later (and in a spirit of bitter hostility to Cromwell, Henry, and the English Reformation) said that it was, and that Cromwell, by reading it, had become an agent of Satan. About this time the story became current that Niccolò Machiavelli gave the devil his popular title of "Old Nick." Though false, the association stuck; not only was Machiavelli regularly described as devilish, but the devil in time came to be described as Machiavellian.

1532: Antonio Blado, having obtained the necessary permission from Pope Clement VII (Giulio de' Medici), began to publish Machiavelli's writings. *The Prince* appeared in Rome on January 4, and on May 8 Bernardo di Giunta published an edition in Florence. He reprinted in 1537 and 1540; and the busy Venetian publishers picked up the text, issuing seven editions (1537, 1540, 1541, 1546, 1550, 1552, 1554) in less than twenty years.

1550: The first *Collected Works* of Machiavelli were published; from its engraved portrait, this is called the Testina edition.

1553: *The Prince* was first translated into a foreign language; a French version by Guillaume Capel appeared in Paris.

1560: *The Prince* was translated into Latin, the international language of scholarship, by Sylvester Telius (Tegli) Fulginatus and published at Basel.

1640: *The Prince* was published in English; Edward Dacres was the translator. There had been previous translations into English, and they survive in the odd manuscript, but none was published till the episcopal censorship broke down in 1640.

II. *The Index and the Bartholomew Massacre*

1559: The entire works of Machiavelli were placed on the Index of Prohibited Books, compiled by the Holy Inquisition in Rome. This act resulted from the decrees of the Council of Trent, which met from 1545 to 1563 in order to stiffen the discipline of the Roman Church against Protestantism. Pope Paul the Fourth, whose entire life had been spent as an inquisitor, and who was a mortal enemy of heresy in any form, urged on the compiling of the Index, and widened its scope, so that it dealt not just with heresy, but with morality and manners in general. Since Machiavellism was sometimes associated in Protestant countries with the Jesuit order, it is interesting to note that at Ingolstadt in Bavaria, the Jesuit college held a book-burning in 1615, at which Machiavelli's works were incinerated.

1572: Beginning on St. Bartholomew's night, and for several weeks thereafter, the Catholic leaders of France made a sudden, concerted effort to wipe out the entire Huguenot (Protestant) population of France. They succeeded, to the extent of approximately fifty thousand murders. Charles IX was King of France at the time, but he was young (twenty-two), weak, and flighty: the power in the country lay with his mother, Catherine de' Medici. She was hated as an Italian and a Medici, as a favorer of Italian and particularly papal courtiers, as a secretive and treacherous person, and finally as a reader of Machiavelli. The Catholic treachery of the Saint Bartholomew's Massacre thus came to be blamed on Machiavelli by the Protestants—just at a time when Catholics were being forbidden to read him, because he was on the Index.

1576: Innocent Gentillet, a French Huguenot enraged by the Massacre of Saint Bartholomew, wrote the book by which Machiavelli was largely to be known for years to come, the *Discours sur les moyens de bien gouverner . . . contre Nicolas Machiavel, Florentin*. As translations into the languages of Protestant countries were many years away, as the Huguenots were dispersed across Europe and carried their hatred of Machiavelli with them, and as Catholics themselves could not read or even possess copies of Machiavelli's text, Gentillet had a major influence. For instance, Antonio Possevino, an Italian Jesuit, wrote in 1592 a Latin *Judgment of Four Authors*, one of whom was Machiavelli. Because Gentillet's book was divided into three parts, Possevino took for granted that *The Prince* was, too—thereby betraying the fact that he had never laid eyes on it, but based his "judgment" on the opinion of one whom he considered a heretic. Gentillet was translated into English thirty-eight years before Machiavelli himself.

III. *Ragion de Stato*

When Machiavelli went on the Index, he did not disappear completely from the Catholic countries; any devout Catholic could read him by getting a dispensation, and not everyone even bothered getting formal permission. Lawyers especially could not help dealing with a version of Machiavelli's thought —that the prince, being responsible for the survival of the state, is entitled to use extraordinary means (as we would say, "executive privilege") toward that end. How extraordinary these means could legitimately become was a typical lawyer's question: it involved qualifying, softening, and moralizing Machiavelli's basic insight, often without mentioning him at all. This was relatively easy to do because, as we must never forget, Machiavellism was but a minor current in the broad stream of political thought, the main body of which runs straight and clear, from Erasmus's *Institution of a Christian Prince* (1515) to Fénelon's *Télémaque* (1699), with indefinite extensions before and after. In this majority view, politics is properly an engine of morality and is entitled to depart from strict morality only in extreme emergencies.

1580s: Paolo Paruta, a Venetian lawyer and historian, wrote a set of *Political Discourses* (not published till 1599) in which he discussed, very much after Machiavelli's manner, a number of case histories. The question was whether the right policy had been followed, under the circumstances, and whether the practical advantages of certain actions did not outweigh their moral obliquity. But in the end Paruta was more a moralist than a politician.

1585: Alberico Gentili, a liberal Italian jurist who ended his career at Oxford, was bold enough to mention Machiavelli directly. In his big book *On Embassies* he declared (III, 9) that Machiavelli exposed the powers of the prince as a deliberate satiric warning against excesses in the use of a power healthy in itself.

1589: Giovanni Botero gave the name *Ragion di stato*, or reason of state, to the book he wrote watering down Machiavelli's doctrine of special princely authority, and the phrase became immensely popular. As Botero worked out his position, it combined faith in a strong central authority with the comfortable expectation that that authority would be used for strictly moral ends and without any undue excesses.

1621: Ludovico Zuccolo in his brief *Ragione di stato* honed Botero's rather unctuous Machiavellism back to something like its original sharpness.

1576: Jean Bodin enters the story of Machiavellism from a special angle. Because Machiavelli was thought to be an atheist, who saw value in religion only as an engine of political influence, anyone in the sixteenth century who spoke for the toleration of several religious creeds was judged to be a Machiavellian. Bodin was a jurist and political theoretician, who espoused religious toleration (known to most true believers of the day as religious indifference) in his big book called *La République*. Thus, though he seems to mention Machiavelli only to refute him, and perhaps accepted the Huguenot story that he was responsible for the massacre of St. Bartholomew's Eve, Bodin was labelled a Machiavellian. As late as 1605, Ben Jonson brings onto the stage of *Volpone* Sir Politic Would-be, who airily explains how to get along abroad in matters of religion:

And then for your religion, professe none;
But wonder, at the diversitie of all;
And, for your part, protest, were there no other
But simply the lawes o'th'land, you could content you:
NIC: MACHIAVEL, and monsieur BODINE, both
Were of this minde.

Act IV, scene 1

IV. *Elizabethan Dramatists and Other Vilifiers*

1589: Elizabethan audiences were used to pretty strong stuff on the tragic stage, partly because one of the dramatists' favorite models was Seneca, partly because one of their favorite locales was Italy. Italians as the Elizabethans saw them were sophisticated, insincere, corrupt, and cruel; they stabbed with stilettos, poisoned with Borgia rings, betrayed their friends, slept with their sisters, and associated with papal agents, all of whom itched to murder and torture high-minded Protestant folk. In short, Italians were natural Machiavellians, and Christopher Marlowe hardly had to introduce Machiavelli at all when he brought the arch villain onstage as prologue to *The Jew of Malta*. Barabas, the hero-villain of that tragedy, is so fierce and unscrupulous that nobody else could possibly introduce him.

MACHIAVEL (*as Prologue*):
Albeit the world think Machiavel is dead,
Yet was his soul but flown beyond the Alps;
And, now the Guise is dead,[1] is come from France
To view this land and frolic with his friends.
To some perhaps my name is odious;
But such as love me guard me from their tongues,
And let them know that I am Machiavel,

---

1. Henry, the third duke of Guise, was a leader in the massacre of St. Bartholomew's Eve; he was murdered by Henry III in 1588.

And weigh not men, and therefore not men's words.
Admired I am of those that hate me most:
Though some speak openly against my books,
Yet will they read me, and thereby attain
To Peter's chair; and when they cast me off,
Are poisoned by my climbing followers.
I count religion but a childish toy,
And hold there is no sin but ignorance. . . .

1592: Robert Greene, in his autobiographical *Groatsworth of Wit*, compares Machiavelli in a single sentence to Cain, Judas, and Julian the Apostate.

1611: John Donne, in *Ignatius his Conclave*, introduces the founder of the Jesuits, Ignatius Loyola, disputing with Machiavelli before Lucifer himself, as to which of them is the more effective agent of evil. Machiavelli is overcome, but not before he has made a strong case for his own supreme villainy.

As these few instances indicate, the figure of Machiavelli and the word Machiavellian quickly became standard, multipurpose terms of abuse, without any more specific meaning than "bad." Edward Meyer, in *Machiavelli and the English Drama*, and Felix Raab, in *The English Face of Machiavelli*, illustrate the range of usage at length; summary views can be had from Mario Praz, "Machiavelli and the Elizabethans" in *The Flaming Heart*—or, for that matter, from half a page of the *Oxford English Dictionary*.

Finally, as usage became looser and looser, the habit spread of attaching Machiavelli's name to any sort of chicanery—as the following titles indicate:

1648: *The Machivilian Cromwellist and Hypocritical Perfidious New Statist*, by William Prynne.

1674: *Machiavellus Gallicus*. Argues that Machiavelli has been metamorphosed into Louis XIV. The author was German.

1679: *Rustic Machiavellism*, by Christian Weiss. A comedy.

1681: *Machiavil Redivivus. Being an exact discovery or narrative of the principles & politics of our bejesuited modern fanatics*.

1683: *Matchiavel Junior or the Secret Acts of the Jesuits*.

1711: *On Medical Machiavellism*, by Valentini.

1713: *On Literary Machiavellism*, by Michael Lilienthal. Apart from these specific titles, there are innumerable usages like *erotic machiavellism*, *marital machiavellism*, *commercial machiavellism*, *popular machiavellism*, and *social machiavellism*, not to mention outright forgeries, like *Napoleon's machiavellism*, which is supposed to consist of Napoleon's annotations on *The Prince*, and is in fact nothing but a flagrant fake.

V. *French Controversialists, English Republicans, and a King of Prussia*

a. In the intricate scrimmages between Catholic and Protestant factions, between Court and Fronde, which fill French history of the early seventeenth century with sectarian clamor, the name of Machiavelli is likely to turn up as a term of abuse, and his ideas as quiet, useful weapons, on any side of any controversy.

> 1638: Henri, Duc de Rohan, hard-bitten general and leader of the Huguenot cause, begins his treatise on *The Interest of Princes and States* with the ringing aphorism, "Nations are governed by princes and princes are governed by interest." The book, a tough, clear assessment of France's national interest vis à vis Spain, was addressed to Cardinal Richelieu; it is written in the spirit of Machiavelli, though it does not invoke his name.

> 1639: Gabriel Naudé, librarian to Cardinal Mazarin and a man of great and miscellaneous learning, wrote *Considerations politiques sur les coups d'état*, meaning by *coups d'état* "tricks or ruses of government." This book, which became very popular, drew on some of Machiavelli's arguments to defend the use of extraordinary measures, including the St. Bartholomew massacre—conditioning the use of these measures only on pious public purposes of manifest importance.

> 1640: Louis Machon wrote, at Richelieu's behest, an *Apologie pour Machiavel* which emphasized the power of the French monarchy, independent of moral or ecclesiastical sanctions, specifically those of the pope. It is a rare and odd instance of Machiavellism walking hand in hand with Gallicanism.

> 1652: Claude Joly, writing a sardonic *Catechism of the Court*, found in Machiavelli a handy stick with which to lash out at Italian-born Cardinal Mazarin, Richelieu's successor in building the structure of centralized French power for Louis XIV. "Maximes italiennes et machiavellistes" are those that Joly thinks Mazarin follows, and that he thinks decent folk will be revolted by. In a parody of the creed, he says that Mazarin was begotten by Machiavelli's ghost upon Cardinal Richelieu.

b. Though Machiavelli was a bogeyman on the English stage, and his name a word of popular abuse, a number of radical English puritans who had taken the trouble to read the *Discourses* and the *Florentine History* found a good deal to admire in him. At first they shrank from saying so openly, but as the decades passed, they become more and more explicit.

    1651: Andrew Marvell, paying tribute to Cromwell in the "Horatian Ode," praised him in the cool, measured tones appropriate to a Machiavellian prince, who, for the good of his cause and the benefit of his people, will ignore religious, political, and moral taboos. It's been argued that because Marvell never mentions Machiavelli, the influence is hypothetical. So it is, but the hypothesis is a strong one, because Marvell was a notably close man. If, like Milton, he had left a commonplace book, it would surely have showed, like Milton's, knowledge of Machiavelli's republicanism and sympathy with it.

    1656: James Harrington in his imaginary commonwealth of *Oceana*, though he sometimes criticized Machiavelli for not seeing deeply enough into the principle of economic and social balance, was generally ecstatic in his praise. Machiavelli is "the learned disciple of the ancients," "the only politician of later ages," and "the incomparable patron of the people."

    1675: Henry Nevile translated Machiavelli's complete works, accurately and sympathetically, and in his political dialogue *Plato Redivivus* (1681) spoke glowingly of "the divine Machiavelli."

    1682: Algernon Sidney, an ardent republican executed for treason in 1683, after a long and stormy career, wrote some *Discourses concering Government*, first published in 1698; he sees Machiavelli as a premature Sidney, a pure idealistic republican.

c. As everyone has seen almost from the beginning, the first step to be taken by anyone who expects to behave like the popular version of a Machiavellian villain is to distance himself as far as possible from Machiavelli. Nobody illustrated this procedure better than Frederick, King of Prussia, later to be known as Frederick the Great.

    1740: The young king, who after a liberal and even rebellious young manhood had just succeeded to the throne, joined with M. de Voltaire to write a book explicitly against Machiavelli. Frederick had literary and musical aspirations— he wrote pretty good French and played at the flute; Voltaire was his cultural adviser, who hoped to steer him toward peaceful and humane pursuits. The book they wrote together was called simply *Anti-Machiavel*. Voltaire's part in it was largely confined to polishing the style and making arrangements for publication. Frederick's reactions to *The Prince* were his own, and they consisted of horrified disapproval.

What he disliked was very much what had distressed English royalists in the political thought of Hobbes; both writers emphasized the authority of the sovereign, but seemed to admit that anyone who could get the sovereignty was entitled to keep and defend it, even against the old sovereign. In *The Prince* Frederick saw a clear blueprint for successful regicide: a reader of Machiavelli's book couldn't help learning how to depose Frederick and wipe out his line. Naturally displeased with this thought, he vigorously denounced Machiavelli as cruel, treacherous, faithless, irreligious, and so forth. Even as he was writing the book, however, he was meditating a treacherous, unannounced attack on his neighbor, Maria Theresa, Queen of Hungary, from whom he wrested Silesia as ruthlessly as if he had been Cesare Borgia himself. Thus began Frederick's long and bloody career of conquest. Voltaire, who had hoped to make his pupil an enlightened and humane ruler, was not pleased; but he was careful not to say anything too explicit about a ruler as powerful as Frederick.

VI. *Before, During, and After the French Revolution*

In the history of Machiavellism, as in almost every other aspect of human life, the French Revolution marks a watershed. For a quarter of a millennium, the major terms in which Machiavelli could be discussed had appeared set; and there seemed little one could do with him except ring changes on the old alternatives. Was he a wicked man, a good man, or a scientifically neutral man? Was he a supporter of tyrants (who could be represented as law and order), or of republican government (which could be represented as regicide)? One could choose among these alternatives or try to combine them, as did the first two figures who follow; but with the second pair, who have fully absorbed the meaning of the Revolution, we're in another world.

1762: Jean Jacques Rousseau, in the *Social Contract*, returned to Gentili's old point, by saying that in *The Prince* Machiavelli professed to teach kings, but it was the people he really taught. *The Prince* was a book for republicans, and by not seeing this fact, previous readers had shown themselves either superficial or corrupt.

1799: Citizen Toussaint Guiraudet, writing at the very crest of the Revolution, brought out an edition of Machiavelli's *Works* in French translation, for which he wrote an uneasy preface. He praised Machiavelli for all the virtues appropriate to the exact moment—as a patriot, a religious neutral, and an authoritarian who, knowing the limits of freedom, would certainly have approved the severe restrictive measures with which Napoleon was in process of putting an end to the Revolution. He actually intimated that Machiavelli would have welcomed the French invasion of Italy. In short, being absorbed in current events himself, Guiraudet submerged Machiavelli in them. Understanding the temper of the early sixteenth century was obviously the last and least of his considerations.

1801–02: In these years, G. W. F. Hegel was delivering to a handful of students at Jena the lectures that later became *The Philosophy of History*. Hitherto, Machiavellism had always meant a readiness to violate, in the interests of a real, immediate state, the general and permanent laws of reason and nature, often identified with those of Christianity. Hegel, by turning this static and uniform law of reason/nature/Christianity into the continually progressing and reconciling dialectic, converted the actual state into an ideal state. Literally, every actual state was the ultimate achievement so far of the world-spirit in the process of working itself out. Thus Hegel could and did acclaim Machiavelli as one who, even in proposing the lower forms of evil, worked effectively toward the higher form of good.

1808: Goethe published *Faust, Part I*. Practically from the first minute of his appearance, Mephisto announces himself as a Hegelian Machiavelli-figure. He is "part of that Power that in always willing evil always procures good." Whether on these terms God is himself the dialectic, or simply a super-Machiavelli manipulating the dialectic and Mephisto within it, may be argued; but it doesn't matter, for the whole premise of Machiavellism—that evil is different from good as politics is different from morality—has evaporated. In the unified version of the dialectic, antithesis contributes as much as thesis to the ongoing, always provisional synthesis.

VII. *Conclusion*

A number of formulas have been invoked to account for the declining influence of Machiavellism in the nineteenth and twentieth centuries. The simplest and most capacious is simply that the world has been Machiavellianized. When moral principles ceased to be independent, unchanging public rules controlling the behavior of those who professed them—when principles were replaced by ideas of interest,

progress, or class solidarity—then Machiavellism lost most
of its point. The modern political liar isn't Machiavellian;
he doesn't even want to deceive; he's simply telling his con-
stituency what it wants to hear: that's his business. Machiavellism is possible only in an age of public morality, or at
least of moral expectations—and that's not our own. The
decisive change has to be dated some time around the French
Revolution.

In his own time, for example, Napoleon, that giant Janus-
figure of modernity, was rarely discussed in Machiavellian
terms, or else only clumsily abused. Some analogies with
The Prince might have seemed appropriate, but overall the
comparison was wrong because the dynamics of the Napo-
leonic situation were entirely different from those of the
Renaissance. Though in the end he betrayed the Revolution,
Napoleon was a revolutionary leader; his strength depended
on the skill with which he evoked and manipulated the
passions of oppressed and frustrated classes. Not so *Il Principe*, not so at all. Machiavelli spoke to the very special
conditions of his own youth. Italy prior to the death of Lorenzo was a closed system of fixed entities, much smaller,
much less stable than the states of eighteenth-century Europe, but similarly organized and having in common the
same essential beliefs. Jockeying, balancing, trading for
power within a little group of established dynastic states was
the true business of Machiavelli's prince, and equally of
princes and diplomats of the European family during the
eighteenth century. Napoleon inaugurated that age of mixed
ideological and imperialist wars through which we are still
trying to live. Mass societies, organized into nations, or ral-
lied behind political dogmas, or identified with particular
races, would have seemed strange and wonderful to Machiavelli. Indeed, the later sixteenth century, with its hideous
wars of religion unleashed by the Reformation, is somewhat
analogous to the twentieth century, with its wars of ideology
unleashed primarily by the French and Russian Revolutions.
One can perhaps see the elements of a recurring cycle in
this alteration. In any case, of all the modern dictators from
Franco to Hitler, Dzhugashvili, Papa Doc, and Saddam
Hussein, only Mussolini has ever so much as paid lip service
to Machiavelli, and as usual with that brutal windbag, it was
all bluff. Mussolini neither knew nor cared anything about
Machiavelli except as intellectual salad dressing for his own
bitter herbs. Wars of ideology, the outcome of deep politics,
tend to create fanatics and demagogues in about equal quan-

tities; and neither class really has much use for Machiavelli.

As an active political influence, Machiavellism has thus been effectively dead and buried for two centuries. That may be one major influence contributing to the new and better understanding of Machiavelli as a figure in his own right— to the growth of reasoned factual scholarship based on acquaintance with all the surviving texts, not just the misunderstanding of one.

MARGINALIA

FRIEDRICH NIETZSCHE

[Morals as Fossilized Violence]†

[The late-nineteenth-century German philosopher had a great admiration for Machiavelli; their styles, their temperaments, their estimates of human nature were much alike. More interesting for our purposes than a mere comparison is the way in which Nietzsche complements Machiavelli's political insights, by arguing that the "autonomous" moral values that the virtuous propose as a standard for judging politics are not in fact heaven-descended. Morality, Nietzsche argues, is the product of acts of violence, repeated over and over again, till social and moral values are literally beaten into men. All religious and moral codes are tainted with cruelty; our search for an origin of moral codes and standards can only take us back to a long and terribly painful conquest as a result of which men gradually learned to interiorize their external compulsions in a conscience. Morals then are simply fossilized violence; and the truly autonomous conscience, like that of Machiavelli's prince, is one that elects its own moral values and imposes them on itself.

Our selection is from the second essay, titled " 'Guilt,' 'Bad Conscience' and Related Matters" in *The Genealogy of Morals*. Nietzsche has been describing the difficulty of breeding an animal (man) with the right to make promises—an animal capable of triumphing over his own deepest and healthiest instinct, which is to forget.]

II

This brings us to the long story of the origin or genesis of responsibility. The task of breeding an animal entitled to make promises involves, as we have already seen, the preparatory task of rendering man up to a certain point regular, uniform, equal among equals, calculable. The tremendous achievement which I have referred to in *Daybreak*[1] as "the custom character of morals," that labor man accomplished upon himself over a vast period of time, receives its meaning and justification here—even despite the brutality, tyranny, and stupidity associated with the process. With the help of custom and the social strait-jacket, man was, in fact, made calculable. However, if we place ourselves at the terminal point of this great process, where society and custom finally reveal their true aim, we shall find the ripest fruit of that tree to be the sovereign individual, equal only to himself, all moral custom left far behind. This autonomous, more than moral individual (the terms *autonomous* and

† From *The Birth of Tragedy and the Genealogy of Morals* by Friedrich Nietzsche. Copyright © 1956 by Doubleday, a division of Bantam, Doubleday, Dell Publishing Group, Inc. Used by permission of Bantam, Doubleday, Dell Publishing Group, Inc.

1. *Morgenröte*, published by Nietzsche in 1881.

moral are mutually exclusive) has developed his own, independent, long-range will, which dares to make promises; he has a proud and vigorous consciousness of what he has achieved, a sense of power and freedom, of absolute accomplishment. This fully emancipated man, master of his will, who dares make promises—how should he not be aware of his superiority over those who are unable to stand security for themselves? Think how much trust, fear, reverence he inspires (all three fully *deserved*), and how, having that sovereign rule over himself, he has mastery too over all weaker-willed and less reliable creatures! Being truly free and possessor of a long-range, pertinacious will, he also possesses a scale of values. Viewing others from the center of his own being, he either honors or disdains them. It is natural to him to honor his strong and reliable peers, all those who promise like sovereigns: rarely and reluctantly; who are chary of their trust; whose trust is a mark of distinction; whose promises are binding because they know that they will make them good in spite of all accidents, in spite of destiny itself. Yet he will inevitably reserve a kick for those paltry windbags who promise irresponsibly and a rod for those liars who break their word even in uttering. His proud awareness of the extraordinary privilege responsibility confers has penetrated deeply and become a dominant instinct. What shall he call that dominant instinct, provided he ever feels impelled to give it a name? Surely he will call it his *conscience*.

III

His conscience? It seems a foregone conclusion that this conscience, which we encounter here in its highest form, has behind it a long history of transformations. The right proudly to stand security for oneself, to approve oneself, is a ripe but also a late fruit; how long did that fruit have to hang green and tart on the tree! Over an even longer period there was not the slightest sign of such a fruit; no one had a right to predict it, although the tree was ready for it, organized in every part to the end of bringing it forth. "How does one create a memory for the human animal? How does one go about to impress anything on that partly dull, partly flighty human intelligence—that incarnation of forgetfulness—so as to make it stick?" As we might well imagine, the means used in solving this age-old problem have been far from delicate: in fact, there is perhaps nothing more terrible in man's earliest history than his mnemotechnics. "A thing is branded on the memory to make it stay there; only what goes on hurting will stick"—this is one of the oldest and, unfortunately, one of the most enduring psychological axioms. In fact, one might say that wherever on earth one still finds solemnity, gravity, secrecy, somber hues in the life of an individual or a nation, one also senses a residuum of that terror with which men must formerly have promised, pledged, vouched. It is the past—the longest, deepest, hardest of pasts—that seems to surge up whenever we turn serious. Whenever man has thought it necessary to create a memory for himself, his effort has been attended with torture, blood, sacrifice. The ghastliest sacrifices and pledges, including the sacrifice of the first-born; the most repulsive mutilations, such as castration; the cruelest rituals in every religious cult (and all religions are at bottom systems of cruelty) —all these have their origin in that instinct which divined pain to be the strongest aid to mnemonics. (All asceticism is really part of the same development: here too the object is to make a few ideas omnipresent, unforgettable, "fixed," to the end of hypnotizing the entire nervous and intellectual system; the ascetic procedures help to effect the dissociation of those ideas from all others.) The poorer the memory of mankind has been, the more terrible have been its customs. The severity of all primitive penal codes gives us some idea how difficult it must have been for man to overcome his forgetfulness and to drum into these slaves of momentary whims and desires a few basic requirements of communal living. Nobody can say that we Germans consider ourselves an especially cruel and brutal nation, much less a frivolous and thriftless one; but it needs only a glance at our ancient penal codes to impress on us what labor it takes to create a nation of thinkers. (I would even say that we are the one European nation among whom is still to be found a maximum of trust, seriousness, insipidity, and matter-of-factness, which should entitle us to breed a mandarin caste for all of Europe.) Germans have resorted to ghastly means in order to triumph over their plebeian instincts and brutal coarseness. We need only recount some of our ancient forms of punishment: stoning (even in earliest legend millstones are dropped on the heads of culprits); breaking on the wheel (Germany's own contribution to the techniques of punishment); piercing with stakes, drawing and quartering, trampling to death with horses, boiling in oil or wine (these were still in use in the fourteenth and fifteenth centuries), the popular flaying alive, cutting out of flesh from the chest, smearing the victim with honey and leaving him out in the sun, a prey to flies. By such methods the individual was finally taught to remember five or six "I won'ts" which entitled him to participate in the benefits of society; and indeed, with the aid of this sort of memory, people eventually "came to their senses." What an enormous price man had to pay for reason, seriousness, control over his emotions—those grand human prerogatives and cultural showpieces! How much blood and horror lies behind all "good things"!

IV

But how about the origin of that other somber phenomenon, the consciousness of guilt, "bad conscience"? Would you turn to our genealogists of morals for illumination? Let me say once again, they are worthless. Completely absorbed in "modern" experience, with no real knowledge of the past, no desire even to understand it, no historical instinct whatever, they presume, all the same, to write the history of ethics! Such an undertaking must produce results which bear not the slightest relation to truth. Have these historians shown any awareness of the fact that the basic moral term *Schuld* (guilt) has its origin in the very material term *Schulden* (to be indebted)? Of the fact that punishment, being a *compensation*, has developed quite independently of any ideas about freedom of the will—indeed, that a very high level of humanization was necessary before even the much more primitive distinctions, "with intent," "through negligence," "by accident," *compos mentis*, and their opposites could be made and allowed to weigh in the judgments of cases? The pat and seemingly natural notion (so natural that it has often been used to account for the origin of the notion of justice itself) that the criminal deserves to be punished *because* he could have acted otherwise, is in fact a very late and refined form of human reasoning; whoever thinks it can be found in archaic law grossly misconstrues the psychology of uncivilized man. For an unconscionably long time culprits were not punished because they were felt to be responsible for their actions; not, that is, on the assumption that only the guilty were to be punished; rather, they were punished the way parents still punish their children, out of rage at some damage suffered, which the doer must pay for. Yet this rage was both moderated and modified by the notion that for every damage there could somehow be found an equivalent, by which that damage might be compensated—if necessary in the pain of the doer. To the question how did that ancient, deep-rooted, still firmly established notion of equivalency between damage and pain arise, the answer is, briefly: it arose in the contractual relation between the creditor and the debtor, which is as old as the notion of "legal subjects" itself and which in its turn points back to the basic practices of purchase, sale, barter, and trade.

V

As we contemplate these contractual relationships we may readily feel both suspicion and repugnance toward the older civilizations which either created or permitted them. Since it was here that promises were made, since it was here that a memory had to be fashioned for the promiser, we must not be surprised to encounter every evidence of brutality, cruelty, pain. In order to inspire the creditor with confidence in his promise to repay, to give a guarantee for the stringency of his promise, but also to enjoin on his own conscience the duty of repayment, the debtor pledged by contract that in case of non-payment he would offer another of his possessions, such as his body, or his wife, or his freedom, or even his life (or, in certain theologically oriented cultures, even his salvation or the sanctity of his tomb; as in Egypt, where the debtor's corpse was not immune from his creditor even in the grave).

The creditor, moreover, had the right to inflict all manner of indignity and pain on the body of the debtor. For example, he could cut out an amount of flesh proportionate to the amount of the debt, and we find, very early, quite detailed legal assessments of the value of individual parts of the body. I consider it already a progress, proof of a freer, more generous, more *Roman* conception of the law, when the Twelve Tables decreed that it made no difference how much or little, in such a case, the creditor cut out—*si plus minusve secuerunt, ne fraude esto.* Let us try to understand the logic of this entire method of compensations; it is strange enough. An equivalence is provided by the creditor's receiving in place of material compensation such as money, land, or other possessions, a kind of *pleasure.* That pleasure is induced by his being able to exercise his power freely upon one who is powerless, by the pleasure of *faire le mal pour le plaisir de le faire*, the pleasure of rape. That pleasure will be increased in proportion to the lowliness of the creditor's own station; it will appear to him as a delicious morsel, a foretaste of a higher rank. In "punishing" the debtor, the creditor shares a seignorial right. For once he is given a chance to bask in the glorious feeling of treating another human being as lower than himself—or, in case the actual punitive power has passed on to a legal "authority," of seeing him despised and mistreated. Thus compensation consists in a legal warrant entitling one man to exercise his cruelty on another.

VI

It is in the sphere of contracts and legal obligations that the moral universe of guilt, conscience, and duty, ("sacred" duty) took on its inception. Those beginnings were liberally sprinkled with blood as are the beginnings of everything great on earth. (And may we not say that ethics has never lost its reek of blood and torture—not even in Kant, whose categorical imperative smacks of cruelty?) It was then that the sinister knitting together of the two ideas *guilt* and *pain* first occurred, which by now have become quite inextricable.

*   *   *

PASQUALE VILLARI

[Learning Diplomacy the Hard Way]

[Machiavelli's first diplomatic assignment came in 1499, when he was thirty. He was to negotiate with Caterina Sforza, countess of Forlì, for some soldiers and military supplies to be used in the Pisan war. The transaction seemed simple. The lady was an ally—sort of; a similar deal had been in effect for

a year, and needed only to be renewed. The problem was simply to get what
Florence wanted as cheaply as possible. But the lady was a Sforza, illegitimate
daughter of the cruel and devious Galeazzo Maria and herself a practiced,
wily operative. Pasquale Villari, whose *Life and Times* (1877–82) was for
long a standard biography of Machiavelli, illustrates in his account of the
mission to Caterina how much young Machiavelli had to learn and how
much of his learning was accomplished by means of hard knocks. In the
manner of an earlier day, Villari's biography is leisured, expansive, and full
of details. Many of the specifics he recorded have been corrected or modified
since he wrote; and no modern biographer would dare to spend two hundred
pages "setting the stage," before getting his hero born. But there's information
as well as entertainment to be picked up from Villari's ample pages. The
comedy of Machiavelli and the Countess Caterina is one of the historian's
particular gems.

In translating this little comedy from the great biography, Mrs. Linda
Villari twice described Caterina's mind as "masculine." Everyone understands the word in this context, but it has acquired a most disagreeable flavor
these days; I have taken the liberty of substituting words free of that ugly
odor.]

*   *   *

On the 12th of July, 1499, he received his first real important commission, being sent with a despatch from the Signory, signed by Marcello
Virgilio, to Caterina Sforza, Countess of Imola and Forlì. The friendship
of this small State was carefully cultivated by the Republic, for not only
was it situated on the high road from Upper to Lower Italy, but also on
that leading into Tuscany by the Val di Lamone. From this side the
Venetians had advanced, from this side the Duke of Valentino had made
threatening demonstrations. That part of the country too was warlike,
and furnished mercenaries to all who asked them of the Countess, who
made almost a trade of it. Her first-born son, Ottaviano Riario, though
a mere youth, was always ready to earn money by taking a command
(*condotta*). In 1498, he had obtained one worth fifteen thousand ducats,
from the Florentines, who were anxious to keep on friendly terms with
his mother. His engagement was to expire at the end of June, but might
be renewed at the pleasure of the Signori for another year. But at the
end of the first period Riario was very discontented. He said that the
Florentines had not observed their bargain, and that he objected to
renewing it. The Countess, however, being a much more prudent person, seeing that the Florentines desired her friendship, and knowing that
Valentino still had designs upon Romagna, showed herself disposed to
ratify the *beneplacito* (formal contract), adding that her uncle the Moor[1]
had sent her a request for men-at-arms, and that she would therefore

---

1. Because of his dark complexion, Lodovico Sforza, duke of Milan, was known as *Il moro*, the
Moor [*Editor*].

be glad of a speedy reply in order to know what she should do. For this reason Machiavelli was sent as Envoy to her Court.

The Countess Caterina was an extraordinary woman, and quite capable of holding her own against the secretary. Born in 1462, an illegitimate daughter of Galeazzo Maria Sforza, by Lucrezia, wife of a certain Sandriani of Milan, she was a woman of handsome, regular features, of great bodily strength, and of incisive intellect. She had gone through many and singular adventures. At a very early age she was married to the dissolute son of Sixtus IV., Girolamo Riario, who, owing to the violent tyranny of his rule, was in continual danger of assassination by conspirators. In 1487 when far advanced in pregnancy, she was nursing her husband in an illness at Imola, when news arrived that the Castle of Forlì had been seized by Codronchi, master of the palace, who had murdered the governor. Whereupon Caterina started the same night, entered the castle, and leaving Tommaso Feo in charge of it, brought Codronchi back with her to Imola, where she gave birth to a child on the following day. On the 14th of April 1488, a conspiracy broke out in Forli, Girolamo Riario was stabbed, and she, left a widow at the age of twenty-six, and with six children, found herself a prisoner in the hands of the Orsi, ringleaders of the revolt. But not even then did her courage fail her. The castle still held out for her, and she was allowed to enter it, in the hope that she would order its surrender to the people, in whose hands she had left her children as hostages. But she had already sent messengers to ask for aid from Milan, and now that she was in safety, she prepared to defend the castle until succor should arrive. To those who sought to subdue her, by threatening the murder of her children, she replied that she was able to give birth to more. The city was recaptured, and the rebellion put down with bloodshed. Afterwards the faithful Castellan who had saved her life was suddenly disarmed and dismissed, and his post given to his brother, Giacomo Feo, a handsome youth whom the Countess soon married.

This second husband also died by assassination in 1495, while driving home with the Countess from the chase. She instantly mounted a horse and galloped into Forli, where she took a sanguinary revenge. Forty persons were put to death, and fifty imprisoned or otherwise persecuted. Yet it was asserted by many that she herself had hired the assassins of her husband, and was now making his death a pretext for ridding herself of her enemies. She answered the accusation by saying, that thanks to the Lord, neither she, nor any other member of the Sforza house had ever found it necessary to make use of common assassins, when they wished to get rid of any man. In 1497 she married for the third time, and became the wife of Giovanni, son of Pier Francesco, one of the younger branch of the Medici, who came to her court as ambassador of the Florentine Republic. On this occasion she was made citizen of

Florence, partly because it was wished to flatter and keep on good terms with her; partly because the old laws prohibiting the marriage of citizens, particularly of powerful citizens, with foreigners, had been revived since the intermarriage of the Medici with the Orsini of Rome had so greatly swelled the pride of that family. In April 1498 Caterina gave birth to another son, afterwards renowned as Giovanni delle Bande Nere, father to Cosimo, first Grand Duke of Tuscany; and towards the end of the same year her third husband also breathed his last. She was therefore at thirty-six years of age, a widow for the third time, the mother of many children, absolute mistress of her little State, and noted as a women of excellent prudence and courage, when Niccolò Machiavelli presented himself at her Court.

The Florentines were disposed to confirm their *beneplacito* to Count Ottaviano, but not to grant him a command exceeding the value of ten thousand ducats, their only object being that of gaining the Countess's good-will. They also commissioned Machiavelli to purchase from her as much powder, saltpetre, and ammunition as she could spare, since perpetual supplies were needed for the camp before Pisa. After a necessary halt at Castrocaro, whence he sent information to the Signory of the factions which divided that place, he reached Forlì on the 16th day of July, and presented himself straightway to the Countess. He found with her the agent of Lodovico, and in his presence set forth the object of his mission, the intentions of his Republic, and its desire to be on friendly terms with her. The Countess listened to him with great attention, said that the words of the Florentines "had always satisfied her, whereas their deeds had always much displeased her," and that she must have time for reflection.

She afterwards let him know that she had been offered better terms by Milan, and then the negotiations began. She had neither powder nor ammunition for sale, not having sufficient for her own needs. On the other hand she had an abundance of soldiers whom she passed daily in review and sent on to Milan. Machiavelli, at the instance of Marcello Virgilio, tried to obtain some of these to send to Pisa, but could not come to terms with the Countess either for the price to be paid, or as to when he could have them. On the 22nd of July he thought that he had concluded the bargain, having raised his offer to twelve thousand ducats; yet he added that he was not certain, because the Countess "had always stood upon her dignity," so that he could never clearly determine whether she inclined towards Florence or Milan. "I see on the one hand," he wrote, "that the Court is crowded with Florentines, who appear to manage all the concerns of the State; also, and what is still more important, the Countess beholds the Duke of Milan attacked, without knowing whether she may rely upon his aid or not; but on the other hand the Moor's agent seems to have authority, and foot soldiers are continually leaving for Milan.

In fact, although by the 23rd of July everything appeared to be con-cluded, and it was settled that the agreement should be signed the following day, when Machiavelli presented himself to ask for her sig-nature, the Countess received him as usual in the presence of the Mil-anese agent, and told him that, "having thought the matter over in the night, it seemed to her better not to fulfil the terms, unless the Florentines would pledge themselves to defend her State. That although she has sent him a message of a different nature the previous day, he ought not to be surprised at the change, since the more things are talked over, the better they are understood." But the Florentine Government had ex-pressly told Machiavelli that it was decided not to undertake any such obligation, therefore there was nothing for him to do but return to Florence, which he accordingly did.

The failure of this mission seems to show that the Countess was more cunning than Machiavelli, who allowed himself to be outwitted by a woman. Nor can that be very astonishing when we remember that Caterina Sforza was a woman of subtle intellect, long sole ruler of her State and of great business experience, whereas the Florentine secretary, notwithstanding his wonderful abilities, was only a man of letters making his first campaign in diplomacy. But at bottom the Florentines had no motive for discontent. Their real object was not the arrangement of the *condotta*, but rather that of winning the Countess's friendship without any expense; and in this their success was complete, for the negotiations were not broken off, a confidential agent from Forlì being sent to con-tinue them. To Machiavelli himself the mission had been most useful, for his letters had been highly praised by all in the Palace. His ever-faithful friend and colleague, Biagio Buonaccorsi, a Republican admirer of Savonarola, of Benivieni, of Pico della Mirandola, wrote to him continually and kept him *au fait* of everything. He was a lover of learning, although but a mediocre writer, author of some poems and of a Diary which gives a very accurate account of Florentine events from 1498 to 1512. "In my opinion," he said in a letter of 19th of July, "you have acquitted yourself so far with much honour of the mission imposed upon you, in the which thing I have taken and am still taking great delight; go on as you have begun, for hitherto you have done us much honour." He repeats the same in other letters, in one of which he asks for a portrait of the Countess, and begs that it may be forwarded "in a roll, to avoid its being spoiled by folding." And he also earnestly begs Machiavelli to return at once, because in his absence there was great disorder in the Chancery, and envy and jealousy were very rife; wherefore "remaining away is not good for you, and here there is a deluge of work such as never was."

*   *   *

FRANCESCO GUICCIARDINI

From *Ricordi*

["Francesco Guicciardini," so writes the great nineteenth-century historian De Sanctis, "though but a few years younger than Machiavelli and Michelangelo, already seems of a different generation. In him one recognizes the precursor of a more flabby and corrupt generation, the testament of which is spelled out in his *Ricordi*.

He has the same program as Machiavelli. He hates the priests. He hates the foreigners. He wants a united Italy. He even wants liberty, conceived after his own fashion as a strict and balanced government, rather on the line of a present-day constitutional or mixed monarchy. But they are nothing but preferences, and he wouldn't lift a finger to bring them about."

In fact, Guicciardini was a couple of rungs higher on the social ladder than Machiavelli; he had more money, he served in more rewarding and influential offices, doing some particularly ugly, unpopular (and therefore well-remunerated) work for popes and tyrants of whom he said he disapproved. Perhaps it was just a coincidence that his philosophy of history encouraged cynicism and inactivity. Anything like the enthusiastic and visionary twenty-sixth chapter of *The Prince* was out of his tonal register entirely. He has in fact no faith that the virtú of the ancient Romans can be revived; hence it's not worthwhile to try to make modern Italy less corrupt. For all his subtle mind and urbane cynicism, Guicciardini feels more like a dead weight than the mercurial, electrifying Machiavelli. Why he never got anything like Machiavelli's reputation as an immoralist is a curious question. *Rircordi* 45, 87, and 149, for example, are more coldly self-centered than anything penned by the Florentine secretary. Very possibly Guicciardini was given a better moral report card than Machiavelli because he did not write as well.]

I

*   *   *

45. Frank and natural sincerity is a noble quality, though sometimes harmful to the practitioner. Dissimulation, on the other hand, is useful and often necessary because men are corrupt, yet it is hateful and ugly, so I know not which to prefer. I suppose a man might use one procedure as a matter of course without wholly abandoning the other. That is, in his ordinary and common course of life, he might follow the path of sincerity in order to acquire the reputation of an honest man, and yet, on certain important and unusual occasions, resort to dissimulation. His deception will be the more useful and will work better because his general good reputation makes him more easily trusted.

*   *   *

51. While ambassador in Spain, I noted that king Ferdinand of Aragon, a wise and successful king, was careful when he had a new and important project in mind, not to announce it and then justify it; but exactly the contrary. Before disclosing his intentions, he contrived to have the opinion diffused that the king for such and such reasons ought to take certain actions. Then when he made known that he proposed to do exactly what everyone said was right and necessary, his decisions were accepted with incredible applause and enthusiasm.

* * *

87. It is honest and manly never to promise what you do not mean to perform. But as a rule the man whose request you deny, though your reasons are of the best, remains dissatisfied. Quite otherwise with the man who scatters his promises around liberally. For many accidents may intervene which render it unnecessary for him to do as he promised, and so the petitioner is satisfied with empty words. There is no lack of excuses for not performing a promise, and many men are so dull they do not even realize they've been given empty talk for solid substance. Still, breaking your own promise is such an ugly action that the discredit of it generally outweighs any advantage. So keep your petitioners encouraged and hopeful by feeding them on fine generalities, and avoid as far as possible specific promises.

* * *

95. Every state, if you consider the matter carefully, originated in violence; hence there is no legitimate authority except in republics, or even in them beyond the limits of their own territory—not even in the emperor, whose power is founded on that of the Romans, who were the greatest usurpers of all. I make no exception here even for the priests, who keep us down with two sorts of weapons, the temporal and the spiritual.

* * *

149. It was a cruel decree of the Syracusans that even the daughters of tyrants should be put to death; but there was a kind of reason in it too. For with the tyrant gone, those who were content to live under him will try to set up another one, even if he has to be made of wax. And since it's hard to bring a new man into credit, they will do everything they can to build on what's left of the old one. Thus a city newly escaped from tyranny has not secured its liberty completely until it wipes out the entire line of the tyrant's descendants. I say this absolutely and without qualification of the male descendants, but as for the women I would distinguish according to circumstances, according to the character of the ladies, and according to the character of the cities.

*   *   *

170. If when a particular event occurred you were to get a wise man
to write down what he thought the consequences would be, and were
to write down the forecast, you would find that when after a time you
turned to look at it, that as little of his forecast had come true as you
might expect at the end of the year when reviewing the forecasts of the
astrologers. The events of this world are too variable to be foreseen.

II

*   *   *

105. Even after a man has got a name as a deceiver and trickster,
you will still find that his frauds sometimes attract a believer. This seems
strange, yet the fact is most certain; and I remember that the Catholic
king who had a great reputation this way never had any trouble finding
fresh dupes. This can only proceed from the simplicity of men or from
their greed; for greedy men believe anything they desire, and simple
men will swallow anything.

*   *   *

110. What a mistake people make who on every occasion bring up
the example of the Romans! To follow their example, we should have
to have a city trained by history like theirs and then governed exactly
on their model; being as different as we are, asking moderns to imitate
ancients is like entering a donkey in a race against horses.

*   *   *

112. Messer Antonio da Venafro used to say, and very rightly, that
if you set six or eight wise men around a table, they would shortly
become so many crazies. For when they disagree among themselves,
they would quickly find more reasons to fight than to agree.

*   *   *

TRAIANO BOCCALINI

From *News Bulletins from Parnassus*†

[Traiano Boccalini, who flourished in Italy during the last years of the
sixteenth and first years of the seventeenth century, got his political expe-

† From *I ragguagli di Parnasso* (Venice, 1630). Translated by the editor.

rience as a Roman judge and administrator for three tough Renaissance popes, Sixtus V, Clement VIII, and Paul V. But when it came time to publish his great satirical work, *I ragguagli di Parnasso*, in 1612, he moved to the freer climate of Venice, and was careful to stay there for the rest of his life. The book is a set of imaginary newsletters from the kingdom of Parnassus, in which animals and books speak their minds and present their problems before the court of King Apollo, while authors, like Niccolò Machiavelli, are revived from the dead to be set on trial. Machiavelli, as the reader will see, is roundly condemned before this tribunal, but on grounds that suggest that Boccalini felt much more sympathy for him than for the court, which in condemning him was so flagrantly serving its own selfish interest.]

(I, 89)

Niccolò Machiavelli, who had been banished from Parnassus on pain of death, is discovered hiding in the library of a friend, and is sentenced to undergo the penalty previously pronounced against him, of death by fire.

Although Niccolò Machiavelli was banished many years ago from Parnassus and its territories under the very gravest penalties both to himself and to those who dared receive in their libraries a man of such pernicious principles, nonetheless last week, in the house of a friend who was secretly harboring him in his library, he was taken prisoner. The criminal judges at once took cognizance of his person, and this morning the fatal fires were about to be lit, when he asked His Majesty that some time be allowed him to say something in his own defense before the tribunal that had condemned him. Apollo, displaying his usual benignity, gave him to understand that he might send his solicitors to court, where they would be courteously heard. Machiavelli replied that he wanted to act as his own lawyer, and that Florentines had no need of lawyers to state their case. Everything he requested was granted. Machiavelli was therefore brought before the bar of justice, where he spoke in his own defense as follows:

"Behold, My Lord of the World of Letters, that Niccolò Machiavelli who has been condemned as a seducer and corrupter of the human race, and a disseminator of scandalous political ideas. I am not present in this court to defend my writings, which I here denounce publicly, and condemn as impious and full of cruel and hateful instructions on how to govern states. So that, if what I have published in my books is doctrine invented by me out of my own head, if it is novel advice, then I demand immediate and unconditional execution of the sentence that the judges have been pleased to pass on me. But in fact my writings contain nothing more than political precepts and rules of state that I have derived from the actions of various princes whom, with Your

Majesty's permission, I'll be glad to name in this court—men of whom it's as much as your life is worth to say an evil word. Now I ask you, what justice, what reason is there that they who invented that furious and desperate political process described by me should be held sacrosanct, while I, who have simply described it, am called a scoundrel and an atheist? I certainly can't see any rationale for adoring the original of a thing as sacred, and denouncing the copy as execrable. Nor do I see why I alone should be persecuted, when the reading of history, which is not only permitted but praised to the skies by everyone, is notoriously capable of converting into so many Machiavellis all those people who look at it through political glasses. Thanks be to God that people aren't all as simple-minded as some would like to think; so that the same people who with the brilliance of their intellects have been able to investigate the deepest secrets of nature, may yet have the wit to discover the true ends of princes in their actions, even though they use the greatest art to conceal them. And if the princes, in order to twist and turn their subjects as seems best to them, want to have them stupid and ignorant, then they will have to make up their minds to the same measures so brutally practiced by the Turks and Muscovites, that is, to prohibit good books. For books are what turn into Arguses those blind eyes that otherwise would never ferret out the true ends of princes' thoughts. Thanks be to God that the hypocrisy so familiar in the world today has power, like the stars, only to incline but not to force human minds to believe what the manipulators of that hypocrisy want us to believe."

The judges were much moved by these words, and it seemed that they were about to revoke the sentence when the Fiscal Advocate advised them that Machiavelli was not only deservedly condemned for the abominable and execrable precepts to be found in his writings, but should be severely punished for another reason, as well. It seems he had been found the other night in a fold full of sheep, to whom he was teaching the way to fit into their mouths the false teeth of dogs—with the evident peril that shepherds might be altogether exterminated, who are persons of such necessity in this world. What an indecent and troublesome thing it would be if this rascal made it necessary for the farmers to arm their breasts with plate mail and to wear iron gauntlets whenever they wanted to milk their sheep or shear them. The price of wool and cheese would rise sky-high if in the future it should become harder for the shepherds to guard themselves from the sheep than from the wolves. No longer able to keep the flock obedient with a whistle and a crook, they would need a regiment of soldiers to do it; and at night, to keep them in order, it wouldn't simply be a matter of stringing a few ropes: walls would be needed, with towers, and moats with counterscarps, after the modern fashion.

These atrocious accusations appeared to the judges so important that they all voted to carry out the original sentence against such a vicious man; and they published it as a fundamental law for the future that any man would be considered an enemy of the human race who ever dared to tell the world such scandalous things. And they all confessed that neither wool nor cheese nor lamb, which derive from sheep, render that animal precious to man, but only its vast simplicity and infinite docility. And that it wasn't possible for a great number of such beasts to be governed by a single shepherd unless they had been deprived of horns, of teeth, and of wit. So that it would set the whole world ablaze if a man should try to make the simpletons clever, and bring light to those dim moles whom Mother Nature had with great circumspection created blind.

✳ ✳ ✳

NORMAN DOUGLAS

From *South Wind*

[Norman Douglas was a pleasure-seeking ironist who gladly exchanged his native Scotland for the Mediterranean resort-island of Capri, not far from Naples. His 1917 novel about English expatriates in this alien environment is amusing and fanciful; one of its special gems is a character of the island's former ruler, the Good Duke. In characterizing this quasi-Renaissance despot, Machiavelli's name is often invoked, usually in the popular, inaccurate formula of a tutor of tyrants and an advocate of ruthlessness. "Nepenthe" is Douglas's fictional name for Capri; the name refers to a drink of the classical gods, which bestowed on one the gift of dreamy forgetfulness.]

The cannon, to be hereinafter described, is not the sole surviving relic of the Good Duke's rule. Turn where you please on the island domain, memories of that charming and incisive personality will meet your eye and ear; memories in stone—schools, convents, decayed castles and bathing chalets; memories in the spoken word—proverbs attributed to him, legends and traditions of his sagacity that still linger among the populace. *In the days of the Duke*: so runs a local saying, much as we speak of the "good old times." His amiable laughter-loving ghost pervades the capital to this hour. His pleasantries still resound among those crumbling theatres and galleries. That gleeful devilry of his, compounded of blood and sunshine, is the epitome of Nepenthe. He is the scarlet thread running through its annals. An incarnation of all that was best in the age, he identified, for wellnigh half a century, his interests with those of his faithful subjects.

He meditated no conquests. It sufficed him to gain and to retain the affection of men in whose eyes he was not so much a prince, a feudal lord, as an indulgent and doting father. He was the ideal despot, a man of wide culture and simple tastes. "A smile," he used to say, "will sway the Universe." Simplicity he declared to be the keynote of his nature, the guiding motive of his governance. In exemplification whereof he would point to his method of collecting taxes—a marvel of simplicity. Each citizen paid what he liked. If the sum proved insufficient he was apprised of the fact next morning by having his left hand amputated; a second error of judgment—it happened rather seldom—was rectified by the mutilation of the remaining member. "Never argue with inferiors," was one of His Highness's most original and pregnant remarks, and it was observed that, whether he condescended to argue or not, he generally gained his point without undue loss of time.

"It's so simple," he would say to those perplexed potentates who flocked to him from the mainland for advice on administrative questions. "So simple! One knock to each nail. And keep smiling."

It was the Good Duke Alfred who, with a shrewd eye to the future prosperity of his dominions, made the first practical experiments with those hot mineral springs—those healing waters whose virtues, up till then, had been unaccountably neglected. Realizing their curative possibilities, he selected fifty of the oldest and wisest of his Privy Councillors to undergo a variety of hydro-thermal tests on their bodies, internal and external. Seven of these gentlemen had the good luck to survive the treatment. They received the Order of the Golden Vine, a coveted distinction. The remaining forty-three, what was left of them, were cremated at night-time and posthumously ennobled.

He was the author of some mighty fine dissertations on falconry, dancing, and architecture. He wrote furthermore, in the flamboyant style of his period, two dozen pastoral plays, as well as a goodly number of verses addressed, for the most part, to ladies of his Court—a Court which was thronged with poets, wits, philosophers and noble women. The island was a gay place in those days! There was always something doing. His Highness had a trick of casting favourites into dungeons, and concubines into the sea, that endeared him to his various legitimate spouses; and the rapidity with which these self-same spouses were beheaded one after the other, to make room for what he mirthfully called "fresh blood," struck his faithful subjects as an ever-recurring miracle of state-craft. "Nothing," he used to say to his intimates, "nothing ages a man like living always with the same woman." Well aware, on the other hand, of the inequality of social conditions and keenly desirous of raising the moral tone of his people, he framed iron laws to restrain those irregularities of married life which had been a disreputable feature of local society prior to his accession.

Not in vain had he pondered in youth the political maxims of the great Florentine. He cultivated assiduously the friendship of Church and Mob; he knew that no throne, however seemingly well-established, can weather the blasts of fortune save by resting on those twin pillars of security. So it came about that, while all Europe was convulsed in savage warfare, his relations with other rulers were marked by rare cordiality and simplicity of intercourse. He never failed to conciliate his more powerful neighbours by timely gifts of local delicacies—gifts of dark-eyed virgins to grace their palaces, and frequent hampers of those succulent *langoustes* (lobsters) for which the coastal waters of the island are renowned, both items of the finest quality obtainable. A born statesman, he extended this ingratiating demeanour even to those minor sovereigns from whom, to all appearances, he had nothing to fear, supplying them likewise with periodical consignments of pretty maidens and well-flavoured crayfish, only of somewhat inferior quality—the crustaceans often too young, the damsels occasionally over-ripe.

His high aspirations made him the precursor of many modern ideas. In educational and military matters, more especially, he ranks as a pioneer. He was a pedagogue by natural instinct. He took a sincere delight in the schoolchildren, limited their weekly half-holidays to five, designed becoming dresses for boys and girls, decreed that lute playing and deportment should become obligatory subjects in the curriculum, and otherwise reformed the scholastic calendar which, before his day, had drifted into sad confusion and laxity. Sometimes he honoured the ceremony of prize-giving with his presence. On the other hand it must be admitted that, judged by modern standards, certain of his methods for punishing disobedience smack of downright pedantry. Thrice a year, on receiving from the Ministry of Education a list containing the names of unsatisfactory scholars of either sex, it was his custom to hoist a flag on a certain hill-top; this was a signal for the Barbary pirates, who then infested the neighbouring ocean, to set sail for the island and buy up these perverse children, at purely nominal rates, for the slave-markets of Stamboul and Argier. They were sold ignominiously—by weight and not by the piece—to mark his unqualified disapproval of talking and scribbling on blotting-pads during school hours.

It is recorded of the Good Duke that on one occasion he returned from the scene looking haggard and careworn, as though the sacrifice of so many young lives weighed on his fatherly spirit. Presently, envisaging his duties towards the State, he restrained these natural but unworthy emotions, smiled his well-known smile, and gave utterance to an apophthegm which has since found its way into a good many copy-books: "In the purity of childhood," he said, "lie the seeds of national prosperity." And if it be enquired by what arts of Machiavellian astuteness he alone, of all Christian princes, contrived to maintain friendly relations with these formidable Oriental sea-rovers, the answer lies at hand. His device was one of extreme simplicity. He appealed to their better natures by sending them, at convenient intervals, shiploads of local delicacies, girls and lobsters—of indifferent quality, it is true, but sufficiently appetising to attest his honourable intentions.

His predecessors, intent only upon their pleasures, had given no thought to the possibility of a hostile invasion of their fair domain. But the Good Duke, despite his popularity, was frequently heard to quote with approval that wise old adage which runs "In peace, prepare for war." Convinced of the instability of all mundane affairs and being, moreover, a man of original notions as well as something of an artist in costumery, he was led to create that picturesque body of men, the local Militia, which survives to this day and would alone entitle him to the grateful notice of posterity. These elegant warriors, he calculated, would serve both for the purpose of infusing terror into the minds of potential enemies, and of acting as a decorative body-guard to enhance his own public appearances on gala days. He threw his whole soul into the enterprise. After the corps had been duly established, he amused himself by drilling them on Sunday afternoons and modelling new buttons for their uniforms; to give them the requisite military stamina he over-fed and starved them by turns, wrapped them in sheepskin overcoats for long route-marches in July, exercised them in sham fights with live grapeshot and unblunted stilettos and otherwise thinned their ranks of undesirables, and hardened their physique, by forcing them to escalade horrible precipices at midnight on horseback. He was a martinet; he knew it; he gloried in the distinction. "All the world loves a disciplinarian," he was wont to say.

Nevertheless, like many great princes, he realized that political reasons might counsel at times an abatement of rigour. He could relent and show mercy. He could interpose his authority in favour of the condemned.

He relented on one celebrated occasion which more than any other helped to gain for him the epithet of "The Good"—when an entire squadron of the Militia was condemned to death for some supposed mistake in giving the salute. The record, unfortunately, is somewhat involved in obscurity and hard to disentangle; so much is clear, however, that the sentence was duly promulgated and carried into effect within half an hour. Then comes the moot question of the officer in command who was obviously destined for execution with the rest of his men and who now profited, as events proved, by the clemency of the Good Duke. It appears that this individual, noted for a child-like horror of bloodshed (especially when practised on his own person) had unaccountably absented himself from the ceremony at the last moment—slipping out of the ranks in order, as he said, to bid a last farewell to his two aged and widowed parents. He was discovered in a wine-shop and brought before a hastily summoned Court-martial. There his old military courage seems to have returned to him. He demonstrated by a reference to the instructions laid down in the Militiaman's Yearbook that no mistake in saluting had been made, that his men had therefore been wrongfully convicted and illegally executed and that he, *a fortiori* (consequently), was innocent of any felonious intent. The Court, while approving his arguments, condemned him none the less to the indignity of a double decapitation for the offence of leaving his post without a signed permit from His Highness.

It was at this point that the Good Duke interposed on his behalf. He rescinded the decree; in other words, he relented. "Enough of bloodshed for one day," he was heard to remark, quite simply.

This speech was one of his happiest inspirations. Instantly it echoed from mouth to mouth; from end to end of his dominions. Enough of bloodshed for one day! That showed his true heart, the people declared. Enough of bloodshed! Their enthusiasm grew wilder when, in an access of princely graciousness, he repaired the lamentable excess of zeal by pinning the order of the Golden Vine to the offending officer's breast; it rose to a veritable frenzy as soon as they learned that, by Letters Patent, the entire defunct squadron had been posthumously ennobled. And this is only one of many occasions on which this ruler, by his intimate knowledge of human nature and the arts of government, was enabled to wrest good from evil, and thereby consolidate his throne. . . .

* * *

ROBERT M. ADAMS

Necessitá/Fortuna

Among the special words that students of Machiavelli have laid under the microscope, *virtú* was one of the first and is still the most important; but *fortuna, stato, ordini, ingegno, astuzia, inganno, ambizione, natura, prudenza, fede, lealtá,* and many others have joined the list. *Necessitá* has not been formally excluded, but it has not seemed to offer many discussable complications. It has in fact an interesting combination of positive as well as negative aspects. Some things we *must* do, others are *verboten.* But in both aspects, the word suggests the policeman's peremptory mitt. We must turn right, we cannot turn left, there is no admission to the place we want to go. External compulsion looming before us and diverting or halting our progress is the image; and when we can't get over the obstacle or around it, there's not much to do but shrug our shoulders and give up. Even when necessity tells us we must do *this*, a strong peripheral negative clings to her command; a big part of her meaning is "and not *that* or *the other thing* or *anything else but this.*"

How different the ways of feckless fortune who drops on us the endless array of happenings each of which can divide and subdivide or reverse direction endlessly. Necessities, if we take the word at full strength, verge on the immutable; fortune commits herself to very little—disaster can turn into triumph and vice versa in the blink of an eye. Surely the two terms stand very close to permanent opposition to one another. Yet necessity is not always a traffic cop; though often just as peremptory as a red light or lines of barbed wire, "necessities" in politics are more often conditional. If you want to reach a particular goal, you have to put up with this, that, or the other preliminary or indispensable condition. A candidate for public office in America has to have or develop a huge tolerance for rubber chicken, meaningless handshakes, and loud platitudes. To rule in the Romagna, one had to deal swiftly and impressively with Vitelozzo, Oliverotto, and Remirro de Orco. These are the theatrical, symbolic, or (one might say) pedagogic forms by which virtú dealt with apparent *necessitá*. (When you strangle Vitelozzo, every bravo in the Romagna rubs his neck.) But behind this flash lie more pedestrian and perhaps measurable routines. Without a lot of Alexander's money, Cesare was bound to deflate like a pricked balloon; without winning a local election or two for a job one doesn't particularly cherish, an American pol can hardly qualify for a higher job, on which (we may presume) his eye is really fixed.

So necessities of different sorts are, as it were, the tough stuff out of which politicians chisel their reputations. To judge their achievements we have to know where they are coming from, what they are starting with, what they are getting at, where they are going to, what they've got to work with, what they've got to work against—all the circumstances, in short, that may help or hinder them. Menaces and inhibitions, superstitions and mythologies may be no less significant in this calculation than bank accounts and artillery. There is, accordingly, no proper Machiavellian doctrine, only a certain preliminary mental clarity that could help one to calculate the real forces at play in an actual situation. This is what Eliot (p. 272) calls innocence.

It's not at all clear that language, with its so-called key words, first principles, ill-defined categories, and latent but powerful value systems, does not block off much of the field one is trying to understand. Among the dimensions with which it can hardly deal at all is the quantitative; how deeply is a supporter committed to a leader or a cause, what makes him stand fast or run away? Commentators speak lightly of Machiavelli's Tuscan militia because they came to grief outside the walls of Prato— as if the enterprise itself was academic or Quixotic. Yet modify a few intangibles, and these despised militia might have become a force as formidable as Garibaldi's "Mille," who years later (and in the face of a thousand humiliating precedents) fulfilled heroically the ancient slogan, "Fuori i barbari." After the event everything was clear; but to measure probabilities in advance, or to assign reasons for the different outcomes of the two ventures, would have been a task of cruel difficulty.

Even when it does not directly mislead us in accounting for human motivation, language has a thousand slippery ways of ignoring what it cannot easily express. Nobody is eager to root out the discreditable motives for action when more flattering ones lie ready to hand. And many of the motives for violent action really are only semi-articulate. Resentment of injuries suffered is one sort of deep motivation; another, almost as strong, is resentment of injuries inflicted. Why do the Fiorentini despise the Pratesi, while the latter hate the former? Whatever original wrongs there may have been have long since been buried under an accumulation of scabs and scratches. Among the deeper motivations to which articulate language can hardly reach are religious prejudice, ethnic hatred, and the thrill of violence for its own sake. Machiavelli himself had little direct experience of the wars of religion and race (as we too carelessly label them); but they tap deep-reaching, many-layered, and complexly striated currents of feeling, and we should not be deluded into thinking that verbal formulas can summarize them.

Nor should we be ashamed to embrace the next corollary, that when it comes to historical motivation we hardly ever know what we're talking about. The best knowledge we have is a guess after the event, not too far after. But as a rule not even the actors in an event can account clearly for their own motives. Just possibly the best use we can make of those key Machiavellian terms, and others like them, is to treat them as transparencies to look through in search of different realities or more finely subdivided reality-screens. What we are satisfied with as a realistic mode of historical motivation depends, naturally, on the patterning of our own contemporary lives. But that falls clearly in the sphere of *fortuna*, who rarely fails to have the last word.

Epigrams, Maxims, and Observations from the Machiavellians

[As with many hard substances, contact with Machiavelli often results in sparks; a random sampling of these brief illuminations is presented herewith. Unless otherwise indicated, translations (where called for) are by the editor.]

In this godless world of Nature (Machiavelli thought), man was left alone with only himself and the powers Nature had given him, to carry on the fight against all the fateful forces wielded by this same Nature.[1]
—Friedrich Meinecke

1. From *Machiavellism*, 1925; trans. Douglas Scott and published with introduction by D. W. Stark (New Haven: Yale University Press, 1957) 35.

The art of government is the organization of idolatry.

Liberty means responsibility. That is why most men dread it.

Vice is waste of life. Poverty, obedience, and celibacy are the canonical vices.

Economy is the art of making the most of life.

The love of economy is the root of all virtue.

Political Economy and Social Economy are amusing intellectual games; but Vital Economy is the Philosopher's Stone.

If you injure, your neighbor, better not do it by halves.

—"The Revolutionist's Handbook and Pocket Companion"[2]

Maybe the Tuscans are wrong about this, but slavery is always in their eyes a form of imbecility; intelligence and liberty being, in Tuscany, synonymous.[3]

—Curzio Malaparte

Machiavelli is no more the inventor of Machiavellism than Graves is the inventor of Grave's disease.[4]

—Mario Praz

O the rare tricks of a Machivillian!
He doth not come like a gross plodding slave
And buffet you to death: no, my quaint knave,
He tickles you to death; makes you die laughing,
As if you had swallowed a pound of saffron.[5]
—Loquitur FLAMINEO in The White Devil
by John Webster

True cynicism is a fault of the temperament of the observer, not a conclusion arising naturally out of the contemplation of the object; it is quite the reverse of "facing facts." In Machiavelli there is no cynicism whatever. . . . Such a view of life as Machiavelli's implies a state of the soul which may be called a state of innocence.[6]

—T. S. Eliot

The continuation of Machiavelli's thought need not be sought among the Machiavellians, who continue his politics of precept and casuistry

2. From "The Revolutionist's Handbook and Pocket Companion, by John Tanner, M.I.R.C. (Member of the Idle Rich Class)," an appendix to G. B. Shaw's play, Man and Superman.
3. From Maledetti Toscani (Florence, 1956) 12.
4. From "Machiavelli and the Elizabethans,"
in Praz's book The Flaming Heart (New York: Doubleday Anchor Books, 1958).
5. From John Webster, The White Devil, act 5, scene 3, lines 196 ff.
6. From "Niccolò Machiavelli," in For Lancelot Andrewes (Garden City, N.Y.: Doubleday Doran, 1929) 50–51.

by writing about "reason of state," often mingling this topic with moralistic trivialities; neither should it be sought among the anti-Machiavellians, auctioneers of the fusion, the identity of politics with morals, who devote themselves to thinking up states founded on pure principles of virtue and justice; nor, finally, among the eclectics, who juxtapose theories of morals and theories of politics, and instead of resolving the antinomies, soften and empiricize them, converting them into accidents and inconveniences which happen in life but can be given the character of accidental things. Instead, the train of Machiavelli's thought must be sought in those who try to clarify the concept of "prudence," of "shrewdness" in short of "political virtue," without mixing it up with "moral virtue" and without making it the mere negation of that quality: for example, among seventeenth-century writers, Zuccolo. And the same train may be found in some potent spirits who theorized that beyond the shrewdness and sagacity of the individual as conceived by Machiavelli lay the divine workings of Providence—such, for example, was Tommaso Campanella. But the true and worthy successor of Machiavelli, the powerful intellect who gathered up these scattered suggestions of the critics, and gave them power by combining them with the undying thought of the Florentine secretary, was another Italian (and indeed in these two Italians can be symbolized the entire philosophy of politics in its seminal form): and this was Vico. Not particularly well disposed toward Machiavelli, yet full of his spirit, he clarified and purified that spirit, integrating its conceptions of politics and history, resolving its hesitations, softening its pessimism.[7]

—Benedetto Croce

We are much beholden to Machiavelli and other writers of that class, who openly and unfeignedly declare or describe what men do, and not what they ought to do. For it is not possible to join the wisdom of the serpent with the innocence of the dove, except men be perfectly acquainted with the nature of evil itself; for without this, virtue is open and unfenced; nay, a virtuous and honest man can do no good upon those that are wicked, to correct and reclaim them, without first exploring all the depths and recesses of their malice.[8]

—Francis Bacon

. . . *Nicholas Machiavel's Prince*, who is a man, (though through the grand corruptions of the age and place in which he lived, and the safety of his own life, was forced as may rationally be judged to write in some kind of unhandsome disguises) I must call for the excellency and usefulness in corrupt times and places for his work's sake, *one of the most wisest, judicious, & true lovers of his country, of Italy's liberties and*

---

7. From *Etica e politica* (Bari, 1945), book 2, section 1, "Machiavelli e Vico," 253–54.

8. From *De Augmentis Scientiarum*, book 7, chapter 2. The translation is by F. R. Headlam.

freedoms, and generally of the good of all mankind that ever I read of in my days. [9]

—John Lilburne

"War is nothing but the continuation of politics by other means." [1]
—Karl von Clausewitz, *Vom Kriege* (1832)

Tuscan Sayings

[Like most medieval towns, Florence was cramped inside its protective walls; outside lay the fields with their garden plots, olive groves, country houses, and *contadini*, or peasants. Within very recent times it was still the custom for farmers to gather by themselves every Sunday morning in a corner of the Signoria to talk politics, argue football, discuss crops, and savor a *goccia* or two of wine with a neighbor. In the days of Machiavelli and Guicciardini, the country was even more closely intertwined with the city; and the idiom of the peasantry had a pervasive influence on the great writers of the city. Folk talk tended, as it still tends, to be dry and sardonic; it is rich in traditional formulas; it is sharp and sour. Much of what the moralists deplore as wicked cynicism, in Machiavelli particularly, is simply Tuscan folk talk, disguised a little and formalized. Even when the core of the thought comes from Livy or Sallust, its flavoring is peasant. Like the wine they drink, the peasants of Tuscany put a little acid edge on everything they say. "Tipo Chianti, eh?" they will say to the man behind the bar—the wine is *like* Chianti. They'll drink it anyway; but nobody's putting anything over on them, and they want that clear. Whether Machiavelli adopted proverbs already in existence or wrote in such a way that his sentences quickly became proverbial, is hard to know; one might study it out if at this date the matter seemed important.]

"Cosa fatta capo ha"; literally, a thing done has a head. In other words, Take a first step, others will follow on their own.
—Machiavelli, *Istorie Fiorentini* 2.1

"Chi ha tempo ha vita"; while there's time, there's life.
—Guicciardini, *Ricordi* 2.54

"Chi fonda in sul popolo fonda in sul fango"; he who builds on the people builds on mud.

—Machiavelli, *Principe* XI

---

9. From *The Upright Man's Vindication* (London, 1653) 7, quoted by Felix Raab, *The English Face of Machiavelli* (London: Routledge and Kegan Paul, 1964) 173–4. The prose is not very neat, but the sentiment is obviously sincere, and "Free-Born John" Lilburne was one of the toughest, most vociferous agitators for freedom against both Charles I and Oliver Cromwell.
1. Since Marxism domesticated the idea of the class struggle, this maxim has been stood on its head. [*Editor*].

"Di cosa nasce cosa"; one thing leads to another.
—Guicciardini, *Ricordi* 1.96

"Poco e buono"; little and good—used especially of talk.
—Guicciardini, *Ricordi* 2.210

"La guerra fa i ladri, la pace gl'impicca"; war makes thieves, peace hangs them.
—Machiavelli, L'Arte della Guerra 1

"Li stati che vengano subito e crescono presto, non possono avere le barbe e corrispondenzie loro"; states that, like natural plants, sprout early and grow quickly don't have strong roots and branches.
—Machiavelli, *Principe* VII

Selected Bibliography

As one might anticipate, the enormous spate of books and articles about Machiavelli includes material written in a great variety of European languages—with the curious exception of Russian. The bibliography is thus challengingly multilingual. Though a great deal of this material has been translated into English, a serious student of Machiavelli cannot go very far without Italian, German, and French. The following list of readings concentrates on works written originally in English or available through translation; but occasionally it is bound to stray into other languages. Even so, it remains a minimal approximation to a bibliography of the subject; so much has been written on or about Machiavelli that a vast volume would be required simply to name the various contributions to the various discussions that have waxed and waned over the centuries.

BIOGRAPHIES

For many years a standard biography on the grand scale, rich in details and relatively unadventurous in outlook, was that of Pasquale Villari, *Niccolò Machiavelli and His Time*, published at Florence in 1877 and translated into English in 1878. A more recent *Life of Niccolò Machiavelli*, incorporating later scholarship and elegantly written, is that of Roberto Ridolfi (Rome, 1954); it too has been translated into English (by Cecil Grayson, for the University of Chicago Press, 1963). Oreste Tommasini, *La vita e gli scritti di Niccolò Machiavelli* (Turin, 1883, with numerous later additions) is a vast and disorderly compendium of information. Edmond Barincou did an intimate study for the French series "So-and-so *par lui-même*"; it has been translated by Helen R. Lind under the simple title *Machiavelli* as Evergreen Profile Book 23 (New York: Grove Press, 1961). A more romantic, semifictionalized volume, which links Machiavelli with Savonarola, Castiglione, and Aretino as lawgivers of their age, is Ralph Roeder's *Man of the Renaissance* (New York: Viking, 1933); though a little florid in its rhetoric (soft minds cannot resist hanging adjectives on Cesare Borgia like decorations on a Christmas tree), it is still vivid and imaginatively compelling. *Machiavelli in Hell* is by Sebastian de Grazia (Princeton, 1989); though unpredictable in its arrangement and wholly independent of the interpretive literature, this book makes some useful points about Machiavelli's language. The title never quite explains itself.

BACKGROUNDS

General accounts of the Renaissance and of Italy's peculiar destiny in the fifteenth and sixteenth centuries must always be headed by two old war horses—Jacob Burckhardt's *Civilization of the Renaissance in Italy*, first published in 1860 and still going strong, with an English translation available in the Modern Library; and John Addington Symonds, *History of the Renaissance in Italy*, published in several volumes between 1875 and 1886. Symond's volumes hardly constitute a proper history, but are full of rich and curious information. Ferdinand Schevill has written, among other books, A *History of Florence* (New York: Harcourt Brace, 1936) with a useful introductory survey of the sources of Florentine history; in 1963 it was reprinted in two volumes as *Medieval and Renaissance Florence*. Garrett Mattingly, *Renaissance Diplomacy* (London, 1955) provides valuable standards for judging Machiavelli's theory and practice in the light of his own times. A fundamental study, which impinges only indirectly, but even so very importantly, on the life and thought of Machiavelli is Hans Baron's monumental *Crisis of the Early Italian Renaissance* (Princeton University Press, two volumes 1955, one volume 1966). A careful introduction to the social background is Lauro Martines, *The Social World of the Florentine Humanists, 1390–1460*; a fascinatingly intimate study of the political background is Nicolai Rubinstein, *The Government of Florence under the Medici 1434–1494* (Oxford University Press, 1960). More popular in its orientation, less accurate, and containing many specifics that the political historians take for granted is a French study of *Daily Life in Florence in the Time of the Medici* by Jean Lucas Dubreton, tr. A. L. Sells (London: Allen & Unwin, 1960). One gets even closer to the world of mercantile Florence as it existed about a century before Machiavelli's time through *Two*

Memoirs of Renaissance Florence, written by Buonaccorso Pitti and Gregorio Dati, translated by Julia Martines, edited by Gene Brucker, and published as Harper Torchbook TB 1333. Finally, although the student cannot go far wrong reading the articles of Felix Gilbert wherever he finds them, two call for particular mention: "Florentine Political Assumptions in the Age of Savonarola and Soderini" in the *Journal of the Warburg and Courtauld Institutes* 20 (1957): 187–214; and "The Concept of Nationalism in Machiavelli's *Prince,*" in *Studies in the Renaissance* 1 (1954): 38–48.

English books on the Borgias tend to be more lurid than accurate, like "Baron Corvo" 's general account of the family and Rafael Sabatini's popular biography of Cesare; in Italian, Gustavo Sacerdote and Clemente Fusero have both written detailed factual accounts of Cesare's career (Milan, 1950, 1958); they tend generally to support Machiavelli's contention that during his brief ascendancy the Romagna was well ruled.

POLITICAL THEORY

A major contribution to the study of Machiavelli as a political theorist was made by Augustin Renaudet, *Machiavel, étude d'histoire des doctrines politiques* (Paris, 1942). The standard study of Machiavellism is that of Friedrich Meinecke, *Die Idee der Staatsräson* (Munich, 1924), translated into lumpy English by Douglas Scott and published as *Machiavellism* (London and New Haven, 1957). Sharp, though dated, is "Luther and Machiavelli," by J. N. Figgis, in *Studies in Political Thought from Gerson to Grotius* (Cambridge, England, 1916) 71–121. Among the important articles are those of Hans Baron, "Machiavelli: the Republican Citizen and the Author of *The Prince*" in *English Historical Review* 76 (1961), and of Myron Gilmore, "Freedom and Determinism in Renaissance Historians," *Studies in the Renaissance* 3 (1956): 47–60. Garrett Mattingly's "Changing Attitudes Toward the State" in *Facets of the Renaissance* (Los Angeles, 1959) 19–40, is more substantial than his "Machiavelli's *Prince*: Political Science or Political Satire?" in *American Scholar* 27 (1957–58): 482–91, which is an academic joke by a most distinguished man. Luigi Russo's annotated edition of *The Prince,* which is a bit hard to find since Sansoni brought it out during the Second World War, contains much sensible and informative commentary.

Hostile critics of Machiavelli's morals are beyond number, and as most of them are frankly uninterested in Machiavelli, but are tilting at other windmills, we shall list only a few. Giuseppe Prezzolini's *Machiavelli anticristo* (Rome, 1954) carries its thesis on its title page; under the more subdued title of *Machiavelli* it has been translated into English (New York, 1967). Herbert Butterfield, *The Statecraft of Machiavelli* (London, 1940); Gerhard Ritter, *Die Dämonie der Macht* (Munich, 1948), translated by F. W. Pick as *The Corrupting Influence of Power* (Hadleigh, England, 1952); and Piero Conte, *L'errore logico di Machiavelli* (Rome, 1955) are all a little less extravagant in their views than Jacques Maritain, "The End of Machiavellianism," variously translated and reprinted but Englished in *The Review of Politics* 4 (1942: 1–33). Father Leslie J. Walker, S.J., has translated the *Discourses* (London, 1950); Yale University Press, 1952) with a corrective introduction and cautionary notes.

LANGUAGE

Instead of thrashing over the morals that Machiavelli didn't have or the political visions that he did have, scholars of recent years have taken to analyzing the language he used as an index to the mind using it. An innovator in this field was Fredi Chiappelli, *Studi sul linguaggio di Machiavelli* (Florence, 1952); this book was shortly followed up by H. de Vries, *Essai sur la terminologie constitutionelle chez Machiavel* (Amsterdam, 1957), and by a great number of detailed studies. Among these we notice J. H. Hexter's study of the meaning of the word *stato* ("state") in "*Il principe* and *lo stato,*" *Studies in the Renaissance* 4 (1956): 113–38, which became chapter 3 in *The Vision of Politics on the Eve of the Reformation* (New York City: Basic Books, 1973). Words like *politica, ordini,* and *fortuna* have been discussed by J. H. Whitfield in *Modern Language Review* 50 (1955): 433–43; in the essay reprinted in this Norton Critical Edition, pp. 193–205; and by Sasso in the *Rivista storica italiana* 64 (1952): 205. Regarding *virtù* there is a whole library of discussion: see the essays by Whitfield in *Modern Language Review* 38 (1943): 222–25 and Allan Gilbert in *Renaissance News* 4 (1951): 53–54, with controversy in the following issue. In *Italian Renaissance Studies,* ed. E. F. Jacob (London, 1960) 48–68, Denys Hay has an account of the complex word *barbarian,* bearing immediately on Machiavelli's use of the term. In Martin Fleisher's symposium *Machiavelli and the Nature of Political Thought* (New York, 1972) there are three studies of Machiavelli's language as a structuring element in his thought, by Fleisher himself, by J. G. A. Pocock, and by Robert Orr. Chiappelli's *Nuovi studi* appeared in Florence, 1969. Finally, it should not be overlooked that Machiavelli himself wrote a little *Dialogo intorno alla nostra lingua,* confirming our sense that he was a literary artist very conscious of his tools and materials. It is set in context by an essay of Cecil Grayson in *Italian Renaissance*

Studies, ed. Jacob, 410–32. The text is in Blasucci, ed., *Opere letterarie* (Milano, 1964) 212–28.

WAR

Machiavelli's ideas on war and its conduct have been discussed by Felix Gilbert, "Machiavelli and the Renaissance of the Art of War," in *Makers of Modern Strategy*, ed. E. M. Earle (Princeton, 1943) and by J. R. Hale, "War and Public Opinion in Renassiance Florence," in *Italian Renaissance Studies*, ed. Jacob, 94–112. C. C. Bayley, *War and Society in Renaissance Florence* (Toronto, 1961) relates the much earlier ideas of Bruni on the subject of militia to those of Machiavelli. See also Piero Pieri, *Il rinascimento e la crisi militare italiana* (Turin, 1952).

CURIOSITIES

A handsome and copiously annotated Italian edition of *Il Principe* (though it is now very hard to locate and much merits reprinting) is that of L. A. Burd (Oxford, 1891). J. R. Hale has written a broad survey of *England and the Italian Renaissance: The Growth of Interest in its History and Art* (London, 1954). Peter S. Donaldson has edited and translated A *Machiavellian Treatise* by Stephen Gardiner. The manuscript was written around 1553–55 but never published; it draws directly on *The Prince* and the *Discorsi*. Since Gardiner was Bishop of Winchester and Lord Chancellor under (Bloody) Mary, this is a specific evidence of Machiavelli actually having influence, if not on a persecution, at least on a persecutor. An important and deeply skeptical critical statement by Benedetto Croce is "Una questione che forse non si chiudera mai" in *Quaderni della critica 14* (1949): 1–16. George Eliot brings Machiavelli on the stage of her Renaissance-Florence novel *Romola*, and there are other efforts at fiction, as by W. H. Woodward, *Elena* (1929), Somerset Maugham (*Then and Now*, 1946), and Maurice Samuel (*Web of Lucifer*, 1947). T. S. Eliot delivers his verdict in the collection titled *For Lancelot Andrewes*. R. H. Buskirk, sensing that the true analogue to Machiavelli's city-state is not the nation any more, but the corporation, has written a potentially funny book, *Modern Management and Machiavelli* (Boston, 1974). Among the five-hundredth anniversary collections, in addition to that edited by Fleisher noted above, should be cited: *Studies on Machiavelli*, ed. M. P. Gilmore (Florence, Sansoni, 1972); *Italy: Machiavelli "500"* (Jamaica, N.Y.: St. John's University Press, 1970), and *The Political Calculus*, ed. A. Parel (Toronto, 1972). Frederick the Great's highly "Machiavellian" attack on Machiavelli (in writing which he was aided by Voltaire), the *Anti-Machiavel*, has appeared under the editorship of Theodore Besterman as volume 5 of *Studies on Voltaire and the 18th century* (Geneva, 1958).

FURTHER READINGS

A full and proper bibliography of Machiavelli is probably by now beyond the power of man or computer to compile. Certainly if one defines "Machiavellism" at all loosely, there is no end to the discussions of war, power, politics, authority, punishment, democracy, morality, leadership, personality structure, international law, freedom, responsibility, etc., etc., within which his name, and more rarely his ideas, may crop up. Still, a reader who is interested in Machiavelli himself, and wants to begin (as sensibly he should) with some fairly recent books, is not without help. Eric W. Cochrane has listed some studies from the years 1940–60 in the *Journal of Modern History*, 33.2 (June 1961): 113–36; and the continental bibliography (not be any means identical with the Anglo-American one) is laid out by Federico Chabod in the last section of *Machiavelli and the Renaissance*, tr. David Moore (1960).

The lack of a compendious bibliographical guide would be more distressing, except that it's true of Machiavelli studies, more than almost any others, that reading one book about him leads you to three or four others that you feel compelled to read. Book-hopping, from Y's footnotes to X's text, from Z's review of F's howler to J's improvement of C's long-inadequate formulation, is the classic way to get into a subject. Adventurous minds will ask nothing better.

Index

Note: Rome and Florence (the Roman empire, the Roman Senate, the Roman armies; the Florentine people, the Florentine government, the city of Florence, the army and allies of Florence) constitute allusions too frequent and too ill-defined to be included in this index. Also omitted are passing references to large national unities, such as Spain, France, Germany, and the United States.

NORTON CRITICAL EDITIONS